To:

know

the

truth

about

ISLAM

The Generous QUR'AN

An accurate,
modern English
translation of
the Qur'an,
Islam's holiest book

The Generous Qur'an

For copyright information:
Usama Dakdok Publishing, LLC
P.O. BOX 244
Venice, FL 34284-0244

ISBN 978-0-9824137-0-8

Dewey decimal system number: 297, Islam

Published in the United States of America

Dedication

This book is first of all dedicated to the families and loved ones of those whose lives were taken in the September 11, 2001, attack. Hopefully, it will give the Western World an illuminating view of that book spawning the beliefs and the hatred which led to that terrible event. Moreover, it is hoped that this book will increase awareness of the greater looming threat posed by those beliefs.

Additionally, this book is dedicated in love to the English-speaking descendants of those who spread Islam by the power of the sword in the invasion of my native country of Egypt 1400 years ago, killing many of my ancestors, and raping their wives and daughters. And although many of the descendants are still today invading and terrorizing the world, before and since September 11, 2001, it is my sincere desire that they come to know the truth, not only about the falsehood contained in the Qur'an, but the truth of the hope of salvation offered to them through the Bible in the person of Jesus Christ. This book is also dedicated to those who are even more dangerous, who deceive the West, as they intentionally alter their book and its teachings to make it more palatable to Western cultures. They began by naming it holy (even though the word holy does not exist in its title in the original Arabic), then they present it as peaceful and loving (even though there is not any peace or love in it) and finally they present their leader, the fabricator of their cult, as a prophet (even though he did not prophesy anything).

I present this true and accurate English translation of the *kareem* (generous) Qur'an so that those who do not know the truth about Islam from its original source of corruption and hate may know the truth that will set them free. I am especially concerned for those who are being deceived and becoming Muslim as a result of false teaching. I pray that as you read this book the Holy Spirit, the Spirit of the true God, may guide you to see the truth about Islam and to see that the Qur'an is little more than a corrupt and repetitive telling of the stories of the Bible and other stories invented by Mohammed and others.

My prayer is that the truth will shine and that abundant and eternal life will be received. Jesus is the way and the truth and the life, as He said in John 14:6: "I am the way, the truth, and the life; no one cometh unto the Father, but by me."

Contents

Foreword

There is perhaps no topic timelier in today's tumultuous geopolitical situation than the study of the modern rise and expansion of Islam. Since the violent assault on the West on September 11, 2001, many in our society have been unwillingly forced to consider and at least *attempt* to understand what is often referred to as Islamic Fundamentalism or the Jihadist Movement. Simultaneously, the airwaves have been filled with well-funded and well-organized spin doctors from such groups as the Council on American-Islamic Relations (CAIR) who make frequent appearances on talk shows and grant sound bites with the repeated mantra that Islam is "the religion of peace." News stories often speak using terms such as "Moderate Muslims" to attempt to separate the average Muslim from those who are labeled as the more extreme elements within the faith of Mohammed.

The confusion concerning the true nature of the religion of Islam is amplified with every terrorist assault and the subsequent attempt to counter-balance with the "take-my-word-for-it" claim that Islam is the religion of peace. Where the modern seeker typically fails to ascertain the truth is the illogical attempt to define a religion by the actions and words of those who profess to follow it, instead of going to the SOURCE of the religion, in this case, the Qur'an. It is only as we read the actual revelations of the "prophet" Mohammed that we can gain an accurate picture of what Islam truly believes and what its nature truly is. It is possible that a group can profess to practice a faith, but in reality they are far removed from the actual teachings of their sacred text. The Lord Jesus made a similar charge against the Jewish religious leaders of His day, when He said that they were not actually practicing Judaism as revealed in the Old Testament scriptures, but He said, "You teach the traditions and doctrines of men as the commandments of God." Hundreds of years of tradition have layered practices and beliefs among Muslims worldwide that are not found within their sacred text, and even run contradictory to it. The actual tenets and articles of faith and practice must be gained by studying the text, not the people, of a revelatory religion, such as Islam.

The explosive growth rate that Islam enjoyed in the early centuries due to the spread of the religion by the sword, in modern times has been replaced by expansive growth due to the plowshare of professed peace.

This has been an increasingly difficult sell, especially in light of the historically aggressive policies of Islam, as well as the clearly unambiguous texts within the Qur'an which speak of intolerance, violence, subjugation of women, polygamy, and the ultimate goal of domination of all religions eventually by Islam. The embarrassing and straightforward nature of the original Arabic text of Islam's Holy Book created a formidable barrier for those seeking to spread Islam in Western (viz a viz English) nations. It is crucial that an accurate English translation (not interpretation) of the Qur'an is produced for the educated seekers of the true nature of Islam.

The concept of replacing the original verses with different, even contradictory verses is a practice that must be understood when dealing with Islam. Muslim methods of interpretation rely on this practice to explain contradictory passages.

The author, Usama Dakdok, knows the power and the darkness that Islam brings to a people. Having been born and raised in the modern Islamic nation of Egypt, Usama spent his childhood in this predominantly Muslim country, was educated in schools saturated with the Qur'an, and even studied Islamic law in college. Usama became a Christian as a youth. He learned English and eventually moved to the United States, with the hopes and prayers of starting a ministry both to educate Christians about the beliefs of Islam and its threat to Christianity, as well as to reach out to western Muslims with the saving Gospel of our Lord Jesus Christ.

Usama studied and received his master's degree in Missiology from New Orleans Baptist Theological Seminary, and the Lord soon opened the door for him and his wife Vicki to fulfill his desire. The Straightway of Grace Ministry was started, with its name derived from the first *surah* of the Qur'an, verse 5, which states: Guide us to the straight way.

With nearly 1.3 billion Muslims worldwide, and the controversy surrounding Islam on the cover of nearly every magazine and newspaper daily, the demand for credible and easy to understand information about Islam, especially the Qur'an, is perhaps at an all-time high. Second, there has perhaps never been a time in history when more Christians have been seeking easily-accessible information about the Qur'an. Note that 87 percent of Muslims around the world do not speak or understand Arabic, but many of them speak English.

Usama has traveled extensively throughout the United States, and much of the Arab world, speaking to groups large and small, challenging Muslims with the truth of God's Word, and using the errors of the Qur'an to point them to Jesus, the true Savior. Doing countless presentations, each dissecting many verses of the Qur'an, one problem consistently appeared: the need for an accurate and unbiased English translation of the Qur'an. Many conference attendees would ask for direction as to which was the best English translation of the Qur'an, and Usama was frustrated that there did not exist a single translation that he could recommend. This led to a prayerful process to begin creating an accurate English translation that could be used by Christians when trying to reach out to Muslims, as well as for Muslims, or those interested in Islam, in order to show them the many errors, contradictions, and perversions in this book of Mohammed.

Working with a team of writers, educators, and scholars around the world, the meticulous process of translating, grammar correction, revising, and further refining began. The Arabic text had to be accurately translated, section headings had to be created, and commentary needed to be made, each requiring diligent research and cross-referencing of the qur'anic text with the biblical text. Finally, the writing of the supplemental sections had to be accomplished.

This new English translation is primarily targeted to the English-speaking Christian world to aid them in both understanding Islam and to help them in sharing their faith with their Muslim contacts. This new translation is secondarily targeted to those who are either studying Islam (such as in a university or Christian college) or are evaluating the claims of Islam in their own personal spiritual journey. Finally, it is the hope and prayer of the author that it will be much used of the Lord to help those caught in the darkness of Islam, especially those who do not speak the Arabic language and rely on the English interpretations, in realizing the false nature of the Qur'an and ultimately pointing them to the truth.

R. Lee

Introduction For The Reader

This book is not just for Jews, Christians, or Muslims, but for everyone who speaks English and lives in the West. It is for atheists, agnostics, or anyone seeking an understanding of what is actually contained in this book that is the basis of the Islamic faith, a faith which is now increasingly impacting the West in so many ways ranging from recruitment and immigration to terrorism.

The reader might ask, "Why do we need another translation of the Qur'an?" After all, there are at least a dozen English translations available for those studying Islam, even if they are not all widely available to the Western reader. However, existent translations are better described as *interpretations*, most of which were not even written by native Arabic speakers, and which generally are written for the approval of prevailing Islamic orthodoxy, copied from each other and with content manipulated to present interpretations that are more acceptable to the Western reader.

The need for a clear understanding of what the Qur'an actually teaches is more important at this time than ever before, now that Islam is being welcomed with open arms and in general ignorance by the West. In these last days some interfaith activists are saying that there are three faiths descended from Abraham: Judaism, Christianity, and Islam, all sharing many of the same beliefs and the same God. This could not be further from the truth because there are not three, but only one faith of Abraham. The Jewish prophets offered numerous prophecies of the coming Messiah and the New Testament records the fulfillment of those prophecies in Jesus Christ. In the back of this book is a table of some of these prophecies and their fulfillments. Throughout this book the reader will discover how the Qur'an and Islam denies both these prophecies and their fulfillments. Moreover, it will be discovered that the Allah of the Qur'an is nothing like the Yahweh of Judaism and Christianity. As the reader will see by the end of this book, Islam cannot be considered "another faith," compatible with either Judaism or Christianity, and it is clearly not the faith of Abraham. The reader will find that, although it draws on some names and stories from Judaism and Christianity, the Qur'an not only denies but is in direct conflict with these two earlier faiths which actually represent the faith of Abraham.

The Generous Qur'an is the first objective translation by a native Arabic speaker attempting to be as literal as possible while still communicating the meaning of the verses, if any. The few exceptions to this literal approach are minor; for example, translating a word for the sexual act as "have sex with" rather than a literal translation which would require use of a very base four letter word in English.

This translation is also as faithful as is possible to the numerous grammatical errors occurring throughout the Arabic text. The reader will, therefore, find tense changes multiple times in the same sentence, gender confusion, and grammatically incorrect sentence construction. One explanation proffered for these errors stems from the fact that Mohammed delivered these verses in Arabic poetry. He may have violated grammatical rules and even created nonsense words to maintain flow and rhyming patterns. Since capitalization and punctuation does not exist in Arabic, the punctuation and capitalization in this English translation attempts to be reflective of the meaning conveyed in Arabic. Furthermore, due to the differences in grammatical structure, some words which are understood when reading the Arabic must be inserted (shown in brackets "[ ]") to accurately convey the meaning in English.

Many words in the Qur'an are either without any meaning or have conflicting interpretations by different scholars. Even though no objective evidence might be found, if a majority of Islamic scholars claimed a meaning for a word, it was accepted. Words which have no meaning or for which the meaning is disputed are used in their Arabic form throughout the text. Arabic uses a completely different alphabet than English; therefore, Arabic words contained in this translation are written using the English alphabet with the commonly accepted spelling of Arabic words where possible and with the author's own spelling of words where necessary. These words are footnoted on their first occurrence.

Two tables in the back of *The Generous Qur'an* will assist the reader in understanding the meaning of Arabic words and phrases used in this translation. The "Words and Idioms" table contains those words which are without meaning or of disputed meaning, as well as proper names. This table also contains words and phrases which are Arabic idioms and in themselves may not convey the same meaning when translated literally into English.

The other table, "Non-Arabic Words," provides the meaning for words used in the Qur'an which are taken from other languages. The inclusion of this table stems from one of the basic objections Islamic leaders raise against translating the Qur'an into any language other than Arabic. They maintain that the Qur'an is written in *pure Arabic*, the only language spoken in paradise, and that its meaning can only be conveyed in Arabic words. For proof they point to such verses as 16:103 (A Portion of a Revelation 16, verse 103), where Mohammed denies accusations that someone has helped him construct the verses he recites, by pointing out that the person they suspect speaks a foreign language, yet the Qur'an is "clear Arabic." During the research for this translation, it was therefore quite interesting to find that there are approximately two hundred and seventy non-Arabic words used in the Qur'an.

The reader should not be alarmed if difficulty is encountered in gaining any meaning from significant portions of the Qur'an because the reader is in good company. Dr. Gerd Rüdiger Puin, a German scholar, a specialist in Arabic calligraphy, and the world's foremost authority on Qur'anic paleography (the study and scholarly interpretation of ancient manuscripts), noted the same problem. In a 1999 Atlantic Monthly article by Toby Lester entitled "What is the Koran?," Dr. Puin is quoted: "...*the fact is that a fifth of the Qur'anic text is just incomprehensible. This is what has caused the traditional anxiety regarding translation. If the Qur'an is not comprehensible, if it can't even be understood in Arabic, then it's not translatable into any language. That is why Muslims are afraid. Since the Qur'an claims repeatedly to be clear but is not—there is an obvious and serious contradiction.*"

Despite this caveat, an awareness of certain aspects of the Qur'an can help the reader gain a greater understanding of how significant conflicts and contradictions between verses are explained away. First, is the concept of abrogation, which is the repeal or annulment of *older* verses by *newer* verses. This is the explanation given by Islamic scholars for some of the obvious conflicts between different verses. For instance, in verse 2:109 Muslims are encouraged to pardon and forgive the Christians and Jews. According to some scholars (see AL-Nahas) this verse is abrogated by verse 9:5, which instructs Muslims to kill, besiege, and ambush them. Consideration was given to the inclusion of a table of abrogated verses in this book. However, research revealed that disagreement between Muslim scholars about many abrogated verses is too great to permit them to be reduced into a meaningful table. Moreover, the order and number of the portions of a revelation give no clue to the order in which they were recited. For instance, A Portion of a Revelation 9, "The Repentant," is considered to be the last portion of a revelation recited by Mohammed. The reader will note that, with the exception of the short first portion of a revelation, the portions of a revelation in the Qur'an are, with some discrepancies, arranged by size, from largest to smallest.

Despite these challenges, readers can gain some insight into the time when a verse was recited by noting *where* Mohammed was when he recited the verses. There is general agreement among Muslim scholars as to whether verses were recited in either Mecca or Medina. This is significant because it reveals to us which verses came earlier when they have conflicting content. When Mohammed lived in Mecca, his recitations were not well received; in fact, they were ridiculed by some, and he did not have enough followers to overcome his neighbors by force of arms. Therefore, his Mecca recitations were tamer and more conciliatory to the Christians and Jews. Mohammed was finally driven out of Mecca, fleeing to Medina with many of his followers. There he had a new audience which was more receptive and he amassed a significant fighting force allowing him to conquer anyone who opposed him. In Medina his recitations became much more inflammatory and full of hatred for Christians, and especially Jews, who opposed him in Mecca. To assist the reader, the contents pages include the location where each portion of a revelation is generally believed to have been recited.

As a final aid to the reader, the author has included comments in bold type to introduce and explain portions of the text. Significantly, the author's comments will frequently reference Bible passages for comparison regarding confused and conflicting statements contained in the Qur'an. Most notable is the often repeated denial that Jesus (whom Mohammed mistakenly calls 'Isā') is the Son of God. The numerous conflicts between the specific teachings of the Bible and statements made by Mohammed will leave the reader with a clear understanding that the Qur'an cannot be *another* revelation adding to what is in the Bible, but rather a rambling and somewhat incoherent text which is in direct conflict with and repeatedly denies essential elements of the Bible. It denies the genuine Abraham, the real Moses, and the true Jesus of the Bible. The Bible and the Qur'an cannot both be correct because they are in such direct conflict. One of these *revelations* has to be terribly wrong. After careful comparison, the reader will understand why the Bible, and not the Qur'an, points the way to Jesus, Who is indeed *the* way, *the* truth, and *the* life.

Doctrine of Abrogation

One of the amazing mysteries of the Qur'an is the doctrine of abrogation. Ironically, this doctrine actually stands against the teaching of the Qur'an itself which clearly says in verse 4:82, "Do they not consider the Qur'an? If it was from other than Allah, they would have found in it many inconsistencies." This verse clearly tells us that the Qur'an is free from any inconsistencies. Moreover, verse 6:34 says, "…no one can change the words of Allah," and verse 85:21-22 reads, "Yet, it is a glorious Qur'an in a kept board." (What is being said here is that the Qur'an is written on a board in heaven and is being kept from change.) From such verses one might think that the words of the Qur'an are written consistently and without any contradiction or any change. But how does one reconcile this concept with the numerous verses in the Qur'an which obviously teach about the doctrine of abrogation? For example, verse 2:106, "Whatever verse we abrogate, or cause it to be forgotten, we bring a better [verse] than it or like it." Also, verse 16:101 states, "And if we exchange one verse in a place of another verse, and Allah knows what he sent down…" Such verses teach that there is a change in Qur'anic verses and abrogation truly exists. Abrogation in the Qur'an is actually the only way to explain the inconsistencies throughout the Qur'an.

What do we mean by abrogation? According to Ibn Kathir's interpretation (part one, page 134), abrogation is defined as "the removal of a verse or the change of a verse with another (newer) verse or to make something lawful which was unlawful or vice versa." How many chapters in the Qur'an contain abrogation? Seventy-one chapters contain abrogation, which is over 60 percent of the Qur'an. Sometimes it is just one verse. For example, verse 9:5, which is called the verse of the sword by all Muslim scholars, abrogates 124 verses of the Qur'an that speak softly about other religions and other people such as the People of the Book (Christians and Jews). There are three different types of abrogation in the Qur'an.

The first type of abrogation is when the verse is removed from the Qur'an and Muslims are not required to practice its teaching. These are verses that Muslims and Mohammed could no longer remember because Allah caused them to be forgotten. It should be noted that there was no effort to compile Mohammed's recitations during his lifetime. Rather, they depended primarily on the memory of Mohammed and his followers, so it is not surprising that some of the verses were forgotten.

The second type of abrogation is when the verse exists but has been superseded by a newer verse and therefore is no longer practiced. This type of abrogated verse includes those verses that Muslims try hard to use in the West to prove that the Qur'an is not a hateful, barbaric book. These are typically the Meccan or early Medinan verses recited prior to Mohammed becoming a strong military leader. According to the Muslim scholars, the verses which Mohammed received later supersede the earlier verses if there is a contradiction. A sample of such superseded verses is verse 2:62 which says, "Surely those who believed (Muslims) and those who are Jews and the Nasara (Christians) and the Sābeen idol worshipers), whoever believed in Allah and the last day and did good deed, so they will have their ajoor (wage) with their lord and no fear on them, and they will not grieve." Such a verse teaches that Christians, Jews, and idol worshipers will have a place in heaven, but this verse was abrogated when Allah says in the Qur'an in verse 3:85, "And whoever desires any other religion except Islam, so it will not be accepted from him, and in the hereafter he will be of the losers." Other examples are in verse 8:61 which says, "And if they lean toward peace (truce), so lean toward it…" and verse 2:256 which states, "No compulsion in religion." These and many other such verses will give the unknowing reader the impression that the Qur'an is a kind book, but the fact is that all these verses have been abrogated by verse 9:5, in one of the last chapters revealed to Mohammed, when Allah said, "So when the forbidden months are passed, so kill the polytheists wherever you find them, and take them (as captives) and besiege them and lay wait for them with every kind of ambush; so if they repent (convert to Islam) and perform the prayer and bring the legal alms, so leave their way free. Surely Allah is forgiving, merciful." Also, in verse 9:29, Allah says, "Engage in war with those who do not believe in Allah nor in the last day…nor believe in the religion of the truth among those who have been given the book…" (Jews and Christians). Such newer verses abrogate the previous verses, and Muslims are commanded to live by the new verses, not the old verses. Therefore, one comes to the conclusion that there is no such thing as soft, kind verses in the Qur'an because Allah has changed his mind and abrogated such verses.

The third type of abrogation is when the written verse is gone but Muslims are still commanded to practice such verses, as we see in practicing the ordinance of stoning the adulterer. When women commit adultery in Islam, Sharia (Islamic law) commands them to be punished by stoning them to death even though the written verse of the Qur'an has been removed. What a strange god! And what strange words of this god – *The Generous Qur'an.*

In God's Word, Jesus says in Matthew 5:17-18, "Think not that I am come to destroy the law, or the prophets: I am not come to destroy, but to fulfill. For verily I say unto you, till heaven and earth pass, one jot or one tittle shall in no wise pass from the law, till all be fulfilled." What a difference the true Word of God makes!!

A portion of a revelation   **The Opening**

In the name of Allah, the merciful, the merciful

Verse 1 indicates that Muslims worship the god of this world who is Satan (See 2 Corinthians 4:4) who is known as the best deceiver (See 3:54 and 8:30), who leads people astray (See 35:8), and who desires to fill hell with all infidels who do not accept Islam (See 7:18 ;11:119, 32:13, and 98:6).

[1]The praise be to Allah, [a] the rabb[b] of the 'ālameen,[c] [2]the rahmān,[d] the raheem,[e] [3]the owner of the day of the dīn.[f] [4]To you we serve and to you we seek assistance. [5]Guide us to the straight sirāt,[g] [6]the way of those whom you have graced (the Muslims), not those whom the wrath is against (the Jews), nor the lost ones (the Christians).

A portion of a revelation   **The Cow**

In the name of Allah, the merciful, the merciful

The Qur'an commands Muslims to believe in the Bible, as well as the Qur'an. This proves that the Bible was correct at the time of Mohammed.

[1]Alm.[h] [2]This is the katab,[i] there is no doubt in it, a guidance to the fearer, [3]those who believe in the unseen and perform the prayer and out of what we provided them they spend; [4]and those who believe in what has been sent down to you and in what has been sent down before you,[j] and who have confidence in the hereafter.

---

[a] god, non-Arabic word of Syriac/Hebrew origin
[b] lord, non-Arabic word of Aramaic/Syriac origin
[c] worlds, non-Arabic word of Aramaic/Hebrew/Syriac origin
[d] merciful, non-Arabic word of Hebrew/Greek origin
[e] merciful, non-Arabic word of Hebrew/Greek origin
[f] judgment, non-Arabic word of Aramaic/Iranian origin
[g] way, non-Arabic word of Greek/Aramaic origin
[h] a word without meaning containing three Arabic letters
[i] book, non-Arabic word of Aramaic origin
[j] the Bible

Allah guides some to believe and prevents others from believing. This theme is repeated throughout the Qur'an. See also verses 14:4; 24:46; 74:31, and 76:3.

[5]Those are on guidance of their lord, and those are the prosperous. [6]Surely those who kafaro,[a] if you warn them or do not warn them, it is the same; they will not believe. [7]Allah has sealed over their hearts and over their hearing and over their eyes a covering, and to them a severe torment. [8]And some people who say, "We āmana[b] in Allah and in the last day." And they are not believers. [9]They deceive Allah and those who have believed, but they do not deceive except themselves, and they do not feel. [10]In their hearts is a sickness, so Allah increased their sickness, and they will have a painful torment because of what they denied. [11]And when it was said to them, "Do not vandalize on the earth." They said, "Surely we are only reformers." [12]Except surely they are the vandals, but they do not feel. [13]And when it was said to them, "Believe as people have believed." They said, "Will we believe as the foolish have believed?" Except surely they are, they are the foolish, and they do not know. [14]And when they met those who believed, they said, "We believed." And when they were apart with their shaiteen,[c] they said, "Surely we are with you; surely we are only scoffing." [15]Allah scoffs at them and keeps them long in their rebellion blindly. [16]Those are they who have purchased the error with the guidance, so their tijāra[d] has not been ribht,[e] and they were not guided. [17]Their parable is like the parable of he who kindles a fire so when it has shined its light all around him, Allah took away their light and left them in darkness; they cannot see. [18]Deaf, dumb, blind; so they will not return. [19]Or like a storm from the heaven, in it is darkness and thunder and lightning, they place their fingers into their ears because of the thunderbolts, fearing the death. And Allah surrounds the infidels. [20]The lightning almost snatches away their sight. Whenever it shines on them, they walk in it; but when darkness closes on them, they stand. And if Allah willed, he would take away their hearing and their sight. Surely Allah has might over all things. [21]O you people, serve your lord who created you and those who were before you, perhaps you may fear. [22]Who has made the earth a bed for you and the heaven a building and sent water from the heaven, so he brought forth by it of the fruit for your rizq.[f] So do not set up rivals with Allah, and you know.

---

[a] became infidels, non-Arabic word of Hebrew/Syriac origin
[b] believed, non-Arabic word of Ethiopian origin
[c] satans—hosts of evil, non-Arabic word of probable Abyssinian origin
[d] merchandise, non-Arabic word of Akkadian/Aramaic origin
[e] profitable, non-Arabic word of Abyssinian origin
[f] bounty—translated as provision, non-Arabic word of Syriac origin

Mohammed claims that the Qur'an is a divine book because no human can write this well, apart from Allah.

[23]And if you were in doubt as to that which we have sent down on our servant, so bring a surah[a] like it and call your witnesses, rather than Allah, if you were truthful. [24]So if you do not do it and you will never do it, so fear the fire whose fuel is people and stones prepared for the infidels.

The Islamic heaven is made up of beautiful gardens, multiple mates of perfect purity (ever-virgin), and constant provision.

[25]And bashshar[b] those who believed and did good deeds, that for them are jannat,[c] below them the rivers flow. Every time they were provided from it a provision of fruit, they said, "This is the provision we had before." And they will be given the likes of it. And they will have in it pure[d] azawaj,[e] and they will abide in it forever. [26]Surely Allah is not ashamed to give a parable about a mosquito or anything above it. So as to those who believed, they will know that it is the truth from their lord; and as to those who became infidels, so they will say, "What does Allah want by this parable?" He will lead many astray by it, and he will guide many by it. And no one will be led astray by it except the transgressors. [27]Those who break the covenant of Allah after it has been established and cut what Allah has amr[f] to associate and vandalize on the earth, those are the losers. [28]How can you become infidels in Allah? And you were dead so he gave you life. Then he will cause you to die; then he will restore you to life; then to him you will return. [29]He is who created for you all of what is on the earth, then went straight to the heaven, so he made them seven heavens. And he is knowledgeable of all things.

The story of Adam is copied from the Bible and corrupted. This story is repeated in the Qur'an in verses 4:1; 7:11-25, 189; 15:26-44; 17:61-65; 20:115-126; 38:71-88; and 49:13. The worship of Adam by the angels contradicts the command of God to worship Him alone. See Matthew 4:10.

[30]And when your lord said to the angels, "Surely I am placing on earth a kalefah."[g] They said, "Will you place in it those who will

---

[a] a portion of a revelation, non-Arabic word of Syriac origin
[b] to give the good news, non-Arabic word of Aramaic/Syriac origin
[c] gardens, non-Arabic word of Semitic origin, e.g. Akkadian, Hebrew, Aramaic, etc.
[d] ever-virgin
[e] wives, non-Arabic word of Greek origin
[f] command, non-Arabic word, when used as a doctrine of revelation, of Aramaic origin
[g] viceroy, non-Arabic word of Berber/Syriac origin

vandalize in it and shed the blood, and [while] we nusabah[a] with your praise and extol your holiness?" He said, "Surely I know what you do not know." [31]And he taught Adam[b] all the names and then set them before the angels, so he said, "Inform me the names of these, if you were truthful." [32]They said, "Praise be to you. We have no knowledge except what you have taught us. Surely you are the knowing, the wise." [33]He said, "O Adam, inform them of their names." So when he informed them of their names, he said, "Did I not say to you that I surely know the unseen of the heavens and the earth, and I know what you reveal and what you were hiding?" [34]And when we said to the angels, "Osjodo[c] to Adam," so they all worshiped except Iblis.[d] He refused and became proud, and he was among the infidels. [35]And we said, "O Adam, askon[e] you and your wife in the garden and eat from it plentifully wherever you will, and do not come near this tree so that you will be of the unjust." [36]So Shaitān[f] made them fall from it, so he got them out from where they were. And we said, "Get down. You will be enemies to one another, and you will have on earth a dwelling place and enjoyment for a while." [37]So Adam received words from his lord, so he tāba[g] toward him. Surely he is the tawwāb,[h] the merciful. [38]We said, "Get down from it, all of you, so either guidance will come to you from me, so whoever follows my guidance, so no fear on them, and they will not grieve. [39]And those who became infidels and denied our āyat,[i] those are companions of the fire; they will abide in it forever."

The story of Moses is copied from the Bible and corrupted. This story is repeated in the Qur'an in verses 5:20-26; 7:103-171; 10:75-94; 17:101-104; 18:60-82; 19:51-53; 20:9-99; 26:10-68; 27:7-14; 28:1-48, 76-83; 40:23-55; 43:46-56; 44:17-59...

[40]O children of Isra'il,[j] remember my grace which I graced on you and fulfill with my covenant; I will fulfill with your covenant, and so be terrified of me.

The following verses state that the Old Testament books, which Allah gave to the Jews, are true and must be believed.

---

[a] praise, non-Arabic word of Aramaic/Hebrew/Syriac origin
[b] non-Arabic word of Hebrew/Syriac origin
[c] worship, non-Arabic word of Aramaic origin
[d] Devil, non-Arabic word of Greek origin
[e] dwell, non-Arabic word of Greek/Syriac origin
[f] Satan, non-Arabic word of probable Abyssinian origin
[g] relented, non-Arabic word of Aramaic origin
[h] relenting
[i] verses, non-Arabic word of Syriac/Aramaic origin
[j] Israel, non-Arabic word of Greek/Syriac origin

[41]And believe in what I have sent down[a] confirming what is with you,[b] and do not be the first to become infidels of it. And do not purchase with my verses[c] a small price.[d] And so fear me. [42]And do not clothe the truth with batal[e] and hide the truth, and you know. [43]And perform the prayer and bring the zakāt[f] and kneel with the kneelers. [44]Will you command the people to be righteous and forget it yourselves? And you who recite the book, do you not understand? [45]And seek assistance with patience and prayer, and surely it is big except to the devout [46]who think that they will meet their lord and that to him they will return.

Allah favored the Jews above all people. This teaching is repeated in the Qur'an in verses 2:122; 27:15; 38:46; and 45:16.

[47]O children of Israel, remember my grace which I graced on you, and I preferred you above the worlds. [48]And fear a day one soul will not benefit another soul anything and intercession will not be accepted from it and it will not take ransom from it, and they will not be helped. [49]And when we delivered you from the family of Fir'aun[g] laying on you an evil torment, slaughtering your sons and sparing your women, and in this was a great trial from your lord. [50]And when we parted the sea for you, so we delivered you and we drowned the family of Pharaoh and you were watching. [51]And when we promised Moses forty nights, then you took the calf after him, and you are unjust. [52]Then we pardoned you; after that, perhaps you might be thankful. [53]And when we gave Moses the book and the furqān,[h] perhaps you might be guided. [54]And when Moses said to his people, "O my people, surely you have done injustice to yourselves by taking the calf. So repent to your creator, so kill yourselves. This is the best for you from your creator." So he relented on you; surely he is the relenting, the merciful.

In these verses the Jews were asking Moses to see Allah. See also verse 4:153 which contradicts the account in the Bible. See Exodus 20:19.

[55]And when you said, "O Moses, we will not believe you until we see Allah openly." So the thunderbolt seized you while you were looking on. [56]Then we raised you up after you had been dead,

---

[a] the Qur'an
[b] the Old Testament
[c] the Qur'an
[d] i.e. gaining a small value from ignoring the verses of the Qur'an
[e] vanity, non-Arabic word of Hebrew origin
[f] legal alms, non-Arabic word of Hebrew/Syriac origin
[g] Pharaoh, non-Arabic word of Hebrew/Syriac origin
[h] discriminator, non-Arabic word of Hebrew/Aramaic/Syriac origin

perhaps you may be thankful. [57]And we caused the clouds to overshadow you, and we sent down the manna and the salwā[a] on you: "Eat from the good things of what we provided to you." And they did not do injustice to us, but they were unjust to themselves. [58]And when we said, "Enter this qarya,[b] so eat there plentifully whatever you will and enter the bāb[c] with worship, and say, 'Hitta.'"[d] We will forgive you your sins, and we will increase the doers of good. [59]So those who were unjust changed the saying to what had not been said to them, so we sent down on those unjust a rujz[e] from the heaven because they were transgressors.

Moses strikes the rock with the rod and twelve springs come out of it. See also verse 7:160. This contradicts the account in Exodus 17:6 which clearly indicates that Moses struck the rock and water came out of it, but it was not twelve springs. Mohammed confused the gushing water with the account of Exodus 15:27 at Elim where there were twelve springs and seventy palm trees.

[60]And when Moses gave drink for his people, so we said, "Strike the rock with your rod." So gushed from it twelve springs; indeed, all humans knew their drinking place: "Eat and drink from Allah's provision, and do not act wickedly in the land, vandalizing." [61]And when you said, "O Moses, we will not be patient with one food, so pray to your lord for us that he would bring forth for us of that which the earth grows: its herbs and its cucumbers and its garlic and its lentils and its onions." He said, "Do you exchange that which is worse for what is better? Go down into Egypt, so surely you will have what you have asked." And the humiliation and poverty were struck on them, and they returned with wrath from Allah because they were infidels with the āyat[f] of Allah; and they killed the prophets unjustly because they disobeyed, and they were transgressors.

Jews, Christians, and Sabians (idol worshipers) are accepted by Allah. Notice the raised mountain. This is subsequently abrogated in the Qur'an by verse 3:85.

[62]Surely those who believed[g] and those who are Jews and the Nasara[h] and the Sābeen,[i] whoever believed in Allah and the last day

---

[a] quail, non-Arabic word of Hebrew origin
[b] village, non-Arabic word of Syriac origin
[c] door, non-Arabic word of Aramaic origin
[d] forgiveness, non-Arabic word of undetermined origin
[e] wrath, non-Arabic word of Syriac origin
[f] signs, non-Arabic word of Syriac/Aramaic origin
[g] Muslims
[h] word made up to mean Christians
[i] Sabians—idol worshipers—uncertain what specific people this represents; may have been a word play on the name of the Sabaean Christians of S. Arabia, non-Arabic

and did good deed, so they will have their ajoor[a] with their lord and no fear on them, and they will not grieve. [63]And when we took your covenant and lifted up the tūr[b] over you: "Take what we gave to you by strength and remember what is in it, perhaps you may fear." [64]Then after this you turned away, so were it not for Allah's bounty and mercy on you, you would have been among the losers.

Allah turned the Jews into monkeys because they did not keep the Sabbath.

[65]And indeed, you know those of you who transgressed in the Sabt;[c] so we said to them, "Become despised monkeys." [66]So we made that[d] an example to what is between her hands[e] and what is behind her[f] and a sermon to the fearers.

The children of Israel and the sacrifice of the cow is a story made up by Mohammed. This was based loosely from three different references in the Bible and was taken out of context. See Genesis 15, Deuteronomy 21, and Numbers 19.

[67]And when Moses said to his people, "Surely Allah commands you to slaughter a cow." They said, "Do you take us as a scoff?" He said, "I seek refuge from Allah that I be of the foolish." [68]They said, "Call on your lord for us that he would inform us what it is." He said, "Surely he said, 'Surely it is a cow, neither old nor young, between the two,' so do what you are commanded." [69]They said, "Call on your lord for us that he would inform us what is its color." He said, "Surely he said, 'Surely she is a yellow cow. Her color is bright; she pleases the beholders. '" [70]They said, "Call on your lord for us that he would inform us what she is. Surely the cows are alike to us, and surely, if Allah wills, we will be guided." [71]He said, "Surely he said, 'Surely she is a cow not worn by plowing the earth or watering the field, submissive, no blemish in her. '" They said, "Now you come with the truth." So they slaughtered her, and they almost did not do [it]. [72]And when you kill a soul and disagree among yourselves about it, and Allah brings forth what you were hiding. [73]So we said, "Strike him with part of it." Likewise, Allah gives life to the dead and shows you his signs, perhaps you may understand. [74]Then your hearts after that became hard so it is like the rocks or much harder, and surely from the rocks have rivers gushed. Others surely have been cracked so

---

word of unknown origin
[a] wage, non-Arabic word of possible Syriac origin
[b] mountain, non-Arabic word of Syriac origin
[c] Saturday, non-Arabic word of Aramaic/Hebrew origin
[d] that, i.e. Allah's punishment
[e] now—the present
[f] the following generations

water comes out of them, and others surely have sunk down through fear of Allah. And Allah is not unaware of what you do. [75]Do you hope that they will believe in you? And indeed, a group of them were hearing the words of Allah; then they altered it after they had understood it, and they know. [76]And when they met those who believed, they said, "We believed." And when they came together privately, they said, "Will you discuss with them that which Allah opened[a] to you that they may dispute with you about it before your lord? Do you not understand?" [77]Do they not know that Allah knows what they hide and what they reveal? [78]And some of them are illiterate who do not know the book[b] except what they desire, and they are only conjecturing. [79]So woe to those who write the book with their hands, then they say, "This is from Allah," to purchase[c] by it a small price.[d] So woe to them for what their hands wrote, and woe to them from what they are earning. [80]And they said, "The fire will not touch us except for numbered days." Say, "Have you taken a covenant from Allah, for Allah will not revoke his covenant, or do you speak against Allah what you do not know?" [81]Yes, whoever earns evil and his sin surrounds him, so those are the companions of the fire; they will abide in it forever. [82]And those who believed and did good deeds, those are the companions of the garden, they will abide in it forever. [83]And when we took a covenant with the children of Israel: "Do not serve except Allah, and be good to your parents and relatives and to orphans and to the poor. And speak good to people and perform the prayer and bring the legal alms." Then you turned away, except for a few among you, and you turned aside. [84]And when we took your covenant: "Do not shed your blood, and do not bring yourselves out of your homes." Then you decided and you were witnesses. [85]Then you are those who are killing yourselves and driving a group from among you from their homes, backing each other up against them with sin and transgression; and if they come to you as captives, you ransom them. And it is forbidden for you to drive them out. Do you believe part of the book and become infidels with part? So what is the reward of he who does this among you, except for disgrace in the world's life. And on the Day of the Qiyāma[e] they will return to the most severe of torments. And Allah is not unaware of what you do. [86]Those are they who purchased the world's life with the hereafter, so the torment will not be reduced for them, and they will not be helped.

---

[a] revealed
[b] Torah
[c] gain
[d] i.e. gaining a small profit from changing the verses of Allah
[e] resurrection, non-Arabic word of Christian-Aramaic origin

Moses' writings came from Allah, and there are "proofs" of 'Isā's (the Jesus of Mohammed) mission. The Jews reject some prophets and kill others.

[87]And indeed, we gave Moses the book. And after him, we sent messengers; and we gave 'Isā,[a] son of Mary, the proofs and supported him by the qudus[b] spirit. Is it every time a messenger came to you with that which yourselves do not desire, you became arrogant, so a group of them you denied and a group you are killing? [88]And they said, "Our hearts are uncircumcised." Yet Allah has cursed them with their infidelity, so little is what they believe. [89]And when a book[c] came to them from Allah confirming what they have,[d] and they were previously praying for assistance against those who became infidels, so when what they knew came to them, they became infidels in it. So the curse of Allah is on the infidels. [90]Evil is what they have purchased by themselves that they become infidels by what Allah has sent down[e] out of envy that Allah will send down from his bounty on whom he wills from his servants. So they have incurred wrath upon wrath. And to the infidels a disgraceful torment. [91]And when it is said to them, "Believe in what Allah has sent down."[f] They said, "We believe what has been sent down[g] on us." And they become infidels by what [has come] after it.[h] And it is the truth, confirming what is with them. Say, "Why then do you kill the prophets of Allah before if you were believers?" [92]And indeed, Moses came to you with proofs; then you took the calf after him, and you are unjust. [93]And when we took your covenant and we lifted the mountain above you: "Take what we have given to you with strength and hear." They said, "We heard and we rebelled." And [they were forced to] drink the calf in their hearts with their infidelity. Say, "Evil is what your belief commands you, if you were believers." [94]Say, "If the home of the hereafter with Allah was exclusively for you, without the people, so wish the death, if you were truthful." [95]And they will never wish for it because of what their hands have sent on before them. And Allah knows the unjust. [96]And surely you will find them, of all people, most covetous of life and from those who are polytheists. One of them wished that he would live for a thousand years, and it will not remove him from the torment to live long. And Allah sees what they do.

---

[a] false name for Jesus, it would be Yasua in Arabic, non-Arabic word of Hebrew/Aramaic origin
[b] holy, non-Arabic word of Aramaic origin
[c] Qur'an
[d] the Torah
[e] the Qur'an
[f] the Qur'an
[g] the Torah
[h] the Qur'an

[97]Say, "Who was an enemy to Gabreel,[a] so surely he sent it[b] down on your heart by Allah's permission confirming what is between his hands[c] and guidance and good news to the believers." [98]Whoever was an enemy to Allah and his angels and his messengers and Gabreel and Mika'il,[d] so surely Allah is an enemy to the infidels. [99]And indeed, we have sent down clear verses[e] to you, and no one becomes an infidel in it except the transgressors. [100]Or whenever they covenant[f] a covenant, a group of them casts it aside, yet most of them do not believe. [101]And when a messenger from Allah[g] came to them, confirming what they had, a group of those who have been given the book came out and cast the book of Allah[h] behind their backs, as if they did not know. [102]And they followed what the satans recited in the kingdom of Sulaimān,[i] and not that Solomon was an infidel, but the satans were infidels. They teach the people al-sahar[j] and what had been sent on the two angels, Harut and Marut, in Bābil.[k] And they did not teach anyone until they said, "Surely we are only a sedition, so do not become infidel." So they learned from them how to cause divisions between the man and his wife, and they are not harming anyone by it except by Allah's permission. They learn what harms them, and it does not profit them; and indeed, they knew who purchased it in the hereafter. He will not have any khalāq.[l] And evil is what they have purchased by themselves, if they were knowing. [103]And if they had believed and feared, their reward from Allah would have been better, if they were knowing. [104]O you who have believed, do not say, "'Rū'ina,'[m] and say, 'Unzurnā,'[n] and listen, and to the infidels a painful torment." [105]Neither those who became infidels among the People of the Book[o] nor the polytheists desire that any good descend on you from your lord. And Allah specifically will give his mercy to whom he wills. And Allah is the possessor of the great bounty.

Allah changes his mind and abrogates his words in the Qur'an. Verse 106 is contradicted later in verse 15:9.

---

[a] some confuse this name with angel Gabriel, but that name is written in Arabic with a different spelling, i.e. Gibrael, non-Arabic word of Hebrew/Syriac origin
[b] the Qur'an
[c] the Bible
[d] Muslim scholars claim Mohammed meant Michael
[e] the Qur'an
[f] make
[g] Mohammed
[h] Qur'an
[i] Solomon, non-Arabic word of Hebrew/Syriac origin
[j] sorcery, non-Arabic word of Akkadian/Aramaic origin
[k] Babel, non-Arabic word of Akkadian origin
[l] portion, non-Arabic word of Hebrew origin
[m] look at us, non-Arabic word of Hebrew origin
[n] behold us, non-Arabic word of Hebrew origin
[o] Jews and Christians

[106]Whatever verse we abrogate, or cause it to be forgotten, we bring a better [verse] than it or like it. Do you not know that Allah has might over all things? [107]Do you not know that Allah has the kingdom of the heavens and the earth and that you do not have a friend nor helper other than Allah? [108]Or do you wish to ask your messenger as Moses was asked before? And whoever changes faith for infidelity, so indeed, he has gone astray from the right sabīl.[a]

Jews and Christians desire to convert Muslims because they are envious of them. In Abo Obyah's interpretation, as stated by the great Muslim scholar Al Qurtobi,[b] he states, "that any verse in the Qur'an that does not include engaging in war is a Mecce verse, and it is abrogated with engaging in war."

[109]Many of the People of the Book desire to turn you back to infidels after you have believed, out of envy from themselves, after the truth has been shown to them. So pardon and forgive them until Allah will come in with his command. Surely Allah has might over all things. [110]And perform the prayer and bring the legal alms and whatever good you present to yourself; you will find it with Allah. Surely Allah sees what you do.

Jews and Christians wish they would be the only ones in the garden.

[111]And they said, "None will enter the garden except who was a Jew or Nasara (Christian)." These are their desires. Say, "Bring your burhan[c] if you were truthful." [112]Yes, whoever aslama[d] his face to Allah while he is doing good, so he will have his wage with his lord, and there is no fear on them. And they will not grieve. [113]And the Jews said, "The Christians are not [standing] on anything." And the Christians said, "The Jews are not [standing] on anything." And they are reciting the book. Likewise said those who do not know [a saying] like their sayings. So Allah will judge between them on the resurrection day about what they were differing. [114]And who is more unjust than those who prevent, in the mosques of Allah, that his name be mentioned in it and strive to destroy it? Those it was not for them to enter it except in fear. They will have shame in this world, and they will have in the hereafter a great torment. [115]And to Allah the east and the west, so wherever you turn there is the face of Allah. Surely Allah is immense, knowing.

---

[a] way, non-Arabic word of Syriac origin
[b] http://quran.al-islam.com/Page.aspx?pageid=221&BookID=14&Page=17, accessed 11/12/2008.
[c] proof, non-Arabic word of Ethiopian/Abyssinian origin
[d] submits, non-Arabic word of Syriac origin

This is a recurring theme throughout the Qur'an: verses 3:45, 64, 157-159; 4:171-172; 5:17-18, 72-73, 75, 110-120; 6:100-102; 9:30-32; 10:68-70; 16:51; 17:111; 18:4-5; 19:35-39, 88-92; 21:26-29; 23:91-92; 25:2; 37:149-157; 39:3-4; 43:81-88; 72:3-4; and 112:1-4. These verses directly contradict the teaching of the Bible. For example, see Isaiah 9:6 in the Old Testament and Luke 1:26-35 in the New Testament.

[116]And they said, "Allah has taken a son. Praise be to him." Yet to him all of what is in the heavens and the earth, all are obedient to him. [117]The originator of the heavens and the earth. And if he decrees an affair, so surely he only says to it, "Be," so it will be. [118]And those who do not know said, "Were it not that Allah would speak to us or a sign come to us." Likewise said those who were before them [a saying] like their sayings. Their hearts became alike. We indeed have shown the signs clearly to people who are certain. [119]Surely we have sent you with the truth, a bearer of good news and a warner, and do not ask about the companions of hell. [120]And the Jews will not be pleased with you nor the Christians until you follow their religion. Say, "Surely the guidance of Allah, he is the guidance." And if you follow their desires after some of the knowledge which came to you, you will not have any friend nor helper against Allah. [121]Those to whom we have given the book, they recite its true recitation. Those believe in it. And whoever becomes an infidel in it, so those are the losers.

Allah raised the Jews high above all people.

[122]O children of Israel, remember my grace which I graced on you, and I have favored you above the worlds. [123]And fear a day a soul cannot reward for another soul anything nor will any ransom be taken from it nor will any intercession profit it, and they will not be helped.

This is the story of Abraham as made up by Mohammed. It is very close to the one written in Chapter 17 of the Jewish book, *Midraush Rabbah*, but it does not match the story as recorded in the Bible in Genesis 12-25. This story is repeated in the Qur'an in verses 6:75-83; 19:41-48; 21:51-70; 26:69-83; 29:16-27; and 37:83-113.

[124]And when Ibrahim[a] was tested by his lord with words, so he fulfilled them. He said, "I am making you an imam[b] to the people." He said, "And who is my offspring?" He said, "My covenant will not be received by the unjust." [125]And when we made the house[c] as a resort

---

[a] Abraham, non-Arabic word which appears 69 times, of Hebrew/Syriac origin
[b] spiritual leader
[c] the Kaaba—the black stone building in Mecca

for people and a haven: "And take from the place of Abraham a place of prayer." And we made a covenant with Abraham and Ishmael.[a] "That purify my house for those who march around it and the dwellers and the kneelers, the worshipers." [126]And when Abraham said, "My lord, make this balad[b] secure and provide its people from the fruit to those who believe among them in Allah and in the last day." He said, "And whoever becomes an infidel, so I will give him a little enjoyment. Then I will force him into the fire of torment, and evil is the final place." [127]And when Abraham was raising the foundations of the house and Ishmael: "Our lord, accept from us, surely you are the hearing, the knowing. [128]Our lord, and make us Muslims to you and among our offspring a Muslim umma[c] to you. And show us our ritual and relent on us. Surely you are the relenting, the merciful. [129]Our lord, and raise to them a messenger from among them who recites your verses to them and teaches them the book and the hikma[d] and purify them. Surely you are the dear, the wise." [130]And who forsakes the religion of Abraham except him who fools himself? And we indeed choose him in this world, and surely in the hereafter he is among the good. [131]When his lord said to him, "Be Muslim." He said, "I became a Muslim to the lord of the worlds."

Jews are warned not to die without becoming Muslims. Ishmael is incorrectly identified as being in the ancestry of Jacob.

[132]And Abraham advised by it[e] his sons and Jacob: "O my sons, surely Allah has chosen the religion for you, so do not die except you are Muslims." [133]Or were you witnesses when death came to Jacob when he said to his sons, "What will you serve after me?" They said, "We will serve your god and the god of your fathers, Abraham and Ishmael and Isaac.[f] One god and to him we are Muslims." [134]This nation indeed passed away. To them what they earned and to you what you earned. And do not ask about what they were doing. [135]And they said, "Become Jews or Christians; you will be guided." Say, "Yet the religion of Abraham is hanifan,[g] and he was not of the polytheists."

There is no difference between 'Isā (the Jesus of Mohammed) and the other prophets.

---

[a] Hebrew name meaning "God hears," non-Arabic word of Greek/ Syriac/ Ethiopian/ Hebrew origin
[b] country, non-Arabic word of Latin/Greek origin
[c] nation, non-Arabic word of Hebrew/Sumerian origin
[d] wisdom, non-Arabic word of Aramaic origin
[e] to become Muslims
[f] Hebrew name meaning "laughter," non-Arabic word of Hebrew origin
[g] a word without meaning

[136]Say, "We believed in Allah and what has been sent down to us, and what has been sent down to Abraham and Ishmael and Isaac and Jacob and the asbāt,[a] and what has been given to Moses and 'Isā, and what has been given to the prophets from their lord. We do not differentiate between any of them, and to him we are Muslims." [137]So if they believed like what you believed, so indeed, they were guided; and if they turn away, so surely they are only in opposition, for Allah is sufficient for you against them. And he is the hearing, the knowing. [138]The sibgha[b] Allah, and is there any better dipping than Allah? And we serve him. [139]Say, "Do you dispute with us about Allah when he is our lord and your lord? And to us our works and to you your works and to him we are devoted." [140]Or do you say, "Surely Abraham and Ishmael and Isaac and Jacob and the tribes were Jews or Christians"? Say, "Do you know better, or Allah? And who is more unjust than he who hides the witness which he has from Allah? And Allah is not unaware of what you do." [141]This is a nation, indeed, passed away. To her what she earned and to you what you earned. And do not ask about what they were doing.

Facing Mecca to pray was copied from old Arabian pagan practices.

[142]The fools among the people will say, "What has turned them from the direction[c] which they were?" Say, "The east and the west to Allah. He guides whom he wills into a straight way." [143]And likewise, we have made you a central nation that you may be witnesses against the people and that the messenger may be a witness against you. And we did not appoint the direction which you were on except that we might know who follows the messenger from him who turns on his heels. And it was a big[d] except to those whom Allah guided. And Allah was not to let your faith be lost. Surely Allah, to the people, is compassionate, merciful. [144]Indeed, we have seen you turning your face toward the heaven. So we will have you turn to a direction which will please you. So turn your face toward the forbidden mosque.[e] And wherever you are, so turn your faces toward that place. And surely those who have been given the book know for sure that this is the truth from their lord. And Allah is not unaware of what they were doing. [145]And even though you bring to the people who have received the book with every sign, they will not follow your direction; and you will not follow their direction, and some of them are not following the direction of others. And if you follow their

---

[a] tribes, non-Arabic word of Hebrew/Syriac origin in its singular form
[b] dipping, non-Arabic word of Syriac origin
[c] of prayer
[d] a difficult task
[e] Masjid ul Haraam at Mecca

desires after some of the knowledge came to you, surely then you will be among the unjust.

Jews and Christians know their Bible as well as they know their own sons.

[146]Those to whom we have given the book, they know it[a] as they know their sons. And surely a group of them will hide the truth, and they know. [147]The truth is from your lord, so do not be of the doubters. [148]And to everyone is a direction to which he should look toward, so hasten to do good deeds wherever you are. Allah will bring you all together. Surely Allah has might over all things. [149]And from whatever place you come out, so turn your face toward the forbidden mosque and surely to the truth from your lord. And Allah is not unaware of what you do. [150]And from whatever place you come out, so turn your face toward the forbidden mosque, and wherever you were, to that part so turn your faces lest people have an excuse against you except those who are unjust among them. So do not fear them. And fear me that I may complete my grace on you, and perhaps you may be guided. [151]As we have sent to you a messenger from among you reciting to you our verses and uzake[b] you and teach you the book and the wisdom and teach you what you were not knowing. [152]So remember me; I will remember you. And give thanks to me, and do not be infidels. [153]O you who have believed, seek assistance with patience and prayer. Surely Allah is with the patient.[c]

Those who die for the sake of Allah (performing jihad—holy war) are not dead, and Allah will pray over them.

[154]And do not say of those who are killed for the sake of Allah:[d] "Dead." Yet they are alive, but you do not feel. [155]And we will surely test you with some of the fear and the hunger and less of the money and the lives and the fruit, and give the good news to the patient. [156]Those, if a misfortune affected them, they said, "Surely we are Allah's and to him we will return." [157]Those on whom are prayers from their lord and mercy, and those are the guided.

Mohammed kept some of the pagan monuments and incorporated them into Islam.

[158]Surely the safa and the marwah[e] are among the monuments of Allah. So whoever then makes a pilgrimage to the house or visits it,

---

[a] the Bible
[b] purify, non-Arabic word of Syriac origin
[c] those who are steadfast in their fighting of holy war
[d] while performing jihad
[e] hills near the Kaaba

there is no sin for him if he goes around them both. And as for him who voluntarily does what is good, so surely Allah is thankful, knowing.

Those who hide any of the truths in Allah's book will be cursed by Allah.

[159]Surely those who hide what we have sent down from the proofs and the guidance after what we have shown to the people in the book, those Allah will curse them, and the cursers will curse them. [160]Except those who repent and reform and reveal, so to those I will relent. And I am the relenting, the merciful. [161]Surely those who became infidels and died while they are infidels, those on them will be the curse of Allah and the angels and all the people. [162]In it they will abide forever, their torment will not be reduced on them, and they will not be delayed. [163]And your god is one god. There is no god except him, the merciful, the merciful. [164]Surely in the creation of the heavens and the earth, and in the changing of the night and the day, and in the fulk[a] which run in the sea with what is useful to people, and what Allah has sent down from the heaven of water so he gives life by it to the earth after its death, and he scattered in it from every creature, and in the change of the winds and in the clouds that are made to be subservient between the heaven and the earth, are signs to people who understand. [165]And some of the people who take idols rather than Allah and love them as the love of Allah, and those who believed are stronger in their love to Allah. And if those who are unjust will see, when they see the torment, that all the power is to Allah and that Allah is severe in the torment. [166]When those who have had followers disown themselves from their followers, and they saw the torment and the ties between them were cut off. [167]And those who follow said, "If only we had a second turn,[b] so we would disown ourselves from them as they have disowned themselves from us." Likewise, Allah will show them their works as a regret to them, and they will not come out of the fire. [168]O you people, eat of what is lawful and good on the earth, and do not follow the steps of Satan; surely he is an obvious enemy to you. [169]Surely he only commands you with evil and indecency and that you speak against Allah what you do not know. [170]And when it was said to them, "Follow what Allah has sent down." They said, "Yet we follow what we are accustomed to our fathers doing." What if their fathers were not understanding anything, and they were not guided? [171]And the parable of those who became infidels is like he who shouts aloud that which cannot be heard except a call and a cry. Deaf, dumb, blind; so they do not understand.

---

[a] ships, non-Arabic word of Greek origin
[b] have a second chance

These are dietary laws copied from the Bible's Old Testament. See Leviticus and Deuteronomy. This passage is in agreement with verse 5:93 but contradicts verse 5:3. (It is lawful to eat pork.)

[172]O you who have believed, eat of the good things which we provided for you, and give thanks to Allah if you were serving him. [173]It is forbidden for you only that which died[a] and the blood and khinzīr[b] meat and what was killed as a sacrifice to other than Allah. So whoever is compelled without desiring nor returning, so it is not a sin for him. Surely Allah is forgiving, merciful. [174]Surely those who hide what Allah has sent down from the book and purchased by it for a little price,[c] those will not eat into their bellies except the fire. And Allah will not speak to them in the resurrection day, nor purify them, and they will have a painful torment. [175]Those are they who have purchased the error with guidance and torment with forgiveness. So how patient are they on the fire! [176]This is because Allah had sent down the book with the truth. And surely those who disagreed in the book are in far dissent. [177]It is not righteousness that you turn your face toward the east or the west, but righteousness is to who have believed in Allah and the last day and the angels and the book and the prophets, and to bring the money, instead of loving it, to his relatives and to the orphans and the needy and the son of the way[d] and the beggars and for the necks (to free slaves), and performing the prayer and bringing the legal alms and who fulfilling their covenant, if they made a covenant, and the patient under ills and hardships and in time of trouble. Those are the ones who are truthful, and those are the fearers.

Allah prescribes retaliation in the case of murder. This is a barbaric way of life.

[178]O you who have believed, retaliation is decreed on you for the murdered, the free [man] for the free, and the slave for the slave, and the female for the female. So whoever pardons his brother in anything, so follow it with fairness, and perform to him with goodness. This is an alleviation from your lord and a mercy. So whoever transgresses after that, so he will have a painful torment. [179]And you will have life in the retaliation, O you who are substantial of understanding, perhaps you may fear. [180]It is decreed for you when death comes to any one of you, if he leaves goods, the will is

---

[a] of itself
[b] swine, non-Arabic word of Aramaic origin
[c] this term, repeated throughout the Qur'an, means that to the infidel the book is considered to be of little value when compared to the enjoyment of the world
[d] traveler

to the parents and relatives, according to fairness. This is a duty for the fearer. [181]So whoever alters it after he has heard it, so surely its sin will only be on those who alter it. Surely Allah is hearing, knowing. [182]So whoever fears any sin or unfair judgment from the executor, so reconcile between them so there is no sin on him. Surely Allah is forgiving, merciful. [183]O you who have believed, siyam[a] is decreed to you as it was decreed to those before you, perhaps you may fear. [184]Numbered days, so whoever among you who was sick or traveling, so [he will fast] same number of other days. And as for those who are not able to keep it, the atonement of this will be the feeding of a poor one. And he who volunteers good, so it is good for him; and if you fast, it is good for you, if you were knowing. [185]The shahr[b] of Ramadan, in which the Qur'ān[c] was sent down a guidance to the people and proofs of the guidance and of the distinguisher, so whoever among you witnesses the month, so let him fast it. And whoever was sick or traveling, so a like number of days. Allah desires the ease for you and does not desire the difficulty for you and that you complete the number. And that you may Kaber Allah[d] for his guidance, and perhaps you may be thankful. [186]And if my servants ask you about me, so surely I am near. I answer the call of the caller, if he calls me, so let them answer me and believe in me, perhaps they may be guided.

The lengths of time of fasting are equal to the hours of daylight. What is the length of fasting for Muslims who live in Greenland or Alaska?

[187]It is lawful for you to have sex with your women the night of the fasting for they are your garment and you are their garment. Allah knows that you were defrauding yourselves in this, so he relents on you and forgives you. So now have a sexual relationship with them and seek that which Allah has decreed to you and eat and drink until you can discern a white thread from a black thread at the daybreak. Then fulfill the fast till night, and do not have sex with them while you are in the mosque. Those are the limits of Allah, so do not come near them. Likewise, Allah makes his verses clear to people, perhaps they may fear. [188]And do not consume your money among yourselves with vanity, nor present it to the judges that you may consume a part of other people's money with sin, and you know. [189]They ask you of the crescents.[e] Say, "They are times fixed for people and for the pilgrimage. It is not righteous for you to enter the houses from their

---

[a] fasting, non-Arabic word of Syriac origin
[b] month, non-Arabic word of Aramaic origin
[c] Qur'an, non-Arabic word of Hebrew/Syriac origin
[d] that is to call "Allah Akber," i.e. Allah is bigger
[e] moon phases

backs, but the righteousness is he who fears and comes to the houses from their doors. And fear Allah, perhaps you may prosper.

Death is the just reward for infidels.

[190]And engage in war for the sake of Allah against those who engage in war against you, and do not transgress. Surely Allah does not love the transgressors. [191]And kill them wherever you find them, and get them out from where they got you out. And the sedition is worse than the killing. And do not engage in war with them at the forbidden mosque until they engage in war with you in it. So if they engage in war with you, so kill them; likewise is the reward of the infidels. [192]So if they desist, so surely Allah is forgiving, merciful.

Never stop waging war until all men worship Allah. Revenge is lawful. This contradicts Matthew 5:38-39, 44; Romans 12:19-21; and I Peter 2:21-23.

[193]And engage in war with them until there be no sedition and the religion[a] be to Allah. So if they desist, so there will be no transgression except on the unjust. [194]The forbidden month for the forbidden month[b] and all the forbidden things are retaliation, so whoever commits transgression against you, so transgress against him similar to how he transgressed against you. And fear Allah, and know that Allah is with the fearer. [195]And spend for the sake of Allah and do not throw with your hands to the destruction and do good deeds. Surely Allah loves the doers of good.

The Muslim Pilgrimage (the Hajj) is copied from ancient pagan practice.

[196]And complete the pilgrimage and the visit to Allah. So if you are prevented, so do whatever offering will be the easiest, and do not shave your heads until the offering reaches the place of sacrifice. So whoever among you was sick or has an injury of his head, so its atonement is fasting or sadaqa[c] or an offering. So when you are secure, so whoever profits himself with the visit to the pilgrimage, so [give] whatever offering will be the easiest. So whoever does not find [something to offer], so fasting three days in the pilgrimage and seven when you return; these are ten complete. This is for whom his family is not present at the forbidden mosque. And fear Allah, and know that Allah is severe in the punishment. [197]The pilgrimage is known months. So whoever determines [to go on] the pilgrimage, let

---

[a] Islam
[b] Mohammed probably meant "months" since there are four months during which engaging in war is suspended
[c] alms, non-Arabic word of possible Christian-Palestinian dialect origin

him not have sexual relations nor fornication nor dispute in the pilgrimage. Whatever good you do, Allah knows it. And tāzawado,[a] so surely the best of the provisions is the fear. And fear me, O you who are substantial of understanding. [198]It will be no sin on you if you seek bounty from your lord. So when you take off from Arafat,[b] so remember Allah near the forbidden monument, and remember him as he has guided you and that before it you were among the lost. [199]Then take off[c] from where the people take off and ask forgiveness of Allah. Surely Allah is forgiving, merciful. [200]So when you have finished your ritual, so remember Allah as you remember your fathers or with even stronger remembrance. So some of the people who say, "Our lord, give us our portion in this world." And he will not have a portion in the hereafter. [201]And some of them who say, "Our lord, give us good in this world and good in the hereafter and save us [from] the torment of the fire." [202]Those will have a portion of what they have earned. And Allah is swift in the reckoning. [203]And remember Allah in numbered days, so whoever starts earlier in two days, so there is no sin on him. And whoever delays, so there is no sin on him who fears. And fear Allah and know that you will be gathered to him. [204]And some of the people whom you like their speech in the world's life, and Allah is a witness to what is in his heart, and he is the most violent of adversaries. [205]And when he turns away, he strives on the earth to vandalize in it and destroys the crops and the decendant, and Allah does not love the vandalization. [206]And when it was said to him, "Fear Allah," the pride of sin seized him. So jahannam[d] is sufficient for him, and evil is the bed. [207]And some of the people sell themselves desiring to please Allah, and Allah is compassionate to the servants. [208]O you who have believed, enter completely into Islam and do not follow the steps of Satan; surely he is an obvious enemy to you. [209]So if you fall after the proofs have come to you, so know that Allah is dear, wise. [210]Do they wait until Allah comes to them in the shadow of the clouds and the angels and their affair has been judged? And to Allah the affairs return. [211]Ask the children of Israel how many clear signs we have given them. And who changes Allah's grace after it has come to him. So surely Allah is severe in the punishment. [212]The world's life is beautified to the infidels, and they scoff at those who believed. And those who feared will be above them on the resurrection day. And Allah provides to whom he wills without accounting. [213]The people were one nation, so Allah raised prophets announcing the good news and warning. And he sent down the book with them with the truth to judge between the people in what they disagreed about, and

---

[a] make provision, non-Arabic word of Aramaic origin
[b] mountain
[c] depart
[d] hell, non-Arabic word of Persian/Hebrew origin

no one disagreed about it except those who received it after the proofs came to them, revolting among themselves. So Allah guided those who believed in what they disagreed about the truth by his permission. And Allah guides whom he wills to a straight way. [214]Or you thought that you will enter the garden, and it did not come to you, the examples of those who passed before you? Distresses touched them and affliction, and they were shaken until the messenger and those who believed with him say, "When is Allah's victory?" But surely the victory of Allah is near. [215]They ask you what they will spend. Say, "Whatever you spend from good is to the parents and the relatives and the orphans and the poor and the son of the way. And whatever good you do, so surely Allah knows it."

Allah orders Muslims to engage in war because it is good for them. Whoever leaves the religion of Islam must be put to death. Notice also the ties between emigration and performing jihad in verse 218.

[216]War is decreed to you, and it is hated by you. And perhaps you may hate something, and it is good for you; and perhaps you love something, and it is evil for you. And Allah knows, and you do not know. [217]They ask you concerning war in the forbidden month.[a] Say, "Engaging in war in it is big, and to prevent [others] from the way of Allah and to become an infidel in him and the forbidden mosque and to get its people out from it is bigger with Allah. And the sedition is bigger than the killing." And they still engage in war with you until they apostate you from your religion, if they can. And whoever apostates among you, from his religion, so he is put to death as an infidel. So those, their works will be voided in this world and in the hereafter. And those are companions of the fire, and they will abide in it forever. [218]Surely those who have believed and those who emigrated and performed jihad[b] for the sake of Allah, those hope for Allah's mercy. And Allah is forgiving, merciful.

There are benefits with alcohol and gambling which are allowed by the following verse. This contradicts verse 5:90.

[219]They ask you concerning khamr[c] and gambling. Say, "In them is big sin and benefits to people, and their sin is bigger than their benefits." And they ask you what they will spend. Say, "What you can spare." Likewise, Allah shows you his verses, perhaps you may reflect. [220]In this world and the hereafter, and they ask you concerning the orphans. Say, "Doing good to them is good, and if

---

[a] months, since there are four
[b] holy war
[c] wine, non-Arabic word of Aramaic/Syriac origin

you mingle with them, so they are your brethren." And Allah knows the vandal from the doer of good; and, if Allah wills, he would cause you to fall into difficulty. Surely Allah is dear, wise.

It is better to marry a slave than an idolatress (including Christians).

[221]And do not have sex (marry) the polytheist females until they believe. A female slave who is a believer is better than a polytheist, even though you like her. And do not have sex (marry) the polytheist males until they believe. And a male slave who is a believer is better than a polytheist, even though you like him. Those invite to the fire, and Allah invites to the garden and the forgiveness by his permission. And he shows his verses to the people, perhaps they may remember. [222]And they ask you about the menstruation. Say, "It is harmful." So separate from the women during menstruation, and do not get near them until they are purified. So when they are purified, so continue sexual relations as Allah has commanded you. Surely Allah loves those who continually repent, and he loves the purified.

A man's women are his field, and he can have sex with his wives as he pleases.

[223]Your women are a field to you, so enter your field[a] as you please and send beforehand [good] for yourselves. And fear Allah and know that you will meet him and give the good news to the believers. [224]And do not make Allah a hindrance for your oath, that you will be virtuous and fear and promote reconciliation among men. And Allah is hearing, knowing.

It is permissible to lie in an oath. This passage also contains various regulations concerning divorce. Mohammed errs when he insists that women must wait past three menstruations to know whether or not they are pregnant.

[225]Allah will not hold you responsible for your mere utterance in an oath, but he will hold you responsible for that which your hearts gained.[b] And Allah is forgiving, forbearing. [226]To those who desire divorce from their women, let them wait[c] for four months, so if they get back together. So surely Allah is forgiving, merciful. [227]And if they decide on a divorce, so surely Allah is hearing, knowing. [228]And the divorced women should keep themselves[d] three menstruations. It is not lawful for them to hide what Allah has created in their wombs if they were believer in Allah and in the last day. And it will be more

---

[a] have sex
[b] what your heart meant
[c] stop having sex with them
[d] from having sex with men

right for their husbands to bring them back when in this state if they desire reconciliation. And they have rights similar to the one over them in fairness. And to the men, a higher degree than them. And Allah is dear, wise. [229]The divorce is twice. So keep them in fairness, or put them away in fairness. And it is not lawful for you to take what you have given to them of anything unless they fear that they cannot keep the limits of Allah. So if you fear that they cannot keep the limits of Allah, so no sin will be on them for what she will herself give for her redemption. These are the limits of Allah, so do not transgress them; and whoever transgresses the limits of Allah, so those are the unjust.

A man cannot marry his wife after their third divorce until she marries and divorces another man. This contradicts the teachings in Deuteronomy 24:1-4.

[230]So if he divorces her [a third time], so it is not lawful for him to take her again until she has sex with another husband. So if he divorces her, then there will be no sin on them if they return to each other if they think that they can keep the limits of Allah. And these are the limits of Allah; he shows them to people who know. [231]And when you divorce the women, so [when] they reach the end of their waiting period, so keep them in fairness or put them away in fairness. And do not keep them in harm[a] to commit transgression, and he who does that, so indeed, did injustice to himself. And do not take the verses of Allah as a scoff, and remember the grace of Allah on you and what he has sent down on you from the book and the wisdom he preaches to you by it. And fear Allah, and know that Allah is the knower of all things. [232]And when you divorce the women, so [when] they reach the end of their period, so do not prevent them from having sex with their husbands when they have agreed among themselves in fairness. This is to be preached with who was among you who believe in Allah and in the last day. This is the most virtuous for you and most pure. And Allah knows, and you do not know.

Men can require women to nurse their babies for two full years, even after they are divorced.

[233]And the mothers breastfeed their children two full years, to who desires[b] that the breastfeeding be completed, and such provision and clothing as is fair for them will be his responsibility. No soul will be charged except within their means. A mother will not be pressed unfairly for her child, nor a father for his child, and the same with the heir. But if they choose to wean the child by consent and by

---

[a] against their will
[b] when the father desires

discussion, so it will be no sin on them. And if you choose to have a
nurse for your children, so no sin on you if you give what you
promised with fairness. And fear Allah, and know that Allah sees
what you do. [234]And those of you who die leaving wives, they[a] must
keep themselves during four months and ten, so when they reach
the end of their waiting period, there is no sin on you for the way in
which they will dispose of themselves with fairness. And Allah is
aware of what you do. [235]And no sin on you in making proposals of
engagement to the women or covering[b] to yourselves. Allah knows
that you will remember them. But do not promise them in secret
unless you speak honorable words. And do not resolve the contract
of having sex (marriage) until the prescribed time is reached. And
know that Allah knows what is in your souls. So beware of him and
know that Allah is forgiving, forbearing. [236]There is no sin on you if
you divorce the women so long as you have not touched them or
appointed to them a portion. And provide for them, he who is wealthy
according to his means and the poor according to his means, a
provision with fairness. A duty to the doers of good. [237]And if you
divorce them before you touch them and have already settled a
portion for them, so half of what you settled, unless they make a
release or the one who holds the contract of having sex (marriage)
makes a release. And if you make a release, it will be closer to piety.
And do not forget to be bountiful among yourselves. Surely Allah
sees what you do. [238]Keep to the prayers and the middle prayer, and
stand in obedience before Allah. [239]So if you fear, so [pray] on foot or
riding. So when you are safe, so remember Allah as he taught you
what you were not knowing. [240]And those of you who die and leave
wives, will to their wives provision for a year without causing them to
get out. So if they get out[c] there is no sin on you concerning what
they have done to themselves of fairness. And Allah is dear, wise.
[241]And for the divorced [women] let there be a fair provision. A duty
to the fearer. [242]Likewise, Allah makes his verses clear to you;
perhaps you may understand. [243]Have you not seen those go forth
from their homes, and they are thousands, for fear of death? So
Allah said to them, "Die." Then he brought them to life. Surely Allah
is bountiful to people, but most people do not give thanks.

Allah commands Muslim believers to engage in war.

[244]And engage in war for the sake of Allah, and know that Allah is
hearing, knowing. [245]Whoever lends Allah an excellent loan, he will

---

[a] the widows
[b] keeping it secret
[c] of the provided lodging

double it to him many doublings, and Allah can close[a] and open[b] and to him you will return.

Mohammed is confused between Tālūt (Saul) and Gideon. The battle between Tālūt and the Philistines is a completely different story than Gideon and the Midianites. See Judges 7:1-8 and 1 Samuel 17.

[246]Have you not seen the gathering of the children of Israel after Moses? When they said to a prophet for them, "Send to us a king, we will engage in war for the sake of Allah." He said, "Will it be that you would not go to war if engaging in war is decreed for you?" They said, "And why should we not engage in war for the sake of Allah, and indeed, we and our children are driven forth from our homes?" So when the engaging in war was decreed to them, they turned back except for a few of them. And Allah knows the unjust. [247]And their prophet said to them, "Surely Allah has sent Tālūt[c] as a king to you." They said, "How can the kingdom be to him over us when we are more worthy of the kingdom than him, and he has no abundance of money?" He said, "Surely Allah has chosen him over you and has given him increase in knowledge and stature. And Allah gives his kingdom to whom he wills. And Allah is large, knowing." [248]And their prophet said to them, "Surely the sign of his kingdom will be that the tābūt[d] will come to you. In it is tranquility from your lord and the relics left by the family of Moses and the family of Aaron. The angels will carry it. Surely in this is a sign to you if you were believers." [249]So when Tālūt marched forth with his jund,[e] he said, "Surely Allah will test you by a river. So whoever drinks of it so is not of me, but he who does not taste it, so surely he is of me except who scoops a scoop by his hand so they drink from it, except a few of them." So when they had passed it, he and those who believed with him, they said, "We have no strength this day with Jālūt[f] and his troops." Those among them who thought that they would meet Allah said, "How many a small group have victory over a large group, by Allah's permission? And Allah is with the patient." [250]And when they went forth against Goliath and his troops, they said, "Our lord, pour out patience on us and set our feet firm and give us victory against the infidel people." [251]So they defeated them by Allah's permission. And Dāwūd[g] killed Goliath, and Allah gave him the kingdom and the

---

[a] his hand, i.e. withhold
[b] his hand, i.e. give
[c] Saul, non-Arabic word created by Mohammed—apparently from a misunderstanding of the Hebrew word meaning tall
[d] ark, non-Arabic word of Egyptian origin
[e] troops, non-Arabic word of Iranian/Aramaic origin
[f] Goliath, non-Arabic word, apparently of garbled Hebrew origin
[g] David, non-Arabic word of Aramaic origin

wisdom. And he taught him from whatever he willed. And were it not that Allah gives conquest to some people over others, then the earth would have been vandalized. But Allah is the possessor of bounty to the worlds. [252]These are the verses of Allah. We recite them to you with the truth, and surely you are of the messengers.

'Isā (the Jesus of Mohammed) performed many signs, but he was still only a messenger. All prophets are not equal.

[253]These are the messengers; we favored some of them above the others. Some of them spoke to Allah, and he exalted some of them by degrees. And we gave 'Isā, the son of Mary, the proofs, and we supported him with the holy spirit. And if Allah willed, they would not engage in war after the proofs came to them. But they differed. So some of them who believed, and some who became infidel. And if Allah willed, they would not engage in war. But Allah does what he wants. [254]O you who have believed, spend from what we provided to you before a day comes when there will be no selling in it and no friendship and no intercession. And the infidels are the unjust. [255]Allah, there is no god but he, the living, the qayyūm,[a] slumber does not take him nor sleep. To him what is in the heavens and what is on the earth. Who is he that can intercede with him except by his permission? He knows what is between their hands[b] and what is behind them, and they cannot surround[c] anything out of his knowledge except by what he wills. His kursiy[d] reaches over the heavens and the earth, and keeping them does not burden him. And he is the high, the great.

There is no compulsion in religion. This early verse was abrogated by subsequent Qur'an verses which include verse 9:5.

[256]No compulsion in religion. Indeed, the right way is made distinct from the error. So whoever becomes an infidel in the taghut[e] and believes in Allah, so indeed, he will have taken hold on a strong handle that will not be broken. And Allah is hearing, knowing. [257]Allah is the friend of those who believed. He will bring them out of the darkness into the light. And those who became infidels, their friend is the idolatry. They will bring them out of the light into the darkness; those are the companions of the fire, in it they will abide forever.

This story of Abraham and some unknown king is made-up by Mohammed.

---

[a] self-subsisting, non-Arabic word of Syriac origin
[b] now before them
[c] comprehend
[d] throne, non-Arabic word of Aramaic origin
[e] idolatry, non-Arabic word of Aramaic/Abyssinian origin

[258]Have you not seen him who disputed with Abraham about his lord, that Allah had given him the kingdom? When Abraham said, "My lord is he who gives life and causes death." He said, "I give life and cause death." Abraham said, "So surely Allah brings the sun from the east, so bring it from the west." So the infidel was confounded. And Allah will not guide the unjust people. [259]Or like this one who passed by a village, and it was empty on its roof.[a] He said, "Will Allah give life to this after its death?" So Allah caused him to die for a hundred years and then raised him to life. And Allah said, "How long were you waiting?" He said, "I have waited a day or part of a day." He said, "Yet you have waited a hundred years. So look at your food and your drink, they are not corrupted, and look to your donkey. We would make you a sign to people. And look on the bones, how we raise them, then clothe them with flesh." So when this was shown to him, he said, "I know that Allah has might over all things."

This story of Abraham and the birds is copied from the Bible and corrupted. See Genesis 15.

[260]And when Abraham said, "My lord, show me how you give life to the dead." He said, "Have you not believed?" He said, "Yes, but so that my heart be assured." He said, "So take four of the birds and cut them and mix them; then place a part of them on every mountain. Then call them, and they will come swiftly to you. And know that Allah is dear, wise." [261]The parable of those who spend their money for the sake of Allah is like the parable of a grain which produces seven sanabul[b] and in each ear of corn a hundred grains, and Allah will multiply to whom he wills. And Allah is large, knowing. [262]Those who spend their money for the sake of Allah, then do not follow what they have spent with reproach or harm, will have their wage with their lord and no fear on them, and they will not grieve. [263]Kind speech and forgiveness is better than alms followed by injury. And Allah is rich, forbearing. [264]O you who have believed, make not your alms void by reproaches and injury like him who spends his money to be seen by people and do not believe in Allah and in the last day. So his parable is like the parable of a rock with dirt on it on which a heavy rain falls but leaves it hard. No profit from their works will they be able to gain. And Allah does not guide the infidel people. [265]And the parable of those who spend their money seeking to please Allah and for the establishing of their souls are like the parable of a garden on a hill on which the heavy rain falls, and it yields its food double. So even if a heavy rain did not fall on it, so a dew. And Allah sees what you do. [266]Does any one of you desire a garden of palms and

---

[a] crumbled
[b] ears of corn, non-Arabic word of Aramaic origin

vines to be his, below them the rivers flow, he will have in it from every fruit and he becomes old and he has weak offspring so that a violent wind struck it, in it fire, so it burned? Likewise, Allah makes his verses clear to you, perhaps you may reflect. [267]O you who have believed, spend of the good things which you have earned and of that which we have brought forth to you from the earth. And do not give the bad from it, such as you yourselves would not take except with closed eyes. And know that Allah is rich, praised. [268]Satan promises you poverty and commands you with indecency. And Allah promises you forgiveness from himself and bounty. And Allah is large, knowing. [269]He gives the wisdom to whom he wills. And whoever receives the wisdom, so indeed, it is given great good, and none will remember except those with understanding.

Alms that are given will atone for sins.

[270]And whatever you spend for spending, or whatever vow you vow, so surely Allah knows it; and to the unjust there are no helpers. [271]If you show the alms openly, it is well. And if you hide them and give them to the poor, so it is good to you and will atone for your evil. And Allah is aware of what you do. [272]It is not your responsibility for their guidance, but Allah guides whom he wills. And whatever you spend from good, so it is to yourself, and whatever you spend, except seeking the face of Allah, and whatever you spend from good will be repaid to you, and you will not be dealt with unjustly. [273]For the poor, who are confined for the sake of Allah, do not have in their might to strike out into the earth. The fool thinks they are rich because of their modesty. You will know them by their sīmā.[a] They will not beg people, and whatever you spend of good, so surely Allah knows it. [274]Those who spend their money, by night and day, secretly and publicly, so they will have their wage with their lord and there is no fear on them and they will not grieve.

Those who charge interest on loans will burn in hell forever.

[275]Those who devour the interest, they will not stand, except like those whom Satan has beaten by his touch will stand. This because they said, "Surely the selling is only like the interest." And Allah made the selling lawful and forbade the interest. So whomever a sermon has come to him from his lord, so he abstains, so to him what has passed and his affair is to Allah. And whoever returns, so those are the companions of the fire; they will abide in it forever.

---

[a] marks, non-Arabic word of Greek origin

Allah does not love an evil person.

[276]Allah will bring the interest to nothing but will increase alms with the interest. And Allah does not love every sinful infidel. [277]Surely those who believed and did good deeds and performed the prayer and brought the legal alms, they will have their wage with their lord, and no fear on them. And they will not grieve. [278]O you who have believed, fear Allah and abandon what remains of the interest, if you were believers. [279]So if you do not do it, so prepare for a war from Allah and his messenger. And if you repent, so you will have the principal of your money. Do not treat others unjustly, and you will not be dealt with unjustly. [280]And if he was in straits [financial stress], then let there be a delay until it be easy for him. And if you could give it as alms, it is good for you if you were knowing. [281]And fear a day in it you will return to Allah. Then will every soul be rewarded what it has earned, and they will not be dealt with unjustly.

The witness of two females equals the witness of one man.

[282]O you who have believed, when you contract a debt at a fixed time, so write it down, and let a writer write between you with fairness and let not the writer refuse to write, even as Allah has taught him. So let him write it down and let the debtor dictate and let him fear Allah his lord and do not diminish anything from it. So if the debtor was mentally deficient or weak or cannot dictate, so let his friend dictate with fairness and call two witnesses from your men; so if there were not two men, so one man and two women of those among whom you are pleased for witnesses so that if one of them[a] should make an error, the other may cause her to remember. And the witnesses will not refuse whenever they are called. And do not tire to put the debt in writing, be it small or large to its time. This is more aqsuit[b] with Allah, better suited for witnessing, and the best for avoiding doubt. But if the merchandise be there present and you pass it among you, so there is no sin on you not to write it down. And have witnesses when you sell, and do not harm the writer nor the witness; and if you do, so surely it is sin to you. And fear Allah. And Allah teaches you, and Allah knows all things. [283]And if you were traveling and did not find a writer, let pledges be taken. So if one of you trusts the other, so let him who is trusted restore what he is trusted with, and let him fear Allah his lord. And do not withhold the testimony. And whoever withholds it, so surely it is a sin in his heart. And Allah knows what you do. [284]To Allah what is in the heavens and what is on the earth, and if you reveal what is in yourselves or hide it, Allah will call you to account by it. So he will forgive whom he wills,

---

[a] the women
[b] just, non-Arabic word of Aramaic origin

and he will torment whom he wills. And Allah is mighty over all things. [285]The messenger believed in that which had been sent down from his lord. And the believers all believed in Allah and his angels and his books and his messengers. We do not differentiate between any of his messengers. And they said, "We heard and obeyed. Your forgiveness, our lord. And to you is the final return." [286]Allah will not burden any soul except its ability. It will receive what it earned, and it will pay what it earned. Our lord, do not hold us responsible if we forget or akhati'na.[a] Our lord, and do not lay on us a load like that which you have laid on those who have been before us. Our lord, and do not lay on us that for which we have not strength, but blot out our sins and forgive us and have mercy on us. You are our friend, so give us victory against the infidel people.

A portion of a revelation   *The Family of Amran*

In the name of Allah, the merciful, the merciful

[1]Alm. [2]Allah, there is no god but him, the living, the self-subsisting,

The Qur'an was sent down to confirm Moses' law and 'Isā's (the Jesus of Mohammed) Ingeel (the Gospel).

[3]has sent down on you the book[b] with the truth, confirming what is between his hands, and has sent down the Taurāh[c] and the Ingeel,[d] [4]before a guidance to the people, and has sent down the discrimination. Surely those who became infidels in the verses of Allah, they will have a severe torment. And Allah is dear, possessor of revenge. [5]Surely nothing can be hidden to Allah on earth or in the heaven. [6]He is who forms you in the womb how he wills. There is no god but him, the dear, the wise.

No one can know the Qur'an except Allah. So why did he send it? See also verse 7:53. These verses both contradict 25:33.

[7]He is who has sent down on you the book;[e] some of its verses are decisive. Those are the mother of the book and others are ambiguous. So those whose hearts deviate, so they will follow what

---

[a] fall into sin, non-Arabic word of Syriac origin
[b] Qur'an
[c] Torah—first five books of the Old Testament, non-Arabic word of Hebrew origin
[d] the Gospel, non-Arabic word of Greek origin
[e] Qur'an

is ambiguous of it, desiring the sedition and desiring its interpretation, and no one knows its interpretation except Allah. And those deeply rooted in knowledge say, "We believed in it, all of it from our lord." But none will remember except those who have understanding. [8]Our lord, do not make our hearts deviate after you have guided us, and grant to us mercy from you. Surely you are the grantor. [9]Our lord, surely you gather the people to a day; there is no doubt in it. Surely Allah will not change the appointed time. [10]Surely those who became infidels, their money and their children will not profit them anything against Allah. And those are the fuel of the fire. [11]Like the habit of the family of Pharaoh and those who before them, they denied our verses. So Allah seized them for their sins. And Allah is severe in the punishment. [12]Say to those who became infidels, "You will be defeated and gathered into hell, and evil is the bed." [13]Indeed, there was a sign in the meeting of the two groups. A group waged war for the sake of Allah, and another is an infidel. They see them twice as many by their eyes. And Allah supports with his victory whom he wills. Surely in this is a lesson for those who have sight. [14]Beautify to people the love of the lusts of women and sons and the qantēr[a] which are moqantarah[b] of gold and silver and horses with marks and livestock and fields. Such is the enjoyment of the world's life. And Allah has the best return.

In the gardens men will have multiple wives of stainless purity (ever-virgin).

[15]Say, "Will I inform you with better than that? To the fearer with their lord gardens, below them the rivers flow, they will abide in it forever. In it are pure[c] wives with Allah's pleasure. And Allah sees the servants." [16]Those who say, "Our lord, we surely believed, so forgive us our sins and guard us from the torment of the fire." [17]The patient and the truthful and the lowly and the spenders and they who ask forgiveness at daybreak. [18]Allah witnessed that there is no god but him. And the angels and those who possess knowledge will stand with qist.[d] There is no god but him, the dear, the wise.

The only true faith in Allah's sight is Islam. Mohammed's only responsibility is to deliver Allah's message. See also verses 6:107 and 10:99-100. These verses contradict 4:89; 9:73; and 47:4.

---

[a] measures, non-Arabic word of Greek origin
[b] measured
[c] ever-virgin
[d] justice, non-Arabic word of Aramaic origin

[19]Surely the religion with Allah is Islam, and they[a] to whom are given the book[b] did not disagree, except after the knowledge came to them, out of envy among themselves. And whoever becomes an infidel in the verses of Allah, so surely Allah is swift in the reckoning. [20]So if they dispute with you, so say, "I have surrendered my face to Allah and those who follow me." And say to those who were given the book[c] and to the Gentiles, "Have you become Muslim?" So if they become Muslims, so indeed, they are guided; and if they turn away, so surely your duty is only the delivering. And Allah sees the servants. [21]Surely those who become infidels in the verses of Allah and kill the prophets unjustly and kill those who command with justice from the people, so give them the good news of a painful torment. [22]Those are they whose works will come to nothing in this world and in the hereafter, and they will have no helpers. [23]Have you not seen those who have received a portion of the book? They are called to the book of Allah that he might judge between them. Then a group of them turn away and they withdraw. [24]This is because they said, "The fire will not touch us except for our numbered days." And whatever they were forging made them proud in their religion. [25]So how, when we will gather them to a day, no doubt in it, and when every soul will be paid what it has earned, and they will not be dealt with unjustly? [26]Say, "Allahumma,[d] owner of the kingdom, you give the kingdom to whom you will and remove the kingdom from whom you will. You exalt whom you will and despise whom you will. In your hand is the good. Surely you have might over everything. [27]You penetrate the night into the day, and you penetrate the day into the night. You bring forth the living out of the dead, and you bring forth the dead out of the living; you provide to whom you will, without accounting."

Muslims who make friends with unbelievers lose their salvation, but Muslims can make temporary friendships with infidels only when the Muslims are weak until they have the upper hand. See verse 47:35.

[28]Believers do not take the infidels for friends, rather than the believers, and whoever does this so he has nothing to do with Allah, except that you should guard yourself from them, cautiously. And Allah himself warns you, and to Allah is the final return. [29]Say, "Whether you hide what is in your chests, or whether you reveal it, Allah knows it. And he knows what is in the heavens and what is on the earth. And Allah has might over all things." [30]A day, [when] every soul will find what it has done from good and what it has done from

---

[a] Jew and Christian
[b] the Bible
[c] the Bible
[d] O Allah, non-Arabic word of Hebrew origin

evil, [will be] brought before it. It wishes that a long time will be between them. And Allah himself warns you. And Allah is compassionate to the servants. [31]Say, "If you were loving Allah, so follow me. Allah will make you loved and forgive you of your sins. And Allah is forgiving, merciful."

Allah does not love those who do not believe. This is contrary to the Bible which teaches that God loves all people. See John 3:16.

[32]Say, "Obey Allah and the messenger." So if they turn away, so surely Allah does not love the infidels. [33]Surely Allah chose Adam and Noah and the family of Abraham and the family of 'Imrān,[a] above the worlds, [34]their offspring, some from the other. And Allah is hearing, knowing.

Mohammed thought that Mary, the mother of Jesus, was the same Mary (Miriam) who was the sister of Moses and Aaron. See also verses 19:28 and 66:12. According to the Bible, the only woman who vowed her child in her belly to the Lord was Hannah, the mother of Samuel. See I Samuel 1:1. Mary, the daughter of Amram, never married nor had children.

[35]When the woman [wife] of Amran said, "My lord, surely I vow to you what is in my belly is to be devoted [to you]. So accept it from me. Surely you are the hearing, the knowing." [36]So when she had given birth to her, she said, "My lord, surely I have delivered her a female, and Allah knows of what I have birthed. And the male is not like the female. And I have named her Mary, and I seek refuge for her and for her offspring from the rajim[b] Satan."

Mohammed was apparently influenced by Chapters 15 and 18 from the Coptic book, *The Story of the Trip of Joseph*. It reports that Mary was living in the Temple of Solomon. Actually, no females lived in the Temple. In fact, they were only allowed as far as the outer courtyard. Because it was God's house, the worshipers could not enter the holy place which was reserved for priests and other worship leaders, much less the holiest place (Holy of Holies) which was to be entered by the high priest only once a year. See Leviticus 16 and Hebrews 9:6.

[37]So her lord accepted her with a good acceptance and planted her a good planting. And Zakariyyā[c] took responsibility for her, and

---

[a] Amran, non-Arabic word of Syriac origin
[b] stoned, non-Arabic word of Ethiopian origin, originally meaning cursed
[c] Zacharias, non-Arabic word of Syriac origin

every time Zacharias entered into her in the mihrab,[a] he found that she had provision. He said, "O Mary, where did this come from?" She said, "It is from Allah. Surely Allah provides for whom he wills, without accounting."

The story of Zacharias and John the Baptist is copied from the Bible and corrupted. See Luke 1:8-25. The story is repeated in the Qur'an in verses 19:1-15 and 21:89-90.

[38]Thereupon Zacharias called his lord and said, "My lord, grant me from yours a good descendant. Surely you are the hearer of the calling." [39]So the angels called to him while he stood usalle[b] in the holy of holies: "That Allah gives you good news of Yahya,[c] confirming by a word from Allah, and a master, celibate, and a prophet from among the good." [40]He said, "My lord, how can I have a son and, indeed, the old age has come to me and my woman [wife] is barren?" He said, "Likewise, Allah does what he wills." [41]He said, "My lord, give me a sign." He said, "Your sign that you will not speak to the people for three days except gestures. And remember your lord much, and praise in the evening and in the morning."

The story of the birth of 'Isā (the Jesus of Mohammed) is copied from the Bible and corrupted. See Luke 1:26-56. These following verses also contradict the account in verses 19:16-40.

[42]And when the angels said, "O Mary, surely Allah has chosen you and purified you and chosen you above the women of the worlds. [43]O Mary, be devout towards your lord and worship and kneel with the kneelers." [44]This is from the unseen news that we reveal to you. And you were not with them when they cast their aqlam[d] for which of them should take responsibility of Mary, and you were not with them when they disputed.

'Isā (the Jesus of Mohammed) was a virgin-born messenger (created by Allah), but not Allah's son. This story is repeated in verses 5:110-120 and 19:16-40. Concerning 'Isā's creation of the birds, Mohammed was influenced by Chapter 2 in the Greek book, *The Gospel of Thomas*, and also by Chapter 36 in an Arabic book, *The Gospel of a Childhood*.

[45]When the angels said, "O Mary, surely Allah gives you the good news with a word from him. His name is the Christ, 'Isā, son of Mary, exalted in this world and in the hereafter, and of the nearer. [46]And he will speak to the people from the cradle and in his old age. And of the good." [47]She said, "My lord, how can I have a son when no man has

---

[a] holy of holies in Solomon's temple
[b] praying, non-Arabic word of Syriac origin
[c] name mistakenly used when John the Baptist was meant
[d] pens, non-Arabic word of Greek/Ethiopian origin

touched me?" He said, "Likewise, Allah creates what he wills. When he makes a command, so he surely only says to it, 'Be,' so it will be. [48]And he will teach him the book and the wisdom and the Torah and the Gospel. [49]And a messenger to the children of Israel." "Indeed, I came to you with a sign from your lord. I create for you the figure of a bird from the tīn.[a] So I breathe into it, so it will become a bird by Allah's permission. And I heal the blind and the leper, and I raise the dead by Allah's permission. And I inform you about what you eat and what you store in your houses. Surely in this is a sign for you, if you were believers. [50]And confirming what is between my hands from the Torah, and make lawful for you some of the things that were forbidden to you. And I came to you with a sign from your lord. So fear Allah and obey me. [51]Surely Allah is my lord and your lord, so serve him. This is a straight way."

'Isā (the Jesus of Mohammed) and the disciples were Muslims, despite the fact that Islam was not established until the seventh century, long after the death and resurrection of Jesus and the death of His disciples.

[52]So when 'Isā sensed infidelity on their part, he said, "Who are my allies in Allah's cause?" The Hawārīyūn[b] said, "We are Allah's allies. We believed in Allah and bear witness that we are Muslims. [53]Our lord, we believed in what you sent down, and we followed the messenger. So write us among the witnesses."

Allah is the best deceiver. Allah reveals his plan for 'Isā's (the Jesus of Mohammed) death and resurrection.

[54]And they deceived, and Allah deceived. And Allah is the best deceiver. [55]When Allah said, "O 'Isā (Jesus), surely I am causing you to die, and I am raising you up to me and purifying you from those who became infidels and make those who follow you above those who became infidels, until the resurrection day. Then to me is your return, so I will judge between you about what you were differing. [56]So as for those who became infidels, so I will torment them with a severe torment in this world and in the hereafter, and they will have no helpers. [57]And as for those who believed and did good deeds, so he will pay them their wages. And Allah does not love the unjust. [58]This we recite to you from the verses and the wise reminder."[c]

---

[a] mud, non-Arabic word of N. Semitic origin
[b] white or pure—Mohammed used it to mean disciples of Jesus, non-Arabic word of probable Abyssinian origin
[c] Qur'an

'Isā (the Jesus of Mohammed) was created from dust, just like Adam.

[59]Surely the example of 'Isā with Allah is like the example of Adam. He created him from dust. Then he said to him, "Be," so he will be. [60]The truth from your lord, so do not be of the doubters. [61]So who disputes with you about him? After that the knowledge has come to you, so say, "Come. Let us call our sons and your sons, our women and your women, and ourselves and yourselves. Then will we invoke, so we make Allah's curse on the liars." [62]Surely this is the true story, and there is no god except Allah. And surely Allah is the dear, the wise. [63]So if they turn away, so surely Allah knows the vandals.

Christians must not take Jesus as Lord, with God.

[64]Say, "O People of the Book, come to an equal word between us and you. That we serve only Allah nor partner anything with him nor take each other as lords rather than Allah." So if they turn away, so say, "Bear witness that we are Muslims." [65]O People of the Book, why do you dispute about Abraham when the Torah and the Gospel were not sent down until after him. Do you not understand?

Mohammed maintains that Abraham, the father of the Jewish race, was not a Jew. See verse 67. He also said Abraham was not a polytheist, which is contradicted in verses 6:76-78.

[66]Here you are, those who disputed about that in which you have knowledge, but why do you dispute about that of which you have no knowledge? And Allah knows, and you do not know. [67]Abraham was not a Jew nor a Nasranyan (Christian), but he was hanifan, a Muslim. And he was not of the polytheists. [68]Surely the most worthy people to Abraham are those who followed him and this prophet[a] and those who believed. And Allah is the friend of the believers.

Jews have been misled and will mislead Muslims.

[69]An assembly among the People of the Book desire to mislead you, but they only mislead themselves. And they do not feel. [70]O People of the Book, why do you become infidels in the verses of Allah,[b] and you are witnesses? [71]O People of the Book, why do you clothe the truth with vanity and hide the truth, and you know? [72]And an assembly of the People of the Book said, "Believe in what has been sent down on those who believed at daybreak and be infidels at its end."[c] Perhaps they will return. [73]"And do not believe except those who followed your religion." Say, "Surely the guidance is

---

[a] Mohammed
[b] the Qur'an
[c] of the day

Allah's guidance, and he gives it to someone, similar to what you have received." Or they dispute with you before your lord. Say, "Surely the bounty is in the hand of Allah. He gives it to whom he wills. And Allah is large, knowing." [74]He makes his mercy special to whom he wills. And Allah is the possessor of the great bounty. [75]And some of the People of the Book who, if you trust him with a qintār,[a] he will pay it back to you. And some of them, if you trust him with a dīnār,[b] he will not pay it back to you unless you keep demanding it. This is because they said, "There is no way upon us in the Gentiles." And they say the lies against Allah, and they know. [76]Yes, whoever fulfills his covenant and fears, so surely Allah loves the fearer. [77]Surely those who purchase their covenant with Allah and their oath for a little price, those have no portion in the hereafter; Allah will not speak to them and will not look at them on the resurrection day and will not purify them. And they will have a painful torment. [78]And surely among them is a group who will twist their tongues with the book in order that you may think it is from the book, and it is not from the book. And they say this is from Allah, and it is not from Allah; and they say the lies against Allah, and they know. [79]It was not for humans that Allah brings to him the book and the wisdom and the prophecy; then he says to the people, "Be my servants rather than Allah, but be rabbānīyun[c] by what you were teaching of the book and by what you were todarasoon."[d]

Those who take angels or prophets like Jesus as lords are infidels. People must believe in Mohammed.

[80]And he does not command you to take the angels and the prophets as lords. Will he command you to infidelity after you are Muslims? [81]And when Allah took a covenant with the prophets, saying, "I brought you from a book and wisdom, then a messenger comes to you, confirming what is with you, so that you may believe in him and that you may give him victory." He said, "Did you affirm and take my covenant?" They said, "We affirmed." He said, "So bear witness, and I am with you of the witnesses. [82]So whoever turns away after this, so those are the transgressors.

Everyone must be obedient to Allah, either willingly or by force. Allah does not differentiate between prophets and Jesus.

[83]Do they desire other than Allah's religion and to him what is in the heavens and the earth have submitted[e] willingly and grudgingly,

---

[a] a measure, non-Arabic word of Greek origin
[b] dinar, a coin, non-Arabic word of Greek origin
[c] Jewish teachers, non-Arabic word of Syriac origin
[d] studying, non-Arabic word of Hebrew origin
[e] have become Muslims

and to him they will return? [84]Say, "We believed in Allah and in what has been sent down on us and what has been sent down on Abraham and Ishmael and Isaac and Jacob and the tribes and in what was given to Moses and 'Isā and the prophets from their lord. We do not differentiate between any one of them. And to him we are Muslims.

All the members of religions, except for Islam, will be lost forever. Allah will not guide any Muslim who becomes an infidel. They will go to hell forever. This is contradicted by verses 2:62 and 3:89.

[85]And whoever desires any other religion except Islam, so it[a] will not be accepted from him, and in the hereafter he will be of the losers. [86]How will Allah guide people who became infidels after they had believed and bore witness that the messenger[b] is true and the clear proofs came to them? And Allah will not guide the unjust people. [87]Those their reward, that the curse of Allah and the angels and the people together is on them. [88]In it they will abide forever, their torment will not be lessened; and they will not be delayed, [89]except those who repent after that and reform. So surely Allah is forgiving, merciful.

Allah will never give a second chance—Mohammed contradicts himself again.

[90]Surely those who become infidels after believing, then they increase in their infidelity. Their repentance will never be accepted, and those are they who have gone astray. [91]Surely those who became infidels and die infidels, none of them will be accepted, even with as much gold as the earth could contain, even though he should offer it in ransom. Those will have a painful torment, and they will have no helpers.

Righteousness is received by doing good deeds. This contradicts the Bible. See Ephesians 2:8-9.

[92]You will never receive the righteousness until you spend from what you love. And whatever you spend of anything, so surely Allah knows it. [93]All food was lawful to the children of Israel, except what Israel forbid for himself before the Torah was sent down. Say, "So bring the Torah, so recite it, if you were truthful." [94]So whoever forges the lies against Allah after this, so those are the unjust. [95]Say, "Allah is truthful." So follow the religion of Abraham, hanifan, and he was not of the polytheists.

---

[a] any other religion
[b] Mohammed

The Islamic Pilgrimage (the Hajj) was copied from pagan practices. Jews and Christians are attempting to convert Muslims into infidels.

[96]Surely the first house that was established for the people was that in Becca,[a] blessed and a guidance to the worlds. [97]In it there are clear signs, the standing place of Abraham. And whoever enters it was secure. People owe to Allah the pilgrimage to the house, who are able to have a way to it. And whoever becomes an infidel, so surely Allah is rich above the worlds. [98]Say, "O People of the Book, why do you become infidels in the verses of Allah? And Allah is a witness of what you do." [99]Say, "O People of the Book, why do you prevent the believers from the way of Allah? You desire to make it crooked, and you are witnesses. And Allah is not unaware of what you do. [100]O you who have believed, if you obey a group from those who have been given the book, they will revert you into infidels after you believed. [101]And how can you become infidels, and you recited to you the verses of Allah, and his messenger is among you? Whoever holds fast to Allah, so indeed, is guided to a straight way. [102]O you who have believed, fear Allah his true fear, and do not die except you are Muslims. [103]And hold fast by the habl[b] of Allah together, and do not be divided. And remember Allah's grace on you when you were enemies, so he attuned between your hearts. So you became brethren by his grace. And you were on the edge of the pit of fire, so he delivered you from it. Likewise, Allah clearly showed you his verses, perhaps you may be guided. [104]And that there will be among you a nation calling to the good and commanding what is right and forbidding from the evil, and those are the prosperous. [105]And do not be like those who are divided and disagree after the proofs came to them, and for those a great torment."

Black faces will mark the damned in hell. White faces will mark the saved in the gardens.

[106]A day faces turned white and faces turned black. So as for those whose faces turned black: "Did you become infidels after you had believed? So taste the torment because you were infidels." [107]And as to those whose faces turned white, so in the mercy of Allah they will abide in it forever. [108]These are the verses of Allah. We recite them to you with the truth. And Allah does not desire injustice to the worlds. [109]And to Allah what is in the heavens and what is on the earth. And to Allah the affairs will return.

---

[a] error, should be Mecca
[b] rope, non-Arabic word of Aramaic origin

The United Arab Empire was (according to Mohammed) the best nation on the earth.

[110]You were the best nation who came forth to the people. You command what is right and you forbid from the evil and you believe in Allah. And if the People of the Book believed, it would have been better for them. Some of them are believers, and most of them are transgressors. [111]They will not inflict on you but harm. And if they engage in war with you, they will turn their backs to you; then they will not be helped. [112]The humiliation is smitten on them wherever they are found, except by a rope from Allah and a rope from the people. And the wrath of Allah they receive, and poverty is smitten on them because they were infidels in the verses of Allah. And they are killing the prophets unjustly; that is because they disobeyed and they were transgressors.

Mohammed declared that some Jews and Christians were true believers, and they were reciting the true (uncorrupted) Bible.

[113]They are not alike. Among the People of the Book is an upright nation who recites the verses of Allah throughout the night as they worship. [114]They believe in Allah and in the last day and command what is right and forbid from the evil and hasten in doing the good deeds. And those are of the good. [115]And whatever good they do, so they will not be denied it. And Allah knows the fearer. [116]Surely those who became infidels, their money and their children will not profit them anything against Allah. And those are the companions of the fire; they will abide in it forever. [117]The likeness which they spend in the world's life is like a cold wind which falls on the fields of people who did injustice to themselves, so it[a] destroyed it.[b] And Allah did not deal with them unjustly, but they dealt unjustly with themselves.

Muslims should not have friends except from among themselves.

[118]O you who have believed, do not take friends other than from yourselves. They will not fail to corrupt you. They desire for your ruin. Hatred indeed has already shown itself out of their mouths, and what is hidden in their chests is bigger. Indeed, we showed the verses to you, if you were understanding. [119]Here you are, love them, and they do not love you. You believe the entire book. And when they met you, they said, "We believed." But when they are apart, they bite their fingers at you out of anger. Say, "Die with your anger." Surely Allah knows what is in the chests. [120]If good touches you, it grieves them; and when evil afflicts you, they rejoice in it. And if you are patient and fear, their schemes will not harm you anything. Surely

---

[a] the wind
[b] the field

Allah surrounds what they do. [121]And when you left your family early in the morning so that you might prepare the believers for their positions for engaging in war. And Allah is hearing, knowing. [122]When two assemblies of you were about to fail, and Allah is their friend. And on Allah, so let the believers depend. [123]And indeed, Allah gave you victory at Badr,[a] and you were humiliated. So fear Allah, perhaps you may be thankful. [124]When you said to the believers, "Is it not enough for you that your lord aids you with three thousand angels sent down?" [125]Yes, if you are patient and fear, and they[b] come on you suddenly, your lord will aid you with five thousand of the marked angels. [126]And Allah did not make it except as good news to you and that your heart may be calmed by it. And the victory is not except from Allah the dear, the wise. [127]That he might cut a portion from those who became infidels or cast them down so they will return failures. [128]It is none of your affair whether he relents on them or he torments them, so surely they are unjust. [129]And to Allah what is in the heavens and what is on the earth. He forgives to whom he wills, and he torments whom he wills. And Allah is forgiving, merciful. [130]O you who have believed, do not consume the interest double and redoubled. And fear Allah, perhaps you may prosper. [131]And fear the fire which is prepared for the infidels. [132]And obey Allah and the messenger,[c] perhaps you will receive mercy. [133]And hasten to forgiveness from your lord and a garden, its width is the heavens and the earth, prepared for the fearers, [134]those who spend in prosperity and in adversity, and who repress their anger and pardon people. And Allah loves the doers of good. [135]And those who, when they commit an indecency or do an injustice to themselves, remember Allah. So they ask forgiveness for their sins. And who will forgive the sins except Allah? And they do not persist in what they have done, and they know. [136]The reward of those is forgiveness from their lord and gardens, below them the rivers flow; they abide in it forever, and blessed is the wage of the workers. [137]Indeed, customs have passed before your time. So walk on the earth, so look how was the end of the deniers. [138]This is a declaration to the people and a guidance and a sermon to the fearer.

True Muslims do not seek peace if they have the upper hand. See also verses 4:104 and 47:35.

[139]And do not be weak, and do not grieve; and you have the upper hand if you were believers.

---

[a] one of Mohammed's battles
[b] the enemy
[c] Mohammed

Allah proves true believers by allowing them to be martyrs.

[140]If a wound has touched you, so indeed, a wound like it has also touched the people before. And such are the days we alternate between the people. And that Allah may know those who believed, and he takes martyrs from among you. And Allah does not love the unjust. [141]And that Allah may purify those who believed and destroy the infidels. [142]Or you thought that you would enter the garden and Allah would not know those among you who performed jihad, and he knows the patient? [143]And indeed, you were desiring the death before you met it. So indeed, you have seen it, and you are looking. [144]And Mohammed is not but a messenger; indeed, the messengers passed before him. If he dies or is killed, will you turn on your heels? And who turns on his heels will not harm Allah anything. And Allah will reward the thankful. [145]And it was not for a soul to die except by Allah's permission, a written decree. And who desires the reward of this world, we will give to him from it; and who desires the reward of the hereafter, we will give to him from it. And we will reward the thankful. [146]And how many a prophet, many ribbīyūn,[a] engaged in war with them. So they never lost courage when they were hurt for the sake of Allah. And they did not weaken, and they did not submit. And Allah loves the patient. [147]And their saying was not, except that they said, "Our lord, forgive us of our sins and our extravagance in our affairs and set our feet firm and give us victory against the infidel people." [148]So Allah gave them the reward of this world and a better reward of the hereafter. And Allah loves the doers of good. [149]O you who have believed, if you obey those who became infidels, they will turn you on your heels so you will fall back losers. [150]Yet Allah is your protector, and he is the best helper.

Islam is the religion behind terror. See also verses 33:26-27.

[151]We will cast the terror into the hearts of those who became infidels because they partner [other gods] with Allah which he did not send down with any sultān.[b] And their abode is the fire, and evil is the place of the unjust.

Those who turn away from battle love this world. Conquest through invasion is a normal way of life for Muslim believers. Also, see verse 3:156.

[152]And indeed, Allah fulfilled his promise to you when you killed them by his permission until you failed and you disputed in the affair and disobeyed after he showed you[c] what you loved. Some of you desired this world, and some desired the hereafter. Then he turned

---

[a] myriads, non-Arabic word of Syriac origin
[b] authority, non-Arabic word of Aramaic origin
[c] of the spoil

you away from them so that he might test you. And indeed, he has pardoned you. And Allah is a possessor of bounty to the believers. [153]When you go up and do not wait for anyone, and the messenger[a] was calling you from your rear [to the fight], so he gave you sorrow on sorrow so that you may not grieve about what you have missed and what has befallen you. And Allah is aware of what you do. [154]Then he sent on you, after the sorrow, security. Sleep covered a group among you; and a group indeed their own passions stirred them up to think, without the truth of Allah, with the thought of ignorance. They said, "Do we have anything in this affair?" Say, "Surely all the affair is to Allah." They will hide in themselves what they did not reveal to you. They say, "If there was anything in this affair for us, we would not have died here." Say, "If you were in your houses, they who were ordained to be killed would have gone forth to the places where they lie in order that Allah might test what was in your chests and that he purifies what is in your hearts. And Allah knows what is in the chests." [155]Surely those among you who turned back the day the two groups met.[b] Surely Satan only caused them to fall by some of what they have earned, and indeed, Allah pardons them. Surely Allah is forgiving, forbearing. [156]O you who have believed, do not be like those who became infidels, and they said to their brethren when they traveled on the earth or if they were invaders, "Had they been with us, they would not have died and would not have been killed." So that Allah makes this a regret in their hearts, and Allah gives life and death. And Allah sees what you do.

Those who die for the sake of Allah receive pardon and mercy. If Allah helps the Muslims, then they cannot be defeated in battle.

[157]And if you are killed for the sake of Allah[c] or die, then forgiveness from Allah and mercy are better than that which they gathered.[d] [158]And if you were to die or be killed, it is to Allah that you will be gathered. [159]So it is by mercy from Allah you became lenient to them. And had you been rough and thick-hearted,[e] they would have left from around you. So pardon them and ask forgiveness for them and consult with them in the affair; so if you have decided, so depend on Allah. Surely Allah loves the dependent. [160]If Allah gives you victory, so no one can defeat you. But if he forsakes you, so who will give you victory after him? And on Allah so let the believers

---

[a] Mohammed
[b] in battle
[c] while performing jihad
[d] spoils
[e] harsh

depend. [161]And it was not to a prophet to cheat,[a] and whoever cheats will bring what he cheated[b] on the resurrection day. Then every soul will be paid what it has earned, and they will not be dealt with unjustly. [162]Is the one who follows the pleasure of Allah like the one who returns with wrath from Allah? And hell is his abode, and evil is the final place. [163]There are degrees with Allah. And Allah sees what they do. [164]Indeed, Allah is gracious to the believers when he raised a messenger[c] from among themselves to recite to them his verses and purify them and teach them the book and the wisdom, and that they were before in an obvious error. [165]Or when a misfortune has befallen you, indeed, you befall twice like it before. You say, "Where did this come from?" Say, "It is from yourselves." Surely Allah has might over all things. [166]And what befell you on the day the two groups met,[d] so by Allah's permission and that he may know the believers.

Muslims who do not go to war for Allah are hypocrites.

[167]And that he might know the hypocrites, and it was said to them, "Come, engage in war for the sake of Allah, or contribute." They said, "If we knew how to engage in war, we would have followed you." They are closer on that day to infidelity than to faith. They say with their mouths what is not in their hearts, and Allah knows best what they hide. [168]Those who said to their brethren and stayed,[e] "Had they obeyed us, they would not have been killed." Say, "Keep the death off yourself, if you were truthful."

Muslims who die while performing jihad will feast with Allah in the gardens.

[169]And do not think that those who were killed for the sake of Allah[f] dead. Yet they are alive with their lord, receiving their provision, [170]rejoicing in what Allah has given them from his bounty. And they receive the good news of those who did not follow them from behind them, except fear on them, and they will not grieve. [171]They receive good news of the grace of Allah and bounty and that Allah will not lose the wage of the believers. [172]Those who respond to Allah and the messenger after being afflicted with wounds, to those who do good among them and fear, a great wage. [173]Those to whom the people said, "Surely the people have gathered against you, so fear them." So he increased their faith. And they said, "Allah is sufficient for us and the best guardian." [174]So they turned away with grace

---

[a] in dividing the spoils
[b] dishonestly gained
[c] Mohammed
[d] in war
[e] at home and did not go to war
[f] in jihad

from Allah and bounty, evil did not touch them, and they followed the pleasure of Allah. And Allah is a possessor of a great bounty.
[175]Surely it is only Satan who puts fear in his friends. So do not fear them, and fear me if you were believers.

Muslims need good luck in the hereafter. See also verse 41:35.

[176]And do not let those who hasten after the infidelity grieve you. Surely they will not harm Allah anything. Allah desires that he will not make luck for them in the hereafter, and they will have a great torment. [177]Surely those who purchase the infidelity with their faith will not harm Allah anything, and they will have a painful torment.

Allah gives unbelievers a long life so that they will sin more and be punished more. This is contrary to the God of the Bible. See 2 Peter 3:9.

[178]And do not let those who became infidels think we only increase for them good for themselves, surely we only increase for them that they may increase in sin. And to them is a disgraceful torment. [179]It was not in Allah to leave the believers in the condition in which you are in, until he distinguishes the bad from the good. And it was not of Allah to show you the unseen, but Allah chooses of his messengers whom he wills. So believe in Allah and his messengers, and if you believe and fear, so you will have a great wage. [180]And do not let the stingy count that what Allah has given them from his bounty is good for them, yet it is evil for them. They will be noosed with that of which they have been stingy on the resurrection day. And to Allah the inheritance of the heavens and the earth. And Allah is aware of what you do. [181]Indeed, Allah has heard the saying of those who said, "Surely Allah is poor, and we are rich." We will write what they said and their killing of the prophets unjustly. And we will say, "Taste the torment of the burning." [182]This is because of what your hands have sent before, and that Allah is not unjust to the servants. [183]Those who said, "Surely Allah made a covenant to us, not to believe in a messenger until he brings to us a qurbān[a] eaten by the fire." Say, "Indeed, messengers came before me with the proofs and with what you said. Then why did you kill them, if you were truthful?" [184]So if they deny you, so indeed, messengers before you were denied, though they came with proofs and with zober[b] and with the illuminating book.[c]

---

[a] sacrifice, non-Arabic word of Hebrew/Syriac origin
[b] in plural form it means scriptures, non-Arabic word of Hebrew/Syriac origin
[c] the Bible

Before entering the garden, Muslims will be in hell for a time.

[185]Every soul tastes the death, and surely you will only receive your wages on the resurrection day. So whoever is removed from the fire and enters the garden, so indeed, he becomes triumphant. And what is the world's life except the enjoyment of the proud.

Hurtful things are assured for those who worship other gods.

[186]You will be surely tested in your money and in yourselves. And you will hear from those to whom were given the book before you and from those who are polytheists much harm. And, if you are patient and fear, so surely this is the determination of the affairs. [187]And when Allah took a covenant with those who were given the book that you may reveal it to the people and to not hide it, so they cast it behind their backs. And they purchased by it a little price. So evil is what they purchased. [188]Do not think that those who rejoice by what they have brought and love to be praised for what they did not do. So do not count them with a triumph from the torment, and they will have a painful torment. [189]And to Allah the kingdom of the heavens and the earth. And Allah has might over all things. [190]Surely in the creation of the heavens and the earth and the change of the night and the day are signs to those who have understanding. [191]Those who remember Allah when standing and sitting and on their side, and they think of the creation of the heavens and the earth: "Our lord, you did not create this in vain, praise be to you. So save us from the fire torment. [192]Our lord, surely those whom you admit into the fire, so indeed, you have disgraced them. And the unjust do not have helpers. [193]Our lord, surely we have heard the announcer who calls to faith, 'that believe in your lord.' So we believed. Our lord, so forgive us our sins and atone our evil deeds and make us die with the righteous. [194]Our lord, and give us what you have promised us by your messengers, and do not put us to shame on the resurrection day. Surely you do not change the appointment."

Those who die while engaged in war for Allah will have their sins blotted out.

[195]So their lord answered them, "I will not lose the work of a worker among you, whether male or female, some of you from the others. So those who emigrate and are forced out of their homes and have suffered in my way (cause) and engaged in war and killed, I will atone for their evils; and I will admit them into gardens, below them the rivers flow, a reward from Allah. And Allah has the best reward." [196]Do not let the change in those who became infidels in the countries deceive you. [197]A little enjoyment, then hell will be their abode, and evil is the bed. [198]But to those who feared their lord are gardens, below them the rivers flow. They abide in it forever as guests of their Allah, and what is with Allah is best for the righteous.

[199]And surely some of the People of the Book are those who believe in Allah and in what he has sent down to you[a] and in what he has sent down to them,[b] humbling themselves to Allah. They will not purchase with the verses of Allah a little price. Those will have their wage with their lord, surely Allah is swift in the reckoning. [200]O you who have believed, be patient and excel in patience and be firm and fear Allah, perhaps you will be prosperous

A portion of a revelation   *The Women*   4

In the name of Allah, the merciful, the merciful

Mohammed differs from the Bible by claiming that people were created from a single soul. The Bible indicates that Adam and Eve were two souls created from one flesh. See Genesis 2:21. Notice that the name of Eve is never mentioned in the Qur'an.

[1]O you people, fear your lord who created you from a single soul and created a wife from it, and from them he spread[c] many men and women. And fear Allah of whom you ask of him and the wombs. Surely Allah was watching over you. [2]And give to the orphans their money and do not substitute the worthless for the good and do not consume their money to your money. Surely this was a great hūb.[d]

Men may have four (or is it nine?) wives if they treat them the same. See also verse 4:129. It is lawful to lust after women. The following verse, 4:3, as well as verses 2:230, 236; and 33:50 contradict the teaching of the Bible. See Matthew 5:27-30.

[3]And if you fear that you cannot deal fairly among the orphans, so have sex (marry) what appeals to you from the women, two and three and four. So if you fear that you will not treat them equally, so one [wife]; or [have sex with] what your right hand possesses,[e] this is near that you may not have hardship. [4]And give the women their dowry as a free gift, so if they give you from their own soul part of it, then consume it with enjoyment and pleasure. [5]And do not give the retarded your money which Allah has placed with you for their

---

[a] the Qur'an
[b] the Bible
[c] abroad
[d] sin, non-Arabic word of probable Syriac origin
[e] concubines and slaves

support. And give provision to them from it and clothe them and speak to them with kind speech. [6]And test the orphans until they reach the age of having sex (marriage), so if you perceive in them a sound judgment, so hand over their money to them. But do not consume it wastefully or by hastily entrusting it to them until they grow up. And whoever was rich, so let him stay away from it; and whoever was poor, so let him consume from it with fairness. So when you give over their money to them, so take witnesses over them. And Allah is a sufficient accounter. [7]To men a portion of what their parents and relatives leave, and to women a portion of what their parents and relatives leave, whether it be little or much, an obligated portion. [8]And when the relatives are present at the division, and the orphans and the poor, so give provision to them from it. And speak to them with kind speech. [9]And let those who, if they left behind them weak offspring, have fear over them, so let them fear Allah, and let them speak correct speech. [10]Surely those who consume the money of the orphans unjustly, surely they only consume fire in their bellies. And they will roast [in] a blaze.

A male receives twice the inheritance of a female. However, mathematical computations in the distribution of inheritance are confusing with unexplained, missing portions. For example, in the case of an only daughter, Mohammed makes a huge mathematical error. He says that the daughter gets one half, and the parents of the deceased each get one sixth. That totals five sixths. Where does the remaining one sixth go?

[11]Allah commands you, concerning your children, to the male the like portion of two females; so if there were more than two females, so they will have two thirds of that which their father left. And, if she was one [daughter], she will have the half, and to his parents to every one of them a sixth part of what he left if there was to him a [surviving] son. So, if he had no son and his parents are his heirs, so his mother will have the third; so if there was to him brothers, so to his mother the sixth after any will[a] was made for it or any debts. [As] to your fathers or your children, you know not which of them is the closest to you in usefulness. [This] is the ordinance of Allah. Surely Allah was knowing, wise. [12]And you will have half of what your wives leave if there was no son to them; so if there was a son to them, then a fourth of what they leave will be yours after any will was made for it or any debts. And your wives will have a fourth part of what you leave if there was no son to you; but if there was a son, then they will have an eighth part of what you leave after any will you made for it or any debts. And if a man or a woman bequeaths, was lacking [heirs], and he has a brother or sister, so to each of them the sixth; so if

---

[a] monies bequeathed

there were more than this, so they will be sharers in a third after any will was made for it or any debts without loss to anyone. [This] is a command from Allah. And Allah is knowing, forbearing. [13]These are the boundaries of Allah and whoever obeys Allah and his messenger, he will admit him to gardens, below them the rivers flow; they abide in it forever, and this is the great triumph. [14]And whoever will disobey Allah and his messenger and will transgress his boundaries, he will admit him into a fire to abide in it forever, and he will have a shameful torment.

This says that adulterous and homosexually active women are to be locked up in their houses until they die. This contradicts verse 24:2 which commands one hundred lashes. It also contradicts the actual practice of Islamic Law (Shariah) found in the hadith (Bukhari, volume 9, #17) which requires them to be stoned to death. This hadith was based on a verse which was in the Qur'an. Unfortunately, the paper on which the verse was written was eaten by a goat when Mohammed's family was dealing with his funeral. Notice that the punishments of men who commit the same sin are much less.

[15]And for those who commit indecency[a] among your women, so call four witnesses from among you against them. So if they testify, so detain them[b] in their houses until death takes them or Allah makes another way for them. [16]And if two[c] among you commit it,[d] then punish them. So if they repent and reform, then leave them alone. Surely Allah was relenting, merciful. [17]Surely the repentance is only from Allah to those who do the evil in ignorance and then soon repent, so those are whom Allah relents on. And Allah was knowing, wise.

No one can be saved by "death-bed" repentance.

[18]And the repentance is not for those who do the evils until, when the death comes to one of them, he says, "Surely I now have repented." And neither to those who die while they are infidels. Those, we have prepared for them a painful torment. [19]O you who have believed, it is not lawful for you to inherit the women grudgingly. And do not hinder them in order to take from them part of what you had given them unless they commit an obvious indecency, and live with them in fairness. So if you hated them, so perhaps you may hate something in which Allah has placed an abundance of good.

---

[a] lesbianism or adultery, see Bukhari hadith #4839-4820
[b] the women
[c] men
[d] homosexuality

Muslims can exchange their wives.

[20]And if you desire to exchange one wife for another wife and have given one of them a measure, do not take anything[a] from it. Would you take it by buhtūn[b] and a manifest sin? [21]And how can you take it when one of you has gone into the other, and they have taken from you a thick[c] covenant? [22]And do not have sex (marry) with women whom your fathers have had sex (marry) with, except what has already passed. Surely this was indecent and hateful and an evil way. [23]Forbidden to you are your mothers and your daughters and your sisters and your paternal aunts and your maternal aunts and the daughters of the brother and the daughters of the sister and your mothers who nursed you[d] and your sisters in the breast feedings[e] and the mothers of your women[f] and your step-daughters who are in your laps, born of your women[g] which you had entered into.[h] So if you were not entered into them,[i] so you are not at fault, and also the wives of your sons who proceed out of your backbone[j] and two sisters together, except what has passed. Surely Allah was forgiving, merciful.

It is lawful for men to have sex with their married slaves and concubines. It is lawful to seek women with money (prostitution – marriage for fun).

[24]And married women [are also forbidden], except all that your right hand possesses. This is the decree of Allah for you. And it is lawful to you, besides this, to seek out women with your money, chaste without fornication. So, whatever you enjoy by it (their sexual parts) from them, so give them their wages; it is an ordinance. And there will be no sin on you about what you have mutually agreed on after the ordinance. Surely Allah was knowing, wise. [25]And whoever among you who cannot have sex (marry) the free believing women, so [marry] those whom your right hand possesses (slaves) from your young believing girls. And Allah knows best your faith, some of you from others. So have sex (marry) with them with the permission of their masters, and give them their wages with fairness, chaste without fornication and not entertainers of lovers. So if they become Muslim, so if they commit indecency, so torment them half of the

---

[a] deduction
[b] slander, non-Arabic word of Syriac origin
[c] firm
[d] any woman who fed a man at least five times becomes his mother
[e] any girl who has been breastfed by a man's mother at least five times becomes his sister
[f] wives
[g] wives
[h] had sex with
[i] not had sex with them
[j] this is believed to be the origin of man's sperm

torment prescribed for [free] married women. This is for those who fear to fall into fornication among you, and if you were patient, it would be good for you. And Allah is forgiving, merciful. [26]Allah desires to show this to you and to guide you into the customs of those who have been before you and relents on you. And Allah is knowing, wise. [27]And Allah desires to relent on you. And those who follow the lusts, they desire that you should swerve with a great swerving. [28]Allah desires to lighten for you, and he created the human weak. [29]O you who have believed, do not consume your money among you with vanity, unless there was merchandise among you by your own consent, and do not kill yourselves. Surely Allah was merciful to you. [30]And whoever does that transgressively and unjustly, so we will roast him [in] a fire, for this was easy for Allah.

Receiving forgiveness for smaller sins is possible, but forgiveness for bigger sins is not possible.

[31]If you avoid the biggest[a] of which you are forbidden, we will atone for your evils, and we will admit you with a generous entry. [32]And do not desire the bounty which Allah has given some of you above the others. The men will have a portion according to what they earn and to the women a portion according to what they earn. And ask Allah for his bounty. Surely Allah was knowing of all things. [33]And to everyone we have appointed heirs of what the parents and relatives left and those with whom you have made an oath, so give them their portion. Surely Allah was a witness over all things.

Men are superior to women. Men must scourge their wives before they become rebellious. See also verses 2:228 and 4:128.

[34]Men are in charge of women by what Allah preferred some of them above the others and by what they spend out of their money. So good [women] are obedient, guarding in secret that which Allah has guarded. And of whom you fear rebellion, so preach to them and separate from them in the beds and scourge them. So if they obey you, so do not seek a way against them. Surely Allah was higher, big. [35]And if you fear a separation between them, so send for a judge from his family and a judge from her family. If they desire reconciliation, Allah will bring them together. Surely Allah was knowing, aware. [36]And serve Allah, and do not partner anything with him. Be good to the parents and the relatives and the orphans and the poor and the related neighbor or the unrelated neighbor and to the companion by your side and the son of the way and what your right hand possesses. Surely Allah does not love who was proud, boastful, [37]those who are stingy and command others to be stingy

---

[a] worst sin

and hide away what Allah has given them of his bounty. And we have prepared for the infidels a shameful torment. [38]And those who spend their money to be seen of men and do not believe in Allah nor in the last day, and whoever Satan was for him a companion, so an evil companion he has! [39]And what would it cost them if they believed in Allah and the last day and spend from what Allah provided them? And Allah was a knower of them. [40]Surely Allah will not treat unjustly the weight of an atom. And if there be any good deed, he will double it, and he will give from himself a great wage. [41]So how when we bring from every nation with a witness, and we bring you up as a witness against those? [42]On that day those who became infidels and disobeyed the messenger, they will wish that the earth was leveled with them. But they will not hide any saying from Allah.

Women in Islam are dirtier than dirt. See also verse 5:6.

[43]O you who have believed, do not come near the prayer while you are drunk until you know what you are saying, nor after sexual orgasm except that you are merely passing by, until you wash. And if you were sick or traveling or one of you has relieved himself or you have touched the women, so you did not find water, so rub your faces and your hands with good dirt. Surely Allah was pardoning, forgiving.

Jews and Christians are sellers of error and enemies to Muslims.

[44]Have you not seen those[a] who have been given a portion from the book?[b] They purchase error and desire for you to go astray from the way. [45]And Allah knows best your enemies. And Allah is a sufficient friend, and Allah is a sufficient helper. [46]Some of the Jews are those who alter the words from their places and say, "We have heard and disobeyed and hear but as one that does not hear," and look at us twisting with their tongues and stabbing[c] in the religion. And if they would say, "We have heard, and we obey and hear and see us," it would have been better for them and more right. But Allah has cursed them because of their infidelity. So they will not believe except for a few.

The Qur'an confirms the Bible to be true.

[47]O you who have been given the book, believe in what we have sent down[d] confirming what is with you[e] before we hide faces and

---

[a] Jews and Christians
[b] the Bible
[c] ridiculing
[d] the Qur'an
[e] the Bible

turn them on their backs or curse them as we cursed the companions of the Sabbath.[a] And the command of Allah was accomplished.

Allah never forgives people who partner him with any other god.

[48]Surely Allah will not forgive partnering[b] with him. But other than this, he will forgive whom he wills. And who partners with Allah, so indeed, he forged a great sin. [49]Have you not seen those who purify themselves? Yet Allah will purify whom he wills, and they will not be dealt with unjustly a thread. [50]Look how they forge the lies against Allah, and that in itself is a clear sin. [51]Have you not seen those to whom a portion of the book has been given? They believe in jibt[c] and the idolatry, and they say to those who became infidels, "Those are more guided in the way than those who believed." [52]Those are they whom Allah has cursed. And whomever Allah curses will not find for him any helper. [53]Or do they have a share in the kingdom? So then they will not bring to the people a naqira.[d] [54]Or they envy the people about what Allah has given them from his bounty. So indeed, we gave the family of Abraham the book and the wisdom, and we gave them a great kingdom. [55]So some of them believed in him. And some prevent [others] from him, and sufficient is the blaze of hell.

Whoever does not believe in the verses of Allah will enter hell.

[56]Surely those who became infidels in our verses, we will roast them [in] a fire so often as their skins are burned; then we will change them for other skins so that they may taste the torment. Surely Allah was dear, wise.

In the garden (Paradise) men will have multiple, purified (ever-virgin) wives.

[57]And those who believed and did good deeds, we will admit them into gardens, below them the rivers flow, they will abide in it forever and ever. In it they will have purified[e] wives, and we will admit them into a shadowy shade. [58]Surely Allah commands you to give back the trusts to their people, and when you judge between the people, to judge with justice. Surely Allah preaches graces by it to you. Surely Allah was hearing, seeing. [59]O you who have believed, obey Allah, and obey the messenger and those among you in charge of your affairs. So if you dispute in anything, so bring it before Allah and the messenger, if you were believing in Allah and the last day. This is

---

[a] i.e. the Jews who have been changed to monkeys
[b] worshiping other gods
[c] unknown meaning in Arabic, non-Arabic word of Abyssinian origin
[d] speck on the back of a pit from a date
[e] ever-virgin

better and a very good interpretation. [60]Have you not seen those who claim that they believed in what has been sent down to you[a] and what has been sent down before you?[b] They desire to be judged before the idolatry; and indeed, they were commanded to become infidels in it, and Satan desires to lead them astray, a faraway straying. [61]And when it is said to them, "Come to that which Allah has sent down and to the messenger," you have seen the hypocrites turning away from you with repetitiveness. [62]So how, when some misfortune befalls them because of what their hand had sent before, then they will come to you swearing by Allah: "That we desire nothing but to promote good and reconciliation"! [63]These are those whom Allah knows what is in their hearts. So turn away from them and preach to them and say to them flawless words about themselves. [64]And we have not sent any messenger but to be obeyed, by Allah's permission. And if they, when they have treated themselves unjustly, come to you, so they ask Allah's forgiveness, and the messenger asks forgiveness for them, they will find that Allah is relenting, merciful.

It is lawful to swear. See also verses 52:1-6; 79:1-4; 84:16-18; 85:1-3; 89:1-4; 91:1-9... This contradicts the Bible which clearly teaches that it is evil to swear. See Matthew 5:33-37.

[65]So no, [I swear] by your lord they will not believe until they have set you up as judge between them in what they dispute. Then they will not find in themselves any embarrassment in your judgments, and they will submit with complete submission. [66]And had we prescribed to them: "Kill yourselves, or get out from your homes," they would not have done it except for a few among them. And if they did what was preached to them, it was better for them and greater strength. [67]And then we surely give to them from us a great wage. [68]And we would have guided them to a straight way. [69]And whoever obeys Allah and the messenger, so those [will be] with those whom Allah has given his grace among the prophets and the siddaquen[c] and the martyrs and the good. And those are an excellent company. [70]Such is the bounty of Allah. And Allah is a sufficient knower.

Allah commands Muslim believers to go to war.

[71]O you who have believed, take your precautions, so go to war in separate groups, or go to war all together. [72]And surely among you there are those who will go slowly, and if a misfortune befalls you, he says, "Indeed, Allah graced me in that I was not a martyr with them."

---

[a] the Qur'an
[b] the Bible
[c] persons of integrity, non-Arabic word of Aramaic origin

[73]And if a bounty[a] from Allah befalls you, they will surely say, as if there had never been any friendship between you and him: "I wish I had been with them so that I would have triumphed a great triumph."

Believers engage in war for Allah. They receive a great reward, whether they live or die.

[74]So let those who purchase the world's life for the hereafter engage in war for the sake of Allah. And whoever engages in war for the sake of Allah, whether he is killed or victorious, so we will give him a great wage. [75]And what is [the matter] with you that you should not engage in war for the sake of Allah? And the weakened among the men and the women and the children who say, "Our lord, get us out of this village where its people are unjust and grant us from you a friend and grant us a helper from you." [76]Those who believed engage in war for the sake of Allah, and those who became infidels engage in war for the sake of the idolatry, so engage in war against the friends of Satan. Surely the scheme of Satan was weak.

Muslims who refuse to go to war fear man more than Allah.

[77]Have you not seen those to whom it was said, "Withhold your hands[b] and perform the prayer and bring the legal alms." So when it was prescribed for them to engage in war, behold, a group of them feared the people like the fear of Allah or a greater fear. And they said, "Our lord, why did you prescribe for us the engagement of war? Were it not that you delay us to a near time." Say, "Little is the enjoyment of this world, but the hereafter is better for him who fears. And you will not be dealt unjustly a thread."

Death will overtake those in "high towers." Note the contradiction between verses 78 and 79. Where does misfortune come from, from Allah or from man himself?

[78]Wherever you may be, death will overtake you even if you were in lofty buruj.[c] If good fortune befalls them, they say, "This is from Allah." And if misfortune befalls them, they say, "This is from you." Say, "All is from Allah." So what is the affair with those people? They are not near to understanding speech. [79]Whatever good fortune befalls you is from Allah, and whatever misfortune befalls you is from your own self. And we have sent you to the people [as] a messenger. And Allah is a sufficient witness. [80]Whoever obeys the messenger, so indeed, he obeyed Allah. And whoever turns away, so we have not sent you a keeper over them. [81]And they say, "Obedience." So

---

[a] spoils of war
[b] from waging in war
[c] towers, non-Arabic word of Latin origin

when they go forth from your presence, during the night a group of them change what you say. And Allah writes down what they do nightly. So turn away from them, and depend on Allah. And Allah is a sufficient guardian.

According to verse 82, finding inconsistencies in the Qur'an proves that the Qur'an is not from Allah.

[82]Do they not consider the Qur'an? If it was from other than Allah, they would have found in it many inconsistencies. [83]And when matters come to them, either of the security or the fear, they spread it abroad. But if they would report them to the messenger and to those who are substantial in the affair, then those among them who desire information would learn it from them. And were it not for the bounty of Allah on you and his mercy, you would have followed Satan except for a few.

Muslim believers are commanded to engage in war for the sake of Allah.

[84]So engage in war for the sake of Allah, lay not burdens on any but yourself, and provoke the believers. Perhaps Allah will restrain the fierceness of those who became infidels, and Allah is the strongest in torment and is the strongest in retribution. [85]Whoever intercedes a good intercession, a portion of it will be his. And whoever intercedes an evil intercession, a portion of it will be his. And Allah was keeper over all things. [86]And when you are greeted with a greeting, so greet with better than it, or return it. Surely, Allah was a sufficient accounter over all things. [87]Allah, there is no god but him. He will surely gather you to the resurrection day. There is no doubt in it. And whose speech is more truthful than Allah's?

Allah deliberately leads people astray.

[88]What is [the matter] with you that you divided into two groups concerning the hypocrites when Allah has cast them off because of what they have earned? Do you desire to guide those whom Allah has led astray? And whomever Allah leads astray, so you will not find for him a way.

These verses indicate that Muslims must kill infidels rather than making friends with them.

[89]They desire that you should become infidels as they are infidels so that you should be alike. So do not take any of them for friends until they emigrate for the sake of Allah. So if they turn away, so seize them and kill them wherever you find them, and do not take from them as friends or helpers. [90]Except those who will arrive to a people between you and them a covenant or those who come to you, their chests shrinking from engaging in war with you or engaging in

war with their own people. And if Allah willed he would have made them dominate you so that they would engage in war with you. So if they withdraw from you, they will not engage in war with you, and they offer you the salām.[a] So Allah will not make for you a way against them.

Muslims must kill those who return to sedition or unbelief after professing to partner with them.

[91]You will find others who desire to be safe from you and safe from their own people. So often as they return to the sedition, they will be overthrown in it. So if they do not leave you nor offer you peace nor withhold their hands, so seize them and kill them wherever you find them. Over those, we have given you clear authority. [92]And it was not for a believer to kill a believer except by khati'a.[b] And whoever kills a believer by mistake so freeing a believer's neck [from slavery], and the blood-money will be paid to the family of the slain unless they give it as alms. So if the [killed] believer was from an enemy people to you, so freeing a believer's neck. And if he was from a people between you and them a covenant, so blood-money is to be paid to his family, and freeing a believer's neck. So who has not the means so fasting two consecutive months' penance from Allah. And Allah was knowing, wise.

Reasons why Muslims should never be allowed to join the military in non-Muslim countries.

[93]And whoever kills a believer intentionally, so his reward will be hell; he will abide in it forever, and Allah's wrath will be on him and will curse him and will prepare for him a great torment. [94]O you who have believed, when you go forth[c] for the sake of Allah, make investigation, and do not say to those who offer you peace, "You are not a believer," seeking the width of the world's life. So with Allah are abundant spoils. Likewise, you were before, so Allah has been gracious to you. So investigate. Surely Allah was aware of what you do.

Allah favors Muslims who perform jihad above other Muslims.

[95]Those believers who stay[d] other than those who are substantially injured are not equal to those who perform jihad for the sake of Allah with their money and their lives. Allah favors those who perform jihad with their money and their lives above those who stay

---

[a] peace, non-Arabic word of Hebrew/Aramaic origin
[b] mistake, non-Arabic word of Syriac origin
[c] to fight, perform jihad
[d] do not fight, jihad

to a higher degree. Allah promises each of them the goods. And Allah favors those who perform jihad, above those who stay, [with] a great wage, [96]degrees from him and forgiveness and mercy. And Allah was forgiving, merciful. [97]Surely those that the angels cause to die while they are unjust to themselves said, "Where were you?" They said, "We were weakened on the earth." They said, "Was not Allah's earth broad enough for you to emigrate in?" So those will have their abode in hell and an evil final place. [98]Except the weakened among the men and the women and the children, they could not find the means of escape and were not guided a way. [99]So those, perhaps Allah will pardon them. And Allah was pardoning, forgiving. [100]And whoever emigrates for the sake of Allah will find on the earth many places of refuge and abundant resources. And whoever leaves from his house emigrating to Allah and his messenger, then death overtakes him, so indeed, his wage is incumbent on Allah. And Allah was forgiving, merciful.

The infidels, those who do not believe in Allah, are the Muslim's enemies.

[101]And when you journey[a] on the earth, so it is not a sin against you to cut short your prayers if you fear that those who became infidels will seduce you. Surely the infidels were your obvious enemies. [102]And if you were among them so you perform for them the prayer, so let a group of them rise up with you. And let them take their weapons so when they worship, so they will be behind you. And let another group that has not prayed come forward. So let them pray with you, and let them take their precautions and their weapons. Those who became infidels desire for you to neglect your weapons and your goods so that they might turn on you at once. And it will be no sin against you if there was any harm of rain, or if you were sick, to put down your weapons and take your precautions. Surely Allah has prepared a shameful torment for the infidels. [103]So when you will have completed the prayer, so remember Allah, standing and sitting and reclining; so when you are secure, so perform the prayer. Surely the prayer is prescribed at fixed times for the believers.

Never tire of pursuing your enemies, the infidels. Mohammed is told to seek forgiveness for his sin. See also verses 47:19 and 48:2.

[104]Do not be weak in pursuing the people. If you are suffering pain, so surely they suffer pain also as you suffer pain, and hope from Allah for what they cannot hope. And Allah was knowing, wise. [105]Surely we have sent down the book to you with the truth that you may judge between the people according to what Allah has shown

---

[a] fight for the sake of Allah, jihad

you. And do not be an advocate for the betrayers. [106]And ask forgiveness of Allah. Surely Allah was forgiving, merciful.

Allah does not love those who are criminals or those who are sinful.

[107]And do not dispute on behalf of those who betray themselves. Surely Allah does not love who was treacherous, sinful. [108]They hide themselves from the people, and they do not hide themselves from Allah. And he is with them when they hold nightly discourses which do not please him. And Allah was encompassing what they do. [109]Here you are, those who dispute in their favor in the world's life. So who will dispute with Allah for them on the resurrection day, or who will be a guardian over them? [110]And whoever does evil or treats himself unjustly, then asks forgiveness of Allah, he will find Allah forgiving, merciful. [111]And whoever earned sin, so surely he earns it against himself. And Allah was knowing, wise. [112]And whoever earns sin, or sins, then throws it on someone innocent, so indeed, he will carry on himself a slander and an obvious sin. [113]And were it not for the bounty of Allah on you and his mercy, a group of them tried to mislead you, and they will not mislead except themselves; they will not harm you at all. And Allah sent down on you the book and the wisdom, and he taught you what you were not knowing. And the bounty of Allah on you was great. [114]There is no good in most of their secret counsels, except him who commands alms or fairness or reconciliation among the people. And whoever does that, seeking Allah's pleasures, so we will give him great wage. [115]And who opposes the messenger after the guidance has been shown to him and follows not the way of the believers, we will let him go to what he chooses. And we will roast him [in] hell and an evil final place.

Allah will not forgive those who worship other gods.

[116]Surely Allah will not forgive the partnering with himself. And he will forgive other than that to whom he wills. And whoever partners with Allah, so indeed, have strayed far away astray. [117]That they call, without him, only females. And that they do not call, except a rebellious Satan. [118]Allah cursed him, and he said, "Surely I will take from your servants a predetermined portion. [119]And I will lead them astray and will stir their desires. And I will command them, so they will cut the ears of livestock; and I will command them, so they will alter the creation of Allah." And whoever takes Satan rather than Allah for a friend, so indeed, has lost a manifest loss. [120]He promises them and stirs their desires, and Satan does not promise them except pride. [121]Those, their abode is hell, and they will not find escape from it. [122]And those who believed and did good deeds, we will admit them to gardens, below them the rivers flow, they will abide

in it forever and ever. The promise of Allah is true. And whose
speech is more truthful than Allah's? [123]Not according to your desires
or the desires of the People of the Book. He who does evil will be
rewarded by it. And they will not find a friend or a helper other than
Allah. [124]And whoever does good deeds, whether male or female,
while he is a believer, so those will enter the garden. They will not be
dealt with unjustly naqira.[a]

There is no better religion than Islam.

[125]And who has a better religion than the one who submits his face
to Allah? Who does what is good and follows the religion of
Abraham, hanifan? And Allah took Abraham for a friend. [126]And to
Allah what is in the heavens and what is on the earth, and Allah was
surrounding all things. [127]And they will consult you concerning the
women. Say, "Allah consults you about them and what is recited to
you in the book concerning female orphans to whom you do not give
what is written for them and you desire to have sex (marry) and with
regard to weak boys and that you deal with justice towards orphans.
And whatever good you do, so surely Allah was a knower of it."

Women are inferior to men and should seek reconciliation with their rebellious husbands. Compare this verse to 4:34.

[128]And if a woman fears rebellion or desertion from her husband,
then there will be no sin on them if they can reconcile between them
a reconciliation and the reconciliation is good. Men's souls are prone
to greed, but if you do good and fear, so surely Allah was aware of
what you do.

It is impossible for Muslims to treat their wives fairly.

[129]And you never can deal fairly between the women even if you
try carefully. So do not turn aside all the way so that you may leave
her as the hanging one. And if you reconcile and fear, so surely Allah
was forgiving, merciful. [130]And if they separate, Allah will make both
rich from his bounty. And Allah was large, wise. [131]And to Allah what
is in the heavens and what is on the earth. And indeed, we have
advised those to whom the books were given before you and to you:
"That fear Allah and if you become infidels, so surely to Allah what is
in the heavens and what is on the earth. And Allah was rich,
praised." [132]And to Allah what is in the heavens and what is on the
earth. And Allah is a sufficient guardian. [133]If he wills, he could cause
you, O people, to pass away and bring others, and Allah was mighty
for that. [134]Whoever was desirous for the reward of this world, so with
Allah is the reward of this world and the hereafter. And Allah was
hearing, seeing. [135]O you who have believed, be standing firmly with

---

[a] speck on the pit of a date, i.e. to the finest detail

justice as a witness to Allah, and even if against yourselves or your parents or your relatives, whether he was rich or poor. So Allah has more right to them. So do not follow the desire, lest you swerve from justice. And if you twist or turn away, so surely Allah was aware of what you do.

Muslims are commanded by Allah to believe in the Bible and its prophets. This is proof that the Bible was correct at the time of Mohammed.

[136]O you who have believed, believe in Allah and his messenger[a] and the book,[b] which he has sent down on his messenger, and the book,[c] which he has sent down before. Whoever becomes an infidel in Allah and his angels and his books and his messengers and the last day, so indeed, he has strayed far away astray. [137]Surely those who believed, then became infidels, then believed, then became infidels, then increased their infidelity, it is not for Allah to forgive them. And he will not guide them [to] a way. [138]Give the good news to the hypocrites that they will have a painful torment. [139]Those who take the infidels for friends, rather than the believers, do they seek the honor with them? So surely all the honor is to Allah. [140]And indeed, he sent it down on you in the book that if you heard the verses of Allah, they become infidels in it, and they scoff at it. So do not sit down with them until they engage in another saying, surely you will then become like them. Surely Allah will gather all the hypocrites and the infidels in hell, [141]those who watch you closely. Then if there was to you a triumph from Allah, they said, "Have we not been with you?" And if there was a portion for the infidels, they say, "Have we not prevailed over you and we prevented you from the believers?" So Allah will judge between you on the resurrection day, and Allah will not make a way for the infidels over the believers.

Hypocrites and Allah deceive each other, and Allah leads people astray. Muslims are commanded not to make friends with infidels.

[142]Surely the hypocrites deceive Allah, and he deceives them. And when they stand up for prayer, they stand lazily, to be seen of people, and they do not remember Allah except a little, [143]wavering between this, belonging neither to these nor to those. And whoever Allah leads astray, so you will not find a way for him. [144]O you who have believed, do not take the infidels as friends rather than believers. Do you desire that Allah will make a clear authority against

---

[a] Mohammed
[b] Qur'an
[c] the Bible

you? [145]Surely the hypocrites are in the lowest areas of the fire, and you will not find for them a helper, [146]except those who repent and reform and hold fast to Allah and they make their religion sincere to Allah. So those [will be] with the believers, and Allah will bring to the believers a great wage. [147]What will Allah do with your torment if you gave thanks and believed? And Allah was thankful, knowing. [148]Allah does not love when you speak of evil out loud, except to the one who was treated unjustly. And Allah was hearing, knowing. [149]If you show good or hide it or forgive evil, so surely Allah was pardoning, mighty. [150]Surely those who are infidels in Allah and his messengers and desire to differentiate between Allah and his messengers and say, "We believe in some and are infidels in some and desire to take a way between that," [151]those are the true infidels, and we prepare for the infidels a shameful torment. [152]And those who believed in Allah and his messengers and did not differentiate between any one of them, those he will bring their wages. And Allah was forgiving, merciful.

Mohammed makes a false accusation against the Jews. Notice the statement about the flying mountain. See also verse 7:171.

[153]The People of the Book ask you to bring down on them a book from the heaven. So indeed, they asked Moses bigger than that. So they said, "Show us Allah openly." So the thunderbolt seized them for their injustice. Then they took the calf. After that our clear signs came to them, so we forgave them this. And we gave Moses a manifest authority. [154]And we uplifted the mountain above them with their covenant, and we said to them, "Enter the door worshiping." And we said to them, "Do not transgress on the Sabbath." And we took from them a thick[a] covenant. [155]So because of their breaking their covenant and being infidels in the verses of Allah and their killing of the prophets unjustly and their saying, "Our hearts are uncircumcised." Yet Allah has taba'a[b] on it for their infidelity so that they will not believe except for a few. [156]And because of their infidelity and their saying against Mary, a great slander.

'Isā (the Jesus of Mohammed) did not die on the cross; someone else, whom Allah made to look like 'Isā, took his place.

[157]And their saying, "Surely we killed the Christ 'Isā, son of Mary, the messenger of Allah." And they did not kill him, and they did not salaba[c] him; but it was made to appear to them, and surely those who disagree about him are in doubt of him. They do not have any knowledge of him except following the conjecture, and they did not

---

[a] firm
[b] sealed, non-Arabic word of Syriac origin
[c] crucify, non-Arabic word of Persian/Syriac origin

kill him for certain. [158]Yet Allah raised him up to himself. And Allah was dear, wise. [159]And none of the People of the Book[a] will believe in him before his death. And on the resurrection day, he will be a witness against them. [160]So with the unjust of the Jews, we have forbidden them good things which were lawful for them and because of their preventing many from the way of Allah. [161]And their taking the interest, and indeed, they were forbidden to do so and their consuming the people's money with vanity. And we prepare for the infidels among them a painful torment. [162]But the men of firm knowledge among them and the believers believe in what has been sent down to you[b] and in what has been sent down before you.[c] And the performer of the prayer and the bringer of the legal alms and the believers in Allah and the last day, those we will bring them a great wage.

This passage shows Mohammed's confusion of names and his incorrect order of historical events.

[163]Surely we have revealed to you as we revealed to Noah and the prophets after him. And we revealed to Abraham and Ishmael and Isaac and Jacob and the tribes and 'Isā and Ayyūb[d] and Yunus[e] and Aaron and Solomon, and to David we gave Zabor.[f] [164]And messengers, we have mentioned their story to you before, and messengers, we have not mentioned their story to you. And Allah spoke to Moses, speaking. [165]Messengers who give good news and warners so that it may not be to the people an excuse against Allah after the messengers. And Allah was dear, wise. [166]But Allah is himself witness of what he sent down to you. He sent it with his knowledge, and the angels are witnesses. And Allah is a sufficient witness. [167]Surely those who became infidels and prevent [others] from the way of Allah, indeed, they have strayed and gone far astray. [168]Surely those who became infidels and act unjustly, it was not for Allah to forgive them. And he will not guide them [to] a way, [169]except the way of hell, they will abide in it forever and ever. And this was easy for Allah. [170]O you people, indeed, the messenger came to you with the truth from your lord. So believe; it is better for you. And if you become infidels, so surely, to Allah what is in the heavens and the earth. And Allah was knowing, wise.

'Isā (the Jesus of Mohammed) was only a messenger. It is far from Allah's glory to have a son. The Trinity is false. Notice that

---

[a] Bible
[b] Qur'an
[c] Bible
[d] Job, non-Arabic word of Greek/Syriac origin
[e] name mistakenly used when Jonah was meant
[f] in singular form = Psalms, non-Arabic word of Hebrew/Syriac origin

the Trinity is clearly taught in this same verse. 1. 'Isā is the messenger, the word of Allah. 2. Allah is the father. 3. The spirit of Allah is the holy spirit. Compare this to the Bible in John 1:1-3, 14.

[171]O People of the Book, do not exaggerate in your religion and do not speak against Allah, except the truth. Surely the Christ 'Isā, son of Mary, is only a messenger of Allah and his word, which he cast to Mary, and a spirit from him. So believe in Allah and his messengers, and do not say, "Three."[a] Cease; it is better for you. Surely Allah is only one god. Praise be to him that there would be to him a son. To him what is in the heavens and what is on the earth, and Allah is a sufficient guardian. [172]The Christ does not disdain to be a servant of Allah, nor do the angels who are close. And whoever disdains his service and is proud, so he will gather them all to himself. [173]So as for those who believed and did good deeds, so he will pay them their wages in full, and he will increase them from his bounty. And as for those who are disdainful and proud, so he will torment them with a painful torment. And they will not find a friend or helper other than Allah. [174]O you people, indeed, an evidence has come to you from your lord, and we have sent down to you a clear light. [175]So as to those who believed in Allah and hold fast to him, so he will admit them into his mercy and bounty, and he will guide them to him a straight way.

Women only receive half t inheritance of a man.

[176]They consult you. Say, "Allah consults you as to the deceased who has no living son or father. If a man died and he had no son and he had a sister, half of what he left will be hers. And he will inherit from her if she did not have a son. But if there are two sisters, they will have two thirds of what he left. And if there are siblings, men and women, so the male will have the portion of two females. Allah shows you so that you will not stray. And Allah knows all things."

A portion of a revelation   **The Table**

In the name of Allah, the merciful, the merciful

Rules for the pilgrimage (the Hajj) were copied from old Arabian paganism.

---

[a] Trinity

¹O you who have believed, fulfill your obligations. The beast of livestock is lawful to you, except that which is recited to you. The hunt is unlawful to you when you are entering on the pilgrimage. Surely Allah judges what he pleases. ²O you who have believed, do not violate the ceremonies of Allah nor the forbidden months nor the guidance nor its ornaments nor those who are the faithful of the forbidden house, seeking bounty from their lord and his good pleasure in them. And when it is lawful for you, then you may hunt. And do not let hatred of people who prevented you from the forbidden mosque lead you to transgress, and be united together to do righteousness and piety. And do not be united to do sin and transgression, and fear Allah. Surely Allah is severe in the punishing.

The dietary laws here are copied from the Old Testament. See Leviticus and Deuteronomy. Islam is the final religion.

³Forbidden to you is that which dies [of itself] and the blood and swine meat and what has been sacrificed to other than Allah and the strangled and the one killed by a blow and by a fall and by goring and that which has been eaten by beasts of prey, except what you make dhakkāūtom,[a] and that which has been slaughtered on Al-Nasb.[b] And to make division of the slain by consulting the arrows is unrighteous for you. Today those who became infidels despair from your religion. So do not fear them, but fear me. Today I have completed your religion for you and have fulfilled on you my grace. And I am pleased to [give] you Islam, a religion, so whoever is compelled by hunger to eat without wanting to transgress. So surely Allah is forgiving, merciful. ⁴They ask you what is lawful for them. Say, "The good things are lawful for you.[c] And what you trained, of the birds [of prey] and the beasts, teaching them as Allah has taught you, so eat of what they will catch for you, and mention the name of Allah on it, and fear Allah. Surely Allah is swift in the reckoning."

It is lawful for Muslim men to marry Christian or Jewish women; however, Jewish or Christian men cannot marry Muslim women.

⁵Today the good is lawful to you, and the foods of those[d] who have been given the book[e] are lawful to you. And your foods are lawful to them. And chaste, believing[f] women and chaste women[g] of

---

[a] ceremonially clean, non-Arabic word of Hebrew origin
[b] stones around the Kaaba
[c] to eat
[d] Jews and Christians
[e] Bible
[f] Muslim
[g] Jews and Christians

those who have received the book[a] before you, when you will have given them their wages, living chastely with them without fornication and without taking secret lovers. And who becomes an infidel of the faith, so indeed, his works will come to nothing, and he will become in the hereafter of the losers.

Touching women makes men "unclean," because women in Islam are dirtier than dirt. Rules for cleanliness were copied from old Arabian paganism.

[6]O you who have believed, when you rise to pray, so wash your faces and your hands up to the elbow, and wipe your heads and your legs to the ankles. And if you had a sexual orgasm, so purify yourselves. And if you were sick or traveling or if one of you has relieved himself or if you have touched the women, so you did not find water, so rub your faces and your hands with good dirt. Allah does not desire to lay a burden on you, but he desires to purify you; and he would fulfill his grace on you, perhaps you may be thankful. [7]And remember the grace of Allah on you and his covenant which he has covenanted with you, when you said, "We have heard and obeyed." And fear Allah, surely Allah knows what is in the chests. [8]O you who have believed, be standing up as witnesses to Allah with fairness, and do not let some people cause you to deal unjustly. Deal justly; it is near to piety. And fear Allah. Surely Allah is aware of what you do. [9]Allah promises those who believed and did good deeds, to them forgiveness and a great wage. [10]And those who became infidels and denied our verses, those are the companions of hell.[11]O you who have believed, remember the grace of Allah on you. They are a people who stretch forth their hands against you, so he kept their hands from you. And fear Allah, and on Allah so let the believers depend. [12]And indeed, Allah took a covenant with the children of Israel, and out of them we raised up twelve chiefs, and Allah said, "Surely I am with you. If you performed the prayer and brought the legal alms and believed in my messengers and 'azzara[b] them and lend Allah a good loan, I will surely atone for you your evils, and I will admit you into gardens, below them the rivers flow. So whoever of you becomes an infidel after that, so indeed, he has gone astray from the right way." [13]So by their breaking of their covenant, we have cursed them and have hardened their hearts. They shift the words from their places, and they have forgotten part of what they were reminded of. You will not cease to discover deceit on their part except in a few of them. So pardon them, and forgive. Surely Allah loves the doers of good. [14]And some of those who say, "Surely we are Nasara (Christians)," we took their covenant. So they have forgotten a part of what they were reminded of, so we have

---

[a] Bible
[b] help, non-Arabic word of Hebrew origin

stirred up enmity and hatred among them until the resurrection day. And Allah will inform them of what they were doing.

Jews and Christians are misled. The Qur'an is a clear book that will guide them straight.

[15]O People[a] of the Book, indeed, our messenger came to you to clear up much that you were hiding from the book[b] and pardons you much. Indeed, a light and a clear book[c] came to you from Allah. [16]Allah will guide with it the one who will follow his pleasure to the ways of peace, and he will bring them out of the darkness to the light by his permission. And he will guide them to a straight way.

Those who believe Jesus is God are infidels. See also verses 5:72-73.

[17]Infidels, indeed, are those who said, "Surely Allah is the Christ, the son of Mary." Say, "So who could have anything against Allah if he desired to destroy the Christ, son of Mary, and his mother and all who are on the earth?" And to Allah the kingdom of the heavens and the earth and what is between them. He creates what he wills. And Allah has might over all things. [18]And the Jews and the Nasara (Christians) said, "We are sons of Allah and his beloved." Say, "So why does he torment you for your sins?" Yet you are human among those created. He will forgive whom he wills and torment whom he wills. And to Allah the kingdom of the heavens and the earth and what is between them, and to him is the final return. [19]O People of the Book, indeed, our messenger came to you to show you after the cessation of the messengers, that you say, "No giver of good news or a warner came to us." So indeed, he[d] came to you as giver of good news and a warner. And Allah has might over all things.

The story of the Jews and their inheritance of the Promised Land is copied from the Bible (see Numbers 13) and corrupted.

[20]And when Moses said to his people, "O my people, remember the grace of Allah on you when he made prophets among you. And he made you kings, and he gave you what he did not give anyone of the world. [21]O my people, enter the holy land which Allah has prescribed for you, and do not turn away on your backs so you will be turned back losers." [22]They said, "O Moses, surely in it are powerful people, and surely we will not enter it until they come out of it. So if they come out of it, so surely we will enter." [23]Two men

---

[a] Jews and Christians
[b] Bible
[c] Qur'an
[d] Mohammed

among the fearers, Allah graced on them, said, "Enter on them the door. So when you enter it, so surely you will be victorious. And on Allah, so depend, if you were believers." [24]They said, "O Moses, surely we will never enter it as long as they are in it. So go, you and your lord. So engage in war. Surely we are sitting down right here." [25]He said, "My lord, surely I do not own anything except myself and my brother, so separate between us and the transgressing people." [26]He said, "So surely it[a] is forbidden to them forty years; they will be lost on the earth. So do not grieve on the transgressing people."

The story of Abel and Cain is copied from the Bible and corrupted. See Genesis 4. Key details are missing. Who are the brothers? What were the sacrifices? Who killed whom?

[27]And recite to them the news with the truth of the sons of Adam when they each offered an offering, so it was accepted from one of them and not accepted from the other. He said, "Surely I will kill you." He said, "Surely Allah only accepts from the fearer. [28]If you stretch your hand against me to kill me, I will not stretch my hand to you to kill you. Surely I fear Allah, the lord of the worlds. [29]Surely I desire that you will bear my sin and your sin so that you will become among the companions of the fire, and that is the reward of the unjust." [30]So his soul persuaded him to kill his brother. So he killed him, so he became of the losers.

In the story about the burial of the deceased brother, the reference to the raven apparently comes from Chapter 21 of a Jewish book, *Pirke Rabbi Eleazar*, which tells of the raven coming to show Adam, not the brother, how to bury his son.

[31]So Allah sent a raven which searched on the earth to show him how he might bury his brother's body. He said, "O woe is to me. Am I unable to become like this raven, so I will hide my brother's body?" So he became of those who regret.

The concept that murder or preservation of a single soul is tantamount to the murder or preservation of an entire people appears to be drawn from the Jewish Mishnah, Sanhedrin 4:5.

[32]For this reason, we inscribed for the children of Israel that he who kills a soul, without a soul, or vandalizes on the earth, so it will be only as though he had killed all the people; and that he who gives it a life, it will be as though he had given life to all the people. And indeed, our messengers came to them with proofs; then surely most of them after that are extravagant on the earth.

---

[a] the Promised Land

The following verse was written in response to the people to whom Mohammed advised to drink his camels' urine and milk as a medicine to heal their sicknesses. Subsequently, they stole those camels after killing his shepherd as explained by the interpretations of Muslim scholars.

[33]Surely the reward of those who war against Allah and his messenger and go about to vandalize on the earth is only that they will be killed or crucified or have their hands and legs cut off on opposite sides or they will be banished from the earth. This is their disgrace in this world, and in the hereafter they will have a great torment. [34]Except those who repent before you overpower them, so know that Allah is forgiving, merciful. [35]O you who have believed, fear Allah and desire the way to him. And perform jihad for his sake, perhaps you may prosper. [36]Surely those who became infidels, if they have what is on the earth together and like it with it, to ransom themselves by it from the torment of the resurrection day, it will not be accepted from them. And they will have a painful torment. [37]They desire to get out from the fire, but they will not come out of it. And they will have a lasting torment

Muslims must cut off the hands of those who steal.

[38]And the male thief and the female thief, so cut off their hands, a reward of what they earned as a punishment from Allah. And Allah is dear, wise. [39]So whoever repents after his injustice and reforms, so surely Allah will relent toward him. Surely Allah is forgiving, merciful. [40]Did you not know that Allah has the kingdom of the heavens and the earth? He torments whom he wills, and he forgives whom he wills. And Allah has might over all things. [41]O you messenger,[a] do not let those who hasten to the infidelity grieve you, of those who say with their mouths, "We believed," but their hearts do not believe. And from those who become Jews, hearers to the lies, hearers to other people, they did not come to you. They shift the words from their places. They say, "If you are giving this, so take it; and if you are not giving it, so beware." And whomever Allah desires to lead into sedition, so you will not have anything for him against Allah. Those whom Allah does not desire to purify their hearts will have in this world disgrace, and in the hereafter they will have great torment. [42]Hearers to the lies and are consuming of the suht.[b] So if they come to you, so judge between them, or turn away from them. And if you turn away from them, so they will not harm you anything. And if you judge, so judge between them with fairness. Surely Allah loves those who deal fairly.

---

[a] Mohammed
[b] unlawful, non-Arabic word of Syriac origin

This passage confirms that the Jewish books (Torah) are true in Mohammed's time.

[43]And how can they make you their judge, and they have the Torah, in it the judgments of Allah? Then they turn away after this, and those are not believers. [44]Surely we have sent down the Torah, in it is guidance and light. The prophets judge by it those who submit themselves to the Jews and the Jewish teachers and the ahbar[a] in what they kept from the book of Allah, and they were witnesses over it. So do not fear the people, and fear me; and do not purchase with my verses a little price. And whoever does not judge by what Allah has sent down,[b] so those are the infidels. [45]And we wrote for them in it: a soul for a soul and an eye for an eye and a nose for a nose and an ear for an ear and a tooth for a tooth and for wounds, retaliation, so whoever gives it as alms, so it is an atonement for him; and whoever will not judge by what Allah has sent down, so those are the unjust.

This passage confirms that the Gospel is from God and is correct in Mohammed's time.

[46]And in their footsteps we sent 'Isā, son of Mary, confirming what is between his hands of the Torah, and we gave him the Gospel, in it is guidance and light, and confirming what was between his hands from the Torah, and a guidance and a sermon to the fearer. [47]And that the people of the Gospel judge by what Allah has sent down in it. And whoever does not judge by what Allah has sent down, so those are the transgressors.

The Qur'an confirms that the previous books of the Bible are and will be true as long as the Qur'an exists.

[48]And to you[c] we have sent down the book[d] with the truth, confirming what is between his hands of the book[e] and as guardian over it. So judge between them by what Allah has sent down, and do not follow their desires about what came to you of the truth. To every one of you we have given a law and a clear way. And if Allah willed, he would have made you one nation but to test you in what he has given to you. So hasten [doing] the goods. To Allah you will all return. So he will inform you about what you were differing. [49]And that [you] judge between them by what Allah has sent down, and do not follow their desires. And be on guard toward them, that they seduce you from some of what Allah has sent down to you; so if they

[a] priests, non-Arabic word of possible Syriac origin
[b] the Torah
[c] Mohammed
[d] the Qur'an
[e] Bible

turn away, so know that Allah only desires to afflict them for some of their sins. And surely many of the people are transgressors. ⁵⁰Do they desire the judgment of ignorance? And who is a better judge than Allah for people who are certain?

Muslims are forbidden from making friends with Christians or Jews.

⁵¹O you who have believed, do not take the Jews and the Nasara (Christians) as friends. They are friends to one another. And whoever among you takes them as friends, so surely he is of them. Surely Allah does not guide the unjust people. ⁵²So you see those who have sickness in their hearts hastening to them saying, "We fear that misfortune will befall us." So perhaps Allah will bring a conquest or a command from himself, so they will become in regret in their souls over what they have done. ⁵³And the believers will say, "Are those who swore to their Allah by their most solemn oath, surely they were with you?" Their works are in vain, so they became losers. ⁵⁴O you who have believed, whoever of you turns back from his religion, so Allah will bring forth a people; he loves them, and they love him. Submissive to the believers, haughty towards the infidels, they perform jihad for the sake of Allah and do not fear the blame of the blamer. This is the favor of Allah. He gives it to whom he wills. And Allah is large, knowing. ⁵⁵Surely your only friends are Allah and his messenger and those who believed, who perform the prayer and bring the legal alms while they are kneeling. ⁵⁶And whoever takes Allah and his messenger and those who believed for friends, so surely the hizbᵃ of Allah are the victors. ⁵⁷O you who have believed, take not those who took your religion as a scoff and sport, among those who have received the bookᵇ before you, and the infidels [as] friends; and fear Allah, if you were believers. ⁵⁸And if you called to the prayer, they took it as a scoff and sport. That is because they are a people who do not understand. ⁵⁹Say, "O People of the Book, do you ridicule us because we believed in Allah and what he has sent down to us and what he has sent down before and that many of you are transgressors?" ⁶⁰Say, "Will I inform you of evil than that as punishment from Allah?" They whom Allah has cursed and on whom he has poured forth his wrath, some of themᶜ he changed into monkeys and swine; and they who worship the idolatry, those are in an evil place and have gone astray from the right way. ⁶¹And when they came to you, they said, "We believed." And indeed, they entered with infidelity, and they left with it. And Allah knows best what they were hiding. ⁶²And you see many of them hastening to

---

ᵃ party, non-Arabic word of Ethiopian origin
ᵇ Jew and Christian
ᶜ Jews

wickedness and malice and to consuming of the unlawful. Evil is what they were doing. [63]Were it not that the Jewish teachers and the priests would forbid their iniquitous speech and their consuming of the unlawful. Evil is what they were doing. [64]And the Jews said, "The hand of Allah is tied." Their hands are tied, and they are cursed because of what they said. Yet his hands are outstretched; he spends however he wills. And he will surely increase many of them. Your lord did not send down to you rebellion and infidelity, and we cast between them enmity and hatred until the resurrection day. As often as they kindled a fire to a war, Allah quenched it. And they strive on the earth vandalizing. And Allah does not love the vandals.

If Jews and Christians believe in God, they will be forgiven. This is more proof that the Bible is infallible.

[65]And if the People of the Book believed and feared, we will surely atone their evils from them and will admit them to the gardens of bliss. [66]And if they perform the Torah and the Gospel and what has been sent down to them from their lord, they will surely eat from above them and from under their legs. Among them is a nation who acts right, but many of them, evil is what they do. [67]O you messenger, proclaim what has been sent down to you from your lord, and if you do not do, so his message will not be delivered. And Allah will protect you from the people. Surely Allah will not guide the infidel people.

Christians and Jews are commanded to believe in the Bible and practice its teaching. The Qur'an will increase the rebellion of many Jews and Christians.

[68]Say, "O People of the Book, you have nothing until you perform the Torah and the Gospel and what has been sent down to you from your lord." And what is sent down to you will increase rebellion and infidelity in many of them. So do not grieve over the infidel people.

Muslims, Jews, Sabians, and Christians being in Paradise contradicts verse 3:85.

[69]Surely those who believed and those who are Jews and the Sabians and the Nasara (Christians), whoever believed in Allah and in the last day and did a good deed, so there is no fear on them. And they will not grieve.

The Jews killed the prophets of God.

[70]Indeed, we took the covenant of the children of Israel and sent messengers to them. Whenever a messenger came to them with what their soul did not desire, a group they denied and a group they are killing. [71]And they thought that there would be no sedition, so they became blind and deaf. Then Allah relented on them; then

many of them became blind and deaf. And Allah is the seer of what they do.

Those who believe that Jesus is God and believe in the Trinity; in other words, all Christians are infidels.

[72]Infidels, indeed, are those who said, "Surely Allah is the Christ, son of Mary." And the Christ said, "O children of Israel, serve Allah, my lord and your lord." Surely whoever partners with Allah, so indeed, Allah forbids him the garden. And his abode is the fire, and the unjust will have no helpers. [73]Infidels, indeed, are those who said, "Surely Allah is the third of three." And there is no god except one god, and if they do not refrain from what they are saying, a painful torment will touch those who became infidels among them. [74]Do they not repent to Allah and ask his forgiveness? And Allah is forgiving, merciful.

'Isā (the Jesus of Mohammed) was nothing more than a messenger because he ate normal human food.

[75]The Christ, son of Mary, is nothing except a messenger; indeed, other messengers have gone before him, and his mother is a siddīqah.[a] They were eating the food. Look at how we show the verses to them, then look at how they turn away! [76]Say, "Will you serve rather than Allah, that do not have a harm nor a profit for you?" And Allah is the hearing, the knowing. [77]Say, "O People of the Book, do not exaggerate in your religion without the truth and do not follow the desire of a people who indeed has gone astray before. And they have caused many to go astray and have themselves gone astray from the right way."

David and 'Isā (the Jesus of Mohammed) cursed the children of Israel.

[78]Cursed are those who became infidels from the children of Israel by the tongue of David and of 'Isā, son of Mary. This is because of their rebellion, and they were transgressors. [79]They were not forbidding each other in committing evil. Evil is what they were doing. [80]You will see many of them make friends with those who became infidels. Evil is what their own souls have sent on before them, that Allah's wrath is on them, and in the torment they will abide forever. [81]And if they were believing in Allah and the prophet and what has been sent down to him, they had not taken them for their friends, but most of them are transgressors.

---

[a] person of integrity, non-Arabic word of Aramaic origin

This passage describes the relationships that Jews, Polytheists, and Christians have with Muslims.

[82]You will find the Jews and those who are polytheistic are the most hostile toward the people who believed, and you will find those who say, "We are Nasara (Christians)," are nearest friends to those who believed. This is because among them are qissīsūn[a] and monks, and surely they are not proud. [83]And when they hear that which has been sent down to the messenger, you see their eyes flow with tears at the truth they know, saying, "O our lord, we believed, so write us down with the witnesses. [84]And why should we not believe in Allah, and what came to us of the truth and hope that our lord would admit us with the good people?" [85]So Allah has rewarded them for what they said with gardens, below them the rivers flow, they will abide in it forever; and this is the reward of the doers of good. [86]And those who became infidels and denied our verses, those are the companions of hell. [87]O you who have believed, do not forbid the good that Allah made lawful for you. And do not transgress. Surely Allah does not love the transgressors. [88]And eat from what Allah has provided you, lawful and good, and fear Allah, in whom you believe.

It is lawful for Muslims to lie in an oath. This contradicts the Bible which commands us not to lie. Liars will not enter into heaven. See Revelation 21:8.

[89]Allah will not hold you responsible for the mere utterance in your oath, but he will hold you responsible in regard to an oath taken seriously. So its atonement will be to feed ten poor persons with such adequate food as you feed your own families with or to clothe them or to set a neck[b] free. So who cannot find means, so fasting three days. This is the atonement of your oaths when you will have sworn. And keep your oaths. Likewise, Allah makes his verses clear to you, perhaps you may give thanks.

Wine and gambling are the Devil's work. This contradicts verses 47:15 and 83:25-26.

[90]O you who have believed, surely the wine and the gambling and the idols and the divining arrows are an abomination of Satan's work. So avoid them, perhaps you may prosper. [91]Surely Satan only desires to stir up enmity and hatred among you, in the wine and the gambling, and prevent you from the remembrance of Allah and from the prayer. So will you desist? [92]And obey Allah, and obey the messenger. And be on your guard. So if you turn away, so know that the duty of our messenger is only the clear delivery.

---

[a] priests/Christian teachers, non-Arabic word of Syriac origin
[b] slave

All food, including pork, is approved. This contradicts verses 2:172 and 5:3.

[93]No junāh[a] will be on those who believed and did good deeds, in regard to any food they have taken, if they feared and believed and did the good deeds, then they feared and believed. Then they feared and did good, and Allah loves the doers of good. [94]O you who have believed, Allah will surely test you with such game as you may catch with your hands or your lances, that Allah may know who fears him in secret; so whoever transgresses after this, so he will have a painful torment. [95]O you who have believed, do not kill game while you are on pilgrimage. Whosoever among you will purposely kill it, so its compensation the like of what he killed from the livestock of equal value, according to the judgment of fair persons among you, to be given as a gift on arriving at the Kaaba; or its atonement feeds the poor,[b] or in fairness to that[c] fasting, so that he may taste the ill consequences of his deed. Allah forgives what is passed, but whoever repeats it, so Allah will take vengeance on him. And Allah is dear, possessor of revenge.

It is lawful to eat all seafood. This is contradicted in Mosaic Law. See Deuteronomy 14:9-10.

[96]Lawful for you the catch of the sea, and its food is enjoyment for you and to the travelers. And it is forbidden for you the catch of the wilderness as long as you are on your pilgrimage, and fear Allah to whom you will be gathered. [97]Allah has made the Kaaba, the forbidden house, to be a standard to the people and the forbidden month and the offering and the ornaments. This, so that you may know that Allah knows what is in the heavens and what is on the earth, and surely Allah is knowing everything. [98]Know that Allah is severe in the punishing and that Allah is forgiving, merciful. [99]The responsibility of the messenger is only the delivering. And Allah knows what you reveal and what you hide. [100]Say, "The evil and the good are not equal, even though the abundance of evil pleases you, so fear Allah. O you who are substantial of understanding, perhaps you may prosper."

Muslims are commanded not to question things in the Qur'an.

[101]O you who have believed, do not ask about things which, if they were revealed to you, it would be harmful to you. And if you ask of it when the Qur'an is sent down, it will be revealed to you. Allah will pardon you for this. And Allah is forgiving, forbearing. [102]The people

---

[a] sin, non-Arabic word of Persian origin
[b] replacement sacrifice to be given at the Kaaba to feed the poor
[c] as an alternative

before you asked such questions, and by them they became infidels.
[103]Allah has not made any Bahira nor Saiba nor Wasila nor Hami,[a]
but those who became infidels forge the lies against Allah, and most
of them do not understand. [104]And when it was said to them, "Come
to what Allah has sent down and to the messenger." They said,
"What we found our fathers doing[b] is sufficient for us," even though
their fathers were not knowing anything, and they were not guided.
[105]O you who have believed, take care of yourselves. He who errs
will not harm you if you have the guidance. To Allah you all will
return, so he will inform you of what you were doing. [106]O you who
have believed, witnesses between you, if the death comes to any of
you, at the time of making the will; two, fair, from among yourselves,
or two others not from yourselves. If you travel on the earth so the
calamity of death surprises you, you will detain them, after the
prayer; and if you doubt them, so they will swear by Allah: "We will
not purchase with it a price even if he was a relative. Neither will we
hide the testimony of Allah. Surely then we would be among the
sinners." [107]So if it will be made clear that they have been guilty of a
sin, so two others will stand in their place against the first two who
sinned, and they will swear by Allah: "Surely our testimony is more
truthful than their testimony. And if we have transgressed, surely
then we will be of the unjust." [108]That is near[c] that they bring the true
testimony, or they will fear that another oath will be given after their
oath. And fear Allah, and hear. And Allah does not guide the
transgressing people. [109]A day Allah gathers the messengers, so he
will say, "What answer were you given?" They said, "We have no
knowledge. Surely you are the knower of the unseen."

**This story of 'Isā (the Jesus of Mohammed) performing miracles
was clearly borrowed out of the Gnostic gospels. Also, note that
the disciples of 'Isā were Muslims.**

[110]When Allah said, "O 'Isā, son of Mary, remember my grace on
you and on your mother when I supported you with the holy spirit;
you spoke to people in the cradle and [as] an old man. And when I
taught you the book and the wisdom and the Torah and the Gospel,
and when you created from the mud the likeness of the bird by my
permission, so you breathed into it, so it will become a bird by my
permission. And you healed the blind and the leper by my
permission. And when you brought forth the dead by my permission,
and when I withheld the children of Israel from you, when you came
to them with the proofs, so those who became infidels among them
said, "That this is but an obvious sorcery." [111]And when I revealed to

---

[a] livestock dedicated to, or liberated in honor of idols
[b] believing
[c] more likely

the Hawārīyūn:[a] "That believe in me and in my messenger." They said, "We believed and bear witness that surely we are Muslims."

The miracle of the descending table, made up by Mohammed, clearly shows Mohammed's confusion and misunderstanding about the account of the Lord's Supper. See Matthew 26:20-29.

[112]When the Hawārīyūn said, "O 'Isā, son of Mary, can your lord send down on us a mā'ida[b] from the heaven?" He said, "Fear Allah, if you were believers." [113]They said, "We desire to eat from it and to have our hearts assured and know that you indeed have told us the truth, and we will be witnesses of it." [114]'Isā, son of Mary, said, "O Allah our lord, send down a table on us from the heaven, that it becomes an 'id[c] for us, to the first of us and to the last of us, and a sign from you. And provide for us, and you are the best of the providers." [115]Allah said, "Surely I will send it down on you, so whoever among you becomes an infidel after that, so surely I will torment him a torment I will not torment any one of the worlds."

'Isā (the Jesus of Mohammed) confessed to Allah that he was not the Son of God.

[116]And when Allah said, "O 'Isā, son of Mary, did you say to the people, 'Take me and my mother as two gods, other than Allah'?" He said, "Praise be unto you. It is not for me that I say what is not true for me; if I had said it, so indeed, you know it. You know what is in my soul, and I do not know what is in your soul. Surely, you are the knower of the unseen.

In the following verses the Qur'an clearly teaches that 'Isā (the Jesus of Mohammed) died. This contradicts verses 4:157-158.

[117]I did not tell them except what you had commanded me, 'That serve Allah, my lord and your lord,' and I was a witness among them as long as I was with them. So when you caused me to die, you were the watcher over them, and you are the witness of all things. [118]If you torment them, so surely they are your servants; and if you forgive them, so surely you are the dear, the wise." [119]Allah said, "This is a day in which the truthfulness will benefit the truthful. They will have gardens, below them the rivers flow, and they abide in it forever and ever. Allah is pleased with them, and they are pleased with him. This is the great triumph." [120]To Allah the kingdoms of the heavens and the earth and what is in them, and he has might over all things.

---

[a] white or pure—Mohammed used it to mean disciples of Jesus, non-Arabic word of probable Abyssinian origin
[b] table, non-Arabic word of Ethiopian origin
[c] festival, non-Arabic word of Syriac origin

A portion of a revelation   *The Livestock*

In the name of Allah, the merciful, the merciful

The creation of the heavens and the earth, the darkness and the light, is copied from Genesis 1:1-4.

[1]The praise be to Allah who created the heavens and the earth and made the darkness and the light. Then those who became infidels set up equals[a] with their lord. [2]He is who created you from mud then decreed a term, and the term is named with him, then you still doubt. [3]And he is Allah in the heavens and on the earth. He knows your secrets and your proclamations, and he knows what you earn. [4]And no verses came to them of the verses of their lord, except they were turning away from it. [5]So indeed, they denied the truth when he came to them. So it will come to them, the news of what they were scoffing at. [6]Have they not seen how many generations before them we have destroyed after we established them on the earth, what we did not establish for you, and we sent the heavens on them in abundance;[b] and we made the rivers to run below them! So we destroyed them for their sins and raised up another generation after them.

Some thought the Qur'an was sorcery.

[7]And if we sent down on you a book on qurtās[c] so that they had touched it with their hands, those who became infidels will say, "This is nothing but obvious sorcery!" [8]And they said, "Were it not that an angel had been sent down on him." And if we sent an angel, he will finish the affair, then they will not delay. [9]And if we made him an angel, we will make him a man, and we will dress them what they dress. [10]And indeed, the messengers before you were scoffed at, so those who were scoffing among them were afflicted with what they were scoffing. [11]Say, "Walk on the earth, then look how was the end of the deniers." [12]Say, "To whom what is in the heavens and the earth?" Say, "To Allah. He has prescribed upon himself the mercy that he will gather you to the resurrection day, no doubt in it. Those who lost their souls, so they will not believe." [13]And to him what dwells in the night and the day, and he is the hearing, the knowing.

---

[a] false gods
[b] rain
[c] parchment, non-Arabic word of Greek/Syriac origin

Mohammed is the first to become a Muslim. Or Adam or who?

[14]Say, "Shall I take a friend other than Allah, fātir[a] of the heavens and the earth, and he feeds and is not fed?" Say, "Surely I am commanded to be the first of those who become Muslim and do not become of the polytheists." [15]Say, "Surely I fear, if I disobey my lord, a torment of a great day." [16]Whoever is spared on that day, so indeed, [he granted] him mercy, and this is the clear triumph. [17]And if Allah touches you with harm, so no one can take it off except him, and if he touches you with good, so he has might over all things. [18]And he is the dominator above his servants, and he is the wise, the aware. [19]Say, "What thing is a bigger testimony?" Say, "Allah is witness between me and you, and this Qur'an has been revealed to me to warn you with it and whoever it reaches. Do you witness that there are other gods with Allah?" Say, "I will not witness." Say, "Surely he is only one god, and I am innocent from what you partner." [20]Those to whom we gave the book, they know it as they know their own sons; those have lost themselves, so they will not believe.

People who do not believe in Islam are wicked and will not prosper.

[21]And who is more unjust than the one who forges a lie against Allah or denies his verses? Surely the unjust will not prosper. [22]And a day, we will gather them together. Then we will say to those who are polytheists, "Where are your shirk[b] whom you were claiming?" [23]Then their sedition was not except that they said, "[We swear] by Allah our lord, we were not polytheists." [24]Look how they lie against themselves, and what they were forging has gone astray from them.

Some said the Qur'an was copied from ancient legends.

[25]And some of them who listened to you, and we made covers on their hearts that they understand it and a deafness in their ears; and if they see every sign, they will not believe in it until when they come to you. They dispute with you. Those who became infidels say, "This is nothing but asātir[c] of the ancients." [26]And they will forbid it and depart from it. And they do not destroy anyone except themselves, and they do not feel. [27]And if you see when they stood over the fire, so they said, "O we wish to return and we will not deny the verses of our lord and we will be of the believers." [28]Yet it appeared to them what they were hiding before. And if they return, they will go back to what they were forbidden, and surely they are liars. [29]And they said,

---

[a] creator, non-Arabic word of Ethiopian origin
[b] partners, non-Arabic word of S. Arabian origin
[c] legends, non-Arabic word of Greek/Syriac origin

"It is only our life of this world, and we will not be raised." [30]And if you see when they stand before their lord, he said, "Is not this the truth?" They said, "Yes, [we swear] by our lord." He said, "So taste the torment because you were infidels." [31]Indeed, those who denied the meeting[a] with Allah are lost until when the sā'a[b] comes suddenly on them. They said, "O our regret of what we neglected of it." And they will carry their burdens on their backs. Is not evil what they carry? [32]And the world's life is not except a sport and fun, and the home of the hereafter is better for those who fear. Do you not understand? [33]Indeed, we know what they say will surely grieve you. So surely they do not deny you, but the unjust disbelieve in the verses of Allah.

God's Word cannot be changed. This is in agreement with verses 10:64; 15:9; and 18:27. However, this contradicts verses 2:106; 13:39; and 16:101.

[34]And indeed, messengers before you were denied, so they were patient on being denied, and they were harmed until our victory came to them. And no one can change the words of Allah. And indeed, some of the news of the messengers came to you. [35]And if their turning away was big for you, so if you are able to seek out a tunnel in the earth or a sullam[c] in the heaven so that you bring them a sign. And if Allah willed, he would gather them to the guidance, so do not be of the ignorant. [36]Surely he answers only those who hear, and the dead, Allah will raise them, then to him they will return. [37]And they said, "Were it not that a sign had been sent down on him from his lord." Say, "Surely Allah is able to send down a sign, but most of them do not know."

Creatures and birds are nations like people. They will also be resurrected.

[38]And there is no creature on earth or bird that flies with its wings, but nations like you. We did not neglect anything in the book. Then to their lord they will be gathered. [39]And those who denied our verses are deaf and dumb in the darkness. Whomever Allah wills, he leads astray; and whom he wills, he makes him on a straight way. [40]Say, "If I show you, if the torment of Allah came to you, or the hour came to you, will you call any rather than Allah, if you were truthful?" [41]Yet to him you call, so he reveals what you call to, if he wills, and you forget what you partner. [42]And indeed, we sent to nations that were before you, so we overtook them with troubles and harms, perhaps they may implore. [43]So were it not that when our torment came to them they implored, but their hearts were hardened. And Satan beautified to them what they were doing. [44]So when they forgot what they were

---

[a] day of judgment
[b] hour, non-Arabic word of Aramaic/Syriac origin
[c] ladder, non-Arabic word of Akkadian/Aramaic origin

reminded with, we opened the doors for them of all things until, when they rejoiced in what they received, we seized them suddenly; so behold, they were in despair. [45]So the remnant of the unjust people were cut off. And the praise be to Allah, the lord of the worlds. [46]Say, "Have you seen, that [if] Allah took your hearing and your sight and sealed on your hearts, which god other than Allah would bring it to you?" Look how we expound on our verses, then they turn away. [47]Say, "Have I shown to you if Allah's torment comes to you suddenly or openly, will any be destroyed except the unjust people?" [48]And we do not send the messengers, except as bearers of good news and warners, so whoever believes and reforms, so there is no fear on them. And they will not grieve. [49]And those who denied our verses, the torment will touch them because they were transgressors. [50]Say, "I will not say to you that you have with me the khazan[a] of Allah nor do I know the unseen nor do I say to you, surely I am an angel. I will only follow what is revealed to me." Say, "Are the blind and the sighted equal? Do you not think?" [51]And warn by it those who fear that they will be gathered before their lord. They will not have other than him a friend nor intercessor, perhaps they may fear. [52]And do not drive out those who call their lord at morning and evening; they desire his face. You are not responsible of their account of anything, and they are not responsible of your account of anything, so that you drive them away, so you will become of the unjust. [53]And likewise, we seduced some of them with others so that they may say, "Are those favored by Allah from among us?" Does Allah not know best who is the thankful? [54]And if those who believe in our verses come to you, so say, "Peace be on you. Your lord has prescribed the mercy on himself," that whoever among you will commit evil through ignorance, then repent after that and reform. So surely he is forgiving, merciful. [55]And likewise, we have expounded on the verses that the way of the criminals might be made known. [56]Say, "Surely I am forbidden to serve those whom you call on rather than Allah." Say, "I will not follow your desires. Indeed, I then have gone astray, and I would not be of the guided." [57]Say, "Surely I have a proof from my lord, and you deny it. I do not have what you hastened with. That the judgment is only to Allah, he relates the truth, and he is the best arbitrator." [58]Say, "If I have what you hasten in, the affair between me and you would be settled. And Allah knows best the unjust." [59]And with him are the keys of the unseen, no one knows them except him. And he knows what is in the shore and the sea, and no leaf falls but he knows it; neither is there a grain in the darkness of the earth nor a green thing or dry, except in a clear book.

---

[a] treasuries, non-Arabic word of Persian/Hebrew origin

All people die when they go to sleep. Also, see verse 39:42.

[60]And he is the one that causes you to die at night and knows what you cut[a] in the day; then he raises you up into it, that the set term of life may be fulfilled. Then to him your return, then he will inform you of what you were doing. [61]And he is the dominator above his servants, and he sends forth keepers over you until when the death comes to one of you, our messengers cause him to die. And they do not fail. [62]Then they returned to Allah their lord, the true. Is not the judgment to him? And he is the swiftest of the accountants. [63]Say, "Who delivers you from the darkness of the shore and the sea? Pleadingly and secretly you call to him, 'If he delivers us from this, we will surely be of the thankful.'" [64]Say, "Allah delivers you from it and from every stress, then you are polytheists." [65]Say, "He is the able who sends on you a torment from above you or from under your legs, or to clothe you in shī'an[b] and to make some of you to taste the fierceness of others." See how we expound on the verses; perhaps they may understand.

Some thought the Qur'an was a falsehood.

[66]And your people denied it, and it is the truth. Say, "I am not a guardian over you." [67]To every news is a time, and you will know.

Satan has power over Mohammed and caused him to forget some verses.

[68]And when you see those who engage in our verses,[c] so withdraw from them until they engage in another speech. And about what Satan causes you to forget, so do not sit with the unjust people for recollection. [69]And those who fear are not accountable to them for anything but to be a reminder, perhaps they may fear. [70]And leave those who make their religion sport and fun, and whom the world's life has deceived. And remind by it that a soul will perish because of what it earned; it does not have a friend or intercessor other than Allah. And that, [if] it ransoms every ransom, it will not be taken from it. Those who perish because of what they earned, they will have a drink of hamem[d] and painful torment because they were infidels. [71]Say, "Will we call rather than Allah who can neither benefit us nor harm us, and will we turn on our heels after that Allah has guided us?" Like someone whom the satans have bewildered on the earth, wandering. He has companions who call him to the guidance: "Come to us." Say, "Surely Allah's guidance, he is the guidance, and we

---

[a] Muslim scholars claim it means earned or commit
[b] sects, non-Arabic word of Syriac origin
[c] in mockery
[d] close-warm, as in the statement close or warm friend. In this context other translators chose the words boiling water

were commanded to surrender to the lord of the worlds. [72]And that
you perform the prayer and fear him. And he is the one to whom you
will be gathered." [73]And he is who created the heavens and the
earth, with the truth and a day he says, "Be," so it will be. His word is
the truth and to him the kingdom. A day the trumpet is blown, the
knower of the unseen and the seen; and he is the wise, the aware.

**The story of Abraham is copied from the Bible and is corrupted.
Note that the correct name of Abraham's father is Terah not
Azar. See Genesis 11:26. Perhaps Mohammed confused
Abraham's father Terah with that of his faithful servant, Eliezer.
See Genesis 15:2. Mohammed describes Abraham as an idol
worshiper.**

[74]And when Abraham said to his father Azar,[a] "Do you take
asnam[b] for gods? Surely I see you and your people are in obvious
error." [75]And likewise, we did show Abraham the kingdom of the
heavens and the earth, and that he might be one of the certain. [76]So
when the night covered him, he saw a planet. He said, "This is my
lord." So when it set, he said, "I do not love the setting one." [77]So
when he saw the moon rising, he said, "This is my lord." So when it
set, he said, "If my lord does not guide me, I will surely be of the
erring people." [78]So when he saw the sun rising, he said, "This is my
lord, this is bigger." So when it set, he said, "O my people, surely I
am innocent of what you partner. [79]Surely I turned my face to him
who has created the heavens and the earth, hanifan, and I am not of
the polytheists." [80]And his people disputed with him. He said, "Do
you dispute with me about Allah, and indeed, he guided me? And I
do not fear what you partner with him, unless my lord wills anything.
My lord embraces all things in knowledge. Do you not remember?
[81]And how should I fear what you partner, and you do not fear what
you partner with Allah, what he did not send down on you with
authority? So which of the two groups are more worthy of security, if
you were knowing?" [82]Those who believed and do not mix their faith
with injustice, those have security, and they are guided. [83]And this is
our argument we gave to Abraham against his people. We raise up
in degrees whom we will. Surely your lord is wise, knowing.

**Mohammed confused names and their relationships to one
another.**

[84]And we granted to him[c] Isaac and Jacob, both we guided, and
Noah we guided before and among his descendants, David and

---

[a] a name, non-Arabic word of Hebrew/Greek origin
[b] idols, non-Arabic word of Aramaic origin
[c] Abraham

Solomon and Job and Joseph and Moses and Aaron. And likewise, we reward the doers of good. [85]And Zacharias and Yahya[a] and 'Isā and Iliyas,[b] all were from the good. [86]And Ishmael and Alyas'a[c] and Yunus and Lūt,[d] and we preferred all those above the worlds. [87]And among their fathers and their descendants and their brethren, and we chose them and guided them into a straight way. [88]This is Allah's guidance; he guides with it whom he wills of his servants, and if they become polytheists, then what they were doing will negate from them. [89]Those are they to whom we gave the book and wisdom and prophecy. So if they become infidels by it, so indeed, we entrusted it to people who will not become infidels by it. [90]Those are they whom Allah has guided, so by their guidance follow. Say, "I do not ask you a wage for it. It is only a reminder to the worlds." [91]And they did not value Allah his true value when they said, "Allah did not send down anything on humans." Say, "Who sends down the book which Moses came by, a light and guidance to the people? You make it parchments, you reveal it, and you hide much, and you taught that which neither you nor your fathers knew." Say, "Allah," then leave them engaging in their play.

The Qur'an confirms that the Bible is the Word of God in Mohammed's days.

[92]And this book which we have sent down is blessed, confirming what is between his hands, and that you may warn the mother of the villages and who are around it. And those who believe in the hereafter will believe in it, and they are keepers of their prayers. [93]And who is more unjust than one who forged a lie against Allah, or said, "It has been revealed to me," when nothing was revealed to him. And who said, "I will send down like that which Allah has sent down"? And if you see when the unjust are in the floods of death and the angels reach forth their hands, "Get your souls out." Today you will be rewarded with a humiliating torment because of what you were saying against Allah without the truth, and you were proud against his verses. [94]And indeed, you came to us, individually, as we created you the first time, and you left behind your back the things which we had given you. And we do not see with you, your intercessors, whom you claim as the partners among you. Indeed, what you were claiming between you is cut and gone astray. [95]Surely Allah falaq[e] the grain and the date pit; he brings forth the living from the dead and brings forth the dead from the living. This is Allah, how is it then you turned away? [96]The splitter of the dawn and maker of

---

[a] John the Baptist
[b] name mistakenly used, Elijah was meant
[c] Elisha, non-Arabic word of Syriac/earlier Semitic origin
[d] Lot, non-Arabic word of Syriac origin
[e] split, non-Arabic word of Syriac origin

night a dwelling and the sun and the moon [for] counting, this is the measure of the dear, the knowing. [97]And he is who has made the stars for you so that you may be guided by it in the darkness of the shore and the sea. Indeed, we expound on the verses for people who know. [98]And he is who has produced you from one soul, so a resting place and a repository. Indeed, we expound on the verses to people who understand. [99]And he is who sends down water from the heaven so that we bring forth by it plants of everything. So we bring forth from it the green foliage; we bring forth the close growing grain and from the palm trees with sheaths of clustering dates and gardens of grapes and the zaytoon[a] and the rummān,[b] like and unlike. Look on their fruit, when they bear fruit. Surely in this is a sign to believing people.

Christians who say God has a Son are ignorant. Notice that Mohammed introduces jinn into the Qur'an which according to the encyclopedia is Islamic mythology. According to some Muslim traditions, they are a class of supernatural creatures, between men and angels, who were created by Allah 2000 years before Adam. Some of them are Muslims.

[100]And they made to Allah partners the jinn and their creation. And they made up for him sons and daughters without knowledge. Praise be to him, and he is exalted above what they describe. [101]The inventor of the heavens and the earth, how can he have a son when he has no female companion? And he created everything, and he is the knower of all things. [102]That is Allah your lord. There is no god except him, the creator of all things. So serve him, and he is the guardian of all things. [103]No vision can reach him, and he reaches the visions. And he is the kind, the aware. [104]Indeed, a clear proof came to you from your lord, so whoever sees it, so it is to himself. And whoever is blind, so it is against it. And I am not a keeper over you.

Some claim that Mohammed obtained the verses of the Qur'an from earlier documents or from discussions with the People of the Book.

[105]And likewise, we expound on the verses, and they will say, "You studied."[c] And we show it to knowing people. [106]Follow what has been revealed to you from your lord. There is no god but him, and turn away from the polytheists. [107]And if Allah willed, they would not become polytheists. And we have not made you a keeper over them,

---

[a] olive, non-Arabic word of Syriac origin
[b] pomegranate, non-Arabic word of uncertain origin
[c] read or learned the verses of the Qur'an from the People of the Book

and you are not a guardian over them. [108]And do not curse those who call rather than Allah, so they wrongfully will curse Allah, without knowledge. Likewise, we adorn to every nation their work, then to their lord their return, so he will inform them of what they were doing. [109]And they swore by Allah with a strong oath, if a sign would come to them, they would believe in it. Say, "Surely signs are only with Allah." And how do you feel it is? If it comes, they will not believe. [110]And we will turn their hearts and their sight as it was when they did not believe in it the first time. And we will leave them in their rebellion blindly. [111]And if we had sent down the angels to them and the dead had spoken to them and we had gathered everything before them, they were not to believe, except if Allah wills, but most of them are ignorant.

Every prophet has enemies who are "satans" of both humans and jinn.

[112]And likewise, we make for every prophet enemies, satans of humans and jinn; they reveal one to another with zukhruf[a] speech to deceive. And if your lord willed, they would not have done it. So leave them in what they forge. [113]And let the hearts of those who do not believe in the hereafter listen to him and please him and earn what they are earning. [114]Will I seek a judge other than Allah, and he is who has sent down to you the expounding book? And those we have given the book know that it is sent down from your lord with the truth. So do not be of the doubters.

Another proof that the Bible is the true Word of God is that no one can change the Word of God.

[115]And the word of your lord has been completed in truth and fairness, and there is no one to change his words. And he is the hearing, the knowing. [116]And if you obey most of those who are on earth, they will mislead you from Allah's way. They follow only the conjecture, and they only lie. [117]Surely your lord, he knows best those who go astray from his way, and he knows best who are the guided.

Any food, including pork, can be eaten if the name of Allah is pronounced over it.

[118]So eat of that which the name of Allah has been pronounced over it, if you were believers in his verses. [119]And why do you not eat of that which the name of Allah has been pronounced over it? And indeed, he expounded to you what he has forbidden to you, except what you are compelled to it. And surely many mislead others by their desire, without knowledge. Surely your lord, he knows best the

---

[a] highly embellished, non-Arabic word of Syriac/Aramaic origin

transgressors. [120]And abandon the open iniquity and its secret. Surely those who earned iniquity, they will be rewarded because of what they were earning. [121]And do not eat from what the name of Allah has not been mentioned over, and surely it is a transgression. And surely the satans will reveal to their friends that they debate you, and if you obey them, surely you will be of the polytheists. [122]Or he who was dead, so we raised him and made for him light, by it he walks among the people like one who is in the darkness and not coming out of it. Likewise, it is beautified to the infidels what they were doing. [123]And likewise, we made in every village, the biggest of its criminals, so that they may deceive in it, and they will not deceive except themselves. And they do not feel. [124]And when a verse comes to them they say, "We will not believe until the like of what was given to the messengers of Allah is given to us." Allah knows best where to place his message. He will afflict those who commit crimes with humiliation from Allah and severe torment because they were deceiving.

Allah leads some people to Islam and restricts others from believing. Only Muslims will have the House of Peace. Others will only have the House of War.

[125]So whomever Allah desires to guide, he opens his chest to Islam; and whomever he desires to mislead, he will make his chest extremely narrow as though he is only ascending to the heaven. Likewise, Allah made the uncleanness on those who do not believe. [126]And this is your lord's straight way. Indeed, we expound on the verses to people who remember. [127]For them is a home of peace with their lord, and he will be their friend because of what they were doing. [128]And a day he will gather them together: "O assembly of jinn, indeed, you took a great number of the humans." And their friends from the humans said, "Our lord, we enjoyed one another, and we have reached our set term which you have set for us." He said, "Your dwelling is the fire, abide in it forever, except what Allah wills. Surely your lord is wise, knowing." [129]And likewise, we make friends among the unjust to one another because of what they were earning.

The Qur'an teaches that Allah has sent messengers to the jinn.

[130]"O assembly of the jinn and the humans, have not messengers come to you from among yourselves relating my verses to you and warning you of the meeting of this your day?" They said, "We bore witness against ourselves." And the world's life deceived them, and they bore witness against themselves that they were infidels. [131]This, because your lord would not destroy the villages unjustly and their people were unaware. [132]And to all are assigned degrees of what

they have done, and your lord is not unaware of what they do. [133]And your lord is the rich, the possessor of mercy. He can send you away if he wills and make whom he wills to be a successor after you, as he raised you up from the offspring of another people. [134]Surely what you are promised will come on you, and you cannot escape. [135]Say, "O my people, do your best, surely I am doing. So you will know for whom will be the final home. Surely the unjust will not prosper." [136]And they assigned to Allah a portion of the harvest and livestock which he has produced. So they said, "This is to Allah," by their claim, "And this is for our partners."[a] So what was for those partners[b] so it will not reach to Allah, and what was for Allah so it reaches to their partners. Evil is what they judge. [137]And likewise, it is beautified to many of the polytheists, the killing of their children [for] their partners, to make them turn away, and they mix for them their religion. And if Allah willed, they would not have done it, so leave them and what they are forging. [138]And they said, "These livestock and crops are forbidden; no one will eat them except whom we will," by their claim. And livestock whose backs were forbidden. And livestock they do not pronounce the name of Allah on it, forgery against him. He will reward them because of what they were forging. [139]And they said, "What is in the belly of these livestock is reserved for our males and forbidden to our wives. And if it was dead, so they partake of it." He will reward them for their assertion. Surely he is wise, knowing. [140]Indeed, those who kill their children foolishly, without knowledge, are lost; and they forbid what Allah has provided them, forging against Allah. Indeed, they have gone astray, and they were not guided.

Allah does not love the extravagant.

[141]And he is who produces gardens, trellised and untrellised, and the palm trees and the different edible plants and olives and pomegranates, like and unlike. Eat of their fruit when they bear fruit, and pay its true[c] on its reaping day. And do not be extravagant, surely he does not love the extravagant. [142]And some of the livestock for burdens and for traveling. Eat from what Allah provided you, and do not follow the steps of Satan. Surely, he is to you an obvious enemy. [143]Eight azawaj,[d] two from the sheep and two from the goats, say, "Are the two males forbidden or the two females or that which the wombs of the two females enclose? Inform me with knowledge, if you were truthful." [144]And from the camels two and from the cows two, say, "Are the two males forbidden or the two females or that which the wombs of the two females enclose, or were you witnesses

---

[a] idols, false gods
[b] their idols
[c] due
[d] pairs, non-Arabic word of Greek origin

when Allah commanded you this?" So who is more unjust than who forged a lie against Allah to mislead the people without knowledge? Surely, Allah does not guide the unjust people.

The dietary laws were copied from the Old Testament of the Bible. It is lawful to eat forbidden food only out of necessity.

[145]Say, "I do not find in what has been revealed to me anything forbidden for the eater to eat, except of that which was dead[a] or blood poured forth or swine meat, so surely this is unclean or profane, being slain in the name of other than Allah. So whoever is compelled without desiring nor returning. So surely your lord is forgiving, merciful." [146]And to those Jews we did forbid every [animal] having a hoof, and of the cows and the sheep we forbade them its fat, except what might be on their backs or their entrails and what is attached to the bone. This we rewarded them for their rebellion, and surely we are truthful. [147]So if they deny you, so say, "Your lord is a possessor of large mercy, but his severity will not be turned aside from the criminal people." [148]Those who are polytheistic will say, "If Allah willed, we did not become polytheists nor our fathers, nor were we forbidden anything." Likewise, those who came before them denied until they had tasted our severity. Say, "Do you have any knowledge that you bring it out to us? You only follow but the conjecture, and you only lie."

Allah chooses not to lead all men in the right way.

[149]Say, "So to Allah is the decisive argument, so if he willed, he would guide you all." [150]Say, "Come your witnesses, those who testify that Allah has forbidden this." So if they testify, so do not testify with them, and do not follow the desires those who denied our verses and those who do not believe in the hereafter, and they set up equals with their lord.

Verses 6:151; 17:33; and 25:68 justify "Honor Killings" of forbidden souls (Muslims) in the instance of murder, adultery, or apostasy.

[151]Say, "Come, I will recite what your lord has forbidden to you so that you will not partner anything with him, and be good to your parents, and do not kill your children because of poverty. We will provide for you and for them. Do not draw near the indecencies what appears from it or what is hidden. And do not kill the soul which Allah forbids except with a just cause. This is what he commanded you, perhaps you may understand." [152]And do not come near the money of the orphan, except with what is good, until he reaches his

---

[a] of itself

strength. And fulfill the kail[a] and the weight with exactness. We will not task a soul beyond its ability. And if you say, so be just, even though he was a kinsman, and fulfill the covenant of Allah. This he has commanded you, perhaps you will remember. [153]And surely this is my straight way. So follow it, and do not follow the ways so it will separate you from his way. This is what he commands you. Perhaps you may fear. [154]Then we gave Moses the book, completely for him who does good, and expounding on everything and a guidance and a mercy. Perhaps with the meeting of their lord they will believe. [155]And this book, we sent it down blessed, so follow it and fear, perhaps you may receive mercy. [156]That you say, "Surely, the book was only sent down to two assemblies[b] before us, and we were not aware of their studying." [157]Or you say, "If the book had been sent down on us, we surely would have been more guided than them." So indeed, a proof came to you from your lord and guidance and mercy. So who is more unjust than he who denies the verses of Allah and turns away from it? We will reward those who turn away from our verses with an evil torment because they were turning away. [158]Do they wait, except for the coming of the angels for them or the coming of your lord or the coming of some signs of your lord? A day some signs of your lord come, the faith of any soul will not profit it unless it has believed before or earned good through its faith. Say, "Wait, surely we are waiting." [159]Surely those who divided their religion, and they were sects, you are not from them at all. Surely their affair is only to Allah. Then he will inform them about what they were doing. [160]Whoever comes with the good, so to him there will be ten like it; and whoever comes with the evil, so he will not be rewarded except like it. And they will not be dealt with unjustly. [161]Say, "Surely my lord has guided me to a straight way, a valuable religion, the religion of Abraham, hanifan, and he was not of the polytheists." [162]Say, "Surely my prayer and my ritual and my life and my death are to Allah, the lord of the worlds. [163]He has no partner. And with that I am commanded, and I am the first of the Muslims." [164]Say, "Will I seek a lord other than Allah, and he is lord of everything? And every soul will not earn except what is against it, that no bearer of a burden bears the burden of another. Then to your lord is your return, so he will inform you about what you were differing." [165]And he is who has made you the viceroys of the earth and has raised some of you above others in degrees so that he may test you in what he gives you. Surely your lord hastens the punishment, and surely he is forgiving, merciful.

---

[a] measure—of food stuff, non-Arabic word of Syriac origin
[b] Jews and Christians

A portion of a revelation   **7**   *Al Araf*

In the name of Allah, the merciful, the merciful

[1]Alms.[a] [2]A book has been sent down to you, so do not let there be stress in your chest from it so that you may warn by it and a reminder to the believers. [3]Follow what has been sent down to you from your lord, and do not follow friends without him. Little is what you remember. [4]And how many a village we have destroyed, so our destruction came to them by night or while they were napping in their midday? [5]So their calling was not when our wrath came to them, except that they said, "Surely we were unjust." [6]So surely, we will ask those we sent them to, and we will surely ask the messengers. [7]So surely, we will relate to them with knowledge, and we were not absent.

Those who do enough good deeds will be happy on Judgment Day.

[8]The weighing on that day is the truth. So whose balances are heavy, so those are the prosperous. [9]And whose balances are light, so those are the ones who lost their souls because they were unjust to our verses. [10]And indeed, we established you on the earth, and we made the supports of life for you, little thanks do you give.

The story of Adam and his wife is copied from the Bible and corrupted again.

[11]And indeed, we created you, then we fashioned you, then we said to the angels, "Worship Adam." So they worshiped except the Devil, he was not of those who worshiped. [12]He said, "What has hindered you that you did not worship when I commanded you?" He said, "I am better than him. You have created me from fire, and you created him from mud." [13]He said, "So get down from it. So it was not for you to be proud in it, so get out. Surely you are of the lowly." [14]He said, "Delay me until a day they will be raised." [15]He said, "Surely you are of the delayed." [16]He said, "Because you have seduced me, I will surely sit down for them on your straight way. [17]Then I will surely come to them from between their hands and from behind them and from their right and from their left, and you will not find most of them thankful." [18]He said, "Get out of it despised, driven away. To all those who follow you from them, I will surely fill hell from all of you."

---

[a] a word containing four Arabic letters without meaning

¹⁹And: "O Adam, dwell you and your wife in the garden, so eat from wherever you will. And do not go near this tree, so you will be of the unjust." ²⁰So Satan whispered to them to show them what was hidden from them in their nakedness. And he said, "Your lord has not forbidden you from this tree except that you become angels or that you become immortal." ²¹And he swore to them: "Surely I am an adviser to you." ²²So he brought them down with pride. So when they tasted the tree, their private parts appeared to them, and they began to cut and glue together leaves of the garden on them.^a And their lord called to them: "Have I not forbidden you of this tree, and I said to you, 'Surely Satan is your obvious enemy'?" ²³They said, "Our lord, we have been unjust to ourselves, and if you do not forgive us and have mercy on us, we will surely be of the losers."

Mohammed stated that Allah created Adam and his wife in the garden in heaven, and they were cast down to earth after they ate from the tree.

²⁴He said, "Get down. The one of you is an enemy to the other, and you will have on earth dwelling and enjoyment for a while." ²⁵He said, "In it will you live, and in it will you die. And from it you will be brought out. ²⁶O children of Adam, indeed, we sent down on you clothing to hide your private parts and feathers and the righteous clothes, this is best." This is of the signs of Allah, perhaps they may remember.

Adam and his wife are wearing clothes prior to the sin. This contradicts the Bible in Genesis 2:25. Note that the following verse 28 contradicts verse 17:16.

²⁷"O children of Adam, do not let Satan seduce you as he got your parents out of the garden by taking their clothes off to show them their private parts. Surely he sees you, he and his host, from where you cannot see them. Surely we have made the satans friends to those who do not believe." ²⁸And if they commit an indecency, they said, "We found our fathers doing it, and Allah has commanded us to do it." Say, "Surely Allah does not command with indecencies. Do you say against Allah what you do not know?" ²⁹Say, "My lord commanded with justice. And lift up your faces at every mosque, and call him, devoted in the religion to him. As he originated you, you will return. ³⁰A group he guided, and a group he led to the error justly. Surely they took the satans for friends rather than Allah, and they think that they are guided. ³¹O children of Adam, take your adornment at every mosque. And eat and drink, and do not be extravagant. Surely he does not love the extravagant." ³²Say, "Who forbids Allah's adornment which he brought out to his servants and the goods of the provision?" Say, "It is for those who believed in the

---

^a their private parts

world's life exclusively on the resurrection day." Likewise, we expound on the verses to people who know. ³³Say, "Surely my lord only forbids the indecencies, whether seen or unseen, and the iniquity and rebellions without the truth and that to partner with Allah what he did not send with authority and that you say against Allah what you do not know."

The time is set for the doom of all secular nations.

³⁴And to every nation is a time. So if their time comes, they will not be delayed an hour, nor they will advance. ³⁵O children of Adam, when messengers come to you from among you and they narrate to you my verses, so whoever fears and reforms, so there will be no fear on them. And they will not grieve. ³⁶And those who denied our verses and were proud against them, those are the companions of the fire; in it they will abide forever. ³⁷So who is more unjust than he who forged a lie against Allah or denied his verses? Those will receive their portion from the book until the time when our messengers come to them causing them to die. They said, "Where is what you were calling rather than Allah?" They said, "They went astray from us." And they witnessed against themselves. Surely they were infidels. ³⁸He said, "Enter in nations who indeed have gone before you of the jinn and the humans into the fire. Every time a nation enters, it curses its sister until when they have all reached in it, their last said to their first, "Our lord, those led us astray, so give them double torment of the fire." He said, "To each double, but you do not know." ³⁹And the first of them said to the last of them, "So you have no favor over us. So taste the torment because of what you were earning."

All those who do not believe in Allah's verses will burn in hell, and the garden is the reward for good work. The story of a camel passing though the eye of a needle is copied and corrupted from Luke 18:25.

⁴⁰Surely those who denied our verses and were proud against them, the heaven's doors will not be opened to them nor will they enter the garden until the camel penetrates the eye of the needle. And likewise, we reward the criminals. ⁴¹They have from hell beds and above them will be coverings, and likewise, we reward the unjust. ⁴²And those who believed and did good deeds, we will not lay on a soul a burden except its capacity. Those are the companions of the garden. They will abide in it forever. ⁴³And we removed hatred from their chests, below them the rivers flow. And they said, "The praise be to Allah who has guided us to this. And we were not to be guided, were it not that Allah had guided us. Indeed, the messengers of our lord came to us with the truth. And they called to them, 'This is

the garden of which you are made heirs because of what you were doing.'" [44]And the companions of the garden called the companions of the fire: "Indeed, we have found what our lord promised us to be true. So have you found what your lord promised you to be true?" They said, "Yes." So, an announcer announced between them: "That the curse of Allah is on the unjust. [45]Those who prevent [others] from the way of Allah and seek to make it crooked, and in the hereafter they are infidels." [46]And between them a veil and on the al-araf[a] are men who knew all by their marks, and they called to the companions of the garden: "That peace be on you." They did not enter it, and they were hoping. [47]And when their eyes were turned toward the companions of the fire, they said, "Our lord, do not place us with the unjust people." [48]And the companions of the al-araf called to the men they knew them by their marks. They said, "What you gathered and what you were proud of did not benefit you. [49]Are those the ones about whom you swore that Allah would not give mercy? Enter the garden. No fear will be on you, and you will not grieve."

Mohammed's story about the companions of the fire calling to the companions of the garden to pour some water on them appears to be a modification of the biblical parable of the rich man and Lazarus. See Luke 16:19-31.

[50]And the companions of the fire called the companions of the garden: "That pour on us some water or from what Allah provided you." They said, "Surely Allah has forbidden them on the infidels, [51]those who took their religion as fun and sport and whom the world's life has deceived. So today we forget them as they forgot the meeting of this their day, and they were disbelieving in our verses." [52]And indeed, we have brought them a book which we expounded on with knowledge, guidance, and mercy to believing people. [53]Do they wait except its interpretation? A day its interpretation comes, those who forgot it before will say, "Indeed, the messengers of our lord came with the truth. So will we have intercessors so they intercede for us, or will we be sent back so we will do other than what we were doing?" Indeed, they have lost their souls, and what they were forging has gone astray from them.

Allah created the heavens and the earth in six days. This is repeated in verses 10:3; 11:7; 25:59; 32:4; 50:38; and 57:4. However, this contradicts verses 41:9-12 which teach that the creation of heavens and earth took eight days.

[54]Surely your lord is Allah who created the heavens and the earth in six days; then he sat on the throne. He covers the night [with] the day, he pursues it swiftly, and the sun and the moon and the stars

[a] the wall between the garden and hell, non-Arabic word of undetermined origin

are subservient by his command. Is it not to him the creation and the commands? Tabārka[a] Allah, the lord of the worlds. [55]Call on your lord pleadingly and secretly; surely he does not love the transgressors. [56]And do not vandalize on the earth after its reformation, and call on him, fearing and hoping. Surely Allah's mercy is near to the doers of good. [57]And he is who sent the wind with good news between the hands of his mercy until when it carries the laden clouds which we drive to a dead country, so we send down with it the water. So we bring forth by it from every fruit; likewise, we will bring forth the dead. Perhaps you may remember. [58]And the good country brings forth its plants by the permission of his lord, and who is wicked does not bring forth except a little. Likewise, we expound on the verses to a thankful people.

Noah's story is copied and corrupted from the Bible. See Genesis 6-8. This story is repeated in Qur'an verses 10:71-73; 11:25-49; 21:76-77; 23:23-30; 26:105-122; 29:14-15; 37:75-82; 54:9-17; 71:1-28...

[59]Indeed, we sent Noah to his people, so he said, "O my people, serve Allah. You have no god other than him. Surely I fear for you the torment of a great day." [60]The leaders of his people said, "Surely we see that you are in obvious error." [61]He said, "O my people, there is no error in me, but I am a messenger from the lord of the worlds. [62]I deliver to you the messages of my lord, and I give you advice. And I know from Allah what you do not know. [63]Or do you wonder that a reminder came to you from your lord upon a man from among you to warn you and that you may fear and perhaps you may receive mercy?" [64]So they denied him. So we delivered him and those who were with him in the ship, and we drowned those who denied our verses. Surely they were a blind people.

The story of Ad and Houd is made-up by Mohammed. The story is repeated in verses 11:50-60; 23:31-41; 26:123-140; 41:15-16; 46:21-25; 51:41-42; 53:50-55; 54:18-22; 69:6-8; and 89:6-14. Who was the prophet? What was the actual message? To whom was it conveyed? Archaeological, historical, contextual, and biblical supports are lacking.

[65]And to Ad, their brother Houd said, "O my people, serve Allah. You have no god other than him. Do you not fear?" [66]The leaders of his people who became infidels said, "Surely we see that you are unsound of mind, and we surely think you are of the liars." [67]He said, "O my people, there is not unsoundness of mind in me, but I am a messenger from the lord of the worlds. [68]I deliver to you the

---

[a] blessed, non-Arabic word of North Semitic origin

messages of my lord, and I am to you a faithful adviser. [69]Or do you wonder that a reminder came to you from your lord upon a man among you to warn you? And remember when he made you viceroys after the people of Noah and increased you in tallness of stature? So remember the favors of Allah, perhaps you may prosper." [70]They said, "Have you come to us that we may serve Allah alone and leave what was our fathers serving? So bring to us what you promise us, if you were of the truthful." [71]He said, "Indeed, vengeance and wrath fell on you from your lord. Do you dispute with me in names that you and your fathers named them which Allah did not send it down with authority? So wait, surely I am with you among those who wait." [72]So we delivered him and those who were with him with mercy from us, and we cut off, to the last, those who denied our verses. And they were not believers.

The story of Themoud and Saleh was made-up by Mohammed. The story is repeated in Qur'an verses 11:61-68; 15:80-84; 17:59; 26:141-159; 27:45-53; 41:17-18; 54:23-32; and 91:11-15. Who was the prophet? What was the actual message? To whom was it conveyed? Archaeological, historical, contextual, and biblical supports are lacking.

[73]And to Themoud, their brother Saleh said, "O my people, serve Allah. You have no god other than him. Indeed, a proof came to you from your lord; this is a camel of Allah, a sign to you. So let her go at large to eat on Allah's earth, and do not touch her with evil so a painful torment will overtake you. [74]And remember when he made you viceroys after Ad and gave you dwellings on the earth, on its plains you take qasuran[a] and hew out of the mountains houses. So remember the favors of Allah, and do not act wickedly in the land, vandalizing." [75]The leaders of his people, who were proud, said, "To those who were weakened, to those of them who believed, do you know that Saleh was sent from his lord?" They said, "Surely we believe by which he has been sent." [76]Those who were proud said, "Surely we are infidels by that in which you believed." [77]So they hamstrung the camel and rebelled against their lord's command and said, "O Saleh, bring on us that which you promise us, if you were of the messengers." [78]So the quake seized them, so they became motionless in their homes. [79]So he turned away from them and said, "O my people, indeed, I delivered to you the message of my lord. And I gave you advice, but you do not love the advisers."

The story of Lot was copied and corrupted from the Bible. See Genesis 18:16-19:38. Variations of this story are also found in Qur'an verses 11:77-83; 15:51-77; 26:160-175; 27:54-58; 29:28-35; 37:133-137; 51:31-37; and 54:33-40.

---

[a] castles, non-Arabic word of Latin origin

[80]And Lot, when he said to his people, "Do you enter into[a] the indecency which no one has committed before you of the worlds? [81]Surely you enter into[b] the men lustfully rather than the women, but you are an extravagant people." [82]And the answer of his people was not, except they said, "Get them out of your village for surely they are purified humans." [83]So we delivered him and his family, except his wife, she was of those who stayed behind. [84]And we rained rain on them, so see how was the end of the criminals.

The story of Midian and Shoaib was made-up by Mohammed. This story is repeated in verses 11:84-95; 15:78-79; and 26:176-191.

[85]And to Midian, their brother Shoaib said, "O my people, serve Allah. You have no god other than him. Indeed, a proof came to you from your lord, so fulfill the measure and the weight. And do not defraud the people their things, and do not vandalize on the earth after its reform. This will be better for you, if you were believers. [86]And do not sit down in every way, threatening and preventing [others] from Allah's way, those who believed in him, nor seek to make it crooked. And remember when you were few, so he multiplied you. And see how was the end of the vandals. [87]And if it was an assembly of you who believed in what I am sent with and an assembly who did not believe, so be patient until Allah judges between us. And he is the best of judges." [88]The leaders of his people who were proud said, "Surely we will get you out, O Shoaib, and those who believed with you, from our village, or you will come back to our religion." He said, "Even though we were hating it? [89]Indeed, we have forged a lie against Allah if we return to your religion after Allah has delivered us from it, and it will not be for us to return to it, except if Allah our lord wills. Our lord's knowledge encompasses everything. On Allah we depend. 'Our lord, open (judge) between us and between our people with the truth. And you are the best opener (judge).'" [90]And the leaders of his people who became infidels said, "If you follow Shoaib, surely you will be losers." [91]So the quake seized them, so they became motionless in their homes. [92]Those who denied Shoaib were as though they never lived in riches in it. They who denied Shoaib, they were the losers. [93]So he turned away from them and said, "O my people, indeed, I delivered to you the messages of my lord, and I advised you. So how should I be grieved for an infidel people?"

---

[a] commit
[b] homosexual lifestyle

It is Allah's will that affliction comes on a village to humble it.

[94]And we did not send a prophet to any village except we seized its people with adversity and harm, perhaps they will implore. [95]Then we changed the good in place of the evil until they were relieved and said, "Indeed, troubles and good did touch our fathers." So we seized them suddenly while they did not feel. [96]If it had been that the people of the villages had believed and feared, we would have opened to them the blessings from the heaven and the earth. But they denied, so we seized them because of what they were earning. [97]Did the people of the villages feel secure that our wrath would come on them by night while they were sleeping? [98]Or were the people of the villages secure that our wrath would come on them in broad day while they were playing?

The losers will escape Allah's deception.

[99]Are they secure from the deception of Allah? So no one can be secure from the deception of Allah except the losing people. [100]Is it not a guide to those who inherit the earth after its family, that if we will, we can afflict them with their sins and seal upon their hearts so that they will not hear? [101]Those the villages, we narrate to you some of their news. And indeed, their messengers came to them with the proofs, so they were not to believe in what they denied before. Likewise, Allah seals the hearts of the infidels. [102]And we did not find in most of them any covenant, and surely we found most of them wicked.

The story of Moses was copied from the Bible and corrupted again. Note that the crucifixion was not implemented for several hundred years after the event as described in verse 124. Also notice that the sorcerers believed in the God of Moses. This is repeated in verse 20:70. This contradicts verse 10:83.

[103]Then we sent after them Moses with our signs to Pharaoh and his leaders, so they treated it unjustly. So see how was the end of the vandals. [104]And Moses said, "O Pharaoh, surely I am a messenger from the lord of the worlds. [105]It is worthy of me that I will not say about Allah except the truth. Indeed, I came to you with proof from your lord, so send with me the children of Israel." [106]He said, "If you have come with a sign, so bring it if you were of the truthful." [107]So he threw down his rod. So behold, it became an obvious serpent. [108]And he drew his hand. So behold, it was white to the onlookers. [109]The leaders from the people of Pharaoh said, "Surely this is a knowing sorcerer. [110]He desires to get you out of your land, so what will you command?" [111]They said, "Delay him and his brother, and send gatherers into the cities. [112]They will bring every knowing sorcerer to you." [113]And the sorcerers came [to] Pharaoh. They said, "Surely we will have a wage if we were the victors." [114]He

said, "Yes, and surely you will be of the nearer." [115]They said, "O Moses, either you cast, or we will be those who cast." [116]He said, "You cast." So when they cast, they bewitched the people's eyes and made them afraid, and they brought a great sorcery. [117]And we revealed to Moses, "That cast your rod." So behold, it pecks what they fabricate. [118]So the truth was vindicated, and vain was what they were doing. [119]So they were defeated thereupon, and they were turned away humiliated. [120]And the sorcerers fell down worshiping. [121]They said, "We believed in the lord of the worlds, [122]the lord of Moses and Aaron." [123]Pharaoh said, "Have you believed in him before I give you permission? Surely, this is a deception you have deceived in the city so that you may get its people out of it, so you will know. [124]I will surely cut off your hands and legs on opposite sides. Then I will crucify you, all of you." [125]They said, "Surely to our lord we will return. [126]And you do not take revenge on us, except because we believed on the signs of our lord when they came to us: 'Our lord, pour out patience on us and cause us to die Muslims.'"

Mohammed describes the killing of the male children of Israel. The timing of this event, as recorded in the following verses, is in agreement with verse 40:25 but is contradicted in 28:4-7.

[127]And the leaders from the people of Pharaoh said, "Will you let Moses and his people to vandalize in the land and desert you and your gods?" He said, "We will kill their sons and spare their women, and surely we are dominant over them." [128]Moses said to his people, "Seek assistance with Allah and be patient, surely the earth is Allah's; he will bequeath it to whom he wills of his servants and the end to the fearer." [129]They said, "We have been oppressed before you came to us and after you came to us." He said, "Perhaps your lord will destroy your enemy and will make you his viceroys in the land. So he will see how you do." [130]And indeed, we seized the family of Pharaoh with the years and less of the fruit, perhaps they may remember. [131]So when good fortune came to them, they said, "This is for us." And if evil befell them, they take Moses and who is with him as a bad omen. But surely their bird[a] is only with Allah, but most of them do not know. [132]And they said, "Whatever signs you bring us to bewitch us, we will not believe in you."

Mohammed is confused between the flood of Noah and the story of Moses and Pharaoh. See Genesis 7. The ten plagues did not include a flood. See Exodus 7:20-12:30.

---

[a] evil omen

[133]So we sent on them the tūfān[a] and the locusts and the lice and the frogs and the blood, expounded signs, so they became proud. And they were a criminal people. [134]And when the wrath fell on them, they said, "O Moses, call for us to your lord, according to that which he has covenanted with you. Surely, if you will take the scourge off of us, then we will surely believe you, and we will surely send the children of Israel with you." [135]So when we lifted the wrath from them for a period which they reached, behold, they broke [their oath]. [136]So we took vengeance on them, so we drowned them in the sea because they denied our signs, and they were unaware of them.

The Jews inherit the land of Egypt, not the Promised Land. Also see verse 26:59. Notice that Pharaoh and his army did not follow the Israelites into the sea in this version of the story.

[137]And we bequeathed to the people who were weakened the eastern and the western lands, which we had blessed; and the good word of your lord was fulfilled on the children of Israel because of their patience, and we destroyed what Pharaoh and his people were making and what they were building. [138]And we caused the children of Israel to cross the sea, so they came on a people who were devoted to their idols. They said, "O Moses, make us a god as they have gods." He said, "Surely you are an ignorant people. [139]Surely those, what they are in would be destroyed, and vain was what they were doing." [140]He said, "Will I seek any other god for you than Allah, and he preferred you above the worlds?" [141]And when we delivered you from the family of Pharaoh, laying on you an evil torment, killing your sons and sparing your women, and in this was a great trial from your lord. [142]And we appointed for Moses thirty nights, and we completed with ten so that his whole time with his lord amounted to forty nights. And Moses said to his brother Aaron, "Be my viceroy among my people, and reform. And do not follow the way of the vandals."

Who was the "first of the believers"? Was it Moses, Mohammed, or could it have been Abraham?

[143]And when Moses came at our set time and his lord spoke with him, he said, "My lord, show me, look to you." He said, "You will not see me, but look to the mountain. So if it dwells in its place, so you will see me." So when his lord tajallā[b] to the mountain, he made it dust, and Moses fell in a swoon. So when he was revived, he said, "Praise be to you. I repented to you, and I am the first of the believers." [144]He said, "O Moses, I have chosen you above all people

---

[a] deluge, non-Arabic word of Hebrew/Syriac origin
[b] appeared in glory, non-Arabic word of Syriac origin

with my messages and with my words, so take what I have given to you and be of the thankful."

The word "alwah" according to Arabic grammar, means three or more tablets. However, in the true story found in Exodus 31:18, the Ten Commandments were written on two tablets. Notice that the tablets in the Qur'an version included not only the Ten Commandments but also contained many other things. Note that the word "alwah" also means wooden boards or planks, not stone, as described in the Bible.

[145]And we wrote for him in the alwah[a] from everything, a sermon and an exposition of everything: "So take it with strength and command your people to take the best part of it. I will show you the home of the transgressors. [146]I will turn away from my signs those who are proud on the earth without the truth, and if they see every sign, they will not believe in it. And if they see the way of guidance, they will not take it a way. And if they see the way of error, they will take it a way. This is because they denied our signs, and they were unaware of them. [147]And those who denied our signs and the meeting of the hereafter, their work will be in vain. Will they be rewarded, except for what they were doing?"

This story about the magic cow with the mooing sound contradicts the account in the Bible. See Exodus 32. See also verses 20:87-88 in the Qur'an.

[148]And Moses' people took, after him, from their ornaments a calf, a body which gave a mooing sound. Did they not see that it could not speak to them, nor guide them a way? They took it, and they were unjust. [149]And when it fell in their hands and they saw that they had gone astray, they said, "If our lord will not have mercy on us and forgive us, we will surely be of the losers."

Moses' anger over Aaron and the absence of the Samaritan proves that Aaron was behind the making of the golden calf. Notice that the boards (tablets) were never broken. This is a contradiction to the biblical account. See Exodus 32:19.

[150]And when Moses returned to his people, wrathful, sorrowful, he said, "Evil is what you have done following my departure. Would you hasten the command of your lord?" And he threw down the boards and seized his brother by the head and dragged him to himself. He said, "Son of my mother, surely the people weakened me and had almost killed me. Therefore, do not make the enemy rejoice at me, and do not place me with the unjust people." [151]He said, "My lord,

---

[a] boards, non-Arabic word of Aramaic origin

forgive me and my brother and admit us into your mercy. And you are the most merciful of the merciful." [152]Surely those who took the calf will receive wrath from their lord and humiliation in the world's life, and likewise, we reward the forgers. [153]And those who did the evils, then repented after it and believed; surely your lord, after that, is forgiving, merciful. [154]And when the wrath of Moses was calmed, he took up the boards, and in their writing was guidance and mercy for those who are terrified of their lord. [155]And Moses chose his people, seventy men, for an appointed time. So when the quake seized them, he said, "My lord, if you will, you had destroyed them before and me. Will you destroy us because of what the fools did among us? It is only your sedition. You will mislead by it whom you will and guide whom you will. You are our friend, so forgive us and have mercy on us, and you are the best of the forgivers. [156]And prescribe for us in this world good, and in the hereafter, surely our guidance is toward you." He said, "I will afflict my torment on whom I will. And my mercy embraces all things, so I will prescribe it to those who fear and bring the legal alms and those who believe in our signs.

References to Mohammed in the Torah and Gospel are alleged.

[157]Those who follow the messenger, the Gentile prophet whom they will find described for them in the Torah and the Gospel. He will command them with fairness and forbid them from the evil and make good things lawful for them and prohibit the impure for them and will ease them of their burdens and of the yokes which were on them so that those who believed in him and strengthened him and helped him and followed the light which has been sent down with him, those are the prosperous." [158]Say, "O you people, surely I am the messenger of Allah to all of you, to whom is the kingdom of the heavens and the earth. There is no god but him. He gives life and causes death, so believe in Allah and his messenger, the Gentile prophet who believes in Allah and his words. And follow him, perhaps you may be guided." [159]And among Moses' people was a nation which guides with the truth, and by it acts fairly. [160]And we divided them into twelve tribes nations, and we revealed to Moses when the people asked drink of him: "That strike the rock with your rod." So gushed forth from it twelve springs; indeed, all humans knew their drinking places. And we caused clouds to shadow them, and we sent down on them the manna and the quail. "Eat of the good things which we provided to you." And they did not treat us unjustly, but they were treating themselves unjustly. [161]And when it was said to them, "Dwell in this village and eat what you will from there and say forgiveness and enter the door worshiping, we will forgive your sins; we will increase the doers of good." [162]So the unjust among them replaced that word

with another, not the same which had been said to them, so we sent a wrath over them from the heaven because they were unjust.

Some of the Jews were cursed and became monkeys until the resurrection day. It is written here that Allah tempts with evil. This contradicts the Bible which clearly teaches that God does not tempt anyone. See James 1:13-14.

[163]And ask them about the village which was present by the sea, when they transgressed on the Sabbath (Saturday), when their whales came to them appearing openly on their Sabbath day; and the day they did not have Sabbath, they (their whales) did not come to them. Likewise, we tempted them because they were transgressors. [164]And when one nation of them said, "Why preach to people whom Allah will destroy or torment them with severe torment?" They said, "[As] an excuse for your lord, and perhaps they may fear." [165]So when they forgot what they had been reminded of, we delivered those who had been forbidden from the evil, and we seized those who did injustice with an evil torment because they were transgressors. [166]So when they revolted against what they were forbidden to do, we said to them, "Become despised monkeys." [167]And when your lord decided to send against them who will subject them to the evil torment until the resurrection day, surely your lord is hasty in the punishment, and surely he is forgiving, merciful. [168]And we have divided them on the earth into nations, some of them are the good and some are otherwise, and we tempted them with the good and the evils, perhaps they may return. [169]So descendants after them descended, and they inherited the book. They will take the width of this below,[a] and they say, "We will be forgiven." And if the width like it comes to them, they will take it. Did they not take against them the covenant of the book? That they will not say about Allah except the truth, and they study what is in it. And the home of the hereafter is best to the fearer. Do you not understand? [170]And whoever holds the book and performs the prayer, surely we will not waste the wage of the reformers.

This is the story of the magic flying mountain.

[171]And when we raised the mountain over them as if it had been a shadow, and they thought it was falling on them: "Take what we give to you with strength. And remember what is in it, perhaps you may fear."

Male sperm comes from the backbone. This is one of many scientific errors in the Qur'an.

---

[a] pleasures of the world

[172] And when your lord took from the children of Adam their descendants from their backs and made them to testify against themselves: "Am I not your lord?" They said, "Yes, we testified." That you should say on the resurrection day, "Surely we were unaware of that." [173] Or you say, "Surely our fathers before partnered [other gods with Allah], and we were their offspring after them. Will you destroy us because of what the liars did?" [174] And likewise, we expound on the verses, and perhaps they may return. [175] And recite to them the news of him to whom we gave our verses, so he departed from it, so that Satan followed him, so he was of the seduced. [176] And if we will, we would lift him up with it, but he clung to the earth and followed his desire, so his parable is like the parable of the dog which pants if you chase him or pants if you leave him alone. Such is the parable of those people who denied our verses. So narrate the stories, perhaps they may reflect. [177] Evil is the likeness of those people who denied our verses, and they were treating themselves unjustly. [178] Whomever Allah guides, so he is the guided; and whomever he leads astray, so those are the losers.

Allah created some people and some jinn to burn in hell.

[179] And indeed, we have created for hell many of the jinn and the humans. They have hearts; they do not understand by it. And they have eyes; they do not see by it. And they have ears; they do not hear by it. Those are like the livestock, but they are even more astray; those are the unaware. [180] And to Allah is the best names, so call on him by them and leave those who pervert in his names. They will be rewarded of what they were doing. [181] And among those whom we created is a nation which guides with the truth and by it acts justly. [182] And those who denied our verses, we will gradually bring them from where they do not know. [183] And I delay them. Surely my scheme is strong.

Some thought Mohammed was possessed by jinn.

[184] Or do they not think that what is in their companion[a] is from the jinn? But he is only a plain warner. [185] Or have they not looked into the kingdom of the heavens and the earth and what Allah created from a thing, and that perhaps their end may be drawing near? So by what speech after this will they believe? [186] Whomever Allah leads astray, so there is no guide for him. And he will leave them in their rebellion blindly. [187] They ask you about the hour, when its arrival will be. Say, "Surely the knowledge of it is only with my lord, and none will make it clear in its time but him. It is heavy in the heavens and the earth; it will not come to you except suddenly." They ask you as if you know about it. Say, "Surely its knowledge is only with Allah, but

---

[a] Mohammed

most people do not know." [188]Say, "I do not have control to benefit or harm myself except what Allah wills. If I were knowing of the unseen, I should increase in the good, and the evil would not touch me. That I am only a warner and an announcer of good news to a believing people." [189]He is who created you from one soul and made from it its wife that he might dwell in[a] her. So when he covered[b] her, she bore a light burden and went about with it, so when it became heavy, they called on Allah their lord: "If you give us Salih,[c] we will surely be of the thankful. [190]So when he gave them Salih, they set up with him partners of what he had given them. So Allah is exalted above what they partnered. [191]Do they partner who cannot create anything, and they are created? [192]And they cannot help them, nor can they help themselves. [193]And if you call on them for guidance, they will not follow you. It is the same to them whether you call them or whether you are silent. [194]Surely those you call on rather than Allah are servants like you, so call on them, so they will answer you if you were truthful. [195]Do they have legs to walk with them or do they have hands to smite with them or do they have eyes to see with them or do they have ears to hear with them? Say, "Call on your partners, then make your scheme against me, so do not delay me." [196]Surely my friend is Allah who has sent down the book, and he is the friend of the good. [197]And they whom you call on rather than him, they cannot help you, nor can they help themselves. [198]And if you call them to the guidance, they will not hear; and you see them looking at you, and they do not see. [199]Take forgiveness, and command with good. And turn away from the fool. [200]And if you are tempted by Satan with temptation, so seek refuge in Allah. Surely he is hearing, knowing. [201]Surely those who feared, when evil thought from Satan touches them, they remember. So behold, they see. [202]And their brethren will increase them in error, then they will not stop short. [203]And if you did not bring a sign to them, they say, "Were it not that you had invented it?" Say, "Surely, I only follow what is revealed to me from my lord. This is proof from your lord, and guidance and mercy to a believing people." [204]And when the Qur'an is read, then listen to it and hear, perhaps you may receive mercy. [205]And remember your lord within yourself, imploring and fearing and in a voice not loud, in the morning and the evening, and do not be of the unaware. [206]Surely those who are with your lord are not too proud to serve him. And they praise him, and to him they worship.

---

[a] have sex with
[b] had sex with
[c] a son's name

A portion of a revelation   **8**   *The Spoils*

In the name of Allah, the merciful, the merciful

[1]They ask you about the spoils, say, "The spoils to Allah and the messenger. So fear Allah and do good among yourselves and obey Allah and his messenger, if you were believers. [2]Surely the believers are only those who, when Allah is mentioned, their hearts fill with fear. And when his verses were recited to them, it increased their faith, and they depend on their lord. [3]Those who perform the prayers and spend from what we provided them, [4]those are the true believers. They have degrees with their lord and forgiveness and a generous provision. [5]As your lord gets you out of your house with the truth, and surely a group of the believers hated it. [6]Disputing with you about the truth after it had been made clear, as if they were driven to death while they were looking on. [7]And when Allah promised you that one of the two assemblies should fall to you and you desired that those who had no thorns (weak) should be yours, and Allah desired to prove the truth with his words and to cut off the last of the infidels. [8]That he establishes the truth and voids the vanity even though the criminals hate it. [9]When you call to your lord, so he answered you, "I will aid you with a thousand angels, rank on rank. [10]And Allah did not make this except as good news and to assure your hearts by it, and the victory did not come except from Allah. Surely Allah is dear, wise. [11]When sleep covers you, it is assurance from him, and he sent down water from the heaven on you to purify you by it and cause the wrath of Satan to pass from you, and that he might tie on your heart and strengthen by it your feet.

Chopping off the heads and fingers of infidels who are opposed to Allah and Mohammed is taught here.

[12]When your lord revealed to the angels: "I am with you, so make firm those who believed. I will cast the terror into the hearts of those who became infidels. So strike above their necks (decapitation), and strike off (chop off) every finger from them." [13]This is because they have opposed Allah and his messenger, and whoever opposes Allah and his messenger, so surely Allah is severe in the punishment. [14]That is, so taste it, and that to the infidels the torment of the fire.

Muslim who turn away from engaging in war with infidels will burn in hell.

[15]O you who have believed, when you meet those who became infidels marching, do not turn your backs to them. [16]And whoever will

turn his back to them on that day, unless he turns away strategically to engage in war or to rally some other group, so indeed, will return with wrath from Allah. And hell will be his abode and wretched is the final place. [17]So it was not you who killed them, but Allah killed them; and you did not throw (weapons of war) when you threw, but Allah threw. And he would give the believer from it a good test. Surely Allah is hearing, knowing. [18]That is and that Allah hinders the scheme of the infidels. [19]If you conquer, so indeed, the conquest has come to you. And if you end it, it is better for you; and if you will return, we will return. And your groups, even though they be many, will not profit you anything. And Allah is with the believers. [20]O you who have believed, obey Allah and his messenger, and do not turn away from him while you hear. [21]And do not be like those who say, "We heard," and they did not hear.

Allah condemns all who cannot hear or talk as the worst creatures because he knows there is no good in them.

[22]Surely, the worst creatures before Allah are the deaf, the dumb, those who do not understand. [23]And if Allah knew of any good in them, he would have made them hear. And if he had made them hear, they would still have turned away and withdrawn. [24]O you who have believed, answer to Allah and to the messenger if he calls you to that which gives you life. And know that Allah comes in between a man and his own heart, and that to him you will be gathered. [25]And fear sedition, though it will not harm those who have specifically been treated unjustly among you, and know that Allah is severe in the punishment. [26]And remember when you were few and weakened on the earth, you feared that people might snatch you, so he sheltered you and supported you with his victory and provided you from the good things, perhaps you may give thanks. [27]O you who have believed, do not betray Allah and the messenger, and betray those who trust you, and you know. [28]And know that your money and your children are only a sedition and that Allah has a great wage. [29]O you who have believed, if you fear Allah, he will make discrimination for you and will atone from you your evils and will forgive you. And Allah is the possessor of the great bounty.

Allah is the best deceiver. It is claimed that the Qur'an is the legends of the ancients.

[30]And when those who became infidels deceive you to detain you or to kill you or to expel you. And they deceive, and Allah deceives. And Allah is the best deceiver. [31]And when our verses are recited to them, they said, "Indeed, we have heard. If we wanted to, we could say like it, this is nothing but the legends of the ancients." [32]And when they said, "O Allah, if this was the truth from you, rain down

stones on us from the heaven, or give us painful torment." [33]And it was not of Allah to torment them while you were with them, and it was not of Allah to torment them while they were asking forgiveness. [34]And what do they have that Allah does not torment them and they prevent [others] from the forbidden mosque and they were not his friends? That his friends but the fearers, but most of them do not know. [35]And their prayer was not at the house, except whistling and clapping, so taste the torment for what you were infidels of. [36]Surely those who became infidels spend their money to prevent [others] from the way of Allah, so they will spend it; then it will become a regret against them. Then they will be defeated. And those who became infidels will be gathered into hell. [37]That Allah may distinguish the bad from the good and puts the bad, some on the other, so he heaps them all together, so he puts him into hell; those are the losers. [38]Say to those who became infidels, if they cease, what is passed will be forgiven them; and if they return, so indeed, the custom of the ancients has passed.

Muslims are commanded to engage in war against the infidels until Islam remains as the only religion.

[39]And engage in war with them until there will not be sedition and the religion[a] will be completely to Allah. So, if they cease, so surely Allah sees what they do. [40]And if they turn away, so know that Allah is your protector. Excellent is the protector, and excellent is the helper.

It is lawful to rob, and Mohammed receives one fifth of the spoil. Also, see verse 8:69.

[41]And know that whatever you take of spoil of anything, so a fifth part to Allah and to the messenger and to the nearest relative and to orphans and to the poor and to the son of the way, if you were believers in Allah, and what we sent down on our servant on the discrimination day, the day of the meeting of the two groups. And Allah has might over all things. [42]While you were on the near side and they were on the far side and the caravan was below you, and if you had made an appointment, you would have failed in the appointment, but that Allah may fulfill an affair that was decreed. That he who should perish might perish with a clear proof, and that he who lives might live with a clear proof. And surely Allah is hearing, knowing. [43]When Allah shows them to you in your sleep as few, and if he had shown them numerous to you, you would fail. And you would have disputed in the affair, but Allah is safe. Surely he knows what is in the chests. [44]And when he showed them to you, when you met as few in your eyes, and diminished you in their eyes that Allah

---

[a] Islam

might carry out the affair that was to be done. And to Allah the affairs will return. [45]O you who have believed, when you meet[a] a group, so hold firm and remember Allah much, perhaps you will prosper. [46]And obey Allah and his messenger, and do not dispute so you become a failure and your smell[b] may go from you. And be patient,[c] surely Allah is with the patient. [47]And do not be like those who came out of their homes boastfully and to be seen of people and who prevent [others] from the way of Allah. And Allah surrounds what they do. [48]And when Satan beautified their works and said, "None of the people will defeat you today, and surely I am a neighbor to you." So when the two groups saw each other, he turned on his heel and said, "Surely I am innocent of you. Surely I see what you do not see. Surely I fear Allah. And Allah is severe in the punishing." [49]When the hypocrites and those who have disease in their hearts said, "Their religion has made them proud." And whoever depends on Allah, so surely Allah is dear, wise. [50]And if you see, when the angels cause those who became infidels to die, they smite their faces and their rear ends: "And taste the torment of the fire." [51]That is because of what your hands have sent on before and that Allah is not unjust to the servants. [52]Like the habit of the family of Pharaoh and of those who were infidels in the signs of Allah before them, so Allah seized them with their sins. Surely Allah is strong, severe in the punishment. [53]This is because Allah does not change the grace with which he graced on a people until they change what is in themselves, and that Allah is hearing, knowing. [54]Like the habit of the family of Pharaoh and those before them who denied the signs of their lord, so we destroyed them with their sins, and we drowned the family of Pharaoh, and all were unjust. [55]Surely the worst creatures before Allah are those who became infidels, so they do not believe.

Mohammed's treatment of conquered people is written here.

[56]Those with whom you had covenants, then they break their covenant at every time, and they do not fear. [57]So if you overtake them in war, then scatter those who are left behind, perhaps they will remember. [58]And should you fear betrayal from any people, so do the same to them. Surely Allah does not love the betrayers. [59]And those who became infidels do not count that they surpass. Surely they will never hinder.

Muslims are commanded to attack and terrorize the infidels. Allah will repay them for what they spend. This is the theme

---

[a] engage in war with
[b] Muslim scholars claim this word means strength or power
[c] steadfast in fighting

which Muslim believers often use as seen in the Brotherhood's logo. Notice that verse 61 is abrogated by 9:5.

[60]And prepare for them whatever power you can and of the tying of horses. Strike terror into the enemy of Allah and your enemy and others, without them you do not know them; Allah knows them. And what you spend from anything for the sake of Allah, it will be repaid to you, and you will not be dealt with unjustly. [61]And if they lean toward peace (truce), so lean toward it. And depend on Allah. Surely he is the hearing, the knowing. [62]And if they desire to deceive you, so surely Allah is sufficient for you. He is who supported you with his victory and with the believers. [63]And he has attuned between their hearts. If you had spent all of what is on the earth, you could not have attuned between their hearts, but Allah has attuned between them. Surely he is dear, wise. [64]O you prophet, Allah is sufficient for you and the believers who follow you.

Allah ordered Mohammed to incite people to kill the infidels. See also verses 2:216, 217, 244; 3:121; 4:76; 8:12, 13, 39, 67; 9:5, 29, 41, 73, 111; 47:4-6, 35... Compare this to Matthew 5:43-48. Notice how Allah changed his mind concerning the number of Muslim fighters as he learned about their weaknesses. This is a great evidence that Allah is not all knowing.

[65]O you prophet, provoke the believers to engage in war. If there will be twenty patient[a] of you, they will have victory over two hundred; and if there will be a hundred of you, they will have victory over a thousand of those who became infidels because they are people who do not understand. [66]Now Allah has lightened for you, and he knows that there is weakness in you. So if there will be a hundred patient ones of you, they will have victory over two hundred; and if there will be a thousand of you, they will have victory over two thousand by Allah's permission. And Allah is with the patient.

Muslims are instructed not to take prisoners (slaves) as they slaughter people throughout the earth until after their victory is assured. Spoil is lawful.

[67]It was not for a prophet to take captives until he had made great slaughter in the land. You desire the widths[b] of this world, and Allah desires the hereafter. And Allah is dear, wise. [68]Were it not for a predetermined decree from Allah, a great torment would have touched you because of what you have taken. [69]So eat of the spoils you have taken lawfully and good, and fear Allah. Surely Allah is forgiving, merciful.

---

[a] steadfast in fighting
[b] riches

Those who engage in war for Allah will receive mercy and noble provision.

[70]O you prophet, say to whoever is in your hands of the captives, "If Allah knows anything good in your heart, he will bring good to you than that which he took from you, and he will forgive you. And Allah is forgiving, merciful." [71]And if they desire to betray you, so indeed, they betrayed Allah before you. So he subdued them. And Allah is knowing, wise. [72]Surely those who have believed and emigrated and performed jihad with their money and their lives for the sake of Allah, and those who gave asylum and helped, those are friends one to another. And those who believed and did not emigrate, you owe no duty or protection at all until they emigrate. And if they seek help from you in the religion, so your duty is to help them, except against the people with whom you have a covenant. And Allah sees what you do.

By going off to war, Muslims prove that they are true believers.

[73]And those who became infidels are friends one to another. If you do not do this,[a] there will be sedition in the land and a big vandalizing. [74]And those who believed and emigrated and performed jihad for the sake of Allah, and those who gave asylum and helped, those are the true believers; they will receive forgiveness and generous provisions. [75]And those who believed afterward and emigrated and performed jihad with you, so those are of you. And those who are united by the wombs (blood relatives), are preferred to each other in the book of Allah. Surely Allah knows all things.

A portion of a revelation   9   *The Repentant*

Notice that this is the final portion of the revelation Mohammed claimed to receive from his angel, Gabreel. It does not include the statement, "In the name of Allah, the merciful, the merciful." It begins with the word "innocent" in the Arabic language. Allah and his messenger, Mohammed, are innocent concerning the killing of the idolaters, the Christians, and the Jews, especially with those whom Mohammed had made a previous covenant not to kill.

---

[a] fighting the infidels and supporting the Muslims

[1]Allah and his messenger are innocent from the polytheists with whom you have a covenant. [2]So travel in the land four months, and know that you will not hinder Allah and that Allah will shame the infidels. [3]And the announcement from Allah and his messenger to the people on the bigger pilgrimage day: "That Allah and his messenger are innocent from the polytheists." So if you repent, so it will be better for you; but if you turn away, so know that you will not hinder Allah. And give the good news to those who became infidels, with a painful torment. [4]Except for the polytheists with whom you made a covenant, then they did not fail anything of you, nor aided anyone against you. So fulfill to them your covenant through their time. Surely Allah loves the fearer.

Muslims are commanded to kill all polytheists who do not accept Islam. According to Muslim scholars, this verse abrogates 124 other verses throughout the entire Qur'an which indicate any compassion for Christians and Jews. Also, notice verse 6 is abrogated by verse 5.

[5]So when the forbidden months are passed,[a] so kill the polytheists wherever you find them, and take them [as captives] and besiege them and lay wait for them with every kind of ambush; so if they repent[b] and perform the prayer and bring the legal alms, so leave their way free. Surely Allah is forgiving, merciful. [6]And if any one of the polytheists asks you for a shelter, so give to him a shelter until he hears the word of Allah, then let him reach his place of safety. This is because they are people who do not know. [7]How can it be that polytheists have a covenant with Allah and with his messenger, except those with whom you had a covenant at the forbidden mosque? So as long as they are straight with you, so be straight with them. Surely Allah loves the fearer. [8]How, if they overcome you, they will not regard with you the kinship or the covenant. They will please you with their mouths and their hearts reject, and most of them are transgressors. [9]They purchased with the verses of Allah a small price, so they prevented [others] from his way. Surely evil is what they were doing. [10]They do not regard in a believer the kinship or a covenant, and those are the transgressors. [11]So if they repent and perform the prayer and bring the legal alms, so they are your brothers in the religion. And we expound on the verses to people who know.

Muslims are commanded to engage in war with those who insult the religion of Islam.

[12]And if they break their oath after their covenant and stab in your

---

[a] pre-Islamic tradition of not fighting during a four month period
[b] convert to Islam

religion, so engage in war with the leaders of the infidelity. Surely there is no oath for them, perhaps they may desist. [13]Will you not engage in war with people who broke their oath and intend to expel the messenger, and they attack you first time? Do you fear them? So Allah is more worthy that you fear him, if you were believers. [14]Engage in war with them. Allah will torment them by your hands and put them to shame and give you victory over them and heal chests of a believing people. [15]And he takes away the rage of their hearts, and Allah relents on whom he wills. And Allah is knowing, wise. [16]Or you thought that you will be left alone while Allah knows those among you who perform jihad? And they did not take strange friends rather than Allah and his messenger and the believers. And Allah is aware of what you do. [17]It was not for polytheists to visit the mosque of Allah; they witness against themselves with infidelity. Those, their works are in vain, and in the fire they will abide forever.

Muslims are not allowed to let anyone into the mosques who do not believe and pay the religious tax. Those who only take the pilgrimage are not on the same high level as those who perform jihad.

[18]Surely only those who believed in Allah and the last day and perform the prayer and bring the legal alms and fear no one except Allah can visit the mosques of Allah, so perhaps those will be among the guided. [19]Do you make the giver of drink to the pilgrims and the guardian of the forbidden mosque like those who believed in Allah and the last day and performed jihad for the sake of Allah? They are not equal before Allah, and Allah will not guide the unjust people.

Muslims who perform jihad with their money and with their lives for the sake of Allah are of greater worth.

[20]Those who believed and emigrated and performed jihad for the sake of Allah with their money and with their lives of the highest degree with Allah, and those are the triumphant. [21]Their lord gives them good news of mercy from himself and of his good pleasure and gardens; they will have in it everlasting bliss. [22]They will abide in it forever and ever. Surely Allah has a great wage.

Muslims are commanded not to take their own family members as friends if those family members are not believers.

[23]O you who have believed, do not take your fathers or your brothers as friends if they love infidelity above belief, and whoever takes them as a friend among you, so those are the unjust. [24]Say, "If your fathers and your sons and your brethren and your wives and your relatives and the money which you have gained and merchandise which you fear may be unsold and dwellings in which

you delight was more loved to you than Allah and his messenger and the performing of jihad for his sake, so wait until Allah brings his command. And Allah does not guide the transgressing people." [25]Indeed, Allah gave you victory in many battlefields and on honein's[a] day when you were pleased with your large numbers, so it did not avail you anything, and the land became so tight against you, despite its width, then you turned back and fled. [26]Then Allah sent down his tranquility on his messenger and on the believers, and he sent down troops which you did not see. And he tormented those who became infidels. And this is the reward of the infidels. [27]Then after this Allah relents on whom he wills. And Allah is forgiving, merciful.

Muslims are commanded not to allow anyone who worships other gods near the forbidden mosque. This includes Christians since Muslims believe that they worship Jesus, the Holy Spirit, and God. This rule is still practiced in Saudi Arabia.

[28]O you who have believed, surely only the polytheists are unclean. So do not let them come near the forbidden mosque after this their year. And if you are afraid of coming to poverty, so Allah will enrich you from his bounty if he wills. Surely Allah is knowing, wise.

Muslims are commanded to kill the Jews and Christians.

[29]Engage in war with those who do not believe in Allah nor in the last day. Nor forbid what Allah and his messenger forbid, nor believe in the religion of the truth[b] among those who have been given the book until they pay the jizya[c] out of hand and they are subdued.

Infidels accept rabbis and monks as lords rather than God and Christ!

[30]And the Jews said, "Uzair[d] is the son of Allah." And the Nasara (Christians) said, "The Christ is the son of Allah." This is their saying with their mouths; they repeat the sayings of those who became infidels before. Allah engages in war with them. How perverted they are! [31]They take their rabbis and their monks as lords rather than Allah and the Christ, the son of Mary. And they are not commanded except to serve one god. There is no god except him. Praise to him above what they partner. [32]They desire to extinguish Allah's light with their mouths, but Allah refused, except that his light be fulfilled, even if the infidels hate it.

---

[a] a battlefield
[b] Islam
[c] tribute, non-Arabic word of Aramaic origin
[d] Ezra, non-Arabic word of Hebrew origin

Allah will give Islam victory over all other religions.

[33]He is who sent his messenger with the guidance and the true religion, so that he may make it prevail over every other religion, even if the polytheists hate it. [34]O you who have believed, surely many of the rabbis and monks do consume people's money with vanity and prevent [others] from the way of Allah. And those who treasure the gold and the silver and do not spend it for the sake of Allah, so give them the good news of a painful torment. [35]On a day they will be heated in the fire of hell, and their foreheads and their sides and their backs will be branded by it: "This is what you treasure to yourself, so taste what you were treasuring." [36]Surely the number of months with Allah is twelve months. In Allah's book, a day he created the heavens and the earth, four of those are forbidden. This is the right religion, so do not do injustice to yourselves during them, and engage in war with all the polytheists as they engage in war with all of you. And know that Allah is with the fearer. [37]Surely the postponing is only added to infidelity. Those who became infidels are led astray by it. They make it lawful for one year and forbid it one year so that they may agree with the number of months which Allah has forbidden, so they make lawful what Allah has forbidden. The evil of their work is beautified to them. And Allah will not guide the infidel people.

This is a warning to those who will not give up this world and go to war for Allah.

[38]O you who have believed, what is [the matter] with you when it was said to you, "March forth for the sake of Allah,"[a] you cling heavily to the earth? Are you satisfied with the world's life rather than the hereafter? So what is the enjoyment of the world's life in the hereafter but a little. [39]If you do not march forth, he will torment you with a painful torment and he will place another people in your place and you will not harm him anything. And Allah has might over everything. [40]If you do not help him, so indeed, Allah helped him when those who became infidels drove him forth in company with a second of two when they were in the cave, when he said to his companion, "Do not grieve. Surely Allah is with us." So Allah sent down his tranquility on him and supported him with troops you did not see and made the word of those who became infidels the lower. And the word of Allah is the highest. And Allah is dear, wise.

Giving money and life to engage in war for Allah is best for Muslims. Those who truly believe in Allah do not ask to be exempt from wars.

---

[a] perform jihad, i.e. holy war

⁴¹March forth lightly or heavily, and perform jihad with your money and your lives for the sake of Allah. This is best for you, if you were knowing. ⁴²If it was an easy spoil to be taken and a short traveling distance, they would surely have followed you, but the way seemed long to them. And they will swear by Allah: "If we were able, we would surely have gone forth with you." They destroy themselves, and Allah knows surely that they are liars. ⁴³Allah pardoned you; why did you give them permission^a until it became clear to you who were the truthful and know the liars? ⁴⁴Those who believe in Allah and the last day, they do not ask permission from performing jihad with their money and their lives. And Allah knows the fearer. ⁴⁵Surely only those who do not believe in Allah and the last day ask permission. And their hearts doubted, so in their doubt they are wavering. ⁴⁶And if they wanted to go forth, they would prepare for it preparation. But Allah hated their going forth, so made them laggards, and it was said, "Sit with those who are sitting." ⁴⁷If they had gone forth with you, they would not have increased you except in discouragement. And had they kept moving among you, they desired the sedition for you. And among you, some will listen to them. And Allah knows the unjust. ⁴⁸Indeed, they desired the sedition before, and they turn affairs upside down for you until the truth arrived and the command of Allah appeared. And they hated [it].

All Muslims who do not go to war will go to hell.

⁴⁹And some of them who say, "Give me permission and do not seduce me." Did they not fall into the sedition? And surely hell will encompass the infidels. ⁵⁰If a good fortune befalls you, it displeased them; and if a misfortune befalls you, they say, "Indeed, we took our own affairs before." And they turn away, and they are rejoicing. ⁵¹Say, "Nothing can befall us except what Allah has prescribed for us. He is our protector, and on Allah so let the believers depend." ⁵²Say, "Do you wait for us other than one of the two best things? And we lie in wait for you that Allah will inflict you by a torment from himself or by our hands. So lie in wait, surely we are lying in wait with you." ⁵³Say, "Spend willingly or grudgingly. It will not be accepted from you; surely you were a transgressing people." ⁵⁴And nothing hinders the acceptance of their spendings, except they became infidels in Allah and his messenger; and they do not come to the prayer, except they are lazy, and they will not spend, except they are grudgingly. ⁵⁵So let not their money or their children please you. Surely Allah only desires to torment them by it in the world's life, and that their souls may depart while they are infidels. ⁵⁶And they swear by Allah that they are surely of you. And they are not of you, but they are divisive people.

---

^a exemption from fighting

Those who swear they are Muslims and hide in caves, rather than engaging in war, are not with Mohammed.

[57]If they find a place of refuge or caves or a doorway, they surely turn toward it and run to it. [58]And some of them blame you in the alms. So if they are given from it, they are pleased; but if they are not given from it, behold, they are full of rage. [59]And if they were pleased with that which Allah and his messenger had given them and said, "Allah is sufficient for us. Allah will bring to us out of his bounty and his messenger, surely our desire is to Allah."

Alms can be used to bribe people to believe in Islam.

[60]Surely alms are only to the poor and the needy and those who collect them and to those whose hearts are inclined[a] and for the necks [ransom for slaves] and for debtors and for the sake of Allah and the son of the way, an ordinance from Allah. And Allah is knowing, wise. [61]And some of them who harm the prophet and say, "He is all ears." Say, "An ear of good to you, he believes in Allah. And believe to the believers, and mercy to those who believed among you." And those who harm the messenger of Allah, they have a painful torment. [62]They swear to you by Allah to please you, but Allah and his messenger are more worthy, that they should please him, if they were believers. [63]Do they not know that who opposes Allah and his messenger, so surely to him hell fire, abide in it forever? This is the great shame. [64]The hypocrites are afraid that a portion of a revelation should be sent down on them, to inform them about what is in their hearts. Say, "Scoff, surely Allah will bring out what you fear." [65]And if you ask them, they will say, "Surely we were only engaging and playing." Say, "Were you scoffing at Allah and his verses and his messenger?" [66]Make no excuse; indeed, you became infidels after you had believed. If we pardon an assembly of you, we will torment the assembly because they were criminals. [67]Hypocritical men and hypocritical women are from one another. They command the evil and forbid what is right and close their hands.[b] They have forgotten Allah, so he has forgotten them. Surely the hypocrites are the transgressors. [68]Allah promises the hypocritical men and hypocritical women and the infidels hell fire, abiding in it forever. It is their reckoning. And Allah cursed them, and they will have a lasting torment. [69]Like those who were before you, they were stronger than you in power and with more money and children. So they enjoyed their portion, so you enjoy your portion as they who were before you enjoyed their portion, and you engaged like they engaged. Those, their works were vain in this world and in the hereafter, and those are

---

[a] the people whom Mohammed bribed to bring to Islam
[b] became stingy

the losers. [70]Has not the news of those who were before them reached them, Noah's people and Ad[a] and Themoud[b] and Abraham's people and the companions of Midian[c] and the Mu'tafikah?[d] Their messengers came to them with the proofs, so it was not of Allah to treat them unjustly, but they were treating themselves unjustly. [71]And the believing men and the believing women are friends to one another. They command what is right and forbid from the evil, and they perform the prayer and bring the legal alms. And they obey Allah and his messenger. Those Allah will give them mercy. Surely Allah is dear, wise. [72]Allah promised the believing men and the believing women gardens, below them the rivers flow, in which they will abide forever, and excellent mansions in the 'Adn's[e] gardens. And pleasure from Allah is bigger. This is the great triumph.

Mohammed was commanded to engage in war and to be harsh against the infidels and the hypocrites.

[73]O you prophet, perform jihad against the infidels and the hypocrites, and be harsh with them. And their abode will be hell, and evil is the final place. [74]They swear by Allah that they did not say, and indeed, they said the word of the infidelity, and they became infidels after they became Muslims. They planned what they could not attain and only disapproved of it because Allah and his messenger had enriched them from his bounty. So if they repent, it will be better for them. And if they turn away, Allah will torment them with a painful torment in this world and the hereafter, and they will not have on earth a friend nor helper. [75]And some of them who made a covenant with Allah: "If he gives us of his bounties, we will surely give alms, and surely we will be of the good." [76]So when he gave to them of his bounty, they became stingy with it and turned away, and they disagreed. [77]So he causes hypocrisy to follow them in their hearts until a day they will meet him because of not fulfilling their promise to Allah and because they were lying. [78]Do they not know that Allah knows their secrets and their private talk and that Allah is the knower of the unseen? [79]Those who taunt such of the faithful who give their alms freely and those who find nothing to give but their hard labor, so they scoff at them. Allah scoffed at them, and they will have a painful torment.

Mohammed has no power to help the hypocrites to receive forgiveness of their sins.

---

[a] non-existent peoples made up by Mohammed
[b] non-existent peoples made up by Mohammed
[c] non-existent peoples made up by Mohammed
[d] meaningless word—Scholars erroneously claimed this to be the name of the cities of Lot, which the Bible clearly teaches were called Sodom and Gomorrah.
[e] Eden, non-Arabic word of Hebrew/Syriac origin

[80]Ask forgiveness for them, or do not ask forgiveness for them; if you ask forgiveness for them seventy times, so Allah will not forgive them. This is because they are infidels in Allah and his messenger, and Allah does not guide the transgressing people.

Muslims who do not go to war do not get a second chance to escape hell.

[81]Those who stayed behind rejoiced by their sitting behind Allah's messenger, and they hated to perform jihad with their money and their lives for the sake of Allah. And they said, "Do not go forth[a] in the heat." Say, "The fire of hell is even hotter, if they were understanding." [82]So they will laugh for a little while, and they will weep much, a reward of what they were earning. [83]So if Allah returns you to a group of them, so they ask your permission to go out [in war]. So say, "You will not go out with me forever, and you will never engage in war with me [against] an enemy. Surely you were pleased to sit the first time, so sit with those who stayed behind." [84]And do not pray over anyone of them who dies ever. And do not stand at his grave. Surely they are infidels in Allah and his messenger, and they died while still transgressors. [85]And do not let their money or their children please you. Surely Allah only desires to torment them by these in this world, and that their souls should depart while they are still infidels.

Muslims who go to war for Allah will go to the gardens.

[86]And when a portion of a revelation was sent down: "That believe in Allah and perform jihad with his messenger." Those of them who are possessed of riches asked permission and said, "Allow us to be with those who are sitting." [87]They were pleased to be with those who stayed behind, and a seal was put on their hearts so they do not understand. [88]But the messenger and those who believed with him performed jihad with their money and their lives. And those have the good things, and those are the prosperous. [89]Allah has prepared gardens for them, below them the rivers flow; they will abide in them forever. This is the great triumph.

Only the weak and sick are exempt from going to war.

[90]And some among the Bedouins who gave excuses came to ask for permission, and those who denied Allah and his messenger stayed. A painful torment will fall on those who became infidels among them. [91]There is no shame for the weak and for the sick and for those who do not find what they spend, if they were faithful to Allah and his messenger, there is no way against the doers of good.

---

[a] in war

And Allah is forgiving, merciful. [92]Nor against those to whom, when they came to you, that you should carry them, you said, "I did not find any way to carry you." They turned away, and their eyes were flooded with tears, grieving, because they found no means to spend.

Muslims who do not go to war are sealed for hell.

[93]Surely the way is only against those who are rich and ask you for permission. They are pleased to be with those who stay behind, and Allah has sealed on their hearts so they do not know. [94]They will apologize to you if you return to them. Say, "Do not apologize. We will never believe you; indeed, Allah has informed us about your news. And Allah and his messenger will see your work. Then you will return to the knower of the unseen and the seen, so he will inform you of what you were doing." [95]They will swear to you by Allah if you return to them so that you may turn away from them. So withdraw from them, surely they are unclean; and their abode is hell, a reward for what they were earning. [96]They will swear to you to be pleased with them, so if you are pleased with them, so surely Allah will not be pleased with the transgressing people. [97]The Bedouins are strong infidels and hypocrites, and they are more disposed to not know the boundary of what Allah has sent down on his messenger. And Allah is knowing, wise. [98]And some of the Bedouins who consider what is spent as a fine, and they lie in wait for misfortune to fall upon you, upon them the evil misfortune may fall. And Allah is hearing, knowing. [99]And some of the Bedouins who believe in Allah and in the last day and take what is spent to get near to Allah and the messenger's prayers, that it surely will bring them near. Allah will admit them to his mercy. Surely Allah is forgiving, merciful. [100]And the first surpassed among the emigrants and the helpers and those who have followed them with good. Allah was pleased with them, and they were pleased with him. And he has prepared for them gardens, below them the rivers flow, to abide there forever and ever. This is the great triumph. [101]And some of the Bedouins around you are hypocrites. And among the people of the Medina, some are trained in hypocrisy. You do not know them; we know them. We will torment them twice, then they will be returned to great torment.

A Muslim could receive purification and sanctification from sin by giving money.

[102] And others have confessed their sins, and they mix good deed with other evil. Perhaps Allah will relent on them. Surely Allah is forgiving, merciful. [103]Take from their money alms, that it will purify them and sanctify them by it, and pray over them for surely your prayers are a relief to them. And Allah is hearing, knowing. [104]Do they not know that Allah, he accepts the repentance from his servants and takes the alms? And that Allah, he is the relenting, the

merciful. [105]And say, "Work so Allah will see your work, and his messenger and the believers. And you will be brought back to the knower of the unseen and the seen. So he will inform you of what you were doing." [106]And others delayed to the command of Allah, whether he will torment them, or whether he will relent on them. And Allah is knowing, wise. [107]And those who took a mosque in resentment and infidelity and caused division between believers and are lying in wait for those who engage in war against Allah and his messenger before that, and they will swear: "That we only desired but the good." And Allah witnesses that surely they are liars. [108]Do not ever stand up in it. For a mosque ussis[a] from its first day in piety, more worthy is it that you stand in it. In it are men who love to be purified. And Allah loves the purified. [109]Is he who founded a bunyanah[b] on the fear of Allah and good pleasure better, or one who founded a building on the edge of a big cliff. So it collapsed with him into the fire of hell? And Allah will not guide the unjust people. [110]Their building which they built will continue to be a doubt in their hearts, unless their hearts are cut into pieces. And Allah is knowing, wise.

Dying in jihad and paying money are two conditions for Muslims to go to the gardens. Jihad is mentioned in the Gospel.

[111]Surely Allah has purchased from the believers their souls and their money so that they may have the garden. They engage in war for the sake of Allah, so they kill and are killed; a promise of this is true in the Torah and in the Gospel and in the Qur'an. And who is more faithful to his covenant than Allah? So receive the good news in your pledge which you have pledged with, and this is the great triumph. [112]The repenters, the servants, the praisers, the travelers, the kneelers, the worshipers, those who command what is right, and those who forbid from the evil, and the keepers to the bounds of Allah. And give the good news to the believers. [113]It was not for the prophet or those who believed to ask forgiveness for the polytheists, even though they were closest relatives, after it has been made clear to them that they are the companions of hell. [114]And the seeking of forgiveness of Abraham for his father was not but in [keeping of] a promise which he had promised to him. So when it was shown to him that he was an enemy to Allah, he declared himself innocent of him. Surely Abraham was very meek. [115]And it was not of Allah to lead people astray after he had guided them until he showed them what they fear. Surely Allah knows all things. [116]Surely Allah has the kingdom of the heavens and the earth. He gives life and causes

---

[a] founded, non-Arabic word of Aramaic origin
[b] building, non-Arabic word of Aramaic origin

death, and you do not have a friend nor helper other than Allah. [117]Indeed, Allah relented on the prophet and the emigrants and the helpers, those who followed him in the hour of distress. After that, the hearts of a group of them almost deviated. Then he relented on them. Surely to them he is compassionate, merciful. [118]And on the three who were left behind until the earth, spacious as it is, became tight (close) against them and their souls became tight, and they thought that there is no refuge from Allah except to him. Then he relented on them so that they might repent. Surely Allah is the relenting, the merciful. [119]O you who have believed, fear Allah and be with the truthful. [120]It was not for the people of the Medina and the Bedouins around them to abandon Allah's messenger or to prefer their lives above his life because neither thirst nor labor nor hunger could come on them for the sake of Allah. Nor do they step a step which may anger the infidels, nor do they receive from the enemy anything but what was prescribed to them as a good work. Surely Allah will not waste the wage of the doers of good. [121]And they do not spend a small or a big expense, and they do not cross a valley, but it is prescribed to them that Allah may reward them with better than what they were doing. [122]And it was not for the believers to go forth [to war] together, so except for a company from each group of them and that they may instruct themselves in their religion and to warn their people if they returned to them, perhaps they may be cautioned.

Muslims are commanded to engage in war against their neighbors who do not believe in Allah.

[123]O you who have believed, engage in war against the infidels who are near to you. And let them find in you harshness, and know that Allah is with the fearer. [124]And if a portion of a revelation is sent down, so some of them who say, "Who among you this increased his faith?" So as for those who believed, so it increased their faith, and they will have the good news. [125]And as for those who have disease in their hearts, so it increased uncleanliness to their uncleanliness, and they died while they were infidels. [126]Do they not see that they are led into sedition in every year once or twice? Then they do not repent, nor do they remember. [127]And if a portion of a revelation is sent down, they look at one another: "And does anyone see you?" Then they turn away. Allah turned away their hearts because they are a people who do not understand. [128]Indeed, a messenger from among yourselves came to you. It is dear to him that you suffer; he cares for you. Compassionate, merciful with the believers. [129]So if they turn away, so say, "Allah is sufficient for me; there is no god but him. I depend on him, and he is the lord of the great throne."

A portion of a revelation   **10**   *Yunus*

In the name of Allah, the merciful, the merciful

Mohammed titled this portion of a revelation Yunus. However, he has the wrong name. Mohammed meant Jonah.

[1]Alr.[a] These are the verses of the wise book. [2]Was it a wonder to the people that we revealed to a man among them that warns the people and gives good news to those who believe, that they will have a true footing with their lord? The infidels said, "Surely this is an obvious sorcerer." [3]Surely your lord is Allah who created the heavens and the earth in six days; then he sat on the throne arranging the affair. There is no intercessor except after his permission. This is Allah your lord, so serve him. Do you not remember? [4]To him you will all return. Allah's promise is true. Surely he began the creation; then he repeated it so that he may reward those who believed and did good deeds with fairness. And those who became infidels will have a drink of hamem and painful torment because they were infidels.

The moon is not a natural satellite reflecting the sun's light, but it produces light of its own and has its own stations. See also verse 71:16. This contradicts the nature of the moon and the Bible which clearly states that the moon does not produce light of its own. See Job 25:5.

[5]He is who has made the sun bright and the moon a light and has ordained its stations so that you may learn the number of years and the reckoning. Allah did not create this except with the truth. He expounds on his signs to a people who know. [6]Surely in the alternations of the night and the day and in what Allah has created in the heavens and the earth, are signs to a fearing people. [7]Surely those who do not hope to meet us and are pleased with the world's life and are secure with it, and those who are unaware of our signs, [8]those, their abode is the fire because of what they were earning. [9]Surely those who believed and did good deeds, their lord guides them with their faith. Below them the rivers flow in gardens of bliss. [10]Their calling in it: "Praise be to you, O Allah." And their greeting in it: "Peace." And they end their calling: "That the praise be to Allah, the lord of the worlds." [11]And if Allah hastens evil to the people as

---

[a] a word containing three Arabic letters without meaning

they would hasten their good, then he would decree for them their end. So warn those who do not hope our meeting, in their rebellion blindly. ¹²When harm touches the human, he prays to us on his side or sitting or standing, so when we remove his harm from him, he passed on as though he had not called to us about the harm which touched him. Likewise, it is beautified to the extravagant what they were doing. ¹³And indeed, we destroyed the generations before you, when they were unjust and their messengers came to them with the proofs, and they were not to believe. Likewise, we reward the criminal people. ¹⁴Then we made you viceroys on the earth after them that we might see how you would do.

Those who would change the Qur'an are rebelling against Allah.

¹⁵And when our clear verses are recited to them, those who do not hope to meet us said, "Bring a different Qur'an than this or change it." Say, "It is not for me to change it on my own. I only follow what is revealed to me. Surely I fear, if I disobey my lord, the torment of a great day." ¹⁶Say, "If Allah willed, I had not recited it to you, neither you know it. So indeed, I have dwelt among you for ages before it. Do you not understand?" ¹⁷So who is more unjust than the one who forged a lie against Allah or denied his verses? Surely he will not prosper the criminals. ¹⁸And they serve rather than Allah, what does not harm them nor profit them, and they say, "Those are our intercessors with Allah." Say, "Will you inform Allah by what he does not know in the heavens nor on the earth?" Praise be to him, and he is exalted above what they partner. ¹⁹And the people were not but one nation, so they differed, and were it not that a word had previously gone forth from your lord, it would have been judged between them in what they differed. ²⁰And they say, "Were it not that a sign had been sent down on him from his lord." So say, "Surely the unseen is only to Allah, so wait, surely I am waiting with you." ²¹And when we make the people taste mercy after harm touches them, though they have deceived in our verses, say, "Allah is faster in deceiving." Surely our messenger writes down what you deceive. ²²He is who makes you travel on the shore and the sea until when you were in the ship and they sail with them with a good wind. And they rejoice by it. A stormy wind comes to them, and the waves come on them from every place. And they thought that they are surrounded with them. They call to Allah, devoted in the religion to him: "If you deliver us from this, surely we will be of the thankful." ²³So when he delivered them, behold, they rebel on the earth without the truth. O you people, surely your rebellion is only against yourself, it is the enjoyment of the world's life. Then to us is your return, so we will inform you of what you were doing. ²⁴Surely the parable of the world's life is only like water we send down from the heaven, so it mixed with the plants of the earth of which people and livestock eat

until the earth has received its raiment and is highly embellished. And its people thought that they are able over it; our command came to it night or day, so we made it a reaping as if it had not flourished yesterday. Likewise, we expound on the verses to a reflecting people.

In eternity, the wicked have black faces. This shows Islam's racism towards the black race.

[25]And Allah calls to the home of peace, and he guides whom he wills to a straight way. [26]To those who did good the best, and more, neither blackness nor humiliation will cover their faces. Those are the companions of the garden; they will abide in it forever. [27]And those who have earned the evils, their reward is evil with the like of it, and humiliation will cover them. They will have no protector against Allah, as though their faces were covered with dark patches of night. Those are the companions of the fire; they will abide in it forever. [28]And a day we will gather them together, then we will say to those who are polytheists, "To your place, you and your partners." So we separated between them. And their partners said, "You were not serving us. [29]So Allah is a sufficient witness between us and between you, for we were unaware of your serving us." [30]Thereupon every soul will taste of what it had done, and they returned to Allah, their true master, and gone astray from them what they were forging. [31]Say, "Who provides to you from the heaven and the earth? Is he who owns the hearing and the sight? And who brings forth the living from the dead and brings forth the dead from the living? And who arranges the affair?" So they will say, "Allah." So say, "Do you not fear?" [32]So this is Allah, your true lord. So what after the truth, except the error? So how can you turn away? [33]Likewise, the word of your lord was established on those who transgress, that they will not believe. [34]Say, "Is there any of your partners who begin the creation then redo it?" Say, "Allah begins the creation, then redoes it. So how can you turn away?" [35]Say, "Is there any of your partners who guide to the truth?" Say, "Allah guides to the truth. Is the one who guides to the truth worthy to be followed; is he who does not guide unless he himself is guided? So what is [the matter] with you? How do you judge?" [36]And most of them do not follow except conjecture; surely the conjecture will not profit anything from the truth. Surely Allah knows what they do.

Only Allah could write a book as great as the Qur'an.

[37]And this Qur'an was not forged without Allah, but it confirms what was between his hands and is an exposition of the book; there is no doubt in it from the lord of the worlds. [38]Or do they say, "He has forged it"? Say, "So bring a portion of a revelation like it, and call on

whom you can rather than Allah, if you were truthful." [39]Yet, they
deny what they do not have knowledge of, and the interpretation of it
has not come to them. Likewise, those who were before them
denied. So look how was the end of the unjust. [40]And some of them
who believe in it, and some of them who do not believe in it. And
your lord knows best those who vandalize. [41]And if they deny you, so
say, "To me my work and to you your work. And you are innocent of
what I do, and I am innocent of what you do." [42]And some of them
who hear you; can you make the deaf to hear even though they were
not understanding? [43]And some of them who look at you, but can
you guide the blind even though they were not seeing? [44]Surely Allah
will not deal with the people unjustly anything. But people deal
unjustly with themselves. [45]And a day he gathers them, they will
seem as though they had waited but an hour of the day, recognizing
each other. Indeed, those who denied the meeting with Allah have
lost, and they were not guided. [46]And if we show you some of what
we promised them, or we cause you to die, so to us is their return.
Then Allah is witness of what they do.

**Every nation has its own messenger. See also verses 16:36, 89.
This contradicts verses 29:27 and 45:16 which clearly teach that
Jews are the only messengers or prophets. Along with this fact,
there have been no prophets sent to Africa, Asia, Europe,
Canada, Australia, North and South America, Russia, China, and
so forth.**

[47]And to every nation a messenger. So when their messenger
comes, it was judged between them with fairness, and they will not
be dealt with unjustly. [48]And they say, "When is this promise if you
were truthful?" [49]Say, "I do not own to myself harm or benefit, except
what Allah wills." To every nation its time, when its time comes, so
they will not delay an hour nor will they advance. [50]Say, "Did you see
if his torment comes to you by night or by day; what portion of it will
the criminal hasten?" [51]Is it then, if it befalls, you believe in him?
Now, and indeed, with it you were hastening! [52]Then it was said to
those who were unjust, "Taste the eternal torment. Will you be
rewarded, except for what you were earning?" [53]And they ask you to
prophesy to them: "Is it true?" Say, "[I swear] by my lord, surely it is
the truth, and you cannot escape." [54]And if every soul that has done
injustice possessed all that is on the earth, it would assuredly
ransom itself with it, and they would proclaim the regret when they
saw the torment. And it was judged between them fairly, and they
are not dealt with unjustly. [55]Is not surely to Allah what is in the
heavens and the earth. Is not surely the promise of Allah true, but
most of them do not know. [56]He gives life, and he causes death. And
to him you will return. [57]O you people, indeed, a sermon has come to
you from your lord and a healing for what is in the chests and a

guidance and a mercy to the believers. [58]Say, "By the bounty of Allah and his mercy, so by that so they may rejoice, it is better than what they gathered." [59]Say, "Have you seen what Allah has sent down to you of provision, so you made of it forbidden and lawful?" Say, "Has Allah given you his permission, or you forge against Allah?" [60]And what is the conjecture of those who forge the lie against Allah on the resurrection day. Surely Allah is bountiful to the people, but most of them are not thankful. [61]And you will not be in any affair, and you do not recite from it, from the Qur'an, and you do not do any work except we were witnesses over you when you engage in it. And not even the weight of an atom on the earth or in the heaven, or smaller than that or bigger, escapes your lord except it is in a clear book. [62]Is not surely no fear on the friends of Allah, and they will not grieve, [63]those who believed and were fearing.

There is no change to the words of Allah.

[64]They have the good news in the world's life and in the hereafter. There is no change to the words of Allah. This is the great triumph. [65]And do not let their saying grieve you. Surely all the honor is to Allah. He is the hearing, the knowing. [66]Is not surely to Allah whoever is in the heavens and whoever is on the earth. And no one follows those who call on partners without Allah. They follow but the conjecture, and that they only lie. [67]He is who made the night for you to dwell in and the day to see. Surely in this are signs to a hearing people.

Allah does not have a son.

[68]They said, "Allah took a son, praise be to him." He is the rich, to him what is in the heavens and what is on the earth. Do you have authority for this? Do you say against Allah what you do not know? [69]Say, "Surely those who forge the lie against Allah do not prosper." [70]Enjoyment in the world, then to us is their return. Then we will make them taste the severe torment because they were infidels.

The story of Noah is copied from the Bible and corrupted once again.

[71]And recite to them the news of Noah when he said to his people, "O my people, if my dwelling with you was big,[a] and my reminding you of the verses of Allah, so on Allah I depended. So gather your affair and your partners; then do not let your affair be a burden on you. Then come to me and do not wait. [72]So if you turn away, so I have not asked you for any wage. My wage is only on Allah. And I am commanded to be of the Muslims." [73]So they denied him. So we

---

[a] bothersome

delivered him and those who were with him in the ship, and we made them viceroys. And we drowned those who denied our verses. So see how was the end of the warned. [74]Then we sent after him messengers to their peoples. So they came to them with proofs, so they were not to believe in what they denied previously. Likewise, we seal on the hearts of the transgressors.

The story of Moses is copied from the Bible and corrupted once again.

[75]Then we sent after them Moses and Aaron to Pharaoh and his leaders with our signs, so they acted proudly, and they were a criminal people. [76]So when the truth came to them from us, they said, "Surely this is obvious sorcery." [77]Moses said, "Do you say to the truth after it has come to you, 'Is this sorcery'? And the sorcerers will not prosper." [78]They said, "Have you come to us to turn us from what we found our fathers on,[a] and to you will be the kibriyā[b] on the earth? And we will not believe in you." [79]And Pharaoh said, "Bring me with every knowing sorcerer." [80]So when the sorcerers came, Moses said to them, "Cast down what you will cast." [81]So when they cast down, Moses said, "Whatever sorceries you brought, surely Allah will demolish it. Surely Allah will not make the work of the vandals to be good. [82]And Allah will establish the truth by his words, even if the criminals hate it."

None of Pharaoh's people (i.e. sorcerers) believed in Moses' Allah. This contradicts verses 26:46-48.

[83]So no one believed to Moses except an offspring from his people because of fear of Pharaoh and his leaders, lest he should seduce them. And surely Pharaoh is exalted in the land, and surely he is of the extravagant. [84]And Moses said, "O my people, if you were believing in Allah, so depend on him if you were Muslims." [85]So they said, "On Allah we depended. Our lord, do not make us a sedition to the unjust people, [86]and deliver us by your mercy from the infidel people." [87]And we revealed to Moses and his brother: "That take your people to houses in Egypt, and in your houses make a kobla[c] and perform the prayer and give good news to the believers." [88]And Moses said, "Our lord, surely you have given Pharaoh and his leaders adornment and money in the world's life, our lord, that they may err from your way. Our lord, hide on their money and harden on their hearts that they will not believe until they see the painful torment." [89]He said, "Indeed, I have answered your calling so be straight and do not follow the way of those who do not know."

---

[a] their faith
[b] glory, non-Arabic word of Ethiopian origin
[c] a direction set toward which you pray

Pharaoh did not drown but became a Muslim by believing in Allah. This contradicts verse 28:40 which clearly teaches that he drowned as an infidel. See also verses 2:50; 7:136; and 17:103.

[90]And we brought the children of Israel through the sea. So Pharaoh and his hosts followed them insolently and with enmity until, when he was about to drown, he said, "I believed that there is no god but him on whom the children of Israel believed, and I am of the Muslims." [91]"Now, and indeed, you disobeyed before, and you were of the vandals. [92]So today we will deliver you with your body that you may become a sign to those who come after you, and surely most people are unaware of our signs." [93]And indeed, we settled the children of Israel a good settlement. And we provided them from the good things, so they did not disagree until the knowledge came to them. Surely your lord judges between them on the resurrection day in what they were differing.

Allah commands Mohammed to check the Qur'an with the Jews and Christians who are reading the Bible. This is proof that the Bible existed and was true in Mohammed's day.

[94]So, if you were in doubt concerning what we have sent down to you, so ask those who are reading the book before you; indeed, the truth came to you from your lord, so do not be of the doubters. [95]And do not be of those who denied the verses of Allah, so you will become of the losers. [96]Surely those on whom the word of your lord established, they will not believe, [97]even if every sign came to them until they see the painful torment. [98]So were it not that a village had believed so its faith profited, except the people of Yunus? When they believed, we removed from them the torment of disgrace in the world's life, and we gave them enjoyment for a while.

Allah could make all men believe if he wanted to.

[99]And if your lord willed, all who are on the earth would have believed together. Will you compel people until they become believers? [100]And it was not for a soul to believe except by Allah's permission, and he will lay the uncleanness on those who will not understand. [101]Say, "Look at what is in the heavens and the earth." And the signs and the warnings will not profit unbelieving people. [102]So do they wait except like the days of those who passed before them? Say, "So wait, surely I am with you among those who wait." [103]Then we will deliver our messengers and those who believed; likewise, it is a duty on us to deliver the believers. [104]Say, "O you people, if you were in doubt in my religion, so I do not serve what you are serving rather than Allah, but I serve Allah who causes you to die. And I have been commanded to be of the believers. [105]And

that: 'Set your face toward the religion, hanifan, and do not be of the polytheists. [106]And do not call rather than Allah what will not benefit you or harm you. So if you did, so surely then you are among the unjust. [107]And if Allah touches you with harm, so none can remove it except him; and if he restores good to you, none can keep back his bounty. He will strike with it whom he wills of his servants, and he is the forgiving, the merciful.'" [108]Say, "O you people, indeed, the truth has come to you from your lord. So whoever is guided, so surely he is only guided to himself; and whoever goes astray, so surely he only strays against it, and I am not a guardian over you." [109]And follow what is revealed to you. And be patient until Allah judges, and he is the best of the judges.

A portion of a revelation   *Houd*

11

In the name of Allah, the merciful, the merciful

[1]Alr.[a] A book whose verses are decisive, then expounded on from the presence of a wise, an aware. [2]That you serve none but Allah, surely I am a warner and a giver of good news to you from him. [3]And that you ask forgiveness of your lord, then repent to him. He causes you to enjoy an excellent enjoyment for a determined time, and he will bring to every worthy one his bounty. And if you turn away, so surely I fear for you a torment of a big day. [4]To Allah is your return, and he has the might over all things. [5]Is it not they surely fold up their chests that they may hide from him. Is it not when they cover themselves in their garments, he knows what they hide and what they reveal. Surely he is the knower of what is in the chests. [6]And there is no creature on the earth except its provision is from Allah, and he knows its resting place and its repository, all in a clear book. [7]And he is who created the heavens and the earth in six days. And his throne was on the water, that he tests you, which of you does the best work. And if you say, "After death you will surely be raised again." Those who became infidels will surely say, "This is nothing but obvious sorcery." [8]And if we delay from them the torment to an accounted period, they will surely say, "What keeps it back?" Is it not a day that will come to them; it will not be averted from them. And what they were scoffing with, afflicted them. [9]And if we cause the human to taste mercy from us, then take it away from him, surely he is despairing, infidel. [10]And if we make him taste grace after harm

---

[a] a word containing three Arabic letters without meaning

has touched him, he will surely say, "The evils are passed away from me." Surely he is joyful, proud.

Forgiveness is the result of patience and good works.

[11]Except those who were patient and did good deeds, those have forgiveness and a big wage. [12]So perhaps you are leaving some of what is being revealed to you, and your chest is stressed by it, that they say, "Were it not that a kanz[a] had been sent down on him or an angel came with him." Surely you are only a warner, and Allah is guardian over all things.

The Qur'an is the word of Allah because no human can write anything that good.

[13]Or they say, "He has forged it." Say, "So bring ten forged portions of a revelation like it, and call on whom you can rather than Allah if you were truthful." [14]So if they did not answer to you, so know that it is only sent down by Allah's knowledge and that there is no god except him. So are you Muslims? [15]Whoever was desiring the world's life and its ornaments, we will fulfill their works in it, and they will not receive less in it. [16]Those who will have nothing in the hereafter except the fire, and what they have done in it will come to nothing. And vain is what they were doing. [17]Is he who was with a proof from his lord and recite it a witness from him and from before him the book of Moses, a guide and a mercy? Those believe in it, and whoever becomes an infidel in it among the parties, so the fire is his promise. So do not be in doubt about it, surely it is the truth from your lord, but most people do not believe. [18]And who is more unjust than the one who forged a lie against Allah? Those will be brought before their lord, and the witnesses will say, "Those are who lied against their lord." Is not Allah's curse on the unjust. [19]Those who prevent [others] from the way of Allah and seek to make it crooked, and they are in the hereafter, they are infidels. [20]Those were not escaping on the earth, and there was not a friend to them other than Allah. The torment will be doubled for them. They were not able to hear, and they were not seeing. [21]Those who have lost their own souls and what they were forging strayed away from them. [22]No doubt, surely in the hereafter, they are the biggest losers. [23]Surely those who believed and did good deeds and akabat[b] before their lord, those are the companions of the garden, they will abide in it forever. [24]The likeness of the two groups is as the blind and the deaf and the sighted and the hearing. Are they equally alike? Do you not remember?

---

[a] treasure, non-Arabic word of Middle Persian/Aramaic origin
[b] a word without meaning, Muslim scholars claim it to be fear, humble, return, reassured, obedient, or humility

The story of Noah was copied from the Bible and corrupted once again.

[25]And indeed, we sent Noah to his people: "Surely I am to you a plain warner, [26]that you do not serve except Allah. Surely I fear a painful torment day for you." [27]So the leaders of those who became infidels from his people said, "We do not see you except a human like us, and we do not see any who follow you except they are the lowliest of us at first thought. And we do not see that you have any favor over us, yet we think you are liars." [28]He said, "O my people, have you seen that if I were with a proof from my lord and he has given me mercy from himself, so it was hidden from you, can we force it on you while you hate it? [29]And, O my people, I do not ask you money for it, that my wage is only except on Allah. And I will not drive away those who believed, surely they will meet their lord. But I see that you are an ignorant people. [30]And, O my people, who will give me help against Allah if I drive them away, do you not remember? [31]And I will not say to you that with me are the treasuries of Allah, nor will I know the unseen, and I will not say that I am an angel, and I will not say to those whom your eyes scorn that Allah will not bring them good. Allah knows best what is in their souls. Then surely I would be of the unjust." [32]They said, "O Noah, indeed, you have disputed with us, so you dispute much with us. So bring on us what you promise us, if you were of the truthful." [33]He said, "Surely only Allah will bring it to you if he wills, and you will not be able to escape. [34]And my advice will not profit you, if I desire to advise you, if Allah was desiring to seduce you. He is your lord, and to him you will return." [35]Or do they say, "He forged it"? Say, "If I have forged it, so my crime is on me. And I am innocent from the crimes you commit." [36]And it was revealed to Noah: "That none of your people will believe except those who have believed, so do not grieve at what they were doing. [37]And make the ship by our eyes and our revelation. And do not speak to me about the unjust, surely they will be drowned." [38]And while making the ship, whenever leaders of his people passed by, they scorned him. He said, "If you scorn us, surely we will scorn you as you scorn. [39]So you will know who will receive torment, it will shame him and will dwell on him, a lasting torment." [40]Until when our command came and the tannūr[a] gushed up.[b] We said, "Carry in it from every pair two and your family, except against whom the word has already gone forth, and those who believed." And no one believes in him, except a few. [41]And he said, "Embark in it. In the name of Allah, its sailing and its anchoring. Surely my lord is forgiving, merciful."

---

[a] oven, non-Arabic word of Persian or Akkadian or Aramaic origin
[b] like froth on milk

Noah's son refused to enter the ship and drowned. This contradicts the Bible. Also, the mountain was Mount Ararat not Al Joudi. See Genesis 5:29-10:32.

[42]And it[a] sailed on with them amid waves like mountains. And Noah called to his son, and he was apart: "O my son, embark with us and do not be with the infidels." [43]He said, "I will take refuge to a mountain that will secure me from the water." He said, "No one will be secure today from the command of Allah except him on whom he will have mercy." And the waves passed between them, so he was among the drowned. [44]And it was said, "O earth, swallow up your water," and "O heaven, desist." And the water abated, and the command was fulfilled. And the ship sat on the Jūdī,[b] and it was said, "Away with the unjust people." [45]And Noah called on his lord, so he said, "My lord, surely my son is of my family, and surely your promise is true. And you are the wisest of the judges." [46]He said, "O Noah, surely he is not of your family, surely he did what is not good. So do not ask what you have no knowledge of. Surely I preach to you, lest you become of the ignorant." [47]He said, "My lord, surely I seek refuge in you, that I ask you of what I do not have knowledge. And unless you forgive me and be merciful to me, I will be of the losers." [48]It was said, "O Noah, go down with peace from us and blessings on you and on nations who are with you. And nations, we will give them enjoyment. Then we will afflict them with a painful torment." [49]This is some of the news of the unseen; we reveal it to you. You did not know it, neither your people before this, so be patient. Surely the end is to the fearer.

The story of Ad, made up by Mohammed, is repeated again.

[50]And to Ad, their brother Houd said, "O my people, serve Allah. You have no god other than him. That you are only forgers. [51]O my people, I do not ask you a wage for it, for my wage is only from him who created me. Do you not understand? [52]And, O my people, ask forgiveness of your lord, then repent to him. He will send down the heaven on you with abundant and increase you power over your power, and do not turn away, criminals." [53]They said, "O Houd, you have not brought us proof. And we will not abandon our gods at your word, and we are not believers in you. [54]We say that some of our gods have smitten you with evil." He said, "Surely I witness Allah. And surely I witness that I am innocent of what you partner [55]without him, so all of you together scheme against me, then you will not be delayed. [56]Surely I depend on Allah, my lord and your lord. There is not a creature except he takes it by her forelock. Surely, my lord is

---

[a] the ship
[b] mountain in Mesopotamia near Mosul, non-Arabic word of possible Syriac origin

on a straight way. [57]So if you turn away, so indeed, I have delivered to you what I was sent with to you. And my lord will raise a successor nation other than you, and you will not harm him anything. Surely my lord is a keeper over all things." [58]And when our command came, we delivered Houd and those who believed with him with a mercy from us, and we delivered them from a thick[a] torment. [59]And this was Ad. They disbelieved in the verses of their lord and rebelled against his messengers and followed the command of every powerful stubborn. [60]And they followed a curse in this world and on the resurrection day. Is it not surely Ad became infidels of their lord, except away with Ad, the people of Houd.

The story of Themoud, made up by Mohammed, is repeated again.

[61]And to Themoud, their brother Saleh said, "O my people, serve Allah. You have no god other than him. He brought you forth from the earth and has settled you in it. So ask forgiveness of him, then repent to him, surely my lord is near answering." [62]They said, "O Saleh, indeed, you were among us and hope was in you before that. Do you forbid us to serve that which our fathers serve? And surely we are in grave doubt of what you are calling us to." [63]He said, "O my people, have you seen that if I were with a proof from my lord, and he gave me from him mercy? So who will help me against Allah if I disobey him? So you will not increase me other than loss. [64]And, O my people, this is Allah's camel, a sign to you. So let her eat in Allah's earth, and do not touch her with evil, so you will be overtaken with a near torment." [65]So they hamstrung her. So he said, "Enjoy [yourself] in your home for three days; this promise will not be denied." [66]So when our command came, we delivered Saleh and those who believed with him, with mercy from us, from disgrace on that day. Surely your lord is the strong, the dear. [67]And the shout seized those who did injustice, so they became motionless in their homes, [68]as if they had never dwelt in it in riches. Is it not surely Themoud became infidels of their lord, except away with Themoud.

The story of Abraham is copied from the Bible and corrupted. Notice that Sarah laughs in verse 71, which contradicts her reaction in verse 51:29 where she slaps her face. See the original true account of Abraham in Genesis 11-25.

[69]And indeed, our messengers came to Abraham with good news. They said, "Peace." He said, "Peace." So he did not delay, but brought a haneez[b] calf. [70]So when he saw that their hands did not reach out to it, he disliked them and grew fearful of them. They said,

---

[a] great
[b] a word without meaning, but Muslim scholars claim it means roasted.

"Do not fear, surely we are sent to the people of Lot." [71]And his woman [wife] was standing by so she laughed. So we gave her the good news of Isaac and after Isaac, Jacob. [72]She said, "Oh, woe is to me! Will I bear a son when I am old and when my husband is old? Surely this is a wonderful thing." [73]They said, "Do you wonder at the command of Allah? The mercy of Allah and his blessings are on you, the people of the house. Surely he is praised, glorious." [74]So when Abraham's fear had gone and the good news had reached him, he disputed with us for the people of Lot. [75]Surely Abraham was meek, awah,[a] often turning. [76]"O Abraham, leave this. Surely indeed, the command of your lord came, and surely the torment will come to them. It will not be turned back."

The story of Lot is copied from the Bible and corrupted. See Genesis 19.

[77]And when our messengers came to Lot, he was troubled because of them. And his arm was tight,[b] and he said, "This is a dreadful day." [78]And his people came hastily toward him, for before they were doing the evils." He said, "O my people, these are my daughters. They are pure for you, so fear Allah, and do not put me to shame to my guests. Is there not among you a man with a right mind?" [79]They said, "Indeed, you know we have no rights to your daughters, and surely you well know what we want." [80]He said, "Would that I had power to resist you or could seek a refuge with a strong supporter." [81]They said, "O Lot, surely we are messengers of your lord. They will not reach to you, so depart with your family a part of the night, and no one of you turn around except your woman [wife]. Surely it will befall on her what will befall on them. Surely their appointed time is in the morning. Is not the morning near?" [82]So when our command came, we made on it its bottom.[c] And we rained down on them rocks of sijjīl,[d] one after another, [83]marked from your lord. And it is not far from the unjust.

The story of Midian, made up by Mohammed, is repeated once again.

[84]And to Midian, their brother Shoaib said, "O my people, serve Allah. You have no god other than him, do not lessen the measure and the weights. Surely I see you are fine, and surely I fear for you the torment of an encompassing day. [85]And, O my people, give full in the measure and the weights with fairness, and do not defraud the people their things. And do not act wickedly in the land, vandalizing.

---

[a] a word without meaning
[b] frustrated because he could not protect them
[c] turned upside down
[d] baked clay, non-Arabic word of Persian origin

[86]What abides with Allah is better for you if you were believers, and I am not a keeper over you." [87]They said, "O Shoaib, does your prayer command you that we should leave what our fathers served or that we do with our money as pleases us? Surely you are the forbearing, the right mind." [88]He said, "O my people, have you seen that if I were with a proof from my lord and he provides for me an excellent provision from him? And I do not want to disagree with you about what he has forbidden you of. That I desire except the reform of which I am able, and my success is not except by Allah, on him I depend and to him I turn. [89]And, O my people, let not my disagreement with you cause you to be stricken as what struck Noah's people or Houd's people or Saleh's people. And the people of Lot are not far from you. [90]And ask forgiveness of your lord, then repent to him. Surely my lord is merciful, friendly." [91]They said, "O Shoaib, we do not understand much of what you say, and we surely see that you are weak among us. And were it not for your family, we surely would have stoned you, and you are not dear to us." [92]He said, "O my people, is my family dearer to you than Allah? And you cast him behind your back. Surely my lord surrounds what you do. [93]And, O my people, do what you are able, surely I will do. You will know who will receive torment which will disgrace him and who is the liar. And watch, surely I am a watcher with you." [94]And when our command came, we delivered Shoaib and those who believed with him, with mercy from us. And a shout seized the unjust, so they became motionless in their homes. [95]As if they had never dwelt in it in riches, is it not away with the Midian, as away with Themoud.

The story of Moses and Pharaoh is copied from the Bible and corrupted once again.

[96]And indeed, we sent Moses with our signs and with a manifest authority [97]to Pharaoh and his leaders, so they followed the command of Pharaoh. And the command of Pharaoh was not right. [98]He will head his people on the resurrection day, so he gave them to the fire. And evil is the entry which they are entering. [99]And they were followed a curse in this and the resurrection day; evil is the gift that will be given. [100]This is some of the news of the villages we relate to you. Some of them are standing and reaped. [101]And we did not treat them unjustly, but they treated themselves unjustly, so their gods on whom they called rather than Allah did not profit them at all. When your lord's command came, they did not increase them except in ruin. [102]And likewise, your lord seized, if he seizes the villages while they are unjust. Surely his seizing is painful, severe. [103]Surely in this is a sign to him who fears the torment of the hereafter. That is a day all people will be gathered to it, and this is a witnessed day. [104]And we do not delay it, except for the calculated time. [105]A day will come when a soul will not talk, except with his permission, so some

of them are wretched and happy. [106]So as for those who are rich, so in the fire they will have in it, inhaling and exhaling. [107]They will abide in it forever, as long as the heavens and the earth will endure, except what your lord wills. Surely your lord is the doer of what he wants. [108]And as for the happy, so in the garden, they will abide in it forever, as long as the heavens and the earth endure, except what your lord wills, a gift which will never stop. [109]So do not be in doubt concerning that which they serve; they do not serve except like what their fathers serve before, and surely we will pay back their portion without reduction. [110]And indeed, we gave Moses the book, so they disagree about it. And were it not that a word had gone forth from your lord, he would have judged between them, and surely they are in grave doubt about it. [111]And surely your lord will repay each their works, surely he is aware of what they do. [112]So stand straight as you have been commanded and who repented with you, and do not exceed the limit. Surely he sees what you do. [113]Do not lean toward the unjust, so the fire will touch you. And you do not have any friends other than Allah, then you will not be helped.

Good deeds wipe away evil deeds.

[114]And perform the prayer at the two edges of the day and at the approach of night. Surely good deeds drive away the evil deeds. This is a reminder to those who remember. [115]And be patient, so surely Allah will not waste the wage of the doers of good. [116]So were it not that some of the generation before you, who possessed favor forbiding against the vandalizing on the earth, except a few from whom we delivered among them. And those unjust followed what they made to enjoy in it, and they were criminals. [117]And your lord was not to destroy the villages unjustly, and their people were reformers.

Allah chose to create some people who would not be Muslims just to fill hell with them.

[118]And if your lord willed, he would have made the people one nation. And they are still different, [119]except whom your lord has given mercy, and that is why he created them. And the word of your lord has been fulfilled: "I will surely fill hell with the jinn and the people together." [120]And all that we have related to you of the news of the messengers is to strengthen your heart with it. And in these the truth has come to you, and a sermon and a reminder to the believers. [121]And say to those who do not believe, "Do whatever you can, surely we are doing. [122]And wait, surely we are waiting. [123]And to Allah, the unseen of the heavens and the earth, and to him all the affair will return. So serve him and depend on him. And your lord is not unaware of what you do."

A portion of a revelation   *Joseph*

In the name of Allah, the merciful, the merciful

[1]Alr.[a] These are verses of the clear book. [2]Surely we have sent it down, an Arabic Qur'an, perhaps you might understand. [3]We narrate to you the best of the stories by which we reveal to you this Qur'an, and before it you were among the unaware.

The story of Joseph is copied from the Bible and corrupted. See Genesis 35-50. Notice that Pharaoh is not mentioned. Mohammed was apparently confused about the ruler's title.

[4]When Joseph said to his father, "O my father, surely I saw eleven stars and the sun and the moon. I saw them worshiping me." [5]He said, "O my son, do not relate your dream to your brothers, so they plot a plot against you. Surely Satan is an obvious enemy to the human." [6]And likewise, your lord will choose you and will teach you the interpretation of the sayings and will fulfill his grace on you and on the family of Jacob as he fulfilled it before on your fathers Abraham and Isaac. Surely your lord is knowing, wise. [7]Indeed, it was in Joseph and his brothers, signs for the inquirers. [8]When they said, "Surely Joseph and his brother are more loved by our father than us, and we are a large group. Surely our father is in obvious error. [9]Kill Joseph or throw him to a land, and to you your father's face will be set, and after this, you will become a good people." [10]A speaker among them said, "Do not kill Joseph, and cast him down to the bottom of the jubb.[b] Some travelers will pick him up if you were doing." [11]They said, "O our father, why do you not trust us with Joseph? And surely we will be advisers to him. [12]Send him with us tomorrow so that he may enjoy and play, and surely we will be keepers to him." [13]He said, "Surely it will grieve me if you take him, and I fear that the wolf will eat him while you are not watching him." [14]They said, "If the wolf eats him, and we are many, surely then we are losers." [15]So when they had gone with him and they agreed to place him at the bottom of the well, and we revealed to him: "You will inform them of this, their affair." And they did not feel.

This is the sad news of Joseph's death and his father's indifference.

---

[a] a word containing three Arabic letters without meaning
[b] well, non-Arabic word, of Aramaic origin

[16]And they came at evening to their father weeping. [17]They said, "O our father, surely we went away racing, and we left Joseph with our goods. So the wolf ate him, and you will not believe us even if we were truthful." [18]And they put on his qamīs[a] with a lie [false] blood. He said, "Yet, your soul lightens the affair. So patience is beautiful, and Allah is the one who is asked for assistance about what you describe."

The discovery and sale of Joseph by the travelers (not Joseph's brothers, as recorded in the Bible) is told here.

[19]And a traveler came there, and so they sent a drawer of water, so he let down his bucket. He said, "Good news, here is a young man!" And they hid him merchandise.[b] And Allah knew in what they are doing. [20]And they bought him for a lesser price of a numbered dirham,[c] and they were not interested in him. [21]And he who bought him in Egypt said to his woman [wife], "Treat him generously, perhaps he may be useful to us, or maybe we can take him a son." And likewise, we did settle Joseph in the land, and we will teach him the interpretation of the sayings. And Allah has victory over his affair, but most people do not know. [22]And when he had reached his age of strength, we gave him judgment and knowledge, and likewise, we reward the doers of good.

The attemped seduction of Joseph and the response of the husband.

[23]The one whom he stayed with in her house sought to seduce him. And she closed the doors, and she said, "I am prepared for you." He said, "Allah's refuge! Surely he is my lord who treats me good, surely the unjust will not prosper." [24]And indeed, she moved to him, and he moved to her,[d] were it not that he saw his lord's[e] proof. Likewise, we averted him from committing the evil and indecency, surely he is of our sincere servants. [25]And they ran for the door, and she tore his shirt behind. And at the door they met her master. She said, "What is the penalty for one who would desire to do evil to your people, except to be put in prison or a painful torment?" [26]He said, "She sought to seduce me." And a witness from her family testified, "If his shirt was torn in the front, so she is truthful, and he is of the liars. [27]And if his shirt was torn from behind, so she lied, and he is of the truthful." [28]So when his lord saw his shirt torn behind, he said, "Surely this is one of your devices, surely your devices are great."

---

[a] shirt, non-Arabic word of Greek/Syriac origin
[b] meaning as an article of merchandise
[c] a coin, non-Arabic word of Greek origin
[d] with lust
[e] her husband's

[29]"Joseph, turn away from this, and[a] ask forgiveness for your sins, surely you were among the sinners."

This describes the gossip by the women and the imprisonment of Joseph.

[30]And the women of the city said, "The woman [wife] of Al-'Aziz has sought to seduce her young man. He has infatuated her with love, surely we see her in obvious error." [31]So when she heard of their deceit, she sent for them and prepared a banquet for them and gave each one of them a sikkin.[b] And she said, "Joseph, come out to them." So when they saw him, they were amazed at him and cut their hands and said, "Allah forbid. This is not a human. This is but a generous angel." [32]She said, "This is he about whom you blamed me. And indeed, I sought to seduce him, so he refused. But if he does not do what I command him, he surely will be imprisoned and be of the disgraced." [33]He said, "My lord, the prison is more loved by me than that which they call me to. And if you do not turn away their devices from me, I will lean toward them, and I will become of the foolish." [34]So his lord answered him, so he took away their devices from him. Surely he is the hearing, the knowing. [35]Then it occurred to them, after they saw the signs, to imprison him for a time. [36]And entered into the prison with him two young men. One of them said, "Surely I saw myself pressing wine." And the other said, "Surely I saw myself carrying khubz[c] above my head, the birds eat from it. Inform us of its interpretation, surely we see that you are of the doers of good." [37]He said, "You will not be provided with food, but I will inform you of its interpretation before it will come to you. This is a part of that which my lord has taught me, surely I have left the religion of people who do not believe in Allah and in the hereafter. They are infidels. [38]And I follow the religion of my fathers, Abraham and Isaac and Jacob, and it was not for us to partner with Allah anything. This is a favor from Allah on us and on the people, but most people do not give thanks. [39]O my two companions of the prison, are disunited lords better, or Allah, the one, the dominant? [40]You do not serve other than him, except names you have named them, you and your fathers; Allah has not sent down with them any authority. That the judgment but to Allah. [He] orders to serve no one but him. This is the right religion, but most people do not know. [41]O my two companions of the prison, as for one of you, so he will give a drink of wine to his lord; but as to the other, so he will be crucified, so the birds will eat from his head. This affair is decreed concerning in which you were consulting me." [42]And he said to the one whom he thought would be delivered, "Remember me to your lord." So Satan

---

[a] addressing the wife
[b] knife, non-Arabic word of Aramaic/Syriac origin
[c] bread, non-Arabic word of Ethiopian origin

caused him to forget the remembrance to his lord, so he abided some years in prison.

This describes the story of the king's dream and Joseph's interpretation while he was still in prison.

[43]And the king said, "Surely I see seven fat cows consumed by seven lean cows and seven green heads of grain and others dried. O you the leaders, consult with me of my dream, if you were interpreters of dreams." [44]They said, "Confused dream. And we do not know the interpretation of dreams." [45]And the one who was delivered of them and remembered after a while said, "I will inform you its interpretation, so send me." [46]"Joseph, O the truthful, consult with us of the seven fat cows which the seven lean consumed and of the seven green heads of grain and others dried; perhaps I may return to the people, perhaps they may know." [47]He said, "You will sow seven years continually. So whatever you hasada,[a] so leave in its heads of grain except a little of what you eat. [48]Then after that will come seven hard years, will consume what you have stored for them except a little of what you will have stored. [49]Then will come after this a year in which people will have rain and in it they will press." [50]And the king said, "Bring him to me." So when the messenger came to him, he said, "Return to your lord, so ask him what the women meant who cut their hands, surely my lord knows well their devices." [51]He said, "What was your purpose when you sought to seduce Joseph?" They said, "Allah forbid. We do not know any evil of him. The woman [wife] of Al-'Aziz said, 'Now the truth hashas.[b] I sought to seduce him, and he is surely of the truthful.'" [52]"That he might know that I have not cheated him in secret, and surely Allah does not guide the device of the betrayers. [53]And I do not declare myself innocent, surely the self commands with the evil, except for those on whom my lord has mercy. Surely my lord is forgiving, merciful." [54]And the king said, "Bring him to me. I will take him for myself." So when he had spoken with him, he said, "Surely today you are with us in a prominent position, secure." [55]He said, "Set me over the treasuries of the land, surely I am a keeper, knowledgeable." [56]And likewise, we established for Joseph in the land that he may choose from it whatever he wills. We give our mercy to whom we will, and we do not waste the wage of the doers of good. [57]And the wage of the hereafter is better to those who believed and were fearers.

---

[a] reap, non-Arabic word of Aramaic origin
[b] a word without meaning

The reunion of Joseph and his brothers is told here.

[58]And Joseph's brothers came, so they entered to him. So he knew them, and they were unaware of him. [59]And when he had provided them with their provision, he said, "Bring me a brother of you from your father. Do you not see that I fill the measure and I am the best of hosts? [60]So if you do not bring him to me, so no measure will there be for you from me, nor will you come near me." [61]They said, "We will persuade his father of him, and we will surely do that." [62]And he said to his young men, "Put their merchandise into their bags. Perhaps they may know it when they return to their family; perhaps they will come back." [63]So when they returned to their father, they said, "O our father, we have been denied our measure, so send our brother with us. And we will have our measure, and surely we will be keepers to him." [64]He said, "Will I entrust you with him except as I entrusted you before with his brother? So Allah is the best keeper, and he is the most merciful of the merciful." [65]And when they opened their bags, they found their merchandise had been returned to them. They said, "O our father, we did not desire that our merchandise would be returned to us. We will bring food to our families, and we will keep our brother and will increase a ba'ir[a] measure. This is an easy measure." [66]He said, "I will not send him with you until you bring to me a firm oath from Allah that you will return him back to me unless you are constrained." So when they brought him their pledge, he said, "Allah is the guardian above what we say." [67]And he said, "O my sons, do not enter by one door. And enter by different doors, and yet I cannot profit you against anything decreed by Allah, for the judgment to Allah alone. On him I depend, and on him, so let the depender depend."

Joseph reveals to his brother (which one?) at the time of the brothers' arrival in Egypt that he is his brother. However, the brothers seem to be unaware of this fact during the rest of these verses.

[68]And when they entered as their father had commanded them, it was not averted from them anything against Allah, but it only served to satisfy a need in the soul of Jacob. And surely he was possessed of knowledge we had taught him, but most people do not know. [69]And when they entered unto Joseph, he took his brother to him. He said, "Surely I am your brother. So do not grieve for what they were doing." [70]So when he had provided them with their supplies, he placed his drinking vessel in his brother's pack. Then a caller called, "O travelers, surely you are thieves!" [71]They said, and they turned back to them, "What did you miss?" [72]They said, "We miss the king's

---

[a] camel, non-Arabic word of Syriac origin

suwā.[a] And to him who will restore it a camel's load, and I guarantee it." [73]They said, "[We swear] by Allah, indeed, you know we did not come to vandalize in the land. And we were not thieves." [74]They said, "So what is the penalty if you were liars?" [75]They said, "His penalty for the one in whose pack you find it, so he is the penalty. Likewise, we reward the unjust." [76]So he began with their bags before his brother's bag. And then he drew it out from his brother's bag. Likewise, we schemed for Joseph that he was not to take his brother into the judgment of the king, except if Allah wills. We raise degrees of whom we will, and above everyone with knowledge more knowledgeable. [77]They said, "If he has stolen, so indeed, his brother has stolen before." So Joseph kept it secret in his soul and did not disclose it to them. He said, "You are in an evil position, and Allah knows what you describe." [78]They said, "O you the dear, surely he has a very aged father. So take one of us instead of him, surely we see that you are of the doers of good." [79]He said, "Allah's refuge! That we should take anyone but him with whom our property was found, for then we should act unjustly." [80]So when they had lost hope of him, they went and spoke privately. The oldest of them said, "Did you not know that your father, indeed, has taken a firm oath from you before Allah and how formerly you failed in your duty with regard to Joseph? So I will not depart the land until my father gives me permission, or may Allah judge for me, and he is the best of the judges. [81]Return to your father, so say, 'O our father, surely your son has stolen. We bear witness only of what we knew; and we were not a keeper to the unseen. [82]And ask the village which we were in and of the caravan with which we have arrived, and surely we are truthful.'" [83]He said, "Yet, you have arranged all this affair among yourselves. So patience is beautiful, perhaps Allah will bring all of them to me. Surely he is the knowing, the wise."

Jacob cries for Joseph, instead of Benjamin, even though he knows Joseph is alive.

[84]And he turned away from them and said, "Oh, my sorrow for Joseph," and his eyes became white from the grief so he was full of anger. [85]They said, "[We swear] by Allah, you will continue to remember Joseph until you are very sick or you be among the perished." [86]He said, "Surely I only complain about my sorrow and grief to Allah, and I know from Allah what you do not know. [87]O my sons, go and inquire of Joseph and his brother and do not give up hope from the spirit of Allah. Surely no one will give up hope from the spirit of Allah except the infidel people." [88]So when they entered into

---

[a] drinking cup, non-Arabic word of Ethiopian origin-same word as from the story of Joseph in the Ethiopian Bible

him, they said, "O you the dear, distress has touched us and our family, and we brought deficient merchandise. So fulfill to us the measure, and be charitable to us. Surely Allah will reward the charitable." [89]He said, "Do you know what you have done to Joseph and his brother when you were ignorant?" [90]They said, "Are you surely Joseph?" He said, "I am Joseph, and this is my brother. Indeed, Allah has been gracious to us. Surely who fears and is patient, so surely Allah will not lose the wage of the doers of good." [91]They said, "[We swear] by Allah indeed. Allah exalted you above us, and that we were surely sinners." [92]He said, "No sin will be on you today. Allah will forgive you, and he is the most merciful of the merciful.

This is the story of the sorcery shirt.

[93]Go with this my shirt, so throw it on my father's face, and he will recover his sight. And bring me all your family." [94]And when the caravan departed, their father said, "I surely found the smell of Joseph, were it not that you refute it." [95]They said, "[We swear] by Allah, you are surely in your old error." [96]So when the bearer of good news came, he cast it on his face, so he regained his sight. He said, "Did I not say to you that surely I knew from Allah what you do not know?" [97]They said, "O our father, ask forgiveness for our sins, surely we were sinners." [98]He said, "I will ask my lord to forgive you. Surely he is the forgiving, the merciful."

Joseph speaks to his father and to his mother (who, according to the Bible, is actually deceased) and welcomes them into Egypt to become royalty.

[99]And when they entered to Joseph, he lodged his parents with him, and said, "Enter Egypt, if Allah is willing, in security." [100]And he raised his parents to the throne, and they fell down worshiping him. And he said, "O my father, this is the interpretation of my previous dream. Indeed, my lord has now made it true, and he has indeed been good to me, since he took me out of the prison and has brought you from the Bedouins. After that, Satan had stirred up strife between me and my brothers. Surely my lord is kind to whom he wills. Surely he is the knowing, the wise. [101]My lord, indeed, you have given to me from the kingdom and have taught me the interpretation of the sayings. Creator of the heavens and the earth, you are my friend in this world and the hereafter. Cause me to die a Muslim, and gather me with the good." [102]This is some of the news of the unseen that we reveal unto you. You were not with them when they gathered their affair, and they were deceivers. [103]And most people, even if you are careful, are not believers. [104]You do not ask of them any wage for it. It is not but a reminder to the worlds. [105]And how many signs in the heavens and the earth, they pass by it, and they turn away from

it. [106]And most of them do not believe in Allah, but they are polytheists. [107]Do they feel secure from receiving the covering of the torment of Allah, or the hour will come to them suddenly, and they will not feel? [108]Say, "This is my way. I call to Allah, with acknowledgement, I and those who follow me. And praise be to Allah, and I am not of the polytheists."

All messengers who came before Mohammed were inspired from God which proves that the Bible is the inspired Word of God. (That is assuming that God is Allah as Muslims claim.)

[109]And we did not send before you, except men whom we revealed to them from the people of the villages. Have they not walked on the earth so they see how was the end of those who were before them? And the home of the hereafter is best to the fearer. Do you not understand? [110]Until when the messengers gave up hope and they thought, they indeed were denied, our victory came to them, so delivered whom we will. And our torment was not turned away from the criminal people. [111]Indeed, in their stories there was a lesson to those who have understanding. It was not a forged saying,

but a confirmation to what is between his hands and an exposition on all things and a guidance and a mercy to believing people.

A portion of a revelation   **13**   *The Thunder*

In the name of Allah, the merciful, the merciful

[1]Almr.[a] These are the verses of the book and that which has been sent down to you from your lord, the truth, but most people do not believe.

Heaven is a structure. The earth is flat and does not move, but the sun and moon each travel. See also verses 15:19; 16:15; 20:53; and 31:10.

[2]Allah is who lifted up the heavens without 'imād.[b] You see it, then he sat on the throne, and he made the sun and the moon subservient, each traveled to its named time. He arranges the affairs. He explains the verses; perhaps you may be certain of meeting your

---

[a] a word containing four Arabic letters without meaning
[b] columns, non-Arabic word of Akkadian/Aramaic origin

lord. [3]And he is who has spread the earth and put stabilizers[a] on it, and rivers and of every fruit he has placed on it two pairs. He makes the night to cover the day. Surely in this are signs to people who reflect. [4]And on the earth are plots next to each other and gardens of grapes and plants and palm trees, with split trunks and without split trunks. They water by one water, and we prefer some of them over the others in the eating. Surely in this are signs for people who understand. [5]And if you wonder, so wonder their saying: "What if we were dust, will we be a new creature?" Those who became infidels in their lord, and those are the chains on their necks. And those are the companions of the fire, and they will abide in it forever. [6]And they will hasten you with the evil before the good, and indeed, punishment was passed before them. And surely your lord is the possessor of forgiveness to people for their injustices. And surely your lord is severe in the punishment. [7]And those who became infidels say, "Were it not that a sign had been sent down on him from his lord." Surely you are only a warner. And to every people is a guide.

According to Muslim scholars, women can be pregnant for a length of time from six months up to four years.[b]

[8]Allah knows what every female bears, and how much their womb lessens and enlarges. And with him everything is by measure. [9]The knower of the unseen and the seen, the big, the highest. [10]It is the same to some of you who hide the saying or speak it loudly, and who hides himself by night and goes forth by day.

Allah will accept only good people after people change themselves.

[11]To him shifts [angels] from between his hands and from behind him, they keep him from the command of Allah. Surely Allah will not change what is in a people until they change what is in themselves. And if Allah wants evil for people, so there is none to avert it. And they do not have a friend other than him. [12]He is who shows you the lightning fearing and hoping and brings up the heavy clouds.

The thunder is angels worshiping Allah.

[13]And the thunder praises with his praise, and the angels, for fear of him. And he sends his thunderbolts, so he smites with it whom he wills while they dispute concerning Allah. And he is severe in prowess. [14]To him is the call of truth. And those who call on other than him, they will not answer them at all, except like as the one who opens his hand toward the water that it may reach his mouth. And it

---

[a] Islamic scholars claim this to mean mountains.
[b] See website: http://quran.al-islam.com/Page.aspx?pageid=221&BookID=14&Page=250, accessed 12/10/2008.

will not reach it. And what is the call of the infidels, except in error. [15]And to Allah, worship all who are in the heavens and the earth, willingly and grudgingly, and their shadows also, morning and evening. [16]Say, "Who is the lord of the heavens and the earth?" Say, "Allah." Say, "Have you then taken friends other than him who do not own to themselves profit or harm themselves?" Say, "Are the blind and the sighted equal, or are the darkness and the light equal? Or have they made partners to Allah who have created as he has created so that their creations appear to them like his?" Say, "Allah is the creator of all things, and he is the one, the dominant." [17]He sent down water from the heaven, so the valleys flow with its measure, so the flood bears along a swelling foam. And from it, that which is molten in the fire for the sake of ornaments or utensils arises a scum like it. Likewise, Allah will set forth the truth and the vanity. So as to the scum, so it is gone in vain. And as to what is useful to the people, so it abides on the earth; likewise, Allah sets forth the parables. [18]To those who answer to their lord, the good, and to those who did not answer to him, if they have what is on the earth together and like it with it, they would give it for their ransom. Those will have the evil reckoning. And hell will be their abode, and evil is the bed. [19]Is the one who knows that the truth has come down to you from your lord like the one who was blind? Surely only the ones with understanding remember. [20]Those who fulfill the promise of Allah and do not break the covenant. [21]And those who join what Allah commanded with to be joined and fear their lord and fear the evil of the reckoning. [22]And those who patiently seek the face of their lord and perform the prayer and spend from what we provided them secretly and publicly and turn away the evil with the good, to those the reward of the final home. [23]Eden's gardens they will enter it with the good among their fathers and their wives and their descendants. And the angels will enter on them from every door. [24]Peace be on you because of your patience, so blessed is the final home. [25]And those who break the covenant of Allah after its confirmation and cut what Allah has commanded to be joined and vandalize on the earth, those will have the curse and will have an evil home. [26]Allah expands and measures the provision to whom he wills. And they rejoice with the world's life. And what is the world's life in the hereafter except enjoyment.

Allah deliberately misleads those whom he chooses.

[27]And those who became infidels say, "Were it not that a sign had been sent down on him from his lord." Say, "Surely Allah misleads whom he wills, and he guides to himself those who turn." [28]Those who believed and whose hearts are secure within the remembrance of Allah. Is it not by the remembrance of Allah the hearts are secure!

[29]Those who believed and did good deeds, tūbā[a] be to them and a good return. [30]Likewise, we sent you to a nation. Indeed, other nations have preceded so that you might recite to them what we revealed to you, and they are becoming infidels in the merciful. Say, "He is my lord. There is no god but him. On him I depend, and to him I return." [31]And if there is a Qur'an by which the mountains could be made to move or the earth to be cut by it or the dead spoken to by it, yet to Allah is all the affair. Did not those who believed despair that if Allah wills he would guide all the people? And still those who became infidels will be afflicted with calamity because of what they have done, or disaster may fall closer to their homes, until the promise of Allah comes. Surely Allah does not change the promise. [32]And indeed, they scoffed at my messengers before you, so I delayed to those who became infidels, then I seized them. So how was my punishment! [33]Is he who stands above every soul because of what it earns and made to Allah partners? Say, "Name them or inform them of what they do not know on the earth or what is revealed from the saying." Yet their deception is beautified for those who became infidels, and they were prevented from the way. And whom Allah leads astray, so he will have no guide. [34]To them is the torment in the world's life, and the torment of the hereafter is harder. And they have no protector from Allah. [35]The parable of the garden which the fearer has been promised: rivers flow under it, its food and its shade are permanent. This is the end of the fearer, and the end of the infidels is the fire. [36]And those to whom we have given the book, rejoice in what has been sent down to you. And some of the parties deny a part of it. Say, "Surely I am only commanded to serve Allah and not to partner with him. To him I do call, and to him my return."

The Qur'an is sent down in the Arabic language. If so, why are there so many foreign words in the Qur'an?

[37]And likewise, we have sent it down, a judgment in the Arabic, and if you follow their desire after what came to you from knowledge, you will not have any friend or protector from Allah. [38]And indeed, we sent messengers before you, and we gave them wives and descendants. And it was not for a messenger to bring a sign except by Allah's permission. For every period is a book.

Allah has a right to erase his words, even though the original copy of the Qur'an is with Allah. This contradicts verse 15:9.

[39]Allah erases what he wills and confirms, and with him is the mother of the book (master copy). [40]And whether we show you some of what we promised them or we cause you to die, so surely your duty is only to deliver. And on us is the reckoning. [41]Or they did not

---

[a] good fortune, non-Arabic word of Syriac origin

see that we come into their land and lessen its borders. And Allah judges, and no one can reverse his judgment. And he is swift in the reckoning. [42]And indeed, those before them deceived, so to Allah all the deception. He knows what every soul earns, and the infidels will know to whom is the reward of the final home. [43]And those who became infidels say, "You are not a missionary." Say, "Allah is a sufficient witness between me and you, and whoever has knowledge of the book."

In the name of Allah, the merciful, the merciful

[1]Alr.[a] A book we have sent down to you that you may bring people out of the darkness into the light, by the permission of their lord, into a way of the dear, the praised. [2]Allah to whom what is in the heavens and what is on the earth, and woe to the infidels from a severe torment. [3]Those who prefer the world's life above the hereafter and prevent [others] from the way of Allah and seek to make it crooked, those are far astray. [4]And we have not sent any messenger except with the tongue (language) of his people to show them. So Allah leads astray whom he wills and guides whom he wills, and he is the dear, the wise.

The story of Moses and Pharaoh is copied from the Bible and is corrupted once again.

[5]And indeed, we sent Moses with our signs: "That bring forth your people from the darkness to the light and remind them of Allah's days." Surely in this are signs to every patient, thankful. [6]And when Moses said to his people, "Remember the grace of Allah on you when he delivered you from the family of Pharaoh, laying on you an evil torment and slaughtering your sons and sparing your women, and in this was a great trial from your lord." [7]And when your lord announced: "If you give thanks, I will surely increase you more; but if you become infidels, surely my torment is severe." [8]And Moses said, "If you and all who are on the earth be infidels, so surely Allah is rich, praised.

---

[a] a word containing three Arabic letters without meaning

They put their hands IN their mouth, not over their ears!

[9]Have you not received the news of those who were before you, the people of Noah and Ad and Themoud, and of those who are after them, no one knows them but Allah? Their messengers came to them with proofs. So they return their hands in their mouths and said, 'Surely we became infidels by what you have been sent with, and surely we are in disturbing doubt of what you call us.'"

Allah will forgive some of their sins. How about the other sins? See also verses 46:31 and 71:4.

[10]Their messengers said, "Is there doubt about Allah, the creator of the heavens and the earth? He calls you to forgive you some of your sins and delays you until an appointed time." They said, "That you are but humans like us, and you desire to prevent us from what our fathers were serving, so bring to us with a manifest authority." [11]Their messengers said to them, "Surely we are but humans like you, but Allah gives favors on whom he wills of his servants. And it was not of us to bring you an authority except by Allah's permission, and on Allah so let the believers depend. [12]And it was not for us except to depend on Allah, and indeed, he guided us in our ways. And we will surely be patient with the harm you put on us, and on Allah, so let the depender depend." [13]And those who became infidels said to their messengers, "We will surely get you out of our land, or you will come back to our religion." So their lord revealed to them: "We will surely destroy the unjust. [14]And surely we will cause you to dwell in the land after them. This is for him who fears my standing and fears my threat." [15]But they sought invasion, and every powerful stubborn was disappointed. [16]Hell will be behind him, and he will be made to drink from pus water. [17]He will drink it sip by sip, and he can barely swallow it. And death will come to him from every place, but he will not die, and behind him, a thick (great) torment. [18]The parable of those who became infidels in their lord, their works are like ashes which the wind scatters on a stormy day. They cannot have anything from what they earned. This is the faraway error. [19]Do you not see that Allah created the heavens and the earth with the truth? If he wills, he could get rid of you and bring a new creation. [20]And this is not dear to Allah. [21]They all went forth before Allah, so the weak said to those who were proud, "Surely we were your followers. So will you then relieve us of some part of the torment of Allah?" They said, "If Allah had guided us, we would have guided you too. It is the same for us whether we be impatient or be patient. We have no escape." [22]And Satan said, when the affair was judged, "Surely Allah promised you a true promise, and I promised you, so I failed you. And it was not for me to have authority over you, except that I called you, so you answered me. So do not blame me, and blame yourselves. I am not crying out for you, and you are not crying out for me. Surely I

became an infidel that you have partnered me before. Surely the unjust will have a painful torment." [23]And those who believed and did good deeds, admitted to the gardens, from below them the rivers flow. They will abide in it forever by the permission of their lord, their greeting in it: "Peace."

The story of the tree is copied from the Bible and twisted into a pseudo-parable. See Psalm 1.

[24]Have you not seen how Allah sets forth a parable of the good word like a good tree, its roots firmly fixed and its branches in the heaven? [25]It brings its fruit all the time by the permission of its lord. Allah sets forth the parables to people, perhaps they may remember. [26]And the parable of an evil word like an evil tree uprooted from the top of the earth, and it has no stability. [27]Allah will strengthen those who believed with a firm word in the world's life and in the hereafter, and Allah leads the unjust astray. And Allah does what he wills. [28]Have you not seen those who change the grace of Allah to infidelity and caused their people to dwell in the home of the perishing? [29]They will roast in hell, and evil is the ending place. [30]And they made rivals to Allah to go astray from his way. Say, "Enjoy, so surely your final place is the fire." [31]Say to my servants who believed, "To perform the prayer and spend from what we provided them, secretly and publicly, before a day comes where there will be no selling in it and no friendship. [32]Allah is who created the heavens and the earth and sent down water from the heaven. So he brought forth by it some of the fruit, a provision for you. And made the ships subservient to you to run in the sea by his command, and he made the rivers subservient to you. [33]And he made the sun and the moon subservient to you continuously and made the night and the day subservient to you. [34]And he gives to you from all of what you ask of him, and if you number the graces of Allah, you cannot count them. Surely the human is unjust, an infidel."

This prayer of Abraham was made-up by Mohammed.

[35]And when Abraham said, "My lord, make this country secure, and protect me and my children lest we serve the idols. [36]My lord, they have surely led astray many of the people. So whoever follows me, so surely he is from me; and whoever disobeys me, so surely you are forgiving, merciful. [37]Our lord, surely I have caused some of my offspring to dwell in a valley which has no plants, near to your forbidden house. Our lord, so that they may perform the prayer, so make the hearts of the people therefore to yearn toward them, and provide them from the fruit, perhaps they may be thankful. [38]Our lord, surely you know what we hide and what we reveal, and there is nothing to be hidden from Allah on the earth, neither in the heaven.

[39]The praise be to Allah who has granted me, in my old age, Ishmael and Isaac. Surely my lord is the hearer of the calling. [40]My lord, make me the performer of prayer and from my offspring. Our lord, and accept my calling. [41]Our lord, forgive me and my parents, and to the believers when the reckoning day will arise." [42]And do not think that Allah is unaware of what the unjust do. Surely he only delays them until a day, which the eyes will look in it. [43]Hastening forward, their heads upraised, their gaze does not return to them, and their hearts air (vacant). [44]And warn the people of a day the torment comes to them, so the unjust will say, "Our lord, delay us for a near time. We will answer your call, and we will follow the messengers." "Were it not that you swore before? There is no ceasing of existence for you." [45]And you dwell in the dwelling of those who were unjust to themselves, and it has appeared clear to you how we dealt with them. And we put forth to you the parables. [46]And indeed, they deceive their deception. And their deception is with Allah, and their deception was such that the mountain would pass away. [47]So do not think that Allah will fail his promise [to] his messengers. Surely Allah is dear, a possessor of revenge. [48]A day the earth will be changed into another earth and the heavens, and they will go forth to Allah, the one, the dominant. [49]And you will see the criminals on that day linked together in chains. [50]Their sirbāl[a] will be of qatirān,[b] and fire will cover their faces. [51]That Allah may reward every soul for what it earned. Surely Allah is swift in the reckoning. [52]This deliver to the people, and let them be warned by it. And that they may know that he is only one god, and to remind the ones with understanding.

A portion of a revelation   15   *The Rock*

In the name of Allah, the merciful, the merciful

[1]Alr.[c] These are the verses of the book and a clear Qur'an.

The infidels will wish they had been Muslims.

[2]Perhaps those who became infidels wish that they were Muslims. [3]Let them eat and enjoy and hope distracts them, so they will know. [4]And we did not destroy a village, except that it had a known written decree. [5]No nation can hasten on their doom nor can they delay it.

---

[a] garments, non-Arabic word of Aramaic origin
[b] pitch, non-Arabic word of Aramaic origin
[c] a word containing three Arabic letters without meaning

Throughout the Qur'an, Mohammed continues to assert that he is not demon-possessed. See verses 26:27; 34:46; 37:36; 44:14; 52:29; 68:2; and 81:22.

[6]And they said, "O you to whom the reminder has been sent down on, surely you are demon-possessed. [7]Why do you not bring to us angels if you were among the truthful?" [8]We will not send down the angels except with the truth. And they were not then delayed.

The Bible cannot be changed. Compare to verses 16:43-44. Also, the stars in the heaven are missiles.

[9]Surely we have sent down the reminder,[a] and surely we will be its keeper. [10]And indeed, we sent before you, in the sects of the ancients. [11]And no messenger came to them, except they were scoffing at him. [12]Likewise, we will instill it into the hearts of the criminals. [13]They do not believe in him, and indeed, the custom of the ancients has passed away. [14]And if we open to them a door from the heaven, they will continue to ascend through it. [15]They would say, "Surely it is only that our eyes are closed, yet we are a bewitched people." [16]And indeed, we have made in the heavens burujan[b] and beautified it to the beholders. [17]And we kept it from every stoned Satan. [18]Except those who eavesdrop, so they are followed by a visible flame.

The earth is flat according to Mohammed.

[19]And the earth, we spread it out and tossed on it stabilizers, and we planted in it from every weighted thing. [20]And we made subsistence in it for you and for those whom you do not give provision. [21]And here is nothing except we have its treasuries with us, and we did not send it down except with known measure. [22]And we send forth the winds as pollinators, so we dropped water from the heaven, so we give you a drink, and you do not store it. [23]And surely we give life, and we cause death. And we are the heirs. [24]And indeed, we know who among you comes before, and indeed, we know who will come later. [25]And surely your lord, he will gather them. Surely he is wise, knowing. [26]And indeed, we created the human from dry mud, from black molded mud. [27]And we created the jinn before from the blazing fire.

Allah commanded angels to worship Adam. The fall of the Devil is told here once again.

---

[a] the Bible
[b] constellations, non-Arabic word of Latin origin

²⁸And when your lord said to the angels, "Surely I am creating a human from dry mud, from black molded mud. ²⁹So when I have fashioned him and breathed into him from my spirit, so fall down, worshiping him." ³⁰So all the angels worshiped him ³¹except the Devil; he refused to be with the worshipers. ³²He said, "O Devil, why were you not with the worshipers?" ³³He said, "I was not to worship a human you created from dry mud, from black molded mud." ³⁴He said, "So get out from it, so surely you are stoned. ³⁵And surely the curse will be on you until the judgment day." ³⁶He said, "My lord, so delay me until a day they will be raised." ³⁷He said, "So surely you are of the delayed ³⁸until the day of the appointed time." ³⁹He said, "My lord, because you seduced me, I will surely adorn to them on earth. And I will surely seduce all of them ⁴⁰except your sincere servants among them." ⁴¹He said, "This is a way on me straight. ⁴²Surely my servants, you have no authority over them except those who follow you from the seduced. ⁴³And surely hell is the promise for them all. ⁴⁴It has seven doors, to every door a portion of them is assigned. ⁴⁵Surely the fearer in gardens and in springs. ⁴⁶Enter it in peace, secure." ⁴⁷And we removed from their chests any jealousy. Brothers, face to face, on beds. ⁴⁸No weariness will reach them, and they will not be driven out of it. ⁴⁹Inform my servants, surely I am the forgiving, the merciful. ⁵⁰And that my torment is the painful torment.

The story of Abraham and Lot is copied from the Bible and corrupted once again.

⁵¹And inform them about Abraham's guest. ⁵²When they entered into him, so they said, "Peace." He said, "Surely we are afraid of you." ⁵³They said, "Do not be afraid. We give you the good news of a boy full of knowledge." ⁵⁴He said, "Did you give me the good news when the old age has touched me? So by what good news do you bring?" ⁵⁵They said, "We gave you the good news with the truth; so do not be of the despairers." ⁵⁶He said, "And who despairs of the mercy of his lord except those who have gone astray?" ⁵⁷He said, "What did you come here for, O messengers?" ⁵⁸They said, "Surely we are sent to a criminal people, ⁵⁹except the family of Lot, of whom we will surely deliver them all ⁶⁰except his woman [wife]. We have decreed that she will be of those who will be left behind." ⁶¹So when the messenger came to the family of Lot, ⁶²he said, "Surely you are an unknown people." ⁶³They said, "Yet we bring to you in what they were doubting in. ⁶⁴And we bring to you with the truth, and surely we are truthful. ⁶⁵So walk with your family a part of the night, and follow their rear. And let none of you turn around, and go where you are commanded." ⁶⁶And this command we gave him because the last of those will be cut off in the morning. ⁶⁷And the inhabitants of the city came rejoicing. ⁶⁸He said, "Surely those are my guests, so do not disgrace me. ⁶⁹And fear Allah, and do not shame me." ⁷⁰They said,

"Have we not forbidden you to any of the worlds?" [71]He said, "Those are my daughters, if you were doing.[a"] [72]By your life, surely they are blinded in their drunkenness. [73]So the shout seized them at the time of sunrise. [74]So we made on it its bottom,[b] and we rained on them rocks of baked clay. [75]Surely in this there are signs for those who ponder. [76]And surely it is an existing road. [77]Surely in this are signs to the believers, [78]and the unjust were companions of the thicket. [79]So we took vengeance on them, and surely they are on an obvious road.

The story about the people of the rock is made-up by Mohammed. Notice that verse 85 contradicts verse 9:73.

[80]And indeed, the people of the rock denied the messengers. [81]And we brought to them our signs, so they were turned away from them. [82]And they were hewing houses from the mountains in security. [83]So a shout seized them in the morning. [84]So what they were earning did not profit them. [85]And we have not created the heavens and the earth and what is between them except with the truth, and surely the hour is coming. So forgive the beautiful forgiveness. [86]Surely your lord is the creator, the knower.

In Mohammed's days there were seven versions of the Qur'an.

[87]And indeed, we have given you seven of the mathānī[c] and the great Qur'an. [88]Do not yearn with your eyes on the wives that we gave to them to enjoy. And do not grieve for them, and lower your wing for the believers. [89]And say, "Surely I am a clear warner." [90]Like we send down on the dividers, [91]those who made the Qur'an into parts. [92]So by your lord, we will surely ask them all [93]about what they were doing. [94]So declare what you are commanded, and turn away from the polytheists.

Those who worship anyone other than Allah (such as Jesus) are scoffers.

[95]Surely we will be sufficient for you against the scoffers, [96]those who make with Allah another god, so they will know. [97]And indeed, we know that your chest became distressed at what they say. [98]So praise with your lord's praise, and be of the worshipers. [99]And serve your lord until the certain comes to you.

---

[a] having sex
[b] turned upside down
[c] repeated, non-Arabic word of possible Aramaic origin

A portion of a revelation   *The Bees*

In the name of Allah, the merciful, the merciful

[1]The command of Allah has come, so do not hasten it. Praise be to him, and he is exalted above what they partner. [2]He sent down the angels with the spirit by his amr[a] on whom he wills of his servants: "That warn there is no god except me, so fear me." [3]He created the heavens and the earth with the truth; he is exalted above what they partner.

Another biological error is recorded in the Qur'an. Mohammed claims that there are two fluids which he called nutfah. Nutfah (male and female sexual discharges) is the combination of white fluid (semen) that was said to originate in the male's backbone and is mixed with yellow fluid which originates in the breasts of the woman. See hadith Saheh Muslim 736, 741, and 742. Also, see the interpretations of Ibn Kathir, Al Galalien, Al Tahindery, and Al Qurtobi. See also verses 86:5-7 for more details.

[4]He created the human from nutfah,[b] so behold, he is an obvious opponent. [5]And the livestock he created for you, in them warmth and gainful uses and from them you eat. [6]And in them you have beauty, when you rest them and when you herd them. [7]And they carry your burdens to a country which you would not be able to otherwise reach except with hardship of soul. Surely your lord is compassionate, merciful. [8]And the horses and the bighal[c] and the donkeys, that you may ride them and an ornament. And he creates what you do not know.

Allah wills for some to be in the right way and for others to be in the wrong way.

[9]And it is on Allah to show the way. Some of them are deviating, and if Allah wills, he would guide you all. [10]He is who sends water from the heaven for you; from it you drink and from it trees on which you feed. [11]By it he planted for you the plants and the olives and the palm trees and the grapes and all the fruit; surely in this is a sign for people who reflect. [12]And he has made the night and the day subservient to you, and the sun and the moon and the stars are subservient by his command; surely in this are the signs for people

---

[a] command, non-Arabic word, when used as a doctrine of revelation, of Aramaic origin
[b] a word without meaning, which scholars claim to mean male and female sexual discharges
[c] mules, non-Arabic word of Abyssinian origin

who understand. [13]And what he created on the earth of different colors, surely in this is a sign for people who remember. [14]And he is who has made the sea subservient to you so that you may eat of its tender meat and take from it ornaments to wear them, and you see the ships sailing through it, and that you may seek of his bounty, and perhaps you will be thankful.

The earth does not move. It sits still.

[15]And he threw the stabilizers on the earth, so that it does not move with you, and rivers and ways, perhaps you may be guided. [16]And marks and by the stars they are guided. [17]Is he who creates like he who does not create, do you not remember? [18]And if you would number the grace of Allah, you could not count it. Surely Allah is forgiving, merciful. [19]And Allah knows what you hide and what you reveal. [20]And those who call on other than Allah, they do not create anything and they are created. [21]Dead, not living, they do not feel when they will be raised. [22]Your god is one god. So those who do not believe in the hereafter, their hearts deny and they are proud. [23]No doubt that Allah knows what they hide and what they reveal. Surely he does not love the proud.

Some say that the Qur'an is the legends of the ancients.

[24]And when it is said to them, "What did your lord send down?" They said, "The legends of the ancients." [25]To carry their burdens completely on the resurrection day and some of the burdens of those whom they misled without knowledge. Is it not evil what they bear! [26]Indeed, the people before them deceived. So Allah annihilated their buildings from the foundations so the roof dropped on them from above them, and the torment came to them from where they did not feel. [27]Then, on the resurrection day, he will shame them and say, "Where are my partners, those with whom you were hostile?" Those who give knowledge say, "Surely the shame is today, and the evil is on the infidels." [28]Those whom the angels caused to die, while they were being unjust to themselves, so they give submission: "We were not doing evil." Yes, surely Allah knows what you were doing. [29]So enter the doors of hell; abide in it forever, so evil is the dwelling place for the proud.

Paradise is the reward for the ones who do good deeds.

[30]And it is said to those who fear, "What did your lord send down?" They said, "Good." To those who do good in this life, good, and in the home of the hereafter, good, and blessed is the home of the fearer. [31]Eden's gardens they will enter them, below them the rivers flow. They have in it everything they desire; likewise, Allah rewards the fearer. [32]Those whom the angels cause to die while they are

good, they will say, "Peace on you, enter the garden because of what you were doing." [33]Will they wait until the angel comes to them or the command of your lord comes? Likewise, those who were before them did. And Allah did not deal with them unjustly, but they were treating themselves unjustly. [34]So the evils of what they had done afflicted them. And they were surrounded by what they were scoffing at. [35]And those who are polytheists said, "If Allah willed, we would not serve anything other than him, neither us nor our fathers, and we did not forbid anything other than him." Likewise, those who were before them did. So what is on the messenger except the clear delivering?

Allah sends a messenger to every nation, and he delivers only those whom he wills.

[36]And indeed, we have sent to every nation a messenger that: "Serve Allah, and turn away from the idolatry." So some of them Allah guided, and some of them, the error established over them. "So walk on the earth, so see how was the end of the deniers." [37]If you care about their guidance, so surely Allah will not guide whom he leads astray. And they will not have any helpers. [38]And they swear by Allah with their most solemn oath that Allah will not raise who died. Yes, the promise on him is truth, but most people do not know. [39]So that he may clear up to them what they disagree in, and that those who became infidels may know that they were liars. [40]Surely only our saying to anything if we desire that we say to it, "Be, so it will be." [41]And those who emigrated for the sake of Allah after they have been treated unjustly, we will surely in this world give them good; and the wage of the hereafter is bigger, if they were knowing. [42]Those who are patient, and on their lord they depend.

All the Bible writers are inspired. This proves that the Bible is the Word of God.

[43]And we did not send before you any except men that we inspired, so ask the people of the reminder,[a] if you were not knowing. [44]With proofs and the scriptures, and we sent down to you the reminder,[b] that you may reveal to the people what has been sent down to them, and perhaps they may reflect. [45]Do those who deceive the evils feel secure that Allah will sink them into the earth or comes to them the torment from where they do not feel? [46]Or will he overtake them in their travel so they will not be able to escape? [47]Or that he may take them fearfully? So surely your lord is compassionate, merciful. [48]Or have they not seen how anything

---

[a] Jews and Christians
[b] Qur'an

which Allah has created yatafyeo,[a] its shades on the right and the left, worshiping Allah, and they were humiliated?

Worship is for Allah alone. Worshiping the Father and the Son, as Christians do, is condemned.

[49]And to Allah all that is in the heavens and on the earth worship, from creature and the angels, and they are not proud. [50]They fear their lord from above them and do what they are commanded. [51]And Allah said, "Do not take two gods; surely he is only one god. So to me, so fear." [52]And to him what is in the heavens and the earth, and to him the religion is always due. Will you then fear any other than Allah? [53]And whatever grace is in you, so it is from Allah; then when harm touches you, so to him you turn for help. [54]Then when he removes the harm from you, then a group from among you partners with their lord [55]to become infidels in what we have given them. So enjoy, so you will know. [56]And they make a portion of what they do not know from what we provided them. [I swear] by Allah, surely you will be asked about what you were forging. [57]And they made the daughters to Allah, praise be to him, and they have what they lust for. [58]And when the birth of a female is announced to any one of them, black shadows settle on his face, and he is grieved. [59]He hides himself from the people because of the evil news he was given. Will he keep it with disgrace or bury it in the dirt? Is not evil what they judge? [60]To those who do not believe in the hereafter, the evil parable, and to Allah is the exalted parable. And he is the dear, the wise. [61]If Allah overtakes the people with their injustices, he would not leave a creature on it, but he will delay them for an appointed time. So when their appointed period comes, they will not delay an hour, nor will they advance. [62]And they made to Allah what they hate, and their tongues describe the lies. That to them is the good; no doubt that they will have the fire, and they will be left. [63][I swear] by Allah, indeed, we have sent[b] to the nations before you, so Satan beautified their works for them. So he is today their friend, and they will have a painful torment. [64]And we did not send down the book on you, except that you clarify to them about what they differed in it, and guidance and mercy to believing people. [65]And Allah sent down water from the heaven, so by it gave life to the earth after its death. Surely in this is a sign to a listening people.

Milk is a solution of blood and excrements. See also verse 23:21. It is lawful to drink wine.

---

[a] a word without meaning
[b] messengers

[66]And surely there is a lesson for you in the livestock. We give you drink from what is in their bellies between excretions and blood; pure milk is agreeable to the drinkers. [67]And from fruit, the palm and the grapes, you take from it sakar[a] and good provisions. Surely in this is a sign to people who understand.

This story describes the prophet of the bees. The honey which comes from the bee's belly is a medicine for every sickness.

[68]And your lord revealed to the bees: "Take houses from the mountains and from the trees and from whatever they build." [69]Then eat from all the fruit, so walk in the ways of your lord despised. From its belly will come out a drink. Its colors are different, in it is a healing to the people. Surely in this is a sign to people who reflect. [70]And Allah created you, then he put you to death. And some of you will be given back to the worst age, so they will not know after knowledge anything. Surely Allah is knowing, mighty. [71]And Allah has preferred some of you above others in the provision, so those whom he preferred, they did not give away of what he provided them to whom their right hands possess.[b] So they are equal in it. Will they disbelieve in the grace of Allah? [72]And Allah made wives for you from your souls and made sons and grandsons from your wives, and he provided you of the good things. Will they believe in the vanity, and by the grace of Allah they become infidels? [73]And they serve rather than Allah, what cannot have provision for them of anything in the heavens and the earth, and they cannot. [74]So do not set forth the parables to Allah. Surely Allah knows, and you do not know. [75]Allah sets forth a parable: an owned slave is not able to do anything, and who from what we provided him from our excellent provisions, so he spends from it secretly and openly. Are they equal? The praise be to Allah, but most of them do not know. [76]And Allah set forth a parable of two men, one of them is mute. He is unable to do anything, and he is a burden on his master; wherever he directed him, he did not bring any good. Should he be equal to the one who is commanded with fairness, and he is on a straight way? [77]And to Allah the unseen of the heavens and the earth. And what is the command of the hour except as the twinkling of the eye, or it is nearer. Surely Allah has might over all things. [78]And Allah brought you out of your mothers' bellies. You do not know anything, and he made to you the hearing and the sight and the hearts, perhaps you may give thanks. [79]Do they not see the birds subservient in the air of the heavens, no one catches them except Allah? Surely in this is a sign to people who believe. [80]And Allah made for you of your houses a dwelling and made for you from the skin of the livestock houses. You find it light in your traveling day and in your settling, and from their wool and their

---

[a] intoxicating drink, non-Arabic word of Syriac origin
[b] concubines and slaves

fur and their hair, furniture, and provisions for a while. [81]And Allah made shades for you from what he created, and he made for you from the mountains places of shelter and made for you garments to protect you [from] the heat and garments to protect you in your violence. Likewise, he fulfills his grace on you, perhaps you may submit [to be Muslims]. [82]So if they turn away, so surely your duty only is the clear delivery. [83]They know the grace of Allah, then they deny it, and most of them are the infidels. [84]And a day we raise from every nation a witness, then no permission will be given to those who became infidels, and they will not be allowed to repent. [85]And when the unjust see the torment, so it will not be reduced for them. And they will not be delayed. [86]And when the polytheists saw their partners they said, "Our lord, those are our partners, which we were calling on rather than you." So they[a] gave them the saying, "Surely you are liars." [87]And they gave to Allah peace on that day, and gone astray from them what they were forging. [88]Those who became infidels and prevent [others] from the way of Allah, we added to them torment above the torment because they were vandals. [89]And a day we raise from every nation a witness against them from among themselves. And we brought you as a witness against those, and we sent down on you the book clarification to everything and a guidance and a mercy and good news to the Muslims. [90]Surely Allah commands with justice and doing the good and giving to relatives, and he forbids indecency and the evil and the aggression. He preaches to you, perhaps you remember. [91]And fulfill the covenant of Allah, if you made a covenant, and do not break your oaths after you have affirmed them. And indeed, you made Allah to stand as witness for you. Surely Allah knows what you do. [92]And do not be like her who unravels her yarn breaking it after it has become strong, taking your oaths a deceit among you because a nation is larger than other nations. Surely Allah only tries you by this, and he will make it clear to you on the resurrection day about what you were differing.

This is a continuing theme that Allah chooses some to be guided and others to go astray.

[93]And if Allah willed, he could have made you one nation. But he leads astray whom he wills, and he guides whom he wills; and surely you will be asked about what you were doing. [94]And do not take your oaths of deceit among you, lest your foot falls after its stability, and you taste the evil because you have prevented [others] from the way of Allah, and to you a great torment. [95]And do not purchase with the covenant of Allah a small price, surely what is with Allah is only better for you, if you were knowing. [96]What is with you will pass

---

[a] false gods

away, but what is with Allah will endure. And surely we will reward those who are patient with their wage with better than what they were doing. [97]Whoever did good deed, whether male or female, while he is a believer, so we will surely make him live a good life. And we will reward them their wage with better than what they were doing. [98]So when you recite the Qur'an, so seek refuge with Allah from the stoned Satan. [99]Surely he has no authority on those who believed, and they depend on their lord. [100]Surely his authority is only over those who befriend him and those who partner with him.

Allah changes his mind about his word. This contradicts verse 15:9. Some believed that Mohammed was helped by another human to write the Qur'an. The Qur'an is in "clear Arabic." This contradicts verse 3:7.

[101]And if we exchange one verse in a place of another verse, and Allah knows what he sent down, they said, "Surely you are only a forger." Yet most of them do not know. [102]Say, "The holy spirit from your lord has sent it down with the truth so that he may strengthen those who have believed and guidance and good news to the Muslims." [103]And indeed, we know that they say, "Surely only a human teaches him." But the tongue of him at whom they hint is foreign while this language is clear Arabic. [104]Surely those who do not believe in the verses of Allah, Allah will not guide them, and to them is a painful torment. [105]Surely they only forge the lie, those who do not believe in the verses of Allah. And those are the liars.

A Muslim who willingly leaves the faith will never be forgiven. It is lawful to deny the faith in the time of persecution if the faith is still sincere in the heart.

[106]Whoever becomes an infidel in Allah after he believed, except one who was compelled and his heart is secure in faith; but whoever opens his chest to the infidelity, so on them wrath from Allah, and they will have great torment. [107]That is because they surely have loved the world's life above the hereafter, and surely Allah will not guide the infidel people. [108]Those are whom Allah has sealed on their hearts and ears and eyes, those are the unaware ones. [109]No doubt, surely in the hereafter they are the losers.

Allah will forgive the sins of those who perform jihad for his cause.

[110]Then surely your lord, for those who emigrated after they were seduced, then perform jihad and were patient. Surely your lord after that is forgiving, merciful. [111]A day every soul will come to argue for itself, and every soul will be paid in full for what it has done. And they will not be dealt with unjustly. [112]And Allah set forth a parable of a village that was safe and secure, its provisions came in plenty from

every place, so it became an infidel of the graces of Allah. So Allah made it taste the clothes of the famine and the fear because of what they were doing. [113]And indeed, a messenger from among them came to them, so they denied him. So the torment seized them, and they were unjust.

Dietary laws are copied from the Jewish laws in the Bible. It is lawful to eat the forbidden food if the person is in need, does not lust for it, and does not return to it for more.

[114]So eat from what Allah provided you, lawful and good, and give thanks for the graces of Allah if you were serving him. [115]Surely unlawful to you is the dead and the blood and the swine meat and that which has been slain to other than Allah. So whoever is compelled without desiring nor returning, so surely Allah is forgiving, merciful. [116]And do not say what the lies your tongues describe: "This is lawful, and this is forbidden," to forge the lies against Allah. Surely those who forge the lies against Allah will not prosper. [117]A little enjoyment and they will have a painful torment. [118]And to the Jews we have forbidden that of which we have related to you before. And we did not treat them unjustly, but they were treating themselves unjustly. [119]Then surely your lord, for those who did the evil with ignorance, then they repented after that. And they reformed, surely your lord after that is forgiving, merciful. [120]Surely Abraham was a leader obedient to Allah, hanifan, and he was not of the polytheists. [121]Thankful for his graces, he has chosen him and guided him to a straight way. [122]And we gave him good in this world, and surely in the hereafter he will be of the good. [123]Then we revealed to you: "That follow the religion of Abraham, hanifan, and he was not of the polytheists." [124]Surely the Sabbath was only ordained for those who differed about it, and surely your lord will judge between them on the resurrection day in what they were differing.

Mohammed is commanded to dispute with others in the best manner. This contradicts many other portions of the Qur'an, such as verse 4:84, where he is told to provoke the believers to wage war against them.

[125]Call to the way of your lord with wisdom and the good sermon, and dispute them by which is best. Surely your lord he knows best of who will go astray from his way, and he knows best of those who are guided. [126]And if you punish, so then punish with the similarity of what you were punished with; and if you are patient, it will be best for the patient. [127]And be patient, and your patience is not, except by Allah. And do not grieve for them, and do not be distressed about what they deceive. [128]Surely Allah is with the fearer and those who do good.

A portion of a revelation   *The Night Journey*

In the name of Allah, the merciful, the merciful

This passage describes Mohammed's trip to Jerusalem and to the seven heavens. Mohammed claimed that he visited the Temple of Solomon and prayed in it. However, the temple was actually demolished 550 years earlier. According to the hadith, Mohammed ascended to the seven heavens riding a mule after his miraculous visit to the temple. Notice in verse 93, when the people requested that Mohammed ascend to heaven as a proof to believe in him, his response was not, "I have already been to heaven," but rather, "I am just a human."

[1]Praise be to him who took his servant by night from the forbidden mosque[a] to the farthest mosque,[b] whom we have blessed that which surrounds him, that we might show him some of our signs. Surely he is the hearing, the seeing.

The books of Moses in the Bible came from God.

[2]And we gave Moses the book, and we made it a guidance to the children of Israel that: "You would take no other guardian than me." [3]The offspring whom we carried on with Noah, surely he was a thankful servant. [4]And we decreed to the children of Israel in the book: "Twice you will vandalize on the earth, and you will be lifted to a big height." [5]So when the first promise came to them, we sent against you our servants with substantial, great strength, so they invaded the innermost parts of the homes, and the promise was accomplished. [6]Then we gave you back what was turned against them and aided you with money and children, and we made you large in number. [7]If you do good, you do good to yourselves; and if you do evil, so for it. So if the promise of the hereafter came to grieve your faces, and they enter the mosque as they entered the first time and bring about tatbīr.[c] [8]Perhaps your lord will have mercy on you. And if you return, we return. And we made hell a prison for the infidels. [9]Surely this Qur'an guides to that which is most upright, and it gives good news to the believers who do good deeds that they will have a big wage. [10]And that those who do not believe in the hereafter, we have prepared for them a painful torment. [11]And the human prays for evil [as] his prayer was for good, and the human

---

[a] of Mecca
[b] Solomon's Temple in Jerusalem
[c] utter destruction, non-Arabic word of Aramaic origin

was hasty. [12]And we have made the night and the day two signs. So we removed the sign of the night. And we made the sign of the day to be seen so that you seek bounty from your lord, and so that you will know the number of the years and the reckoning. And we expound on everything, expounding. [13]And every human, we fastened his bird[a] to his neck, and on the resurrection day we will bring forth a book which he will find spread open. [14]Read your book; your soul today is a sufficient accounter against you. [15]Whoever is guided, so surely he is only guided for himself; and whoever goes astray, so surely he is only going astray against it. And no bearer of a burden can bear the burden of another. And we were not tormenting until we sent a messenger.

Allah is a deceiver who leads people to sin so that he may destroy them.

[16]And if we desire to destroy a village, we command its affluence so they live in transgression in it. So the word will be established against it, so we destroyed it with an utter destruction. [17]And how many generations have we destroyed after Noah! And your lord is sufficient as knower, seer to his servant's sins. [18]Whoever was desiring the hasty, we hastened to him in it what we will, to whom we will. Then we made hell to be his. He will roast in it, despised and rejected. [19]And whoever desires the hereafter and strives after its striving while he is a believer, so those striving there was appreciated. [20]We will aid all those, and those are a gift from your lord. And the gift of your lord was not restricted. [21]See how we preferred some of them over others, and to the hereafter will be bigger in degrees and bigger in preferences. [22]Do not set up another god with Allah, so you will sit despised, disgraced. [23]And your lord has decreed that you do not serve except him. And kindness to the parents, whether one or both of them attain to old age with you, and do not say to them, "Ouf,"[b] and do not shout at them. And say to them generous words. [24]And lower to them the wings of humiliation out of mercy and say, "My lord, have mercy on them as they raised me a[c] little." [25]Your lord knows best what is in your souls if you are good, so surely he was forgiving to those who are repenting. [26]And bring to the relative his due, and to the poor and the son of the way. And do not spend wastefully, extravagantly. [27]Surely the extravagant were brothers of the satans, and Satan was an infidel to his lord. [28]And if you turn away from them, seeking mercy from your lord and wish it, so say to them an easy saying. [29]And do not keep your hand shackled to your neck, nor stretch it all the stretch, so you will sit

---

[a] evil omen
[b] Ugh! - a word exclaimed in a state of frustration
[c] when I was

down blamed, regretful. [30]Surely your lord expands and measures the provision to whom he wills. Surely he was aware and seeing to his servants. [31]And do not kill your children for fear of poverty; we will provide for them and for you. Surely killing them was a big sin. [32]And do not get near the fornication, surely it was indecent and an evil way. [33]And do not kill the soul which Allah has forbidden, except with a just cause. And whoever was killed unjustly, so indeed, we made to his heir an authority. So he will not exceed in the killing, surely he was made victorious. [34]And do not draw near to the money of the orphans, except in what is good, until he reaches his strength. And fulfills the covenant, surely the covenanter was questioned. [35]And fulfill the measure when you measure, and weigh with a straight qistās.[a] This is better and a good interpretation. [36]And do not pursue that of which you have no knowledge. Surely the hearing and the sight and the hearts, every one of those was questioned about it. [37]And do not walk in the land proudly, surely you will not cut the earth, and you will not reach the mountain's height. [38]All this was evil and hated by your lord. [39]This is a part of what your lord revealed to you from the wisdom. And do not set up with Allah another god, so you will be thrown into hell, blamed and rejected. [40]Has Allah preferred sons for you and took from the angels females? You surely say great sayings. [41]And indeed, we have expounded in this Qur'an so that they may remember, and it will not increase them except in aversion. [42]Say, "If there was with him gods as they say, surely they will seek a way to the throne." [43]Praise be to him, and he is exalted above what they say, a big height. [44]The seven heavens and the earth and all who are in them, praise to him; there is not anything except praise with his praise, but you do not understand their praises. Surely he was forbearing, forgiving. [45]And when you read the Qur'an, we have made a hidden veil between you and those who do not believe in the hereafter. [46]And we made covers on their hearts that they understand it and a deafness in their ears, and if you mention your lord in the Qur'an alone, they turn their backs in aversion.

Some people believed that Mohammed was demon-possessed.

[47]We know best what they hear with when they listen to you and when they conspire, the unjust will say, "You only follow a bewitched man." [48]Look how they give to you the parables. So they went astray, so they cannot [find] a way. [49]And they said, "If we become bones and dust, will we surely be raised up a new creation?" [50]Say, "Be stones or iron [51]or creature which grows in your chests." So they will say, "Who will return us?" Say, "The one who created you the first time." So they will nod their heads at you, and they will say, "When

---

[a] balance, non-Arabic word of Greek/Syriac origin

will that be?" Say, "Perhaps it will be soon. [52]A day he will call you, so you will answer with his praise, and you think that you will abide only a little." [53]And say to my servants to say what is good, surely Satan stirs up among them. Surely Satan was an obvious enemy to the human. [54]Your lord knows you best. If he wills, he will give you mercy; and if he wills, he will torment you. And we did not send you as a guardian over them. [55]And your lord knows best of who are in the heavens and the earth, and indeed, we favored some of the prophets above the others. And we gave David Psalms. [56]Say, "Call on those whom you claimed other than him, so they will not be able to remove the harm from you nor alteration." [57]Those whom you call on, they are seeking the way to their lord, which of them is closer to him. They hope for his mercy and fear his torment. Surely the torment of your lord was feared. [58]There is no village which we do not destroy before the resurrection day or torment it with a severe torment. This was mastour[a] in the book.

Mohammed did not perform any sign. See also verses 2:118; 2:145; 6:37, 109, 134; 7:203; 13:7, 27, 31; 17:90-93; and 29:50-51. This contradicts verse 17:1.

[59]And nothing prevented us from sending the signs except that the ancients denied them. And we gave the camel to Themoud, a visible,[b] so they treated her unjustly. And we do not send with the signs except to make fear. [60]And when we said to you, "Surely your lord surrounds the people. And we did not ordain the vision which we showed you except a sedition for people and the cursed tree in the Qur'an. And we will cause them to fear, so it will not increase them except a big rebellion."

Allah commands the angels to worship Adam (again).

[61]And when we said to the angels, "Worship Adam." So they worshiped, except the Devil. He said, "Will I worship him that you have created of mud?" [62]He said, "Did I show you this which you have honored above me? If you delay me until the resurrection day, I will surely sway his offspring except for a few." [63]He said, "Be gone. So whoever of them follows you, so surely hell will be your reward and an ample reward. [64]And entice such of them as you can with your voice, and assault them with your horsemen and your footmen. Be their partner in the money and the children, and make them promises, but Satan will not promise them anything except pride. [65]Surely you will have no authority over my servants, and your lord will be their sufficient guardian." [66]Your lord is the one who drives the

---

[a] written, non-Arabic word of possible Aramaic origin
[b] miracle

ships for you in the sea so that you may seek of his bounty. Surely he was merciful to you. [67]And if the harm touches you in the sea, all those you call on will go astray except him. So when he delivers you to the shore you turn away, and the human was infidel. [68]Have you believed then, that he causes you to sink under the side of the shore or will send a sandstorm on you, then you will not find for yourself a guardian? [69]Or have you believed that he will return you back into it another time, so he sends a stormy wind against you, so he drowns you because of your infidelity? Then you will not find anyone to help you against us. [70]And indeed, we have honored the children of Adam; we have carried them on the land and the sea. And we have provided them from the good things, and we favored them above many of our creatures, with a favor. [71]A day we will call all humans with their leaders, so whoever receives his book by his right hand, so those will read their books and not be treated unjustly even a thread. [72]And whoever was blind in this, so he will be blind in the hereafter and will be more astray from the way. [73]And they were about to seduce you from what we revealed to you and cause you to forge against us another one,[a] and then they would surely have taken you a friend. [74]And were it not that we strengthened you, you would indeed have been inclined a little something toward them. [75]Then we would cause you to taste of double life and of double death; then you will not find a helper for you against us. [76]And that they were about to provoke you to get out of the land. And then they will not stay behind you except a little. [77]Custom of whom we sent before you from our messengers, and you will not find to our custom alteration. [78]Perform the prayer from sundown until the darkness of the night, and the Qur'an of the dawn. Surely the Qur'an of the dawn was witnessed. [79]And during part of the night, so pray with it as an extra ordinance to you. Perhaps your lord will raise you to a praised position. [80]And say, "My lord, admit me with a truthful entry, and get me out with a truthful exit. And grant to me an authority to help." [81]And say, "The truth came, and the vanity has vanished. Surely the vanity was vanishing." [82]And we send down from the Qur'an what is a healing and a mercy to the believers and will not increase the unjust except a loss. [83]And when we graced on the human, he withdraws and goes aside; and when evil touches him, he was in despair. [84]Say, "Everyone acts after his own manner, so your lord knows best who is in a best guided way." [85]And they ask you about the spirit. Say, "The spirit is of the affair of my lord, and you did not receive from knowledge, except a little." [86]And if we will, we surely take away that which we revealed to you. Then you will not find to you by it a guardian against us. [87]Except a mercy from your lord, surely his bounty on you was big.

---

[a] another revelation

Once again the Qur'an claims that no one can write a book like it.

[88]Say, "Surely if the humans and the jinn gathered so that they might bring forth the likeness of this Qur'an, they cannot bring forth the likeness of it, even if they were backing one another." [89]And indeed, we have expounded to the people in this Qur'an from every parable, so most people reject but infidelity. [90]And they said, "We will not believe you until you gush a spring from the earth. [91]Or, a garden of palm trees and grapes will be yours, so you gush the rivers gushing through it. [92]Or you make the heavens to fall on us in pieces, as you claim, or you bring Allah and the angels to face us. [93]Or you have a highly embellished house, or you ascend to the heaven. And we will not believe in your ascension until you send down on us a book we read." Say, "Praise be to my lord. Was I except a human messenger?" [94]And people were not prevented from believing if the guidance came to them, except that they said, "Has Allah sent a human messenger?" [95]Say, "If there was on the earth angels walking in security, we will send down on them an angelic messenger from the heaven." [96]Say, "Allah is a sufficient witness between me and you. Surely he was an aware seer to his servant." [97]And whomever Allah guided, so he is the guided, and whomever he leads astray, so you will never find friends for them other than him. We will gather them on the resurrection day, on their faces, blind and dumb and deaf. Hell will be their abode, so as often as it abates, we increase for them a blaze. [98]This is their reward because they became infidels in our verses, and they said, "If we become bones and dust, will we be raised a new creation?" [99]Have they not seen that Allah who created the heavens and the earth is able to create like them, and he made to them a term? There is no doubt of it, so the unjust refuse, except infidelity. [100]Say, "If you own the treasuries of my lord's mercy, you would surely withhold through fear of spending," and the human was stingy.

The story of Moses is copied from the Bible and corrupted once again. Notice that the Qur'an claims there are nine plagues, but only named five of them. One of the five is a flood which is incorrect. See verse 7:133. This contradicts the Bible which clearly teaches that there were ten plagues. See Exodus 7:14-11:10. Notice also in verse 103 where Pharaoh desires to expel the Jews out of Egypt. This contradicts the account in Exodus.

[101]And indeed, we gave Moses nine clear signs. So ask the children of Israel when he came to them. So Pharaoh said to him, "Surely I think you are bewitched, O Moses." [102]He said, "Indeed, you know that nothing of those sent down except from the lord of the heavens and the earth as proof, and surely I think that you, O

Pharaoh, are doomed." [103]So he desired to expel them out of the land, so we drowned him and all those who were with him. [104]And we said after him to the children of Israel, "Dwell in the land, so when the promise of the hereafter comes to pass, we bring you all together." [105]And with the truth we sent it down, and with the truth it is sent down. And we did not send you except as a giver of good news and a warner. [106]And a Qur'an we divided so that you may recite it to the people by small increments, and we sent it down, descending. [107]Say, "Believe in it, or do not believe it. Surely those who have been given the knowledge before it, when it is recited to them, they will fall on their chins worshiping." [108]And they will say, "Praise be to our lord, surely the promise of our lord was fulfilled." [109]And they fall down on their chins weeping, and it makes them more humble. [110]Say, "Call on Allah, or call on the merciful. By whatever you call, so to him are the best names." And do not be loud in your prayer, neither be soft in it, but follow a middle way between those.

'Isā (the Jesus of Mohammed) is not the Son of God because God has no children.

[111]And say, "Praise be to Allah who has not taken a son, and it was not for him to have a partner in the kingdom. And it was not for him to have a friend from the humiliated." And magnify him[a] magnificently.

A portion of a revelation **18** *The Cave*

In the name of Allah, the merciful, the merciful

[1]The praise be to Allah who has sent down the book on his servant and has not made in it crookedness, [2]valuable to warn of a grievous woe from him and to give the believers good news, those who do good deeds, that they will have an excellent wage; [3]wherein they will dwell forever.

A warning is given to Christians who say God has a Son.

[4]And he warns those who said, "Allah has taken a son." [5]They have no knowledge of this, neither their fathers, a dreadful word to come out of their mouths that they say except a lie. [6]So perhaps you will kill yourself on their footsteps with sorrow if they do not believe by this saying. [7]Surely we have made all that is on the earth as an

---

[a] that is to call "Allah Akbar," i.e. Allah is bigger

adornment for it so that we may test them to see which of them does the best work. [8]And surely we are about to reduce what is on it to dust.

The story of the several sleepers is copied from a fifth century myth which was taken from a Greek book, *The Glory of the Martyrs,* Book 1, Chapter 95, by Gergerous.

[9]Or did you think that the companions of the cave and al rakim[a] were of the wonders of our signs? [10]When the young men took refuge in the cave, so they said, "Our lord, grant us mercy from you and prepare a right course for us in our affair." [11]So we struck on their ears in the cave for many years. [12]Then we raised them up so that we might know which of the two parties could best discern the time they stayed. [13]We will relate to you their news with the truth. Surely they were young men who believed in their lord, and we increased them guidance. [14]And we tied on their hearts when they stood up, so they said, "Our lord is the lord of the heavens and the earth. We will not call any god other than him; indeed, if we did, then we said a transgression." [15]Those our people have taken other gods than him. Were it not that they had brought to them a clear authority. So who is more unjust than one who forged a lie against Allah? [16]And if you separate from them and what they serve except Allah, so take refuge in the cave. Your lord will unfold his mercy to you and will prepare a way for your affair. [17]And you see the sun when it rose bending to the right of their cave, and when it set going from them on the left side, and they are in a wide space in it. This is from the signs of Allah. Whomever Allah guided, so he is the guided. And whomever he leads astray, so you will not find for him a guided friend. [18]And you think that they were awake, but they were sleeping. And we turned them to the right and to the left. And in the entry lay their dog with paws outstretched. Had you looked at them, you would surely have turned away from them in flight, and you would have been filled with fear of them. [19]And likewise, we raised them up that they might ask one another. One of them said, "How long have you stayed here?" They said, "We have stayed a day or part of a day." They said, "Your lord knows best how long you have stayed. So send now one of you with this your paper[b] into the city. So let him see who in it has the purest food, so he will bring to you a provision from it. And let him be courteous, and let not anyone feel you. [20]Surely if they prevail against you, they will stone you or turn you back into their religion, and then you will never prosper." [21]And likewise, we made their adventure known[c] so that they might know

---

[a] a word without meaning
[b] money
[c] to their fellow citizens

that the promise of Allah is true and that the hour, there is no doubt in it. When they disputed among themselves concerning their affair, so they said, "Build a building over them, their lord knows best about them." Those who prevailed in the affair said, "We will surely raise over them a place of worship."

Did Allah know how many there were? Why was this not revealed?

[22]They will say, "Three, their dog is their fourth." And they say, "Five, their dog is their sixth," guessing of the unseen, and they say, "Seven, and their dog is their eighth." Say, "My lord knows best their number; no one knows them except a few." So do not dispute in them except with reference to that which appeared, and do not consult anyone about them.

Before planning anything say, "If God wills." This is copied from the Bible. See James 4:13-15.

[23]And do not say about anything, "I will surely do it tomorrow." [24]Only if Allah wills. And remember your lord when you forget and say, "Perhaps my lord will guide me so that I may come near the right answer of this." [25]And they abided in their cave three hundred years and add nine. [26]Say, "Allah knows how long they abided." To him are the unseen things of the heavens and the earth. See by him and hear. They do not have any friend other than him, and no one partners in his judgment.

If the Bible is God's Word and the Qur'an teaches that no one can change God's Words, then the Bible is infallible.

[27]And recite what had been revealed to you from the book of your lord; no one can change his words, and you will not find a refuge other than him. [28]And let yourself be patient with those who call on their lord at morning and evening, desiring his face. And do not let your eyes wander away from them, desiring the beauty of the world's life. And do not obey him whose heart we have made careless of our remembrance. And who follows his own desire, and whose affair was unbridled.

Men have the will to believe or to become infidels. This contradicts verses 5:40; 6:39; 6:88; 9:27; 10:25; 13:27; 14:4; 16:93...

[29]And say, "The truth is from your lord," so whoever wills, so let him believe; and whoever wills, so let him be an infidel. Surely we have prepared a fire for the unjust whose surādiq[a] will enclose them, and if they call out, they will be relieved with water like molten metal

---

[a] awning, non-Arabic word of Iranian/Aramaic origin

which will scald the faces. Evil is the drink, and evil is that place! [30]Surely those who believed and did good deeds, surely we will not lose the wage of him who did better work. [31]Those will have the Eden's gardens, below them the rivers flow. They will be adorned in it with asawer[a] of gold, and they will be dressed in green robes of sundus[b] and istabraq[c] they will wear. They will be reclining there on the ara'ikah.[d] Blessed is the reward, and good is that place. [32]And give them the parable of two men: to one of them we made two gardens of grape vines and surrounded them with palm trees and placed plants between them. [33]Each of the two gardens yielded its food, and not anything failed in it. And we caused a river to gush forth through them. [34]And to him there was fruit, so he said to his companion as he conversed with him, "I have more money than you and mightier followers." [35]And he entered his garden, and he was unjust to himself. He said, "I do not think that this will ever perish. [36]And I do not think that the hour is coming, and even if I be taken back to my lord, I will surely find a better place than this." [37]His companion said to him as he conversed with him, "Did you become an infidel by him who created you from dust, then from nutfah, then fashioned you as a man? [38]But as for me, he is Allah my lord, and I will not partner anyone with my lord. [39]And were it not that if you entered your garden said, 'What Allah wills. There is no might except by Allah.' Though you see that I have less money and children than you, [40]so perhaps my lord may give to me better than your garden and will send on it his counting (judgment) from the heaven so that it will become a barren wasteland; [41]or its water will become sinking so that you are unable to seek it." [42]And he was surrounded with his fruit, so then he remained alternating his hands[e] over what he had spent on it, and it was empty on its trellises. And he said, "Oh, I wish I had not partnered anyone with my lord." [43]And there was not a group to help him other than Allah, and he was not helped. [44]Thereupon is protection from the true god, and he is best for reward and best for the final end. [45]And give them a parable of the world's life. Like water which we send down from the heaven, so it mingled with the earth's plants. So it becomes dry stubble; the wind scatters it. And Allah was mighty over all things. [46]The money and the children are the adornment of the world's life. And the lasting good deeds are better reward with your lord and better hope. [47]And a day we will cause the mountains to walk and you will see the earth going forth and we gathered them, so we did not leave anyone of

---

[a] bracelets, non-Arabic word of Akkadian origin
[b] fine silk, non-Arabic word of Greek/Akkadian origin
[c] brocade, non-Arabic word of Persian origin
[d] couches, non-Arabic word of Abyssinian/Persian origin
[e] clapping his hands in sorrow

them. [48]And they will be shown before your lord in ranks. "Indeed, you came to us as we created you the first time, yet you claimed that we did not make an appointment for you." [49]And the book will be placed so you will see the criminal afraid at that which is in it, and they will say, "O woe to us, what book is this! There was nothing small or big left out, but he counted it." And they found what they had done is present, and your lord will not deal unjustly with anyone.

Allah commands the angels to worship Adam again. Notice that in this instance Mohammed considered the Devil, who is an angel, to be one of the jinn who also had offspring. This clearly shows that Mohammed was confused between angels and jinn. This raises the question, "Is there really such a thing as jinn?"

[50]And when we said to the angels, "Worship Adam," so they worshiped, except the Devil; he was from the jinn, so he transgressed from the command of his lord. "Will you then take him[a] and his offspring as friends rather than me? And they are an enemy to you. This is an evil exchange for the unjust." [51]I have not made them witnesses of the creation of the heavens and the earth nor the creation of themselves, and you were not taking those who lead astray for supporters. [52]And a day, he will say, "Call on my partners whom you claimed." So they called them, so they did not answer them, and we made between them a destruction. [53]And the criminals saw the fire, so they thought that they would fall into it, and they did not find a place to turn away from it. [54]And indeed, we have expounded in this Qur'an to the people from every parable, and the human was the most contentious thing. [55]And nothing prevents people from believing when the guidance comes to them and asking forgiveness from their lord, except that the customs of the ancients come to them or the torment will come to them face-to-face. [56]And we do not send the messengers except as bearers of good news and warners, and they dispute with those who became infidels with vanity to refute with it the truth. And they took my verses and what they were warned with as a scoff. [57]And who is more unjust than he, who when he is reminded of the verses of his lord, so he turns away from them and forgets what his hands have wrought. Surely we made covers on their hearts that they understand it and a deafness in their ears, and if you call them to the guidance, so they will not be guided then forever. [58]And your lord is the forgiving, the possessor of mercy. If he tormented them because of what they have earned, he would hasten the torment to them. Yet they have an appointed time. They will not find rather than it an escape. [59]And those villages we destroyed when they became unjust, and we made for its destruction an appointed time.

---

[a] the Devil

This is an invented story about Moses by Mohammed. Notice that Allah punishes the innocent by death before any sin is committed.

[60]And when Moses said to his young man, "I will not stop until I reach the confluence of the two seas, or I will be traveling for years." [61]So when they reached their confluence, they forgot their whale. So it got its way into the sea going away. [62]So when they had gone farther, he said to his young man, "Bring our lunch to us, indeed, we have incurred weariness from this our traveling." [63]He said, "Did you see when we took refuge in the rock, so surely I have forgotten the whale. No one causes me to forget to mention it except Satan, and it has taken its way in the sea wondrously." [64]He said, "It is this we were seeking." So they went back retracing their footsteps. [65]Then they found a servant from our servants whom we had given mercy from us and whom we had instructed with our knowledge. [66]And Moses said to him, "Will I follow you so that you will teach me guidance from what you have been taught?" [67]He said, "Surely you cannot have patience with me. [68]And how can you be patient in that you do not have knowledge of?" [69]He said, "You will find me patient if Allah wills, and I will not disobey your command." [70]He said, "So if you follow me, so do not ask me about anything until I mention to you something about it." [71]So they went on until they embarked in a safīna,[a] and he made a hole in it. He said, "Have you made a hole in it so that you may drown its people? Indeed, you have done an idiotic thing!" [72]He said, "Did I not tell you that you surely would not have patience with me?" [73]He said, "Pardon me for my forgetfulness, and do not overburden me of my difficult affair." [74]So they went on until they met a young man, so he killed him. So he said, "Have you killed a pure soul, without a soul?[b] Indeed, you have done a horrible thing!" [75]He said, "Did I not tell you that surely you would not have patience with me?" [76]He said, "If I ask you about anything after this, so do not accompany me. Indeed, you have received an excuse from me." [77]So they went on until they came to the people of a village. They asked these people for food, but they refused to host them. So they found in it a wall that was about to fall so he set it upright. He said, "If you had willed, you might have obtained a wage for this." [78]He said, "This is the parting between you and me. But I will first tell you the interpretation of that with which you could not be patient. [79]As to the ship, so it was owned by poor men who worked on the sea, and I was minded to damage it, for in their rear was a king who seized every ship by force. [80]And as to the young man, so his parents were believers so we feared lest he should trouble them by

---

[a] ship, non-Arabic word of Aramaic origin
[b] who did not commit murder

rebellion and infidelity. [81]So we desired that their lord might exchange in his place, better than he was in virtue and closer in mercy. [82]And as to the wall, so it was owned by two young men, orphaned in the city, and under it was a treasure to them. And their father was a righteous man, so your lord desired that they should reach the age of strength and take forth their treasure as a mercy from your lord. And I did not do it of my own affair. This is the interpretation of that which you could not have patience."

Ze Al Qarnain, Alexander the Great, is a prophet. This section explains that the sun sets in a muddy spring.

[83]They ask you about Ze Al Qarnain.[a] Say, "I will recite to you an account of him." [84]Surely we established him on the earth, and we gave him from everything a way. [85]So he followed a way, [86]until when he reached the setting of the sun, he found it set in a muddy spring, and he found a people by it. We said, "O Za Al Qarnain, either that you torment them or that you do good to them." [87]He said, "As for those who are unjust so we will torment. Then he will be returned to his lord, so he will torment him with a horrible torment. [88]And as to him who believed and did good deed, so he will have the reward of the good, and we will say to him from our easy command." [89]Then he followed a way, [90]until when he reached the rising of the sun, he found that it rose on a people to whom we had given no shelter from it. [91]Likewise, and indeed, we were aware of what he had of news. [92]Then he followed a way, [93]until he came between the two mountains under which he found a people who could not understand a saying. [94]They said, "O Za Al Qarnain, surely Ya'juj[b] and Ma'juj[c] are vandalizing in the land. Shall we make to you a tribute that you make between us and them a barrier?" [95]He said, "That in which my lord has established me is better, so assist me with strength. I will make a barrier between you and them. [96]Bring me blocks of iron," until it equalizes between the two sides. He said, "Blow," until when he made it a fire. He said, "Bring me brass that I may pour over it." [97]And they were not able to scale it, neither were they able to dig through it. [98]He said, "This is a mercy from my lord. So when the promise of my lord comes to pass, he will make it dust. And the promise of my lord was true." [99]On that day we will let them dash like billows, one over another, and it was blown into the trumpet, so we gathered them gathering. [100]And we show hell on that day to the infidels showing. [101]Whose eyes were veiled from my reminder, and they were not able to hear. [102]Do those who became

---

[a] the one with two horns and according to Muslim scholars this is Alexander the Great. See http://quran.al-islam.com/Page.aspx?pageid=221&BookID=13&Page=302, accessed 12/14/2008.
[b] Gog
[c] Magog

infidels think that they can take my servants without me as friends? Surely we prepared hell as a dwelling place for the infidels. [103]Say, "Will we inform you with the works of the losers? [104]Those who their strife in the world's life has gone astray, and they think that what they do is right. [105]They are those who became infidels in the verses of their lord and his meeting. So vain is their works, so we will not account them any weight on the resurrection day. [106]That is their reward, hell, because they were infidels and took my verses and my messengers [as] a scoff. [107]Surely those who believed and did the good deeds, the gardens of Firdaws[a] was for them a dwelling. [108]They abide in it forever; they desire no change from it. [109]Say, "If the sea was ink for the words of my lord, the sea had run out before the words of my lord would run out, even if we brought one like it as an aid." [110]Say, "Surely I am only a human like you. It is revealed to me that your god is only one god. So whoever was hoping the meeting of his lord, so he does good deed, and he does not partner anyone in the service of his lord."

A portion of a revelation   19   *Mary*

In the name of Allah, the merciful, the merciful

The story of Zacharias and John the Baptist is copied from the Bible and corrupted. See Luke 1.

[1]Khyas.[c] [2]A reminder of your lord's mercy to his servant Zacharias. [3]When he called on his lord with a whispered calling. [4]He said, "My lord, surely my bones are brittle, and my head is aflame with gray hair. And I was not miserable with my calling on you. [5]And surely I have fears for my relatives after me, and my woman [wife] was barren. So grant me from yourself an heir, [6]to inherit me and inherit the family of Jacob, and make him pleasing, my lord." [7]"O Zacharias, surely we give you good news of a son; his name is Yahya.[d] That name we have given to none before him." [8]He said, "My lord, how can I have a son, and my woman [wife] was barren and, indeed, when I have now reached old age?" [9]He said, "Likewise, your lord says, it is easy for me; and indeed, I created you before, and you

---

[a] Paradise, non-Arabic word of Greek/Syriac origin
[b] Mary
[c] a word containing five Arabic letters without meaning
[d] wrong name, he meant John the Baptist

were not anything." ¹⁰He said, "My lord, give me a sign." He said, "Your sign will be that you will not speak to the people three nights together."¹¹So he came out of the holy of holies to his people, so he revealed to them to praise morning and evening. ¹²O Yahya, take the book with strength, and we gave him the wisdom [as] a child ¹³and compassion from us and purity. And he was fearing ¹⁴and righteous to his parents, and he was not powerful, disobedient. ¹⁵And peace be on him the day he was born and the day he dies and the day he is raised alive.

The story of Mary and 'Isā (the Jesus of Mohammed) is copied from the Bible and corrupted once again.

¹⁶And remember in the book Miriam, when she went apart from her family to an eastern place. ¹⁷So she took a veil apart from them. So we sent our spirit to her, so he appeared to her a normal human. ¹⁸She said, "Surely I seek refuge with the merciful from you if you were a fearer." ¹⁹He said, "Surely I am only a messenger of your lord that I may grant to you a righteous son."

'Isā (the Jesus of Mohammed) was born of a virgin under a palm tree, not in a manger. See Luke 2:1-20. In Mohammed's account, 'Isā, as a baby, speaks immediately after his birth. The false book, *The Story of the Baby of Mary and the Childhood of the Savior,* influenced Mohammed. He is also confused between Mary the mother of Jesus and Mary (Miriam) the sister of Moses and Aaron.

²⁰She said, "How can I have a son when no man has touched me, and I was not unchaste?" ²¹He said, "Likewise, your lord says, 'It is easy for me, and we will make him a sign to the people and a mercy from us.'" And it was a decreed matter. ²²So she conceived him, so she withdrew with him to a remote place. ²³So the pain of childbirth came on her by the trunk of a palm tree. She said, "Oh, I wish that I had died before this, and I was forgotten, forgetting." ²⁴So he called her from below her, "Do not grieve. Indeed, your lord has made a creek under you. ²⁵And shake the trunk of the palm tree toward you; it will drop fresh, ripe dates on you. ²⁶So eat and drink and please eye. So if you see any human, so say, 'Surely I have vowed a fast to the merciful, so I will not talk to any human today.'" ²⁷So she came to her people with him, carrying him. They said, "O Mary, indeed, you have brought a strange thing. ²⁸O sister of Aaron, your father was not an evil man, and your mother was not unchaste!" ²⁹So she pointed to him. They said, "How can we talk with him who was in the cradle, an infant?" ³⁰He said, "Surely I am the servant of Allah; he gave me the book and made me a prophet. ³¹And he made me blessed wherever I was and commanded me with the prayer and the legal alms as long

as I live [32]and [to be] righteous to my mother. And he has not made me powerful, miserable."

This is Mohammed's report about 'Isā's (the Jesus of Mohammed) birth, death, and resurrection.

[33]"And the peace be on me the day I was born and the day I die and the day I am raised alive." [34]This is 'Isā, son of Mary, the saying of truth about which they doubt.

'Isā (the Jesus of Mohammed) was not the Son of God. It would be unbecoming for God to have a son.

[35]It was not to Allah to take some son. Praise be to him. When he decrees a matter, so surely he only says to it, "Be," so it will be. [36]And surely Allah is my lord and your lord, so serve him. This is a straight way. [37]So parties among them disagree. So woe to those who became infidels from the vision of a great day. [38]Hear by them and see on a day they come to us, but today the unjust are in obvious error. [39]And warn them of the regret day when the command will be accomplished while they are unaware, and they do not believe. [40]Surely we will inherit the earth and all who are on it. And to us they will be returned.

The story of Abraham is copied from the Bible and corrupted again.

[41]And remember in the book Abraham, surely he was a friend, a prophet. [42]When he said to his father, "O my father, why do you serve that which neither hears nor sees nor profits you anything? [43]O my father, surely indeed, some knowledge came to me which has not come to you. So follow me; I will guide you to a straight way. [44]O my father, do not serve Satan; surely Satan was a rebel against the merciful. [45]O my father, surely I fear lest a torment from the merciful touches you, so you will become a friend to Satan." [46]He said, "Are you forsaking my gods, O Abraham? If you do not stop that, I will stone you, and depart from me for a long time!" [47]He said, "Peace be on you. I will ask forgiveness for you from my lord, surely he was kind to me. [48]And I will separate from you and what you call on rather than Allah. And I will call to my lord. Perhaps I will not become miserable by calling to my lord." [49]So when he had separated from them and what they served rather than Allah, we granted to him Isaac and Jacob, and each of them we made a prophet. [50]And we granted them from our mercy and gave them the lofty tongue of truth.

The stories of Moses, Ishmael, Enoch, Adam, and Abraham are loosely copied from the Bible and corrupted again. Notice Mohammed's confusion of the true name of Idris, which is

Enoch. See Genesis 5:21-24. Also, Mohammed considered Ishmael to be a prophet. Compare this to Genesis 16:12.

[51]And remember in the book Moses, surely he was faithful. And he was a messenger, prophet. [52]And we called him from the right side of the mountain and gave him close communication. [53]And we granted to him out of our mercy his brother Aaron, a prophet. [54]And remember in the book Ishmael, surely he was true to his promise and was a messenger, prophet. [55]And he was commanding his family with the prayer and the legal alms and was well-pleasing to his lord. [56]And remember in the book Idris,[a] surely he was a friend, a prophet. [57]And we raised him to a high place. [58]Those are the ones whom Allah graced among the prophets from the descendants of Adam and among whom we carried with Noah and among the descendants of Abraham and Israel and among those whom we have guided and chosen. When the verses of the merciful were recited to them, they bowed down worshiping and weeping. [59]So others have come in their place after them. They have lost the prayer and follow the lusts, so they will meet with error, [60]except those who repented and believed and did a good deed, so those will enter the garden and will not be dealt with unjustly anything. [61]Eden's gardens, which the merciful has promised to his servants in the unseen, surely his promise was to come. [62]They will not hear in it any vain discourse, except "Peace," and they will have their provision in it morning and evening. [63]This is the garden which we bequeath to some of our servants who were fearing. [64]We do not descend, except by the command of your lord, to him what is between our hands and what is behind us and what is between that. And your lord was not forgetful. [65]Lord of the heavens and the earth and what is between them, so serve him and be patient in his service. Do you know to him a name? [66]And the human says, "After I am dead, will I come out alive?" [67]Does the human not remember that we created him before, and he was not anything? [68]So [I swear] by your lord, we will surely gather them and the satans. Then we will bring them surrounding hell on their knees. [69]Then we will seize from each sect those of them who have been strongest in rebellion against the merciful. [70]Then surely we know of those who are most deserving to be roasted.

All Muslims will burn in hell for a while; only the fearer of Allah will ever get out. See also verse 3:185. This contradicts the Bible. See Matthew 25:46 and Luke 16:26.

[71]And there is none of you who will not go down into it.[b] This was an unavoidable decree of your lord. [72]Then we will deliver those who

---

[a] wrong name, he meant Enoch, non-Arabic word of Greek/Syriac/Arabic origin
[b] hell

fear and warn the unjust in it on their knees. [73]And when we recite our clear verses to them, those who became infidels said to those who believed, "Which of the two groups are in the best position and in fairer company?" [74]And how many generations have we destroyed before them who surpassed them in furnishings and appearances? [75]Say, "Whoever was in error, so the merciful will lengthen out to them a length until when they see what they are promised, whether the torment or the hour, so they will know who is in the worse place and the weaker armies." [76]And Allah will increase guidance to those who were guided. And the lasting good deeds are better rewarding with your lord and a better return. [77]Have you seen who became an infidel in our verses and said, "I will surely be given money and son"? [78]Does he have knowledge of the unseen, or has he made a covenant with the merciful? [79]Certainly not, we will prescribe what he will say and will lengthen to him the time of the torment. [80]And we will inherit from him what he says, and he will come to us alone. [81]And they took gods rather than Allah so that they become strength to them. [82]Certainly not, they will be infidels by serving them, and they will be turning against them.

Allah sends satans (demons) to urge people to sin.

[83]Have you not seen that we send the satans against the infidels to incite them incitingly? [84]So do not hasten against them. Surely we only count to them counting. [85]A day we will gather the fearing to the merciful group. [86]And we will drive the criminals thirsty into hell. [87]They will not have the intercession except those who took a covenant with the merciful.

Heaven will be torn apart, and the earth will split from saying, "God has a son."

[88]And they said, "The merciful has taken a son." [89]Indeed, you have brought a wicked thing. [90]The heavens might almost be torn apart from it. And the earth splits, and the mountains fall to pieces [91]because they ascribe a son to the merciful. [92]It must not be to the merciful that he takes a son. [93]That all what is in the heavens and the earth but comes to the merciful as a slave. [94]Indeed, he counted them and numbered them numbering. [95]And all of them will come to him on the resurrection day alone. [96]Surely those who believed and did good deeds, the merciful will make for them friendship. [97]So surely, we made it easy with your tongue so you may give the good news by it to the fearer and warn by it a contentious people. [98]And how many generations have we destroyed before them? Can you feel one of them or hear a whisper from them?

A portion of a revelation   *Taha*

In the name of Allah, the merciful, the merciful

¹Taha.ᵃ ²We did not send down on you the Qur'an that you become miserable, ³except as a reminder for him who fears, ⁴descending from who created the earth and the high heavens. ⁵The merciful sat on the throne. ⁶To him what is in the heavens and what is on the earth and what is between them and what is under the ground. ⁷And if you speak loud, so surely he knows the secret and what is hidden. ⁸Allah, there is no god but him, to him the best names.

The story of Moses is copied from the Bible and corrupted once again. Notice that the location of the fire is in the valley of Tuwa, but the Bible indicates that it was on the mountain of God, Horeb. See Exodus 3:1-5.

⁹And have the sayings of Moses come to you? ¹⁰When he saw a fire, so he said to his family, "Stay, surely I perceive a fire. Perhaps I may bring you a lighted torch from it or find guidance at the fire." ¹¹So when he came to it, he was called, "O Moses, ¹²surely I am your lord. So take off your sandals. Surely you are in the holy valley of Tuwa. ¹³And I have chosen you, so hear what will be revealed. ¹⁴Surely I am Allah; there is no god except me, so serve me and perform the prayer for my remembrance. ¹⁵Surely the hour is coming. I almost hid it, that every soul may be rewarded for what it strives. ¹⁶So do not let those who do not believe prevent you from it and follow his desire so that you should perish. ¹⁷And what is that in your right hand, O Moses?" ¹⁸He said, "It is my rod which I lean on and with which I beat by itᵇ to my sheep, and I have other uses for it." ¹⁹He said, "Cast it down, O Moses." ²⁰So he cast it down, so behold! It became a serpent that slithers. ²¹He said, "Take it and fear not. We will restore it to the first state. ²²And gather your hand to your wings,ᶜ it will come out white without evil as another sign, ²³that we may show you some of our bigger signs. ²⁴Go to Pharaoh, surely he has transgressed. ²⁵He said, "My lord, enlarge my chest, ²⁶and make my affair easy for me. ²⁷And loose the knot from my tongue ²⁸[that] they may understand my saying. ²⁹And make me a prince from my family, ³⁰Aaron my brother. ³¹Increase my strength by him. ³²And I partner

---

ᵃ a word containing two Arabic letters without meaning (which is pronounced as the four letters above)
ᵇ to bring leaves down from the tree for the sheep
ᶜ side

him in my affair. [33]That we praise you much. [34]And remember you much. [35]Surely you were a seer of us." [36]He said, "O Moses, indeed, you are given your request. [37]And indeed, we put on you a favor another time. [38]When we revealed to your mother what is revealed [39]that, 'Cast him into the ark, so cast him into the river, so the river will cast him to the shore. An enemy to me and an enemy to him will take him, and I will bestow love on you from me. And you will be made before my eyes.' [40]When your sister walks, so she will say, 'Will I guide you to someone to take care of him?' So we returned you to your mother so her eyes might be pleased and will not grieve. And you killed a soul, so we delivered you from the grief. And we seduced you [with] seditions so you stayed years among the people of Madyen.[a] Then you came as decreed, O Moses. [41]And I have made[b] you for myself. [42]Go, you and your brother, with my signs, and do not remember me less. [43]Go to Pharaoh, surely he has rebelled. [44]So [both] speak to him with gentle speech, perhaps he will remember or fear." [45]They said, "O our lord, surely we fear that he may exceed against us or he may rebel!" [46]He said, "Do not fear, surely I am with you. I hear, and I see. [47]So you [both] go to him, so say, 'Surely we are messengers of your lord, so send with us the children of Israel, and do not torment them. Indeed, we have brought you a sign from your lord, and the peace is on who follows the guidance.'" [48]"Surely indeed, it has been revealed to us that the torment is on those who denied and turned away." [49]He said, "Who is your lord, O Moses?" [50]He said, "Our lord is he who has given everything its creation, then guided it." [51]He said, "Then what is the state of the first generations?" [52]He said, "Its knowledge is with my lord in a book. My lord does not err and does not forget." [53]He who made the earth for you flat and has traced out ways for you in it and has sent down water from the heaven, so we bring forth as pairs of different plants by it. [54]Eat and pasture your livestock. Surely in this is a sign to those who have forbidding. [55]From it we created you. And in it we will return you, and from it we will bring you forth another time. [56]And indeed, we showed him all of our signs, so he denied and refused.

Mohammed misunderstood which land the Israelites were to inherit.

[57]He said, "Did you come to drive us out from our land by your sorcery, O Moses? [58]So we will bring a sorcery to you like it. So make an appointment between us and you; we will not break and neither will you, a central location." [59]He said, "Your appointment is

---

[a] close to the spelling of the name of the actual Midian people found in Exodus 3:1
[b] chosen

the adornment day, and the people will be gathered in the early afternoon." ⁶⁰So Pharaoh turned away and collected his plots; then he came. ⁶¹Moses said to them, "Woe to you. Do not forge a lie against Allah, so he will destroy you with torment. And indeed, he who forged, failed." ⁶²So they disagreed among themselves in the affair and discussed their plan secretly. ⁶³They said, "Those two are sorcerers. They want to get you out of your land by their sorcery and take away your good traditions. ⁶⁴So gather your schemes, then come standing in line, and indeed, those who become exalted will prosper today." ⁶⁵They said, "O Moses, will you cast, or will we be those who will cast first?" ⁶⁶He said, "Yet you cast." So their ropes and their sticks appeared to him as slithering from their sorcery. ⁶⁷So Moses conceived a fear in his soul. ⁶⁸We said, "Fear not, surely you are the uppermost. ⁶⁹And cast what is in your right hand. It will peck what they have produced. Surely they only produced the plot of sorcery, and the sorcerer will not prosper wherever he comes."

In this version of the story, Mohammed said the Egyptian sorcerers became believers in the god of Moses.

⁷⁰So the sorcerers fell down worshiping. They said, "We believed in the lord of Aaron and Moses." ⁷¹He said, "Have you believed in him before I give you permission? Surely he is your biggest who taught you the sorcery. So I will surely cut off your hands and your legs on opposite sides, and I will surely crucify you on trunks of the palm tree. And you will surely know which of us is more harsh in torment and more abiding." ⁷²They said, "We will not choose you above what came to us of the proofs and him who created us. So judge what you judge, surely you judge only in this the world's life." ⁷³Surely we have believed on our lord that he may forgive us our sins and the sorcery which you compelled us to do. And Allah is better and more abiding. ⁷⁴Surely, whoever comes to his lord as a criminal, so surely he will receive hell; he will not die in it, and he will not live. ⁷⁵And whoever comes to him [as] a believer, indeed did good deeds, so those will have the higher degrees. ⁷⁶Eden's gardens, under it the river flows, they abide in it forever. And this is the reward of the one who is purified. ⁷⁷And indeed, we revealed to Moses to walk with my servants at night, so strike a dry way in the sea. Do not fear to be overtaken, neither be you afraid. ⁷⁸So Pharaoh followed them with his troops, so covered them from the sea that covered them. ⁷⁹And Pharaoh misled his people and did not guide. ⁸⁰"O children of Israel, indeed, we have delivered you from your enemy. And we made a covenant with you on the right side of the mountain, and we caused the manna and the quail to descend on you. ⁸¹Eat of the good things which we provided to you, and do not rebel in them, lest my wrath falls on you. For on whom my wrath does fall, so indeed, destroyed. ⁸²And I am surely forgiving to who repented and believed and did

good deed, then guided. [83]"And what has hastened you from your people, O Moses?" [84]He said, "They were following me closely, and I hastened to you, my lord, that you may be pleased."

This is the story of the Samaritan and Moses' people, even though the Samaritans did not exist as a people until hundreds of years later. This story contradicts the Bible which clearly teaches that it was Aaron, not the Samaritan, who fashioned the golden calf. See Exodus 32. Mohammed confused Hosea 8:5-6 with the calf of the Exodus rebellion!

[85]He said, "So surely indeed, we seduced your people after you, and the Sāmirī[a] led them astray." [86]So Moses returned to his people, wrathful, sorrowful. He said, "O my people, did not your lord promise you a good promise? Was the covenant so long to you, or you desired that wrath from your lord should fall on you so that you broke your promise to me?" [87]They said, "We did not break your promise by our choice, but we carry loads of the people's trinkets, so we threw them, so likewise, the Samaritan threw." [88]So this gave forth a calf to them, a body which had a mooing sound, so they said, "This is your god and the god of Moses." So he forgot. [89]"Do they not see that it does not return to them saying and it does not have for them a harm or benefit?" [90]And indeed, Aaron said to them before that, "O my people, surely you are only seduced by it, and surely your lord is the merciful. So follow me, and obey my commands." [91]They said, "We will not stop worshiping it until Moses returns to us." [92]He said, "O Aaron, what hindered you when you saw them go astray? [93]Will you not follow me? Did you disobey my command?" [94]He said, "O son of my mother, do not seize me by my beard nor by my head. Surely I feared, lest you should say, 'You divided between the children of Israel, and you did not watch my word.'" [95]He said, "So what is the affair with you, O Samaritan?" [96]He said, "I saw what they have not seen, so I took a handful of dust from the path of the messenger, so I made it. And likewise, my soul prompted me to do." [97]He said, "So be gone, so surely to you in this life that you say, 'No touch.' And surely you have a promise that you will not break. And look at your god whom you continue worshiping. Surely we will burn him; then we will blast it into the sea, blasting. [98]Surely your god is only Allah; there is no god except him. His knowledge surrounds all things. [99]Likewise, we recite to you from the news of what has gone before you, and indeed, we give you from ourselves a reminder. [100]Whoever will turn away from it, so he will surely carry a burden on the resurrection day. [101]They will abide in it forever, and it is an evil burden to them to bear on the resurrection day. [102]A day the trumpet

---

[a] Samaritan, non-Arabic word of Hebrew/Syriac origin

will be blown, and we will gather the criminals on that day, blue.
[103]Whispering one to another, you tarried, except ten. [104]We know best what they say when the perfect one among them says, "You have only stayed except a day." [105]And they ask you about the mountains, so say, "My lord will blast them, blasting." [106]So he will leave it as a plain, smooth level. [107]You will not see crookedness or elevation in it. [108]On that day they follow the caller, there is no crookedness in him, and their voices will be hushed to the merciful, so you will not hear except whispering. [109]On that day, the intercession will not profit, except to whom the merciful gives permission to and whose sayings pleases him. [110]He knows what is between their hands and what is behind them, and they do not surround knowledge by him. [111]And the faces submit to the living, the self-subsisting, and indeed, failed are those who carry injustice.
[112]And he who does good deeds while a believer, so he will not fear injustice or to be decreased. [113]And likewise, we sent it down to you an Arabic Qur'an, and we expounded in it some of the warnings, perhaps they may fear, or that it may be a reminder for them. [114]So Allah is exalted, the king, the truth. And do not hasten by the Qur'an before its revelation is completed[a] to you, and say, "My lord, increase me in knowledge."

The story of Adam is copied from the Bible and corrupted once again.

[115]And indeed, we covenanted Adam before, so he forgot; and we did not find any determination in him. [116]And when we said to the angels, "Worship Adam," so they worshiped, except the Devil refused. [117]So we said, "O Adam, surely this is an enemy to you and to your wife. So do not [let him] get you out of the garden, so you will be in misery. [118]Surely you will not be hungry in it, neither will you be naked. [119]And you will not be thirsty in it, neither will you feel the heat of the sun." [120]So Satan whispered to him and said, "O Adam, will I show you the tree of immortality and of the kingdom that will not perish?" [121]So they ate from it, so their nakedness appeared to them, and they began to cut and glue together leaves of the garden on them.[b] And Adam disobeyed his lord, so he was seduced. [122]Then his lord chose him, so he relented on him and guided. [123]He said, "Go all of you down from it; each of you is an enemy to the other. So whatever guidance comes to you from me, so whoever follows my guidance, so he will not go astray nor be in misery. [124]And whoever will turn away from my reminder, so surely to him a life of hardship. And we will gather him blind on the resurrection day." [125]He said, "My lord, why did you gather me blind, and indeed, I was seeing?" [126]He said, "Likewise, our verses came to you, so you forgot it, and

---

[a] given
[b] their private parts

likewise, today you will be forgotten.[127]And likewise, we reward those who are extravagant and do not believe in the verses of his lord, and the torment of the hereafter is more severe and more lasting." [128]Did not he guide them how many generations we destroyed before them? They walk in their dwellings. Surely in this are signs to those who have forbidding. [129]And were it not that a word proceeded from your lord; it was appointed and at a fixed time. [130]So be patient about what they say, and praise with your lord's praise before the sunrise and before its setting and some of the night. So praise to him, and in the edges of the day, perhaps you will be pleased. [131]And do not strain your eyes to what we have enjoyed on some of the wives, the flowers of the world's life, that we may seduce them in it. And the provision of your lord is better and more lasting. [132]And command your family with the prayer and patiently adhere to it. We do not ask you to give provision. We will provide for you, and the end is to the piety.

Once again, people ask Mohammed to prove his claim to be a prophet by performing signs. Note his strange response!

[133]And they said, "Were it not that he would bring us a sign from his lord. Have not proofs come to them in the first suhuf?"[a] [134]And had we destroyed them by a torment before him, they would surely have said, "Our lord, were it not that you had sent to us a messenger that we might follow your verses before we were despised and disgraced!" [135]Say, "All are waiting, so wait. So you will know who are the companions of the even way and who has been guided."

A portion of a revelation   **The Prophets**

In the name of Allah, the merciful, the merciful

[1]The reckoning of the people has drawn near, and they are heedless in turning away. [2]No new reminder comes to them from their lord, but they listen to it while they are sporting. [3]Their hearts are occupied and confer in secret, those who are unjust: "Is that but a human like you, do you bring the sorcery, and you are seeing?" [4]Say, "My lord knows the saying in the heaven and the earth. And he is the hearing, the knowing."

---

[a] pages of writing, non-Arabic word of S. Arabia origin

Some point out that Mohammed did not perform any signs like the previous prophets. They also say that his Qur'an is just a forgery and poetry.

[5]"Yet," they said, "it is the medley of dreams, yet he forged it. Yet he is a poet. So let him bring to us with a sign as the ancients were sent." [6]No village before them believed; we destroyed it. Will they believe?

The Bible is the inspired Word of God. Notice the Bible is identified as the reminder. Also see verse 25.

[7]And we did not send before you, except men whom we revealed to them. So ask the people of the reminder, if you were not knowing. [8]We did not make them bodies, they do not eat the food, and they were not immortal. [9]Then we fulfilled the promise to them, so we delivered them and whom we willed, and we destroyed the extravagant.[10]Indeed, we have sent down to you a book, in it your reminder. Do you not understand? [11]And how many a village was unjust we destroyed, and we raised up after it another people. [12]So when they felt our torment, then they ran away from it. [13]"Do not run and return to what you enjoyed in it and your dwellings. Perhaps you may be asked." [14]They said, "O woe to us, surely we were unjust!" [15]So this was still their calling until we made them as extinguished reaping. [16]And we did not create the heaven and the earth and what is between them sporting. [17]Had it been our will to find fun, we surely would take it from ourselves, if we were doing. [18]Yet we cast with the truth against vanity so it will crush its head, so it vanished and the woe to you for what you describe. [19]And to him who is in the heavens and the earth and who is with him, will not be proud of serving him, nor they regret. [20]They praise the night and the day and do not cease. [21]Or they take gods from the earth who can raise the dead. [22]If there were gods in them except Allah, it would be vandalized. So praise be to Allah, the lord of the throne, above what they describe. [23]He is not asked about what he does, and they will be asked. [24]Or have they taken gods other than him? Say, "Bring your proofs." This is a reminder of those who are with me and a reminder of those who were before me, yet most of them do not know the truth, so they turn away. [25]And we have not sent before you any messenger, except that we reveal to him. Surely there is no god except me, so serve me.

Mohammed denies the deity of Jesus Christ, once again, and 'Isā (the Jesus of Mohammed) will burn in hell.

[26]And they said, "The merciful has taken a son, praise be to him." Yet they are honorable servants. [27]They do not go before him with the speech, and they work with his command. [28]He knows what is between their hands and what is behind them, and they do not

intercede except to whom he pleases. And they tremble from his fear. [29]And whoever says from among them, "Surely I am a god, without him." So such a one we will reward him hell; likewise, we reward the unjust.

Heaven, as a place, is a solid structure like a ceiling. The earth does not move. It sits still. See also verses 22:65 and 50:6.

[30]Or have not those who became infidels seen that the heavens and the earth were a solid mass, so we parted them, and we made every living thing from the water? Do they not believe? [31]And we made stabilizers on the earth, lest it move with them, and we made ways between them on it, perhaps they may be guided. [32]And we made the heaven a kept ceiling, and they turn away from its signs. [33]And he is who created the night and the day and the sun and the moon, each swimming in the sky. [34]And we did not make it for humans before you to dwell forever. If you die, are they immortal? [35]Every soul will taste the death, and we will test you with evil and with good [as] sedition, and unto us you will return. [36]And when those who became infidels see you, they take you but as a scoff. "Is this who remembers your gods?" And they are with the remembrance of the merciful; they are infidels. [37]The human was created of haste. I will show you my signs, so do not hasten. [38]And they say, "When will this promise be, if you were truthful?" [39]If those who became infidels knew the time when they will not be able to keep the fire from their faces or from their backs, and they will not be helped. [40]Yet it will come on them suddenly and will confound them so they will not be able to put it back, neither will they be delayed. [41]And indeed, the messengers before you were scoffed at, so afflict those who scoffed at them with what they were scoffing with. [42]Say, "Who will keep you by night and by day from the merciful?" Yet they were turned away from the remembrance of their lord. [43]Or do they have gods who can defend them without us? They cannot help themselves, and they will not be befriended by us.

When Islam comes to a land, the natives are defeated, and their borders are reduced.

[44]Yet we gave those and their fathers enjoyment until they had a long age. Do they not see that we came to the earth to lessen its borders? Are they the victorious? [45]Say, "Surely I am only warning you with the revelation, and the deaf cannot hear the call when they are warned." [46]And if a little of the torment of your lord touches them, they will surely say, "O woe to us, surely we were unjust!"

Men save themselves by doing good deeds for Allah.

[47]And we set up the scales with justice for the resurrection day so that no soul will be dealt with unjustly anything, even if it was the weight of a khardal[a] seed, we will bring it. And sufficient is the reckoning to us. [48]And indeed, we gave Moses and Aaron the discriminator and a light and a reminder for the fearer, [49]those who fear their lord in the unseen. And they are in fear of the hour. [50]And this is a blessed reminder, we sent it down. Are you then denying it?

The story of Abraham is given here once again. Mohammed invented the story of the fire which occurs as a result of a misunderstanding of the word "Ur" (meaning *city*) because it was mistranslated by the Jewish interpreter Johnathan, son of Azreel. He translated the word as "light" into the Chaldean language. So it said, "I am the lord who got you out from the *light of the fire* of the Chaldeans," instead of saying "...the *city* of the Chaldeans." Notice that Mohammed confused Abraham's story with Gideon's story in Judges 6:22-32.

[51]And indeed, we gave Abraham his guidance before, and we were knowing him well. [52]When he said to his father and to his people, "What are those statues which you are devoted to?" [53]They said, "We found our fathers serving them." [54]He said, "Indeed, you and your fathers were in obvious error." [55]They said, "Have you come to us with the truth, or are you of the sporters?" [56]He said, "Yet your lord is the lord of the heavens and the earth who created them, and I am of the witnesses to this. [57]And [I swear] by Allah, I will surely lay a plot against your idols after you turn your backs." [58]So he made them pieces except the biggest of them, perhaps they may return to it. [59]They said, "Who has done this to our gods? Surely he is of the unjust." [60]They said, "We heard a youth speak of them. He is called Abraham." [61]They said, "So bring him before the people's eyes, perhaps they may witness." [62]They said, "Have you done this to our gods, O Abraham?" [63]He said, "Yet their biggest, this did it, so ask them if they were speaking." [64]So they returned to themselves, so they said, "Surely you are the unjust!" [65]Then they hung down their heads: "Indeed, you know that those cannot talk." [66]He said, "Do you serve without Allah that which does not profit you anything nor harm you?" [67]"Ouf to you and what you serve without Allah. Do you not understand?" [68]They said, "Burn him, and help your gods if you were doing." [69]We said, "O fire, be cold, and peace on Abraham." [70]And they sought to lay a plot against him, but we made them the losers.

---

[a] mustard, non-Arabic word of Syriac origin

Stories from the Old Testament are jumbled and misquoted in these verses.

[71]And we delivered him and Lot to the land which we blessed in it to the worlds. [72]And we granted him Isaac and Jacob as extra, and we made them both doers of good. [73]And we made them leaders who guide by our command. And we revealed to them doing the good deeds and the performing of the prayer and bringing the legal alms, and they were serving us. [74]And we gave Lot wisdom and knowledge, and we delivered him from the village which was doing the abominations. Surely they were an evil, transgressing people.[75]And we admitted him in our mercy, surely he was of the good. [76]And Noah, when he called before, so we answered and delivered him and his family from the great calamity. [77]And we helped him against the people who denied our verses. Surely they were an evil people, so we drowned them all.

This passage has Solomon and David judging at the same time. Mohammed confused Solomon with Absalom. See 2 Samuel 15:1-6. The story of the ninety-nine sheep is completely mixed up with the account found in 2 Samuel 12:1-7 which tells about Nathan the prophet rebuking David for his sin with Bathsheba.

[78]And David and Solomon, when they judged concerning the crop when the sheep of the people pastured in it, and we were to their judgment a witness. [79]So we caused Solomon to understand it, and to each of them we gave wisdom and knowledge. And we made subservient with David the mountains and the birds to praise, and we were the doers. [80]And we taught him the making of clothes for you to protect you from your violence. So are you thankful?

What a mighty wind! What are the diving satans?

[81]And to Solomon, the strongly blowing wind will run according to his command to the earth which we blessed in it, and we were knowing of all things. [82]And some of the satans, who would dive for him and they would do works without that, and we were keepers for them.

The story of Job is taken from the Bible. It was condensed from 42 chapters and corrupted. The story is repeated in verses 38:41-44. For the actual account, read the book of Job in the Bible. Notice, as usual, Mohammed uses names of prophets without giving any details of their stories.

[83]And Job, when he called his lord: "Surely harm has touched me, and you are the most merciful of the merciful!" [84]So we answered him. So we removed what is in him from harm, and we gave him his

family and like them with them, a mercy from us and a reminder to the servants. [85]And Ishmael and Idris[a] and Za Al Kafel,[b] all were among the patient. [86]And we admitted them in our mercy, surely they were of the good.

The story of Jonah is copied from the Bible and corrupted once again, this time with a new name, Za Al Nōn.

[87]And Za Al Nōn,[c] when he went in wrath, so he thought that we had no power over him. So he called from the darkness, "There is no god except you; praise be to you, surely I was of the unjust!" [88]So we answered to him and delivered him from the grief, and likewise, we deliver the believers. [89]And Zacharias, when he called on his lord: "My lord, do not leave me alone,[d] and you are the best of the inheritors." [90]So we answered him and granted him Yahya,[e] and we fixed his wife for him. Surely they were hastened in the good deeds, and they called on us with affection and fear. And they were humble to us. [91]And she who guarded her private parts, so we breathed into her[f] of our spirit,[g] and we made her and her son a sign to the worlds. [92]Surely this is your nation, one nation; and I am your lord, so serve me. [93]And they cut off their affair among them, and to us they will all return. [94]So whoever will do good deeds, while he is a believer. So we will not deny his striving, and surely we are prescribing for him. [95]And it is forbidden for a village which we have destroyed, surely they will not return [96]until if Gog and Magog are opened and they speed up from every elevated place. [97]And the true promise draws near. So behold, eyes of those who became infidels will stare: "O woe to us, indeed, we were heedless of this; yet we were unjust."

'Isā (the Jesus of Mohammed) and any others who are served will burn in hell.

[98]Surely you and whatever you serve, without Allah, will be the fuel of the fire for hell, and into it you will arrive. [99]If those were gods, they would not enter it, and everyone in it will abide there forever. [100]They will exhale in it, and they will not hear in it. [101]Surely those of whom the good preceded from us, those are kept away from it. [102]They will not hear its crackling, and they will abide forever in what their soul lusts for. [103]The biggest terror will not grieve them, and the angels will meet them: "This is your day which you were promised."

---

[a] wrong name, he meant Enoch
[b] wrong name, he meant Isaiah
[c] wrong name, he meant Jonah
[d] without offspring
[e] the Baptist
[f] her vagina, see Qur'an 66:12
[g] the holy spirit

The rolling of the heavens is copied from the Bible. See Isaiah 34:4. Notice that verse 105 is copied from a quotation found in Psalm 37:29.

[104]A day we will roll up the heavens as rolling books of written sijill.[a] As we made the first creation, so we will bring it forth again. This promise binds us, surely we were doing. [105]And indeed, we wrote in the Psalms after the reminder: "Surely my good servant will inherit the earth." [106]Surely there is in this a message to a servant people. [107]And we did not send you except as a mercy to the worlds. [108]Say, "Surely it is only revealed to me that your god is only one god. So are you Muslims?" [109]So if they turn away, so say, "I have warned you all alike, and I do not know if what you have been promised is near or far away." [110]Surely he knows what is spoken openly, and he knows what you conceal. [111]And I do not know, perhaps it is a seduction for you and an enjoyment for a time. [112]He said, "My lord judges with the truth, and our lord is the merciful whose assistance is to be sought against what you describe."

A portion of a revelation — **22** — *The Pilgrimage*

In the name of Allah, the merciful, the merciful

[1]O you people, fear your lord. Surely the shaking of the hour is a great thing. [2]A day you see it, every nursing [female] will become shocked of what she had nursed and everyone who is pregnant will deliver what she is carrying and you will see the people drunk and they are not drunk, but the torment of Allah is severe. [3]And some of the people who dispute about Allah without knowledge and follow every rebellious satan. [4]It is prescribed against him, whoever takes him for a friend, so he will lead him astray, and he will guide him to the torment of the blaze.

Mohammed's concept of conception is written here. See also verses 23:12-14.

[5]O you people, if you were in doubt, of the resurrection, so surely we created you from dirt, then from nutfah, then from a clot, then pieces of flesh, created and uncreated, to show you. And we cause whom we will to remain in the wombs for an appointed time. Then we

---

[a] edict, non-Arabic word of Greek origin

will bring you forth as infants, then permit you to reach your age of strength. And some of you will die, and some of you will be given back to the worst age, so they will not know after knowledge anything. And you have seen the earth barren, so when we send down the water on it, it stirs and swells and grows every kind of beautiful pair. [6]This is because Allah is the truth. And he will give life to the dead, and he has might over everything. [7]And that the hour is coming, no doubt about it, and that Allah will raise up who are in the tombs. [8]And among the people are those who dispute about Allah without knowledge or guidance or an enlightening book, [9]turning aside to mislead others from the way of Allah. In the world he will have disgrace. And on the resurrection day we will make him taste the torment of the fire. [10]This is because of what your hand has advanced, and surely Allah is not unjust to the servants. [11]And some of the people who serve Allah on the edge, so if good falls on him, he is confident in it; and if sedition comes on him, he turns on his face. He lost this world and the hereafter, this is the clear loss. [12]He calls on without Allah, which can neither hurt him nor profit him, this is the far error. [13]He calls on him whose harm is closer than his profit. Wretched is the lord, and wretched is the associate! [14]Surely Allah will admit those who believed and did good deeds into gardens, below them the rivers flow. Surely Allah does what he wants. [15]Whoever was thinking that Allah will not help him in this world and in the hereafter, so let him stretch a rope to the heaven, then let him cut it off, so he will see if it can remove that which enrages him. [16]And likewise, we send it down clear verses, and surely Allah guides whom he wants. [17]Surely those who believed and those who are Jews and the Sabians and the Nasara (Christians) and the Magians[a] and those who are polytheists, surely Allah will separate between them on the resurrection day. Surely Allah is a witness of all things. [18]Have you not seen that who is in the heavens and who is on the earth and the sun and the moon and the stars and the mountains and the trees and the creatures and many of the people worship Allah. And many the torment is established against him. And whomever Allah humiliates, so he will not have anyone to give him honor. Surely Allah does what he wills. [19]Those are two debaters who dispute[b] concerning their lord. So those who became infidels, garments of fire will be cut out for them, above their heads the hamem will be poured. [20]By it will melt what is in their bellies and their skin. [21]And there are whips of iron for them. [22]Whenever they wanted to get out of it from gloom, they were brought back to it: "And taste the torment of the fire." [23]Surely Allah will admit those who believed and did good deeds into gardens, below them the rivers flow. They will be adorned in it with golden bracelets and with pearls,

---

[a] ancient Persian polytheists
[b] verb indicates three or more—grammatical error in Qur'an

and their clothes in it are silk. [24]And they are guided to the good of the speech, and they are guided to the praised way. [25]Surely those who became infidels and prevent [others] from the way of Allah and from the forbidden mosque, which we have appointed to the people alike for those who dwell in it and for the stranger and those who desire to profane it unjustly, we will cause them to taste a painful torment.

The Pilgrimage to Mecca and the circling of the mosque in Mecca are copied from ancient pagan practices.

[26]And when we showed to Abraham the place of the house that you will not partner anything with me, and purify my house to those who march around and to those who stand or kneel in worship. [27]And proclaim the pilgrimage to the people. They will come to you on foot and on every lean mount, arriving by every deep way. [28]To bear witness of its benefits to them and may remember Allah's name on known days for what he provided them from the bahīma[a] of the livestock, so eat from it, and feed the despondent, the poor. [29]Then let them complete the prescribed duties for them and perform their vows and march around the 'atīq[b] house. [30]That and he who honors the forbidden ordinances of Allah, so it is good for him with his lord. And the livestock is lawful for you except those already specified to you. So avoid the uncleanness of the idols, and avoid the zūr[c] speech.

Those who unite 'Isā (the Jesus of Mohammed) or anyone else with Allah will be destroyed.

[31]Hanifa[d] to Allah and do not partner with him. And whoever partners with Allah, so it is like one falling down from the heavens, so the bird will snatch him or the wind will carry him off to a far distant place. [32]That and whoever honors the rites of Allah, so surely it is of the piety of the hearts. [33]You have in them benefits until a fixed time, and then its place is the ancient house. [34]And to every nation we have appointed religious ceremonies so that they may remember the name of Allah over the beast of livestock which he provided them. So your god is one god, so be Muslim to him and give the good news to the humble. [35]Those, when Allah's name is mentioned, their hearts tremble and the patient about whatever falls on them and the performers of the prayer, and they spend from what we provided them.

---

[a] animals, non-Arabic word of Hebrew origin
[b] ancient, non-Arabic word of Aramaic origin
[c] falsehood, non-Arabic word of probable Middle Persian origin
[d] word without meaning

The rules for animal sacrifices were copied from Arabian paganistic practices. Eating camel meat is lawful in the Qur'an, but it is forbidden in Mosaic Law. See Leviticus 11:4.

[36]And the camels we have made for you for the sacrifice to Allah, you have good in them. So mention the name of Allah over them as they stand in a row, so that when they fall over on their sides, so eat from them and feed the content and the beggar. Likewise, we made them subservient to you, perhaps you will give thanks. [37]Allah will not receive their meat or their blood, but he will receive the piety from you. Likewise, he has made it subservient to you so that you might magnify Allah[a] for his guidance and give the good news to the doers of good. [38]Surely, Allah defends those who believed. Surely, Allah does not love any traitor, infidel. [39]Permission is given to those who engage in war because they were wronged, and surely Allah is capable of helping them.

Allah ordained war to prevent the ungodly from destroying all godly things.

[40]Those who have been driven from their homes unjustly, except they said, "Our lord is Allah." And were it not that Allah had repelled some people by others, sawāmi'[b] and biya'[c] and salawāt[d] and mosques, in which the name of Allah is ever remembered, would surely have been destroyed. And indeed, Allah will help those who help him. Surely Allah is strong, dear. [41]Those who, if we establish them on the earth, performed the prayer and brought the legal alms and commanded what is right and forbade from the evil, and to Allah the end of the affairs. [42]And if they deny you, so indeed, before them, the people of Noah and Ad and Themoud denied. [43]And the people of Abraham and the people of Lot [44]and the companions of Midian. And Moses was denied. So I delayed to the infidels, then I seized them. So how was my repudiation? [45]So how many a village we destroyed when it was unjust, so it became empty on its trellises and its wells have been abandoned and its lofty castles? [46]Have they not walked on the earth, so it will be to them hearts to understand with or ears to hear with? So surely it will not blind the eyes, but it will blind the hearts which is in the chests.

Mohammed has copied a well-known verse from the Bible found in 2 Peter 3:8.

[47]And they hasten you with the torment, and Allah will not change his promise. And surely one day with your lord is like a thousand

---

[a] that is to call "Allah Akbar," i.e. Allah is bigger
[b] cloisters, non-Arabic word of Ethiopian origin
[c] churches, non-Arabic word of Syriac origin
[d] synagogues, non-Arabic word of Syriac origin

years of what you count. [48]And how many a village have I delayed to it,[a] and it was unjust; then I seized it, and the final return is to me. [49]Say, "O you people, surely I am only a plain warner to you. [50]So those who believed and did good deeds, they have forgiveness and a generous provision. [51]And those who strove to hinder our verses, they are the companions of hell."

Mohammed defends himself concerning his quotation of the Satanic Verses in verses 53:19-23 by claiming that it is a normal thing which took place with many prophets before him. However, this claim is unsubstantiated.

[52]And we did not send before you any messenger nor prophet except that when he wishes, Satan casts in his wishes, so Allah abrogates what Satan casts. Then Allah fixed his verses. And Allah is knowing, wise. [53]So he made what Satan casts a sedition to those who have sickness in their hearts and those who their hearts are hardened and surely the unjust are in far opposition. [54]And so that those who have been given the knowledge know that it is the truth from your lord, so they believe in it. And their hearts may be humble to it, and surely Allah will guide those who believed into a straight way. [55]And still those who became infidels in doubt of it until the hour comes to them suddenly or the torment will come on them on a barren day. [56]The kingdom on that day is to Allah. He will judge between them, so those who believed and did good deeds are in the gardens of bliss. [57]And those who became infidels and denied our verses, so those will have a disgraceful torment.

Those who leave home to engage in war for Allah will be rewarded—a recurring theme.

[58]And those who emigrated for the sake of Allah then were killed or died, Allah will surely provide for them an excellent provision. And surely Allah is the best of the providers. [59]He will admit them an entrance which will please them. And surely Allah is knowing, forbearing. [60]That and whoever punishes like what he was punished with, then he was oppressed, Allah will help him. Surely Allah is pardoning, forgiving. [61]That is because Allah penetrates the night into the day and penetrates the day into the night. And that Allah is hearing, seeing. [62]That is because Allah is the truth, and that what they call on other than him is the vanity. And surely Allah is the high, the big. [63]Do you not see that Allah sends down water from heaven so the earth becomes green? Surely Allah is kind, aware. [64]To him what is in the heavens and what is on the earth. And surely Allah is the rich, the praised.

---

[a] its punishment

Heaven is a structure that Allah is holding by his hand.

[65]Do you not see that Allah has made subservient to you what is on the earth and the ships run in the sea with his command? And he holds the heaven so that it will not fall on the earth except with his permission. Surely Allah is with the people, compassionate, merciful. [66]And he is who has given you life, then will cause you to die, then will give you life. Surely the human is an infidel. [67]To every nation we have appointed religious ceremonies that they observe. So do not let them dispute with you in the affair, and call on your lord, surely you are on a straight guidance. [68]But if they dispute with you, so say, "Allah knows best what you are doing." [69]Allah will judge between you on the resurrection day about what you were differing. [70]Do you not know that Allah knows what is in the heaven and the earth? Surely that is in a book. Surely that is easy for Allah.

There is no help for those who serve anyone but Allah.

[71]And they are serving without Allah, what he did not send down with authority and what they did not have knowledge of, and the unjust have no helper. [72]And when our clear verses are recited to them, you will know the disgraceful deed in the faces of those who became infidels. They will almost attack those who recite to them our verses. Say, "Will I inform you about evil from this fire? Allah promises it to those who became infidels, and evil is the final place." [73]O you people, a parable is set for you, so listen to it. Surely those whom you call on without Allah, they cannot create flies even if they were gathered to it, and if the flies snatched something away, they cannot rescue it away from them. Weak is the seeker and the sought. [74]They did not value Allah his true value. Surely Allah is strong, dear. [75]Allah chooses messengers from the angels and from the people. Surely Allah is hearing, seeing. [76]He knows what is between their hands and what is behind them, and all the affairs will return to Allah.

Muslims are named by Abraham. Also, believers must worship humbly and engage in true jihad.

[77]O you who have believed, kneel and worship and serve your lord and do good, perhaps you will prosper. [78]And perform jihad in Allah, his true jihad. He elected you, and he did not place on you any hardship in the religion, the religion of your father Abraham. He has named you the Muslims, before and in this, that the messengers may be a witness against you and that you may be witnesses against the people. So perform the prayer and bring the legal alms and hold fast to Allah. He is your protector. So blessed is the protector, and blessed is the helper.

A portion of a revelation **23** *The Believers*

In the name of Allah, the merciful, the merciful

[1]Indeed, the believers have prospered, [2]those who are humble in their prayers, [3]and those who turn away from vain words, [4]and those who to the legal alms are doing.

Believers, male and female, must restrain themselves from sex with anyone except their spouses and their concubines or slaves, whether married or single.

[5]And those who are keeping their private parts (maintain their chastity), [6]except from their wives or what their right hands possess, so surely they are not blamed. [7]So whoever desires to reach more than that, so those are the transgressors. [8]And those who to their trusts and their covenants are watchful, [9]and those who to their prayers are keeping, [10]those who are the heirs, [11]those who inherit the paradise, they will abide in it forever.

This is a scientific misconception concerning the formation of the fetus. Also, Allah is one of many creators.

[12]And indeed, we created the human from an extract of mud. [13]Then we made him a nutfah in a secure place. [14]Then we created the nutfah into a clot. So we created the clot into a piece of flesh, so we created the piece of flesh into bones, so we clothed the bones with flesh. Then we made it another creature. So blessed be Allah, the best of the creators. [15]Then after that, surely you will die. [16]Then you will surely be raised on the resurrection day. [17]And indeed, we have created above you seven ways, and we were not heedless about the creation. [18]And we send down water by measure from the heaven. So we cause it to dwell on the earth, and surely we are able to take it away. [19]So we produce to you by it gardens of palm trees and grapes. You have in it much fruit, and from it you eat.

Mohammed tells about an olive tree on Mount Sinai, but no tree grew on Mount Sinai.

[20]And a tree comes from Mount Sainā,[a] which yields oil and a juice for eaters. [21]And surely there is a lesson for you in the livestock: we give you to drink of what is in their bellies and you have many

---

[a] Sinai, non-Arabic word of Syriac origin

benefits and of them you eat. [22]And on them and on ships you are carried.

The story of Noah is copied from the Bible and corrupted again. Notice that the order of events described the water coming up and then the animals were put aboard. This opposes the Bible which clearly teaches that at God's direction, the animals were loaded one week prior to the flood. Also, a mistake was made when no mention was given to the fact that there were also seven of each of the pure animals and birds. See Genesis 7.

[23]And indeed, we sent Noah to his people. So he said, "O my people, serve Allah. You have no god other than him. Do you not fear?" [24]So the leaders of those who became infidels among his people said, "What is this except a human like you, who desires to be preferred over you. And, if Allah willed, he would send angels. We did not hear of this from our ancient fathers. [25]He is only a man in whom is jinn, so watch him for a time." [26]He said, "Lord, help me, for they denied me!" [27]So we revealed to him that, "Make the ship by our eyes and our revelation, so when our command comes and the oven boils up,[a] so walk into it from every pair two and your family, except for him on whom our saying has already passed among them. And do not speak to me for those unjust, surely they will be drowned. [28]So when you are seated with those who are with you on the ship, so say, "The praise be to Allah who has delivered us from the unjust people." [29]And say, "My lord, send me down with a blessed descending, and you are the best of the senders." [30]Surely in this are signs, and we were the testers.

This describes the unknown messenger with the unknown message to the unknown people.

[31]Then we raised up after them another generation. [32]So we sent to them a messenger from among them: "That serve Allah, you have no god other than him. Do you not fear?" [33]And the leaders of his people, those who became infidels, and they denied the meeting[b] of the hereafter, and though we give them plenty of enjoyment in the world's life, said, "This is just a human like you. He eats from what you eat from and drinks from what you drink. [34]And if you obey a human like yourselves, then surely you will be losers. [35]Does he promise you that if you die and were dust and bones, you will be coming out? [36]Far away, far away is what you promised. [37]This is only our life of this world: we die and we live and we will not be raised. [38]He is just a man who forged lies against Allah, and we will not believe in him." [39]He said, "Lord, help me for they denied me!"

---

[a] like froth on milk
[b] day of judgment

[40]He said, "In a little while, they will surely become regretful." [41]So the shout seized them with the truth, so we made them as scum. So away with the unjust people! [42]Then, after them, we raised up other generations. [43]No nation will hasten their appointed time, and neither will they delay it. [44]Then we sent our messengers one after another. And every time a nation's messenger arrived, they denied him. So we made some of them to follow others, and we made them tales, so away with the people who do not believe.

The story of Moses is copied from the Bible and corrupted again.

[45]Then we sent Moses and his brother Aaron with our signs and a manifest authority [46]to Pharaoh and his leaders, so they became proud, and they were a haughty people. [47]So they said, "Will we believe in two humans like ourselves, and their people to us are serving?" [48]So they denied them, so they were among the destroyed. [49]And indeed, we gave Moses the book, perhaps they may be guided. [50]And we made the son of Mary and his mother a sign, and we sheltered them in a high place with security and with a spring. [51]O you messengers, eat of things that are good and do good deed, surely I know what you do. [52]And surely this is your nation, one nation, and I am your lord, so fear me. [53]So they cut off their affairs among them into Zober,[a] every party rejoicing by what they had. [54]So leave them in their depths of error until a time. [55]Do they think that we only provided them with money and sons? [56]We hasten to them in the good, yet they do not feel. [57]Surely those who are from the awe of their lord, fearing. [58]And those who believe in the verses of their lord, [59]and those who do not have partners with their lord, [60]and those who give what they gave and their hearts filled with dread, surely to their lord they will return; [61]those hasten to do good deeds and are the first to do it. [62]And we will not burden a soul beyond its capacity, and with us is a book that speaks with the truth. And they will not be dealt with unjustly. [63]Yet their hearts are overwhelmed in that, and they have their works, without this, that they continue to do, [64]until when we seize those who have a luxurious life with torment, then they groan. [65]Do not groan today, surely you will not be helped. [66]Indeed, my verses were recited to you, so you were turning back on your heels, [67]acting proudly against it, and leaving it by night. [68]Did they contemplate the words or did it come to them, that which did not come to their ancient fathers? [69]Or did they not know their messenger, so they are denying him? [70]Or they say, "There is a jinn in him." Yet he came to them with the truth, and most of them to the

---

[a] translated throughout the Qur'an as "scriptures," but in this verse only is translated as "sects"

truth are haters. [71]And if the truth had followed their desires, surely the heavens and the earth and all that is in them would be vandalized. Yet we have brought them their reminder, so they turn away from their reminder. [72]Or you ask them for a tribute, the tribute of your lord is the best. And he is the best of the providers. [73]And you will surely invite them to a straight way. [74]And surely those who do not believe in the hereafter are deviating from the way. [75]And if we had taken mercy on them and lifted the harm that is in them, they would have plunged on in their rebellion blindly. [76]And indeed, we seized them with a torment, so they did not submit to their lord, And they did not implore [77]until, when we have opened on them the door of a severe torment, behold, they are in it moblesun.[a] [78]And he is who made the hearing and the sight and the hearts for you, little you give thanks. [79]And he is who multiplied you on the earth, and you will be gathered to him. [80]And he is who gives life and causes death and to him the alternation of the night and the day. Do you not understand? [81]Yet they said like what the ancients said. [82]They said, "If we died and we were dust and bones, will we then be raised? [83]Indeed, we were promised this, we and our fathers before. This is nothing but the legends of the ancients." [84]Say, "To whom is the earth and who is in it, if you were knowing?" [85]They will say, "To Allah." Say, "Do you not remember?" [86]Say, "Who is the lord of the seven heavens and the lord of the great throne?" [87]They will say, "To Allah." Say, "Do you not fear?" [88]Say, "In whose hand is the kingdom of all things and who protects, but against him there is no protection, if you were knowing?" [89]They will say, "To Allah." Say, "So how are you bewitched?" [90]Yet, we brought them with the truth, but surely they are liars.

The Qur'an clearly teaches that Allah has no son.

[91]Allah has not taken some son. And there was not any other god with him or else each god would go with what he created, and perhaps some of them will be against the others. Praise be to Allah, above what they describe. [92]The knower of the unseen and the seen, so he is higher above what they partner. [93]Say, "My lord, will you show me what they promised? [94]My lord, do not make me of the unjust people." [95]And surely, we are able to show you what we promised them. [96]Pay the evil by that which is better. We know best what they describe. [97]And say, "My lord, I seek refuge in you against the suggestion of the satans. [98]And I seek refuge with you, my lord, lest they come to me." [99]Until, when death comes to one of them, he says, "My lord, return me. [100]Perhaps I may do a good deed with what I have left." Certainly not, surely this is a word which he will speak. And behind them will be a berzah[b] until a day they will be

---

[a] a word without meaning
[b] barrier, non-Arabic word of Pahlavi origin

raised. [101]So when they blow in the trumpet, so no ties of family between them on that day. Neither will they ask each other.

Salvation comes to those whose good deeds outweigh their bad deeds on the scales.

[102]So whose scales are heavy, so those are the prosperous. [103]And whose scales are light, so those are they who lost their souls in hell forever. [104]The fire will scorch their faces, and they will shrivel in it. [105]"Were not my verses recited to you, so you were denying them?" [106]They said, "Our lord, our misery prevailed against us, and we were a strayed people. [107]Our lord, get us out of it. So if we then return, so surely we will be unjust." [108]He says, "Stay in it, and do not speak to me. [109]Surely there was a group among my servants who were saying, 'Our lord, we believed, so forgive us and have mercy on us, and you are the best of the merciful.' [110]So you took them for a scoff until they made you forget my remembrance, and you were laughing at them. [111]Surely I have rewarded them today for their patience. Surely they are the triumphant." [112]He said, "How many number of years did you stay on the earth?" [113]They said, "We stayed a day or part of a day, so ask those who count." [114]He said, "You only stayed a little while, if you were knowing. [115]Did you think that we created you for nothing and that you would not return to us?" [116]So Allah is exalted, the king, the truth. There is no god except him, the lord of the generous throne.

It will be bad for the unbelievers who worship 'Isā (the Jesus of Mohammed) or any god along with Allah.

[117]And whoever calls with Allah another god, he has no proof in him, so surely his reckoning is only with his lord. Surely the infidels will not prosper. [118]And say, "My lord, forgive and have mercy. And you are the best of the merciful."

A portion of a revelation   *The Light*

In the name of Allah, the merciful, the merciful

[1]A portion of a revelation we have sent down and made mandatory, and we sent it down in very clear verses, perhaps you may remember.

People who have sex outside of marriage must be beaten. This verse has been superseded by the practice of stoning to death which used to be a written verse of the Qur'an. However, the scrap of parchment containing this verse was eaten by a goat.

[2]The female fornicator and the male fornicator, so scourge each of them with one hundred stripes, and do not let compassion keep you from carrying out the religion of Allah, if you were believers in Allah and the last day. And let an assembly of the believers witness their torment.

Muslims who have committed fornication cannot marry chaste Muslims.

[3]The male fornicator cannot have sex (marry) except with a female fornicator or a female polytheist, and the female fornicator cannot have sex (marry) except with a male fornicator or a male polytheist. And this is forbidden for the believers. [4]And those who accuse virtuous women, then they cannot bring four witnesses, then scourge them with eighty stripes, and do not receive their testimony forever, for those are transgressors, [5]except those who repent and reform after that. So surely Allah is forgiving, merciful. [6]And those who accuse their wives and there was not for them witnesses but themselves, so the testimony of each of them will be a testimony by swearing by Allah four times, that surely he is of the truthful. [7]And the fifth time, the curse of Allah will be on him, if he was one of the liars. [8]But the torment will not be on her if she swears four swearings by Allah, that surely he is of the liars. [9]And a fifth time the wrath of Allah on her, if he was among the truthful. [10]And were it not for the bounty of Allah on you and his mercy. And Allah is the relenting, wise.

This is the alleged slander of Mohammed's favorite wife, Aisha, when three witnesses accused her of adultery. Mohammed then increased the required number of witnesses to four, so that he would not have to punish her. When Mohammed married Aisha, she was six and he was fifty-one.

[11]Surely those who came with the slander were a group among you, do not consider it evil for you. Yet, it is good for you, to everyone of them what he earned of the sin, and as for him who had the biggest share among them, he will have a great torment. [12]Were it not that when you heard it,[a] the believing men and the believing women had thought of themselves good and said, "This is manifest slander." [13]Were it not that they had brought four witnesses against it, but since they did not bring the witnesses, so those with Allah[b] are the liars. [14]And were it not for the bounty of Allah on you, and his

---

[a] the slander
[b] in Allah's sight

mercy in this world and the hereafter, a great torment would have touched you because of what you have plunged into. [15]When you threw it[a] with your tongue and you say by your mouth what you do not have knowledge of and you consider it a light thing, and it is great with Allah. [16]And were it not that you heard it, you said, "It is not for us to speak of this. Praise be to you. This is a great slander." [17]Allah preaches to you that you will never return to the like of it if you were believers. [18]And Allah makes his verses clear to you. And Allah is knowing, wise. [19]Surely those who love to spread indecency among those who believed will have a painful torment in the world and in the hereafter. And Allah knows, and you do not know. [20]And were it not for the bounty of Allah on you and his mercy. And Allah is the compassionate, the merciful. [21]O you who have believed, do not follow the steps of Satan. And whoever follows the steps of Satan, so surely he is commanded with indecency and the evil. And were it not for the bounty of Allah on you and his mercy, none of you would have ever been pure, but Allah purifies whom he wills. And Allah is hearing, knowing. [22]And do not let persons of wealth and plenty among you swear that they will not give to the closest of their kinsman and the poor and the emigrants for the sake of Allah, but let them rather pardon and forgive. Do you not love that Allah forgave you? And Allah is forgiving, merciful. [23]Surely those who threw[b] the married, the unaware, the believing women, they are cursed in this world and in the hereafter, and they will have a great torment. [24]A day their tongues and their hands and their legs will witness against them because of what they were doing. [25]On that day, Allah will pay them back their true debt, and they will know that Allah is the clear truth. [26]Devious women for devious men and devious men for devious women, and kind women for kind men and kind men for kind women. Those will be acquitted from what they said, to them forgiveness and a generous provision. [27]O you who have believed, do not enter houses that are not your houses until you ask permission and greet its family. This is good for you, perhaps you will remember. [28]So if you did not find anyone in it, so do not enter it until you receive permission; and if it is said to you, "Return," so return. This is purest for you, and Allah is the knower of what you do. [29]It is not a sin for you to enter houses not dwelt in. In it there is enjoyment for you, and Allah knows what you show and what you hide. [30]Say to the believing men that they restrain their eyes and keep their private parts (maintain their chastity). This is purest for them. Surely Allah is aware of what they do.

---

[a] say the slander
[b] accuse with slander

Women must hide their bosoms and not display their ornaments. They may, however, expose themselves to certain members of their family and to male slaves.

[31]And say to the believing women to restrain their eyes and to keep their private parts (maintain their chastity) and do not display their ornaments, except that which appears from it, and that they throw their veils over their bosoms and do not display their ornaments, except to their husbands or their fathers or their husbands' fathers or their sons or their husbands' sons or their brothers or their brothers' sons or their sisters' sons or their women or what their right hand possessed or the male followers who have no substantial sexual desire or to children who have not looked at the women's private parts. And not stomp with their legs so that their hidden ornaments may be known. And repent to Allah together, O you believers, perhaps you may prosper. [32]And have sex (marry) with the unmarried among you and the good among your slaves and the maidservants. If they are poor, Allah will enrich them from his bounty. And Allah is bountiful, knowing.

Slaves should not be used in prostitution unless they are willing.

[33]And let those who cannot afford to have sex (marry) keep themselves chaste until Allah enriches them of his bounty. And those of whom your right hand possesses[a] who desire a book,[b] so write it for them if you know that there is some good in them and give to them from Allah's money what he gave you. And do not compel your young females to become prostitutes if they want to keep chaste so that you seek the material of the world's life. And whoever compels them,[c] so surely after they were compelled, Allah is forgiving, merciful. [34]And indeed, we have sent down to you clear verses and an example of those who passed away before you and a sermon to the fearer. [35]Allah is the light of the heavens and the earth. His light is like a niche in which is a lamp. The lamp is encased in zujāja,[d] the glass vessel, as it were a glistening planet. It is lighted from a blessed zaytonah[e] tree, neither of the east nor of the west, whose zuit[f] would almost shine out, even though fire did not touch it, light on light. Allah guides whom he wills to his light. And Allah gives the parables to men, and Allah has knowledge of everything. [36]In houses which Allah has allowed to be raised and his name is remembered in it, praise will be lifted to him in it, in the morning and the evening.

---

[a] slaves-concubines
[b] a document to be set free
[c] to prostitution
[d] glass vessel, non-Arabic word of Syriac origin
[e] olive, non-Arabic word of Syriac origin
[f] oil, non-Arabic word of Syriac origin

[37]Men, who neither merchandise nor selling, distract the remembrance of Allah and the performing of the prayer and the bringing of the legal alms. They fear a day in which their hearts and eyes will be turned around. [38]That Allah will reward them the best for what they have done, and he will increase them from his bounty. And Allah provides to whom he wills without accounting. [39]And those who became infidels, their works are like a mirage in flat land which the thirsty thinks to be water until when he comes to it, he did not find it anything, and found Allah there. So he gave him back his reckoning, and Allah is swift in the reckoning. [40]Or like darkness on the deep sea when covered by waves on waves, on top of it clouds, darkness; some of it is above others. If he pulls out his hand, he can hardly see it. And whomever Allah does not make to him light, so he will not have any light. [41]Have you not seen that Allah, all that is in the heavens and the earth and the birds in flight praise him. Everyone indeed knows their prayer and his praises, and Allah knows what they do. [42]And to Allah the kingdom of the heavens and the earth, and to Allah is their final return. [43]Have you not seen that Allah drives the clouds, then blends them together, then piles them in masses, so you see the rain coming from their midst? And he brings mountains of hail from the heavens, and he gives it to whom he wills and turns it away from whom he wills. The brightness of his lightning almost takes away the sight. [44]Allah alternates the night and the day. Surely in this is a lesson to those who have sight.

All beasts were created from water. This is taken from Genesis 1:20-25. No explanation is given for animals such as the kangaroo which hops rather than walks or slithers.

[45]And Allah created every creature from water; some walk on their bellies and some of them walk on two legs and some walk on four. Allah creates what he wills. Surely Allah has might over all things. [46]Indeed, we sent down our clear verses, and Allah guides whom he wills to a straight way. [47]And they say, "We believed in Allah and in the messenger, and we obeyed." Then a group of them turns away after that, and those are not believers. [48]And when they are called to Allah and his messenger, to judge between them, then a group of them turns away. [49]And if there is truth to them, they will come to him in obedience. [50]Is there in their heart a disease or are they in doubt or are they in fear that Allah and his messenger treats them unjustly? Yet those are the unjust. [51]Surely the words of the believers, when they were called to Allah and his messenger that he may judge between them, was that they only said, "We heard, and we obeyed." And those are the prosperous. [52]And whoever obeys Allah and his messenger and reveres Allah and fears him, so those are the triumphant. [53]And they swear by Allah with a most solemn oath, that

if you command them, they will go forth.[a] Say, "Do not swear a known obedience. Surely Allah is aware of what you do." [54]Say, "Obey Allah, and obey the messenger. So if they turn away, so surely on him only what he carries and on you what you carry. And if you obey him, you will be guided, and the messenger's responsibility is only the clear delivery." [55]Allah promised those who believed among you and did good deeds that he will cause them to be successors on the earth, as he also gave successors to those who were before them, and that he will surely establish their religion for them, which he pleased for them, and that he will change them, after their fear, security. "They will serve me, they will not partner anything with me, and who becomes an infidel after that, so those are the transgressors." [56]And perform the prayer and bring the legal alms and obey the messenger, perhaps you will receive mercy. [57]Do not think that those who became infidels hinder on the earth. Their abode is the fire, and evil is their final place.

Here are some rules for privacy.

[58]O you who have believed, let those whom your right hand possess[b] and those who have not come to the age of puberty among you ask permission of you three times: before the dawn prayer and when you lay aside your garments at midday and after the evening prayer. Three nudity to you. No sin will attach to you or to them if after those times, when you go around to visit each other, they come in without permission. Likewise, Allah makes clear his verses to you. And Allah is knowing, wise. [59]And when your children come of age in maturity, let them seek permission as those who were before them seek permission. Likewise, Allah clearly shows you his verses. And Allah is knowing, wise.

Older women can stop wearing the modest outer garment.

[60]And to women who are past childbearing who do not wish to have sex (marriage), there is no sin on them if they lay aside their clothes, but not showing their ornaments. Yet if they abstain from this, it will be better for them. And Allah is hearing, knowing. [61]There is no sin on the blind and no sin on the lame and no sin on the sick and not on yourselves to eat from your houses or the houses of your fathers or the houses of your mothers or the houses of your brothers or the houses of your sisters or the houses of your paternal uncles or the houses of your paternal aunts or the houses of your maternal uncles or the houses of your maternal aunts or of those of which you possess his keys or your friends. No sin will be attached to you whether you eat together or separate. So, when you enter houses,

---

[a] perform jihad-holy war
[b] slaves and concubines

so salute one another with a good and blessed greeting from Allah.
Likewise, Allah makes his verses clear to you, perhaps you may
understand. [62]Surely the believers are only those who believed in
Allah and his messenger, and if they were with him on any affair of
common interest, they do not depart until they ask his permission.
Surely those who ask your permission are those who believe in Allah
and his messenger. So if they ask your permission for some of their
own affairs, so give permission to whom you will among them and
ask Allah forgiveness for them. Surely Allah is forgiving, merciful.
[63]Do not make the call of the messenger among you like the calling
of one another. Indeed, Allah knows those who withdraw quietly from
you, hiding themselves behind others. So those who disobey his
command, be aware lest sedition befall them or a painful torment
falls on them. [64]Is it not surely to Allah what is in the heavens and the
earth. Indeed, he knows all about you and a day they will return to
him, so he will inform them of what they did. And Allah knows all
things.

*A portion
of a revelation* — **25** — *The Discriminator*

In the name of Allah, the merciful, the merciful

[1]Blessed is he who has sent down the discriminator on his servant
so that he may be a warner to the worlds.

God has no Son. This includes Jesus and any partners in His kingdom.

[2]He who has the kingdom of the heavens and the earth, and he
did not take a son. And it was not for him to have a partner in the
kingdom, and he created everything, so he determined it,
determining. [3]And they took without him gods, who do not create
anything, and they are themselves created. And they do not possess
to themselves harm nor good, and they do not possess death nor life
nor resurrection.

Infidels say that the Qur'an is a fraud and is copied from earlier books.

[4]And those who became infidels said, "This is but a fraud of his
own devising and other people assisted him." So indeed, they came
unjustly and with falsehood. [5]And they said, "The legends of the
ancients that he has written down, so it is dictated to him morning

and evening." ⁶Say, "He has sent it down, who knows the secrets of
the heavens and the earth. Surely he was forgiving, merciful."

Some believed Mohammed was bewitched.

⁷And they said, "What sort of messenger is this? He eats food,
and he walks in the aswaq.^a Were it not that an angel had been sent
down, so he will be a warner with him; ⁸or a treasure would be cast
to him or to him was a garden, he eats from it." And the unjust said,
"That you are following but bewitched man!" ⁹See how they give
parables to you, so they have gone astray, so they cannot [find] a
way. ¹⁰Blessed is he who if he wills makes to you better than that,
gardens, below them the rivers flow, and he will make castles for
you. ¹¹Yet they denied the hour, and we have prepared a blaze for
those who denied the hour. ¹²When it^b sees them from a far place,
they hear its raging and exhaling. ¹³And when they are thrown into a
narrow place in it, bound together, they call thereupon perdition.
¹⁴Today, do not call one perdition, but call many perdition. ¹⁵Say, "Is
this good or the eternal garden which is promised for the fearer? It
was a reward and a final place for them. ¹⁶They will have what they
desire in it forever; it was a responsible promise from your lord."
¹⁷And a day he will gather them and what they serve without Allah,
so he will say, "Did you lead those my servants astray, or have they
strayed from the way?" ¹⁸They said, "Praise be to you. It was not
right for us to take any other friends than you, but you gave them and
their fathers enjoyment until they forgot the reminder and they were a
būr^c people." ¹⁹So indeed, they denied you in what you are saying,
so you cannot turn away or help. And whoever among you who does
injustice, we will make him taste a big torment. ²⁰And we did not
send before you of the messengers, except surely they ate food and
walked in the streets, and we made some of you to be a sedition to
some others. Will you be patient? And your lord was seeing. ²¹And
those who do not hope for our meeting said, "Were it not that the
angels had been sent down on us or we see our lord." Indeed, they
became proud in themselves and revolted with a big revolt. ²²A day
they will see the angels, there will be no good news for the criminals
on that day, and they will say, "Unlawful, forbidden." ²³And we
proceed to what they did of work, so we made it scattered dust.
²⁴The companions of the garden on that day have a good abiding
place and the best resting place. ²⁵And a day the heavens will be
split by the clouds and the angels are sent, descending. ²⁶The true
kingdom on that day is to the merciful, and it was a difficult day for
the infidels. ²⁷And a day the unjust will bite on his hand saying, "I
wish I had taken the way with the messenger. ²⁸O woe is me, I wish I

---

^a streets, non-Arabic word of Aramaic/Syriac origin
^b hell
^c ignorant, non-Arabic word of Hebrew or Syriac origin

did not take so-and-so for a friend. [29]Indeed, he led me astray from the reminder after it came to me, and Satan was a failure to the human." [30]And the messenger said, "O my lord, surely my people have considered this Qur'an to be deserted." [31]And likewise, we have appointed to every prophet an enemy among the criminals. And your lord is sufficient as a guide and a helper. [32]And those who became infidels said, "Were it not that the Qur'an had been sent down on him all at once." Likewise, we strengthened your heart with it, and we chanted it, chanting. [33]And they will not bring to you a parable, but we bring to you the truth and the best tafsīr.[a] [34]Those who are gathered on their faces into hell, those [are in] the most evil place and are farther strayed from the way.

Once again Mohammed repeats the stories of Moses, Noah, Ad, and Themoud, as well as the Companion of the Rass.

[35]And indeed, we gave Moses the book, and we made with him his brother Aaron a prince. [36]So we said, "Go to the people who deny our verses." So we destroyed them with utter destruction. [37]And Noah's people, when they denied the messengers, we drowned them, and we made them a sign to the people. And we prepared a painful torment for the unjust. [38]And Ad and Themoud and the companion of the Rass and many generations between them. [39]And we gave parables to each of them, and each we destroyed with utter destruction. [40]And indeed, they came on the village which we rained the evil rain. Were they not seeing it? Yet, they were not hoping for resurrection. [41]And when they see you, they take you, but as a scoff: "Is this the one whom Allah sent as a messenger? [42]He was about to lead us astray from our gods, were it not that we were patient with it." And they will know, when they see the torment, who is farther erred from the way. [43]Have you seen who takes his god at his own desire? Will you be a guardian for him? [44]Or do you think that most of them will hear or understand? That they are but like livestock; yet, they are farther erred from the way. [45]Have you not seen how your lord extends the shadow, and if he willed, he could have made it stationary? Then we made the sun to be an evidence for him. [46]Then we drew it[b] toward us, easily drawing. [47]And he is who made the night for you as a garment and sleep for rest and made the day for raising up. [48]And he is who sent the winds as good news between the mercies of his hands. And we sent down pure water from the heavens [49]to give life by it to a dead country, and we give it for drink for whom we have created, livestock and many humans. [50]And indeed, we distribute it among them so that they may remember, so

---

[a] interpretation, non-Arabic word of Syriac origin
[b] the shadow

most people refuse, but infidelity. [51]And if we will, we would send to every village a warner. [52]So do not obey the infidels, and perform jihad against them with it a big jihad.

Some consider the following verse as a great proof of Mohammed's prophetic ability. However, the knowledge of the separation between fresh water and salt water was not a new discovery. Pliny the Elder, the noted Roman naturalist, senator, and commander of the Imperial Fleet in the 1st century A.D., observed this peculiar behavior of fishermen's nets in the Strait of Bosphorus near Istanbul. Pliny deduced that surface and bottom currents were flowing in opposite directions. He provided the first written documentation of what is now called the "estuarine circulation." Additionally, it can be shown from simple logic that the fresh and salt waters do eventually combine. If they did not, there would be huge oceans of fresh water continually growing out from every major river. Simple studies show that fresh water flowing out from rivers slowly mixes with and becomes increasingly salinated over time and distance until it reaches equilibrium with the normal salt levels of the greater body of water. The speed of this changeover varies according to temperature as well.

[53]And he is who mixed the two seas, this is fresh, furāt,[a] and this salty and bitter, and has put a barrier between them and forced repelling.

The interpretation of the following verse by the Muslim scholar, Al Qurtobi, clearly teaches that a man can marry his own daughter or his sister who was conceived from an adulterous relationship.

[54]And he is who created people from the water, so he made it[b] a relative and a kinship, and your lord was mighty. [55]And they serve without Allah that which did not profit them nor harm them, and the infidel was a backer against his lord. [56]And we did not send you except a giver of good news and a warner. [57]Say, "I do not ask you any wage for it, except for him who wills to take a way to his lord." [58]And depend on the living who does not die, and praise with his praise. And he is sufficient; he is aware of the sin of his servants. [59]Who created the heavens and the earth and whatever is between them in six days; then he sat on the throne, the merciful, so ask about him, the knower. [60]And when it is said to them, "Worship to the merciful." They said, "And what is the merciful? Will we worship whom you command us?" And it increased their rejection. [61]Blessed

---

[a] sweet river water, non-Arabic word of Akkadian origin
[b] the infant

who made in the heaven constellations and made in it a sirāj[a] and a shining moon. [62]And he is who made the night and the day behind it for those who desire to remember or desire to be thankful. [63]And the servants of the merciful are those who walk on the earth gently, and, when the fool addressed them, they say, "Peace." [64]And those that pass the night worshiping and standing to their lord. [65]And those who say, "Our lord, turn the torment of hell away from us." Surely its torment was inevitable. [66]Surely it is an evil abode and place. [67]And those when they spend, they are not extravagant and they are not stingy, and are standing in the middle between that. [68]And those who do not call with Allah another god and do not kill the soul, which Allah has forbidden except with a just cause, and they do not commit fornication, and who does that will meet sin. [69]The torment will be doubled for him on the resurrection day, and he will abide shamefully in it forever. [70]Except who repented and believed and did a good deed, so those Allah will exchange their evil deeds for good deeds. And Allah was forgiving, merciful. [71]And whoever repents and does a good deed, so he surely repents to Allah a repentance. [72]And those who do not bear false witness; and if they pass by what is vain, they pass by honorably. [73]And those who, if reminded by the verses of their lord, they did not fall down on them[b] deaf and blind. [74]And those who say, "Our lord, grant us from our wives and our offspring, the pleasure of our eyes, and make us to the fearing imam." [75]Those will be rewarded with a room because of their patience, and in it they will meet with greetings and peace. [76]They will abide in it forever, an excellent abode and place. [77]Say, "My lord will not notice, were it not for your calling. So indeed, you denied, so it will be inevitable."

A portion of a revelation   26   *The Poets*

In the name of Allah, the merciful, the merciful

[1]Tsm.[c] [2]These are the verses of the clear book. [3]Perhaps you are killing yourself[d] because they will not be believers. [4]If we willed, we could send down a sign on them from the heaven so that their necks will continue to be submissive to it. [5]And there is not a new reminder

---

[a] lamp, non-Arabic word of Syriac origin
[b] the verses
[c] a word containing three Arabic letters without meaning
[d] with grief

that has come to them from the merciful, except that they were turning away from it. ⁶So indeed, they denied. So the news will come to them of what they were scoffing at. ⁷Have they not seen how many generous pairs we planted in it? ⁸Surely in this is a sign, and most of them were not believers. ⁹And surely your lord is the dear, the merciful.

The story of Moses and Aaron is copied from the Bible and corrupted once again. In this version Mohammed does not have a grasp of the timeline in this story and assumes that this is the same Pharaoh. However, Moses has been gone for forty years, and the Pharaoh who knew of him has died. See Exodus 2:23.

¹⁰And when your lord called Moses, "That go to the unjust people. ¹¹Pharaoh's people, will they not fear?"¹²He said, "My lord, surely I fear that they will deny me. ¹³And my chest will be tightened, and my tongue does not speak, so send to me Aaron. ¹⁴And they have on me a guilt, so I fear that they may kill me." ¹⁵He said, "Certainly not. So go, [both of you] with our signs. Surely we are with you listening. ¹⁶So go [both of you] to Pharaoh, so say, 'Surely we are a messenger of the lord of the worlds, ¹⁷that send the children of Israel with us.'" ¹⁸He said, "Did we not see you as a child among us, and you stayed among us many years of your life? ¹⁹And you did your act which you did, and you are of the infidels." ²⁰He said, "I did it indeed, and I am of the lost. ²¹So I fled from you when I feared you, so my lord granted me wisdom and made me of the messengers. ²²And this is a grace that he has favored on me that has enslaved the children of Israel." ²³Pharaoh said, "And what then is the lord of the worlds?" ²⁴He said, "Lord of the heavens and the earth and what is between them, if you were certain." ²⁵He said to those around him, "Will you not hear?" ²⁶He said, "Your lord and the lord of your ancient fathers." ²⁷He said, "Surely your messenger who has been sent to you is a demon-possessed." ²⁸He said, "Lord of the east and the west and what is between them, if you were understanding." ²⁹He said, "If you take any god instead of me, I will make you of the prisoners." ³⁰He said, "What if I bring to you something manifest?" ³¹He said, "So bring it if you were of the truthful." ³²So he threw down his rod, so behold, it is an obvious serpent. ³³And he drew out his hand, so behold, it was white to the onlookers. ³⁴He said to the leaders around him, "Surely this is a knowing sorcerer. ³⁵He desires to get you out of your land with his sorcery. So what do you command?" ³⁶They said, "Put him and his brother off for awhile, and send gatherers into the cities. ³⁷They will bring every knowing sorcerer to you." ³⁸So the sorcerers were gathered on an appointed, known day. ³⁹And it was said to the people, "Are you gathered? ⁴⁰Perhaps we will follow the sorcerers if they were the victors." ⁴¹So when the sorcerers came, they said to Pharaoh, "Will we have our wage if we are the victors?"

[42]He said, "Yes, and surely then you will become of the nearer." [43]Moses said to them, "Cast down what you are casting." [44]So they cast down their ropes and rods, and they said, "[We swear] by Pharaoh's might we will surely be the victors." [45]So Moses threw down his rod, so behold, it pecks what they fabricate. [46]So the sorcerers fell down worshiping. [47]They said, "We believed in the lord of the worlds, [48]the lord of Moses and Aaron." [49]He said, "Have you believed on him before I gave you permission? Surely he is your biggest who has taught you the sorcery. So surely you will know I will cut off your hands and legs on opposite sides, and I will crucify you, all of you." [50]They said, "It cannot harm us, surely we will return to our lord. [51]Surely we hope that our lord will forgive us of our sins, that we were the first of the believers." [52]And we revealed to Moses: "That go forth by night with my servants, surely you will be followed."

Mohammed describes inheriting the land of Egypt, rather than the Promised Land. See also verse 44:28. This is affirmed by the interpretations of Ibn Kathir, Al Galalien, Al Tahindery, and Al Qurtobi.

[53]So Pharaoh sent to the cities gathering: [54]"Surely they are a small group. [55]And surely they are enraging us. [56]And surely we must be on guard together." [57]So we got them out of gardens and springs [58]and treasures and generous dwellings, [59]likewise, and we bequeathed it to the children of Israel. [60]So they followed them at sunrise. [61]So when the two groups saw each other, the companion of Moses said, "Surely we are overtaken!" [62]He said, "Certainly not, surely my lord is with me, and he will guide me." [63]So we revealed to Moses: "That strike the sea with your rod." So it split, so each side was as a great mound. [64]And we moved toward, then the others. [65]And we delivered Moses and all those with him. [66]Then we drowned the others. [67]Surely in this is a sign, and most of them were not believers. [68]And surely your lord is the dear, the merciful.

The story of Abraham is copied from the Bible and corrupted once again.

[69]And recite to them the news of Abraham, [70]when he said to his father and his people, "What do you serve?" [71]They said, "We serve idols, so our devotion is constant to them." [72]He said, "Do they hear you when you call, [73]or do they profit you or harm?" [74]They said, "Yet, we found our fathers doing likewise." [75]He said, "Have you seen what you were serving, [76]you and your ancient fathers? [77]So surely they are an enemy to me, except the lord of the worlds [78]who has created me, so he will guide me. [79]And he who feeds me and gives me a drink. [80]And when I am sick, so he heals me. [81]And he who put me to death, then gives me life. [82]And who, I hope, will

forgive me of my sins in the judgment day. [83]My lord, grant me wisdom and join me with the good. [84]And give me a truthful tongue among the others. [85]And make me of the heirs of the garden of bliss. [86]And forgive my father, surely he was of the lost. [87]And do not put me to shame a day they are raised, [88]a day neither money nor children will benefit, [89]except to him who comes to Allah with a whole heart, [90]when the garden will be brought near to the fearer. [91]And hell went forth for the seduced." [92]And it was said to them, "Where are those whom you were serving [93]without Allah? Will they help you or will they win?" [94]So they will be poured into it, them and the seduced [95]and the devil's troops together. [96]They said while they were quarreling in it, [97]"[We swear] by Allah, surely we were in obvious error [98]when we made you equal with the lord of the worlds. [99]And none led us astray except the criminals. [100]So we will not have intercessors, [101]and no intimate friend. [102]But if we have a second turn, so surely we will be among the believers." [103]Surely in this is a sign, and most of them were not believers. [104]And surely your lord, he is the dear, the merciful.

The story of Noah is copied from the Bible and corrupted once again.

[105]The people of Noah denied the messengers. [106]When their brother Noah said to them, "Will you not fear? [107]Surely I am a faithful messenger to you. [108]So fear Allah, and obey me. [109]And I do not ask you any wage for it; my wage is but on the lord of the worlds. [110]So fear Allah, and obey me."

Evidently, Mohammed was not aware of who the "believers" of Noah were. According to the Bible, they were only his wife, his three sons, and his sons' wives. See Genesis 7:7.

[111]They said, "Will we believe in you, and your followers are the lowliest?" [112]He said, "But I have no knowledge of what they were doing. [113]Their judgment is only on my lord, if you feel. [114]And I am not driving away the believers. [115]That I am, except a plain warner." [116]They said, "Now, unless you desist, O Noah, you will become of the stoned." [117]He said, "My lord, surely my people denied me. [118]So fath[a] between me and them, judging, and deliver me and the believers who are with me." [119]So we delivered him and those who were with him in the loaded ship. [120]Then we drowned the rest after that. [121]Surely in this is a sign, and most of them were not believers. [122]And surely your lord, he is the dear, the merciful.

The story of Ad was invented by Mohammed and repeated once again.

---

[a] judge, non-Arabic word of Ethiopian origin

[123]Ad denied the messengers. [124]And when their brother Houd said to them, "Will you not fear? [125]Surely I am a faithful messenger to you.[126]So fear Allah, and obey me. [127]And I do not ask you any wage for it; my wage is but on the lord of the worlds. [128]Do you build in every high place a wasteful masterpiece? [129]And you take castles, perhaps you will live forever; [130]and when you attack, you attacked powerfully.[131]So fear Allah, and obey me. [132]And fear who aided you in what you know. [133]He aided you with livestock and sons [134]and gardens and springs. [135]Surely I fear for you a torment of a great day." [136]They said, "It is the same to us if you preach or if you were not of the preachers. [137]This is only the custom of the ancients, [138]and we will not be tormented." [139]So they denied him, so we destroyed them. Surely in this is a sign, and most of them were not believers. [140]And surely your lord he is the dear, the merciful.

The story of Themoud was invented by Mohammed and repeated once again.

[141]Themoud denied the messengers. [142]And when their brother Saleh said to them, "Will you not fear? [143]Surely I am a faithful messenger to you. [144]So fear Allah, and obey me. [145]And I do not ask you any wage for it; my wage is but on the lord of the worlds. [146]Will you be left secure in what is here? [147]In gardens and springs [148]and plants and palm trees with tender shoots of flowers. [149]And you carve skillful houses in the mountains. [150]So fear Allah, and obey me. [151]And do not obey the command of the extravagant, [152]those who vandalized on the earth and do not reform." [153]They said, "Surely you are only from the bewitched! [154]You are only a human like us, so bring a sign if you were of the truthful." [155]He said, "This is a camel. To her a drink, and to you a drink, a known day. [156]And do not touch her with evil so the torment of a great day will overtake you." [157]So they hamstrung her. So they became regretful. [158]So the torment seized them, surely in this is a sign, and most of them were not believers.[159]And surely, your lord, he is the dear, the merciful.

The story of Lot is copied from the Bible, corrupted, and repeated once again.

[160]The people of Lot denied the messengers. [161]When their brother Lot said to them, "Will you not fear? [162]Surely I am a faithful messenger to you. [163]So fear Allah, and obey me. [164]And I do not ask you any wage for it; for my wage is but on the lord of the worlds. [165]Do you enter into[a] the males from the worlds, [166]and forsaking what your lord created for you from your wives? Yet you are a transgressing people!" [167]They said, "O Lot, if you do not desist, you

---

[a] have sex with in a homosexual lifestyle

will become of the expelled." [168]He said, "Surely I am of those who detest what you are doing. [169]My lord, deliver me and my family from what they do." [170]So we delivered him and his whole family together, [171]except an elder among those who tarried. [172]Then we destroyed the others. [173]And we rained on them rain, so evil is the rain of the warned. [174]Surely in this is a sign, and most of them were not believers. [175]And surely your lord, he is the dear, the merciful.

The story of Shoaib was invented by Mohammed and repeated once again.

[176]The dwellers of the woods denied the messengers. [177]When Shoaib said to them, "Will you not fear? [178]Surely I am a faithful messenger to you. [179]So fear Allah, and obey me. [180] And I do not ask you any wage for it; my wage is but on the lord of the worlds. [181]Fulfill the measure, and do not be of those who give less. [182]Weigh with the straight balance. [183]And do not defraud people their things, and do not act wickedly in the land, vandalizing. [184]And fear who created you and the ancient generations." [185]They said, "Surely you are only of the bewitched. [186]And you are only a human like us, and we think that you are surely among the liars. [187]So drop on us a part of the heaven if you were of the truthful." [188]He said, "My lord knows best what you do." [189]So they denied him, so the torment seized them on the covering day. Surely it was a day of great torment. [190]Surely in this is a sign, and most of them were not believers. [191]And surely your lord, he is the dear, the merciful.

The entire Qur'an exists in the Bible, the ancient Scriptures.

[192]And surely this is descended from the lord of the worlds, [193]descended by the faithful spirit [194]on your heart so that you may be among the warners, [195]with a clear Arabic tongue. [196]And surely it is in the ancient scriptures. [197]Or was it not a sign to them that the scholars of the children of Israel know it? [198]If we had sent it down on some foreigner, [199]so he had read it to them, and they were not to believe in it. [200]Likewise, we have made it to enter the hearts of the criminals. [201]They will not believe in it until they see the painful torment. [202]So it will come on them suddenly, and they do not feel. [203]So they will say, "Will we be delayed?" [204]Will they hasten on our torment? [205]Have you seen that we give them enjoyment for years? [206]It came to them, what they were promised. [207]It did not profit them what they were enjoying. [208]We did not destroy a village except it had its warners, [209]a reminder, and we were not unjust.

The Qur'an defends itself, claiming that it is not a Satanic book. Also, compare verse 212 with verse 223. Can the satans hear or not?

²¹⁰And it was not sent down by the satans. ²¹¹And they must not, and they could not. ²¹²Surely they are separated from the hearing. ²¹³So do not call with Allah another god, so you will become of the tormented. ²¹⁴And warn your nearest relatives. ²¹⁵And lower your wings to those who follow you of the believers. ²¹⁶So if they disobey you, so say, "Surely I am innocent of what you do." ²¹⁷And depend on the dear, the merciful, ²¹⁸who sees you when you stand up, ²¹⁹and when you change movement among the worshipers. ²²⁰Surely he is the hearing, the knowing. ²²¹Will I inform you about on whom the satans descended? ²²²They descended on every sinful liar. ²²³They listen, and most of them are liars. ²²⁴And the poets, the seduced follow them. ²²⁵Have you not seen them wandering in every valley? ²²⁶And they say what they do not do, ²²⁷except those who believed and did good deeds and remembered Allah often, and they had help after they were treated unjustly. And those who act unjustly will know what outcome they will come to.

A portion of a revelation   **27**   *The Ants*

In the name of Allah, the merciful, the merciful

¹Ts.ᵃ Those are the verses of the Qur'an and a clear book. ²A guidance and good news to the believers. ³Those who perform the prayer and bring the legal alms, and they in the hereafter, they are assured. ⁴Surely those who do not believe in the hereafter, we adorn to them their works so they are blind. ⁵Those are the ones who will have the evil torment, and they in the hereafter, they are the losers. ⁶And surely you receive the Qur'an from the presence of a wise, knowing.

The story of Moses is copied from the Bible, corrupted, and repeated once again. The "white hand" of Moses is erroneously presented as one of the "nine" plagues!

⁷When Moses said to his family, "Surely I have perceived a fire. I will bring you news from it, or I will bring you a blazing brand, perhaps you warm yourselves." ⁸So when he came to it, he was called, "Blessed is he who is in the fire and those who surround it, and praise be to Allah, the lord of the worlds. ⁹O Moses, surely I am Allah, the dear, the wise. ¹⁰And throw down your rod!" So when he

---

ᵃ a word containing two Arabic letters without meaning

saw it shaking as though it were a jinn, he retreated backward and did not return. "O Moses, do not fear, surely the messengers will not fear in my presence, [11]except for those who did injustice, then changed, doing good after evil. So surely I am forgiving, merciful. [12]And enter your hand into your pocket. It will come forth white, without evil, as one in nine signs to Pharaoh and his people, surely they were a transgressing people. [13]So when our signs came to their very sight, they said, "This is obvious sorcery." [14]And they disbelieved in them, and their souls know it for certain, unjustly and proudly. So look how was the end of the vandals.

The story of David and Solomon is copied from the Bible and corrupted. This story is also found in verses 21:79-82; 34:12-14; and 38:30-40. The original story of Solomon is found in the Bible in 1 Kings 1-11. Note: the myth about the birds comes from a book, *The Second Tergemon of the book of Esther*, which identified the bird as a rooster instead of a "hoopoe." Also notice the story of Esther copied from the Bible in 1Kings 10:1-10.

[15]And indeed, we gave knowledge to David and Solomon, and they said, "Praise be to Allah who has favored us above many of his believing servants." [16]And Solomon inherited David, and he said, "O you people, we have been taught the speech of the birds, and we have been given from everything. Surely this is the manifest bounty." [17]And to Solomon were gathered his troops of the jinn and the humans and the birds, so they were spread, [18]until they reached the Valley of the Ants. An ant said, "O you ants, enter into your dwellings, lest Solomon and his troops crush you, and they do not feel." [19]So he smiled, laughing at her (the ant) sayings, and he said, "My lord, inspire me to thank your grace which you graced on me and on my parents, and that I do good deed that will be pleasing to you. And admit me, by your mercy, among your good servants."

This is the story of the "philosopher" hoopoe, the bird that talked and traveled the world.

[20]And he inspected the birds, so he said, "Why is it that I do not see the hoopoe? Or was he of the absent? [21]Surely I will torment him with a severe torment. Or I will surely slaughter him, or he brings to me a manifest authority." [22]So he did not tarry long, so he said, "I have gained the knowledge that you do not know, and I have come to you from Sabā[a] with sure news. [23]Surely I have found a woman reigning over them, gifted with everything, and she has a great throne. [24]I found her and her people worshiping to the sun without Allah, and Satan adorns their works so that he prevented them from

---

[a] Sheba, non-Arabic word of probable Hebrew/Syriac origin

the way, so they are not guided. ^{25}Will they not worship to Allah who brings the secret things of the heavens and the earth, and who knows what you hide and what you reveal? ^{26}Allah, there is no god but him, the lord of the great throne." ^{27}He said, "We will see if you are truthful, or you were among the liars. ^{28}Go with this my book. So throw it down to them, then turn away from them, so see what is their return." ^{29}She^a said, "O you the leaders, a generous book has been thrown down to me. ^{30}Surely it is from Solomon, and surely it is, 'In the name of Allah, the merciful, the merciful. ^{31}Do not exalt yourselves above me, and come to me as Muslims.'" ^{32}She said, "O you the leaders, consult with me in my affair. I was not to make any command unless you bear witness to me." ^{33}They said, "We are imbued with strength and are imbued with mighty valor, and the command is to you, so see what you command." ^{34}She said, "Surely when kings enter a village they vandalized it and made the noblest of its family to be humiliated, and likewise, they do. ^{35}And surely I will send to them a gift, so I will see what the messenger will return." ^{36}So when he (the bird) came to Solomon, he said, "Do you supply me with money? So what Allah has given to me is better than what he gave you, yet you rejoice in your gifts. ^{37}Return to them, for we will surely come to them with troops which they cannot withstand, and we will drive them from it humiliated while they are subdued."

Solomon requests that the kingdom of the Queen of Sheba and the jinn are brought to him in the blink of an eye.

^{38}He said, "O you the leaders, which of you will bring me her throne before they come to me as Muslims?" ^{39}An 'ifrīt^b of the jinn said, "I will bring it to you before you rise from your seat, and surely I am strong and faithful for it." ^{40}The one who had the knowledge of the book said, "I will bring it to you before the blinking of your eyes." So when he saw it set before him, he said, "This is of the bounty of my lord, to test me, whether I will be thankful or become an infidel. And who gives thanks, so surely he only gives thanks to himself and who became an infidel. So surely my lord is rich, generous." ^{41}He said, "Disguise her throne for her. We will see if she will be guided or become one who is not guided." ^{42}So when she came, it was said to her, "Is your throne like this?" She said, "It looks similar to it." And we were given the knowledge before her, and we were Muslims. ^{43}And what she was worshiping without Allah prevented her, surely she was among an infidel people. ^{44}It was said to her, "Enter the sarh."^{c} So when she saw it, she thought it was a pool of water and uncovered her legs. He said, "Surely it is a palace paved with glass."

---

^{a} the queen of Sheba
^{b} demon, non-Arabic word of Persian, derived from Pahlavic origin
^{c} tower, non-Arabic word of Ethiopian origin

She said, "My lord, surely I have been unjust to myself, and I surrender with Solomon to Allah, the lord of the worlds."

This is the story of Themoud as invented by Mohammed and is repeated once again.

⁴⁵And indeed, we sent to Themoud their brother Saleh: "That you serve Allah." So they became two groups quarreling. ⁴⁶He said, "O my people, why do you hasten with the evil before the good? Were it not that you ask forgiveness from Allah, perhaps you will receive mercy." ⁴⁷They said, "Is our bird with you and those who are with you?" He said, "Your bird is with Allah. Yet you are a people who are seduced." ⁴⁸And there was in the city nine persons who vandalized in the land and did not reform. ⁴⁹They said, "Swear one to another by Allah that we will surely fall on him and on his family by night. Then we will tell his guardian, 'We did not witness the destruction of his family, and surely we are truthful.'"

Men deceive, and Allah is also a deceiver.

⁵⁰And they deceived a deception, and we deceived a deception. And they did not feel. ⁵¹So see how was the end of their deception. We destroyed them and all their people. ⁵²So these, their houses are ruins because of their injustice. Surely in this is a sign to a knowing people. ⁵³And we delivered those who believed, and they were fearing.

The story of Lot is copied from the Bible, corrupted, and repeated once again.

⁵⁴And Lot, when he said to his people, "Do you come to the indecency while you see? ⁵⁵Do you come to the men in lust instead of the women? Yet, you are an ignorant people!" ⁵⁶So the answer of his people was not, except they said, "Cast out the family of Lot from your village. They surely are purified humans." ⁵⁷So we delivered him and his family except his woman [wife]; we decreed her of the lingered. ⁵⁸And we rained a rain on them, so evil is the rain of the warners. ⁵⁹Say, "The praise be to Allah and peace on his servants that he has chosen. Is Allah good, or what they partner [with him]?" ⁶⁰Is the one who created the heavens and the earth and sent water down to you from the heaven so that we cause the gardens of delight to grow by it? It was not for you to grow its trees. Is there a god with Allah? Yet they are people who are transformed. ⁶¹Is the one who made the earth a resting place and has made rivers in its midst and made stabilizers on it and made a barrier between the two seas? Is there a god with Allah? Yet most of them do not know. ⁶²Is the one who answers the distressed, if he calls him, and removes the evil and makes you to be viceroys on the earth? Is there a god with Allah? Little is what you remember! ⁶³Is the one who guides you in

the darkness of the shore and the sea and who sends forth the winds with good news between the hands of his mercy? Is there a god with Allah? Allah is exalted above what they partner [with him]. [64]Is the one who begins the creation, then repeats it, and who provides you from the heaven and the earth? Is there a god with Allah? Say, "Bring your proofs, if you were truthful." [65]Say, "No one knows the unseen in the heavens and the earth except Allah. And they do not feel when they will be raised. [66]Yet attaining their knowledge in the hereafter. Yet they are in doubt about it. Yet they are blind about it. [67]And those who became infidels said, "If we and our fathers were dust, will we surely come forth? [68]We indeed have been promised this, we and our fathers before, this is only the legends of the ancients." [69]Say, "Walk on the earth, so see how the end was of the criminals." [70]And do not grieve for them, and do not be in distress from what they deceive. [71]And they say, "When will this promise be, if you were truthful?" [72]Say, "Perhaps some of what you hastened may be drawing near." [73]And surely your lord is possessor of bounty to the people, but most of them do not give thanks. [74]And surely your lord knows well what their chests hide and what they show. [75]And there is nothing absent in the heaven and the earth, except in a clear book. [76]Surely this Qur'an relates to the children of Israel most of what they disagree about. [77]And surely it is a guidance and a mercy to the believers. [78]Surely your lord judges between them by his judgment. And he is the dear, the knowing. [79]So depend on Allah, surely you are on the clear truth. [80]Surely you cannot make the dead to hear, and you cannot make the deaf to hear the call if they turn their backs. [81]And you are not to guide the blind from their errors. You cause only those who believe in our verses to hear, so they are Muslims.

Mohammed wrote about a speaking beast among the prophets.

[82]And when the word falls on them, we will cause a creature to come forth to them out of the earth to speak to them: "That the people were not certain of our verses." [83]And a day we will gather from every nation a group of those who deny our verses. So they will be spread, [84]until when they come, he says, "Did you deny my verses? And you did not comprehend them, or what were you doing?" [85]And the words fall on them because they were unjust, so they do not speak. [86]Have they not seen that we made the night that they may dwell in it and the day to see? Surely in this are signs to believing people. [87]And a day the trumpet will be blown, so panicked is who is in the heavens and who is on the earth, except whom Allah wills, and everyone will come to him humbly. [88]And you see the mountains which you think are firm. They will pass away as the passing of the clouds, the work of Allah who perfected everything.

Surely he is aware of what you do. [89]Whoever comes with the good deed, so he will have better than it, and they become secure from the panic on that day. [90]And whoever comes with the evil, so their faces were poured into the fire. Will you be rewarded except for what you were doing? [91]Surely I am commanded to serve the lord of this country which he made forbidden. And to him everything, and I am commanded to be of the Muslims [92]and to recite the Qur'an so that whoever is guided, so surely he will be only guided for himself, and whoever goes astray, so say, "Surely I am only of the warners." [93]And say, "The praise be to Allah. He will show you his signs, so you will know it. And your lord is not unaware of what you do."

A portion of a revelation   **28**   *The Narrative*

In the name of Allah, the merciful, the merciful

[1]Tsm.[a] [2]Those are the verses of the clear book.

The story of Moses and Pharaoh is copied from the Bible and corrupted once again. See also verse 40:36. There is no record that an Egyptian existed by the name of Haman, especially at the time of Moses. Rather, he lived in the Babylonian Kingdom. See also the book of Esther from the Bible.

[3]We will recite to you some of the news of Moses and Pharaoh with the truth to the believing people. [4]Surely Pharaoh exalted himself in the land and made its people into sects, weakening a group of them, slaughtering their sons, and sparing their women, surely he was of the vandals. [5]And we desired to show favor to those who were weakened on the earth and to make them leaders and to make them the heirs [6]and to establish them in the land, and we showed Pharaoh and Haman and their troops among them what they were fearing. [7]And we revealed to Moses' mother: "That breastfeeds him, so when you fear for him, so cast him into the river, and do not fear and do not grieve. Surely we will bring him back to you and make him of the messengers." [8]So the family of Pharaoh picked him up so that he may become an enemy to them and a grief. Surely Pharaoh and Haman and their troops were khati'aeen.[b]

---

[a] a word containing three Arabic letters without meaning
[b] sinners, non-Arabic word of Syriac origin

Mohammed confused Pharaoh's daughter with his wife. See Exodus 2:5-10.

[9]And Pharaoh's woman [wife] said, "He is the pleasure of the eye to me and you. Do not kill him, perhaps he will be useful to us, or we may take him [as] a son." And they did not feel. [10]And the heart of Moses' mother became empty that she almost exposed him were it not that we tied on her heart that she will be of the believers. [11]And she said to his sister, "Follow him." So she watched him from alongside, and they did not feel. [12]And we forbid him the breastfeeding [from other women] before that, so she said, "Will I point out to you the family of a house who will take care of him for you, and they will be an advisor to him?" [13]So we returned him to his mother, so her eyes may be pleased, and she will not grieve; and she might know that the promise of Allah is true. But most of them do not know. [14]And when he reached his strength and became settled, we gave him wisdom and knowledge; and likewise, we reward the doers of good. [15]And he entered the city at a time when its inhabitants did not notice him, so he found in it two men fighting, this is of his sect and this of his enemies. So he was called for help by the one of his sect against him who was of his enemies. So Moses struck him,[a] so he killed him. He said, "This is of satans' work. Surely he is an obviously misleading enemy." [16]He said, "My lord, surely I have done an injustice to myself, so forgive me." So he forgave him. Surely he is the forgiving, the merciful. [17]He said, "My lord, because you have graced on me, so I will not be a backer to the criminal." [18]So he became fearful and vigilant in the city. So when the one that he helped the day before called out to him, Moses said to him, "Surely you are an obvious seducer." [19]So when he desired to seize the one who is an enemy to them, he said, "O Moses, do you desire to kill me as you killed a soul yesterday? Do you only desire to become a powerful in the land, and you do not desire to become of the good?" [20]And a man from the remotest part of the city came running. He said, "O Moses, surely the leaders are consulting to kill you. So get out! Surely I am an advisor to you." [21]So he got out from it in fear, vigilant. He said, "My lord, deliver me from the unjust people!" [22]And when he journeyed toward Midian, he said, "Perhaps my lord will guide me in the right way." [23]And when he arrived at the water of Midian, he found there a nation of people watering. And apart from them he found two women who were keeping back. He said, "What is [the matter] with you?" They said, "We will not water until the shepherds have left, and our father is a very old man." [24]So he watered for them, then turned away to the shade. So he said, "My lord, surely I am poor for whatever good you send down to me." [25]So

---

[a] the enemy

one of them came to him, walking bashfully. She said, "Surely my father invites you so that he may reward you a wage for watering for us." So when he came to him and related to him the narrative, he said, "Do not be afraid. You are delivered from the unjust people." [26]One of them said, "O my father, hire him, surely he will be the best of whom you hired, the strong, the faithful."

In the following verses, Moses marries one of two daughters. This contradicts Exodus 1:16, which clearly teaches that she was one of seven daughters. Additionally, Moses was not required to work in order to marry his wife. See Exodus 2:16-22. Mohammed has confused Moses with Jacob who worked seven years in order to marry his wife. See Genesis 29:18.

[27]He said, "Surely I desire that you have sex (marry) with one of these my two daughters, that you should be employed by me for eight years. So, if you fulfill ten, it is of your own doing,[a] for I do not desire a hardship for you. You will find me, if Allah wills, among the good." [28]He said, "This is between me and you. Whichever of the two terms I fulfill, there will be no wrongdoing against me. And Allah is the guardian of what we say." [29]So when Moses had fulfilled the term and departed with his family, he saw a fire on the mountainside. He said to his family, "Stay, surely I see a fire. Perhaps I may bring you news from it or a brand from the fire, perhaps you will be warmed." [30]So when he came to it, he was called from the right side of the valley in the blessed spot from the tree: "That, O Moses, surely I am Allah, the lord of the worlds. [31]And throw down your rod." So when he saw it shake as if it were a jinn, he turned away and fled and did not return. "O Moses, come and do not be afraid, surely you are of the faithful. [32]Insert your hand into your pocket. It will come out white, without evil, and fold your wings toward you from the fear. So these are two proofs from your lord to Pharaoh and his leaders. Surely they were a transgressing people." [33]He said, "My lord, surely I have killed a soul among them, so I fear they might kill me. [34]And my brother Aaron is more eloquent in speech than I. So send him with me as an assistant to affirm me. Surely I am afraid that they will deny me." [35]He said, "We will strengthen your arm with your brother, and we will give authority to both of you so that they will not reach to you. With our signs, both of you and whoever follows you are the victorious." [36]So when Moses came to them with our clear signs, they said, "This is nothing but forged sorcery. And we have never heard the like of it among our ancient fathers." [37]And Moses said, "My lord knows best who came with guidance from him and to whom will be the final home. Surely he will not prosper the unjust."

---

[a] as a tip

Mohammed confuses the building of the Tower of Babel of Noah's time with the time of Moses and Pharaoh. See also verse 40:36. Compare this to the actual account found in Genesis 11.

[38]And Pharaoh said, "O you the leaders, you have no other god that I know of but me. So kindle a fire to me, O Haman, on the mud. So make to me a tower so perhaps I may go up to the god of Moses, and surely I think he is of the liars." [39]And he became proud with his troops in the land without the truth, and they thought that they will not return to us.

In this version of the story, Pharaoh drowned as an infidel.

[40]So we seized him and his troops, so we cast them into the sea. So see how was the end of the unjust. [41]And we made them leaders who were invited to the fire and on the resurrection day they will not be helped. [42]And we followed them in this world with a curse, and on the resurrection day they will be among the despised. [43]And indeed, we gave Moses the book after we had destroyed the first generations to become to the people a guidance and a mercy, perhaps they may remember. [44]And you were not on the western side when we completed the commandments to Moses, and you were not among the witnesses. [45]But we raised up generations whose age were lengthened, and you were not dwelling among the family of Midian to recite our verses to them. But we were the senders. [46]And you were not on the side of the mountain when we called to him, but a mercy of your lord that you may warn people to whom no warner had come before you, perhaps they may remember. [47]And were it not that a misfortune had befallen them because of what their hands had done, so they will say, "Our lord, were it not that you had sent to us a messenger so that we might follow your signs and become of the believers." [48]So when the truth came to them from us, they said, "Were it not that he was given [signs] as Moses was given." Had they not become infidels of what Moses received before? They said, "Two sorcerers backing each other up." And they said, "Surely we are infidels to each of them."

Here is proof that the Torah had not changed at the time of Mohammed in the 7th century.

[49]Say, "So bring a book from Allah which will be a better guide than both of them that I may follow it, if you were truthful." [50]So if they did not answer you, so know that they are only following their own desires. And who goes more astray than the one who follows his own desire without guidance from Allah. Surely Allah will not guide the unjust people. [51]And indeed, we delivered the word to them, perhaps they may remember. [52]Those to whom we gave the book before it, they are believers in it. [53]And when it is recited to them,

they said, "We believed in it, surely it is the truth from our lord. Surely we were Muslims before it." [54]Those will be given their wage twice because of their patience, and they repelled the evil with the good. And they spend from what we provided them. [55]And when they heard idle talk, they withdrew from it, and they said, "To us our works and to you your works. Peace be on you. We do not desire the foolish." [56]Surely you cannot guide those whom you love. But Allah guides whom he wills, and he knows best the guided. [57]And they said, "If we follow the guidance with you, we will be snatched from our land." Have we not established for them a forbidden, secure place, to which fruit of every kind come to it [as] a provision from us? But most of them do not know. [58]And how many a village rebelled in its living we destroyed, so this is their dwelling. No one dwelt in it after them except a few, and we were the heirs. [59]And your lord was not to destroy the villages until he raised in its mother a messenger reciting to them our verses, and we were not to destroy the villages unless its families are unjust. [60]And whatever things you have been given, so the enjoyment of the world's life and its adornment, and what is with Allah is better and more lasting. Do you not understand? [61]Is he whom we promised a good promise, so he will meet it as the one whom we granted the enjoyment of the world's life; then on the resurrection day, he will be of those who will be brought? [62]And a day he will call them, so he will say, "Where are my partners whom you were claiming?" [63]Those on whom the word is established said, "Our lord, those whom we seduced, we seduced them as we have been seduced. We are innocent to you. They were not serving us." [64]And it was said, "Call on your partners." So they called on them, so they did not answer them. And they saw the torment if they were guided. [65]And a day he will call them, so he will say, "What did you answer the messengers?" [66]So the news was obscured from them on that day, so they will not ask each other. [67]So as for him who repented and believed and did good deed, so perhaps he may become among the prosperous. [68]And your lord creates what he wills and chooses what was good for them. Praise be to Allah, and he is exalted above what they partner. [69]And your lord knows what their chests hide and what they show. [70]And he is Allah. There is no god but him, to him the praise in the first and in the hereafter. And to him the judgment, and to him you will return. [71]Say, "Have you seen that Allah made the night above you continuing until the resurrection day? Who is god other than Allah who brings you light? Do you not hear?" [72]Say, "Have you seen that Allah made the day above you continuing until the resurrection day? Who is god other than Allah? Who brings the night to you in which you may dwell in it? Do you not see?" [73]And from his mercy he has made to you the night and the day that you may dwell in it and that you may seek from his bounty, and perhaps you may give thanks. [74]And a day he will call them, so he will say, "Where are my partners whom you were claiming?"

[75]And we removed a witness from every nation, so we said, "Bring your evidence." So they knew that the truth is to Allah. And what they were forging went astray from them.

The story of Qūrūn (Korah) is copied from the Bible and corrupted. Notice in this version, Mohammed considered Korah to be of Moses' people (a Jew). This contradicts verses 29:39 and 40:23-25 which clearly indicates that Korah was an Egyptian. He also confuses this character with Korah found in the Bible. See Numbers 16:1-40.

[76]Surely Qūrūn[a] was one of Moses' people, so he rebelled against them. We gave to him of the treasures what surely its keys would have burdened a strong, substantial company. When his people said to him, "Do not rejoice, surely Allah does not love the rejoicing. [77]And seek in what Allah has given you, the home of the hereafter, and do not forget your portion from this world. And do good as Allah has done good to you, and do not seek the vandalizing in the land. Surely Allah does not love the vandals." [78]He said, "Surely I have been given it only because of the knowledge that I possess." Did he know that Allah indeed destroyed before him some generations that were mightier than he in strength and more gathering,[b] and the criminals will not be asked about their sins. [79]So he went forth to his people in his adornment. So those who desire the world's life said, "Oh, we wish we had the like of that which has been given to Qūrūn, surely he has a great luck." [80]And those who have been given the knowledge said, "Woe to you! The reward of Allah is better for him who believed and did good deed, and no [one] will receive it, except the patient." [81]So we sunk him and his home into the earth. So there was not any group to help him without Allah, and he was not of the helped. [82]And those who desired his position yesterday were saying, "No wonder that Allah expands and measures the provision to whom he wills of his servants. Were it not for Allah's grace on us, he may sink us! No wonder that the infidels do not prosper." [83]This is the home of the hereafter. We made it for those who do not desire exaltation on the earth nor vandalization, and the end is to the fearer. [84]Whoever comes with the good, so he will have good from it; and whoever comes with the evil, so those who did the evils will not be rewarded except for what they were doing. [85]Surely who made the Qur'an mandatory on you will bring you back at the appointed time. Say, "My lord knows best who came with the guidance and who is in obvious error." [86]And you were not hoping that the book would be cast to you, except as mercy from your lord, so do not become a

---

[a] Korah, non-Arabic word of Hebrew origin and modified
[b] richer

backer to the infidels. [87]And do not let them turn you away from the verses of Allah after they have been sent down to you. And call to your lord, and do not become of the polytheists. [88]And do not call with Allah on another god. There is no god but him. Everything will perish except his face. To him the judgment, and to him you will return.

A portion of a revelation   **29**   *The Spider*

In the name of Allah, the merciful, the merciful

[1]Alm.[a] [2]Do the people think that they will be left alone when they say, "We believed," and they will not be seduced? [3]And indeed, we seduced those who were before them, so surely Allah knows those who believed, and surely he knows the liars. [4]Or those who do evil, do they think that they will get ahead of us? Evil is what they judge. [5]Whoever was hoping to meet Allah, so surely the appointed time of Allah will come. And he is the hearing, the knowing. [6]And whoever performs jihad, so surely he will only perform jihad for himself. Surely Allah is rich above the worlds. [7]And those who believed and did good deeds, we will surely atone for their evils, and we will surely reward them with the best of what they were doing. [8]And we have commanded the human [to show] kindness to his parents. And if they perform jihad against you to partner with me, of which you have no knowledge, so do not obey them. To me is your return, so I will inform you of what you were doing. [9]And those who believed and did good deeds, we will surely admit them among the good. [10]And some of the people say, "We believed in Allah." So if he suffers in the cause of Allah, they consider the people's sedition as the torment of Allah. And if a help comes from your lord, they surely say, "Surely we were with you." Or does not Allah know best what is in the chests of the worlds? [11]And surely Allah knows those who believed, and surely he knows the hypocrites. [12]And those who became infidels said to those who believed, "Follow our way, and we will bear your sins." And they are not bearing any of their sins, surely they are liars. [13]And surely they will bear their own burdens and burdens with their own burdens. And surely they will be asked on the resurrection day about what they were forging.

The stories of Noah, Abraham, Lot, and Moses are copied from the Bible and corrupted again.

---

[a] a word containing three Arabic letters without meaning

[14]And indeed, we sent Noah to his people, so he stayed among them a thousand years less fifty. So the deluge seized them, and they were unjust. [15]So we delivered him and the companions of the ship, and we made it as a sign to the worlds. [16]And Abraham, when he said to his people, "Serve Allah and fear him. This is best for you, if you were knowing. [17]Surely you only serve idols without Allah, and you create a lie. Surely those whom you serve without Allah do not have provision for you, so seek from Allah the provision and serve him and give thanks to him. To him you will return. [18]And if you deny, so indeed, nations before you denied. And the messenger's duty is only the clear delivery." [19]Or have they not seen how Allah begins the creation then repeats it? Surely this is easy for Allah. [20]Say, "Walk on the earth, so look how the creation began. Then Allah will create the hereafter creation. Surely Allah has might over all things." [21]He torments whom he wills and will have mercy on whom he wills, and to him you will be returned. [22]And you will not escape on the earth nor in the heaven, and you do not have any friend nor helper without Allah. [23]And those who became infidels in the verses of Allah and his meeting, those will despair from my mercy, and those will have a painful torment. [24]So the answer of his people was not except that they said, "Kill him or burn him." So Allah delivered him from the fire. Surely in this are signs to a believing people. [25]And he said, "Surely you only took idols without Allah as your friendship between you in the world's life. Then on the resurrection day, some of you will become an infidel of the others, and some of you will curse the others. And your abode is the fire, and you will not have any helpers." [26]So Lot believed in him, and he said, "Surely I am emigrating to my lord; surely he is the dear, the wise."

The "prophethood" and the book (the Bible) were ordained to the descendants of Jacob, the Jews.

[27]And we granted him Isaac and Jacob, and we assigned the prophethood and the book to his descendants. And we gave him his wage in this world, and surely in the hereafter he is among the good. [28]And Lot, when he said to his people, "Surely you enter into the indecency.[a] No one before you of the worlds has ever done that. [29]Do you enter into[b] men and you cut the way[c] and you enter into the evils in your assemblies?" So the answer of his people was not, except that they said, "Bring the torment of Allah on us if you were of the truthful." [30]He said, "My lord, help me against the vandalizing people." [31]And when our messengers came to Abraham with the good news, they said, "Surely we are destroying the people of this

---

[a] have sex with men
[b] have sex
[c] robbing travelers

village. Surely its people were unjust." [32]He said, "Surely Lot is in it." They said, "We know best who is in it. We surely will deliver him and his family except his woman [wife]; she was of those who stayed behind." [33]And when our messengers came to Lot, he was troubled because of them, and his arm was tight.[a] And they said, "Do not fear, and do not grieve. Surely we will deliver you and your family except your woman [wife]; she was of those who stayed behind." [34]Surely we will bring down wrath from the heaven on the people in this village because they were transgressors. [35]And indeed, we left from it a clear sign to people who understand.

The story of Midian, Ad, and Themoud are invented by Mohammed. What country? What time? What message? What people? What was their sin?

[36]And to Midian we sent their brother Shoaib. So he said, "O my people, serve Allah and hope [for] the last day and do not act wickedly in the land, vandalizing." [37]So they denied him, so an earthquake seized them. So they became motionless in their homes. [38]And Ad and Themoud, and indeed, it became clear to you in their dwellings, and Satan adorned their works to them. So he prevented them from the way, and they were clearly sighted.

Notice Mohammed considered Haman and Korah (Qūrūn) to be Egyptian. Also notice that four punishments are given to three people.

[39]And Qūrūn and Pharaoh and Haman, and indeed, Moses came to them with the proofs. So they became proud on the earth, and they were not ahead. [40]So we seized each one with his sin. So some of them we sent on him a hailstorm, and some of them were seized by the shout. And some of them we sank him into the earth, and some of them we drowned. And Allah was not to treat them unjustly, but they were treating themselves unjustly.

Mohammed claims that the spider web is a frail house! This is in error. It is on record that a spider web is strong enough to capture hummingbirds and will hold them long enough for the spider to kill and eat them. (From *The World of Nature*, "Character Sketches," Volume II, p. 48).

[41]The parable of those who took friends without Allah is like the 'ankabūt[b] that took a house. And surely the frailest of all the houses is the house of the spider, if they were knowing. [42]Surely Allah knows what they call on, of anything without him, and he is the dear, the wise. [43]And these are the parables we inform to the people, and no

---

[a] frustrated because he could not protect them
[b] spider, non-Arabic word of Aramaic origin

one will understand it except the learned. ⁴⁴Allah created the
heavens and the earth with the truth. Surely in this is a sign to the
believers.

**Prayer alone can wipe away sin. Muslims must believe in the
Bible. This is another proof of the infallibility of the Bible in
Mohammed's day. Note that verse 46 is abrogated; see all
Muslim scholars' interpretations.**

⁴⁵Recite what has been revealed to you from the book, and
perform the prayer. Surely the prayer wipes out the indecency and
the evil, and the remembrance of Allah is bigger. And Allah knows
what you do. ⁴⁶And do not dispute with the People of the Book
except with what is good, except to those who have done injustices
among them, and say, "We believed in what has been sent down to
us and has been sent down to you. And our god and your god is one,
and we are Muslims to him."

Those who reject the Qur'an are infidels.

⁴⁷And likewise, we sent the book down to you. So those, we gave
them the book, believe in it and some of those who believe in it, and
no one disbelieves in our verses except the infidels. ⁴⁸And you were
not reciting any book before it, and you did not write it with your right
hand. Then the liars would doubt. ⁴⁹Yet, it is clear verses in the
chests of those who have gained the knowledge, and no one
disbelieves in our verses except the unjust.

Mohammed offered no signs as proof except the Qur'an.

⁵⁰And they said, "Were it not that signs are sent down on him from
his lord." Say, "Surely the signs are only with Allah, and surely I am
only a clear warner." ⁵¹Is it not sufficient for them that we have sent
down the book on you to be recited to them? Surely in this is a mercy
and a reminder to a believing people. ⁵²Say, "Allah is sufficient
witness between me and you. He knows what is in the heavens and
the earth. And those who believed in the vanities and became
infidels in Allah, those are the losers." ⁵³And they hasten you with the
torment, and were it not for an appointed time, that torment would
surely have come on them, and it will come on them suddenly while
they did not feel. ⁵⁴They hasten you with the torment, and surely hell
will surround the infidels. ⁵⁵A day the torment covers them from
above them and from below their legs, and he will say, "Taste what
you were doing." ⁵⁶O my servants who believed, surely my earth is
vast, so to me so serve me. ⁵⁷Every soul will taste the death. Then to
us you will return. ⁵⁸And those who believed and did good deeds, we
will lodge them in rooms in the garden, below them the rivers flow.
They will abide in it forever. Blessed is the wage of the workers.

[59]Those who were patient, and they depend on their lord. [60]And how many a creature does not carry her provision? Allah provided for her and for you, and he is the hearing, the knowing. [61]And if you ask them: "Who created the heavens and the earth and has made the sun and the moon subservient?" They will surely say, "Allah." So how then can they turn away? [62]Allah expands the provision to whom he wills from his servants and measures out to him. Surely Allah knows all things. [63]And if you ask them: "Who sends down water from the heaven, so by it brings life to the earth after its death?" They will surely say, "Allah." Say, "The praise be to Allah," yet most of them do not understand. [64]And what is the world's life, except fun and sport, and surely the home of the hereafter is the animal, if they were knowing. [65]So when they embark on ships, they call on Allah, devout in the religion to him. So when he delivers them to the shore, they become polytheists. [66]To become infidels of what we gave to them, and they will have enjoyment, so they will know. [67]Do they not see that we have made a forbidden safe and the people around them are snatched away? Do they believe in the vanity and become infidels in Allah's grace? [68]And who is more unjust than who forged a lie against Allah or denied the truth when it comes to him? Is not hell the dwelling of the infidels? [69]And those who perform jihad for our sake, we will guide them in our ways. And surely Allah is with the doers of good.

A portion of a revelation   30   *The Byzantines*

In the name of Allah, the merciful, the merciful

[1]Alm.[a] [2]The Rūm[b] are defeated. [3]In a near part of the land and after having been defeated, they will be victorious. [4]Within a few years, to Allah is the affair, before and after and on that day, the believers will rejoice. [5]With the victory of Allah, he will give victory [to] whom he wills, and he is the dear, the merciful. [6]The promise of Allah. Allah does not change his promise, but most people do not know. [7]They know the visible of the world's life, and they are unaware about the hereafter. [8]Have they not considered in themselves that Allah did not create the heavens and the earth and what is between them, except with the truth and for an appointed time? And surely most people are infidels in the meeting of their lord.

---

[a] a word containing three Arabic letters without meaning
[b] Byzantines, a non-Arabic word of Greek origin

[9]Have they not walked on the earth, so they see how was the end of those who were before them? They were mightier than them in strength, and those who plowed the earth and constructed it more than they constructed it. And their messengers came to them with the proofs. So it was not for Allah to treat them unjustly, but they were treating themselves unjustly. [10]Then evil was the end of those who did the evil because they denied Allah's verses, and they were scoffing at it. [11]Allah began the creation, then he repeats it, then to him you will return. [12]And a day the hour will rise, the criminals will be in despair. [13]And it was not for them any intercessors from their partners, and they were infidels with their partners. [14]And a day the hour will rise, on that day they will be separated. [15]So as for those who believed and did good deeds, so they are happy in the rauda.[a] [16]And as for those who became infidels and denied our verses and the meeting of the hereafter, so those will be brought to the torment. [17]So praise be to Allah when you come to the evening and when you come to the morning. [18]And to him the praise in the heavens and the earth and at night and when you come to the noon. [19]He brings forth the living out of the dead, and he brings forth the dead out of the living. And he gives the earth life after its death, and likewise, you will be brought forth. [20]And of his signs that he created you from dust, then behold, you are scattered humans. [21]And of his signs that he created to you from your souls wives so that you may dwell in her, and he has established friendship and mercy between you. Surely in this are signs to a reflecting people. [22]And of his signs, the creation of the heavens and the earth, and your variety of tongues and colors. Surely in this are signs to those who know. [23]And of his signs is your sleep, by night and day, and your seeking of his bounty. Surely in these are signs to a hearing people. [24]And of his signs are that he shows you the lightning, fearing, and hoping. And he sends water from the heaven, so he gives life by it to the earth after its death. Surely in this are signs to understanding people. [25]And of his signs that the heaven and the earth stand at his command. Then if he calls you with a call from the earth, behold, you come forth. [26]And to him what is in the heavens and the earth. All to him are obedient. [27]And he is who begins the creation, and then he repeats it, and to him it is easy. And to him the highest example in the heavens and the earth, and he is the dear, the wise. [28]He sets forth a parable to you from among yourselves. Do you have from what your right hand possessed, of partners in what we provided you, so you are alike in it? You fear them as you fear yourselves. Likewise, we expound the verses to an understanding people. [29]Yet the unjust follow their desires without knowledge. So who can guide whom Allah misled?

---

[a] luxurious garden, non-Arabic word of Pahlavic origin

And they do not have any helpers. [30]So set your face to the religion, hanifan, the natural instinct of Allah which people grow up into it. There is no exchange in the creation of Allah. This is the right religion, but most people do not know. [31]Turning to him and fear him and perform the prayer and do not be of the polytheists. [32]Of those who have split up their religion, and they were parties where every group rejoices in what they have. [33]And when some harm touches the people, they call on their lord turning to him. Then if he caused them to taste mercy from him, behold, a group of them have other partners with their lord [34]to become infidels in what we gave them. So enjoy, so you will know. [35]Or we have sent down an authority on them, so he will speak about what they were partnering. [36]And when we cause the people to taste mercy, they rejoice in it; and if an evil touches them because of what their hand has produced, behold, they are in despair. [37]Have they not seen that Allah expands and measures the provision to whom he wills? Surely in this are signs to a believing people. [38]So give to the nearest relative his due and to the needy and the son of the way. This is best to those who desire the face of Allah, and those are the prosperous.

Allah will not bless those who accept interest on investments.

[39]And whatever you have been given of interest to increase in the people's money, so they will not increase with Allah. And whatever you have brought of legal alms, desiring the face of Allah, so those are the ones who will be doubled. [40]Allah who created you, then provided for you, then will cause you to die, then gives you life. Is there any of your partners who do any of those things? Praise be to him, and he is exalted above what they partner. [41]Vandalism has appeared in the shore and the sea because of what the hands of the people have earned so that he may cause them to taste some of what they have done, perhaps they may return. [42]Say, "Walk on the earth, so see how was the end of those before you, most of them were polytheists." [43]So set your face to the right religion before a day will come in which none can turn away from Allah. On that day they will be separated. [44]Whoever becomes an infidel, so his infidelity is on him, and whoever did good deed, so it is for themselves they prepare. [45]That he may reward from his bounty those who have believed and did good deeds, surely he does not love the infidels. [46]And of his signs, that he sends the winds with good news so that he may cause you to taste of his mercy and that ships may sail at his command and that you may seek from his bounty, and perhaps you may give thanks. [47]And indeed, we sent messengers before you to their people, so they came to them with proofs. So we took revenge on those criminals, and it was our duty to help the believers. [48]Allah is who sends the winds, so they raise clouds. So he spreads them in the heaven however he wills. And he made them break, so you see

the rain issuing from their midst. So when he pours it down as he wills on his servants, behold, they rejoice. [49]And before it came down on them, they were in despair. [50]So look then at the traces of Allah's mercy, how he brings life to the earth after its death. Surely this will give life to the dead, and he has might over all things. [51]And if we send a wind, so they see it yellow, they surely continue to be infidels after it.

Mohammed could not perform miracles. Compare this to the miracles of 'Isā (the Jesus of Mohammed) in verse 5:110.

[52]So surely you cannot make the dead hear, and you cannot make the deaf hear the call when they turn their backs. [53]And you cannot guide the blind out of their error. You will make none to hear, except who will believe in our verses, so they are Muslims. [54]Allah is who created you from weakness; then he makes strength after weakness. Then he makes weakness after the strength and gray hair. He created what he wills, and he is the knowing, the mighty. [55]And a day the hour will arise, the criminals will swear that they did not stay but an hour. Likewise, they were lying. [56]But those who are given the knowledge and the faith said, "Indeed, you have waited according to the book of Allah, until the sending (resurrection) day, so this is the sending day, but you were not knowing." [57]So on that day, their excuses will not profit the unjust, and neither will they be allowed to repent. [58]And indeed, we gave in this Qur'an from every parable to the people, and if you bring to them a sign, those who became infidels will surely say, "You are but a purveyor of lies." [59]Likewise, Allah seals on the hearts of those who do not know. [60]So be patient, surely the promise of Allah is true. And do not let those who have no certainty unsettle you.

A portion of a revelation **31** *Lokman*

In the name of Allah, the merciful, the merciful

[1]Alm.[a] [2]These are the verses of the wise book, [3]guidance and mercy to the doers of good, [4]those who perform the prayer and bring the legal alms, and they are certain of the hereafter. [5]Those are on guidance from their lord, and those are the prosperous. [6]And some of the people, who purchase fun talk to lead astray from the way of

---

[a] a word containing three Arabic letters without meaning

Allah without knowledge, and they take it as scoff, those will have a shameful torment. [7]And when our verses are recited to him, he turns away proudly as if he had not heard it, as if in his ears are heaviness. So give him the good news of a painful torment. [8]Surely those who believed and did good deeds have the gardens of bliss, [9]dwelling in it forever. Allah's promise is true. And he is the dear, the wise.

Heaven is a structure. Earth does not move; it sits still.

[10]He created the heavens without columns, you see it, and he threw stabilizers on the earth lest it should move with you. And he scattered in it of every creature. And he sent down water from the heaven, so we grow plants in it from every generous pair. [11]This is the creation of Allah, so show me what others have created without him. Yet the unjust are in obvious error.

The story of Lokman was invented by Mohammed.

[12]And indeed, we gave Lokman the wisdom: "That give thanks to Allah." And whoever gives thanks, so surely he only gives thanks to himself, and whoever becomes an infidel, so surely Allah is rich, praised. [13]And when Lokman said to his son while preaching to him, "O my son, do not partner with Allah, surely the partnering is a great injustice." [14]We have commanded the human concerning his parents. His mother carried him with weakness on weakness and his weaning in two years: "That be thankful to me and to your parents. To me is the final return. [15]And if they perform jihad against you to get you to partner with me of which you have no knowledge, so do not obey them and be in companionship with them in this world with kindness. And follow a way of him who turns to me. Then your return is to me, so I will inform you of what you were doing. [16]O my son, surely if it is the weight of the grain of the mustard seed, so it will be in a rock or in the heavens or on the earth, Allah will bring it. Surely Allah is kind, aware. [17]O my son, perform the prayer and command with the right and forbid from the evil and be patient under whatever will befall you. Surely this is from the determination of the affairs. [18]And do not turn your cheek to the people,[a] and do not walk in the land arrogantly. Surely Allah does not love every arrogant, proud. [19]And let your pace be moderate and lower your voice, surely the most hideous voice is the voice of the donkeys." [20]Have you not seen how that Allah has made what is in the heavens and what is on the earth subservient to you and has been bounteous to you of his graces, its shown and its hidden? And some of the people who dispute in Allah without knowledge and without guidance and without an enlightening book. [21]And when it is said to them, "Follow what Allah has sent down."

---

[a] with pride

They said, "Yet we will follow what we found our fathers doing." It was as if Satan was inviting them to the torment of the blaze. [22]And whoever submits his face to Allah while doing good, so indeed, he takes hold of the firmest handle. And to Allah is the end of the affairs. [23]And whoever becomes an infidel, so do not let his infidelity grieve you. They will return to us, so we will inform them about what they did. Surely, Allah knows what is in the chests. [24]We give them enjoyment for a little while. Then we will force them into a thick[a] torment. [25]And if you ask them: "Who created the heavens and the earth?" They will surely say, "Allah." Say, "The praise be to Allah." Yet most of them do not know. [26]To Allah what is in the heavens and the earth. Surely Allah is the rich, the praised. [27]And if all what is on the earth from trees were pens and the sea providing after it seven more seas,[b] the words of Allah would not be exhausted. Surely Allah is dear, wise. [28]He did not create you and did not raise you, except as one soul. Surely Allah is hearing, seeing. [29]Have you not seen that Allah penetrates the night into the day and penetrates the day into the night and that he made the sun and the moon each run subservient to an appointed time and that Allah is aware of what you do? [30]This is because Allah is surely the truth and that what they call on without him is the vanity. And that Allah is the highest, the big. [31]Have you not seen the ships sailing in the sea by the grace of Allah that he may show you some of his signs? Surely in this are signs to every patient, thankful. [32]And if the waves cover them like shadows, they call to Allah, devoted in the religion to him. So when he delivered them to the shore, so some of them fulfill the promise, and no one disbelieves in our verses except every traitorous, infidel.[33]O you people, fear your lord and dread a day in which a father will not compensate for his son, neither will an infant compensate anything for his father. Surely the promise of Allah is true. So do not let the world's life deceive you, and do not let pride deceive you regarding Allah. [34]Surely Allah has with him the knowledge of the hour, and he sends down the rain. And he knows what is in the wombs, and no soul knows what it will gain tomorrow. And no soul will know in what land it will die. Surely Allah is knowing, aware.

---

[a] great
[b] of ink

A portion of a revelation   *The Worship*

In the name of Allah, the merciful, the merciful

[1]Alm.[a] [2]The descending of the book, there is no doubt in it from the lord of the worlds. [3]Or they say, "He has forged it." Yet it is the truth from your lord so that you may warn a people to whom no warner had come before you, perhaps they may be guided. [4]Allah who created the heavens and the earth and what is between them in six days; then he sat on the throne, you have no friends or intercessors without him. Do you not remember?

The trip from heaven to earth takes angles 1,000 years. This is contradicted in verse 70:4 which indicates that it takes 50,000 years.

[5]He arranges the affair from the heaven to the earth. Then it ascends to him in a day, its duration was one thousand years from what you count. [6]That is the knower of the unseen and the seen, the dear, the merciful, [7]who best created everything. And he began the creation of the human from mud. [8]Then he made his seed from worthless water. [9]Then he shaped him and blew into him from his spirit. And he made to you the hearing and the sight and the hearts. Little thanks you give. [10]And they said, "If we went astray on the earth, then will we become a new creation?" Yet they are infidels of the meeting of their lord. [11]Say, "The angel of death, who is in charge over you, will cause you to die. Then you will return to your lord." [12]And if you could see the criminals hang their heads before their lord: "Our lord, we have seen and heard, so return us. We will do good. Surely we are certain."

Allah's will is not to guide all the people but to fill hell with jinn and people.

[13]And if we had willed, we would surely give to every soul its guidance. But the word which has gone forth from me was established: "I will surely fill hell with jinn and people together." [14]So taste, because you forgot the meeting of this your day, surely we will forget you, and taste the torment of the eternity because of what you were doing. [15]Surely, the only people who believe in our verses are those who fall worshiping when reminded of them and praise with their lord's praise, and they are not proud. [16]Their side goes up from the beds, they call on their lord with fear and hope, and they spend

---

[a] a word containing three Arabic letters without meaning

from what we provided them. [17]So no soul knows what is hidden from them of the pleasure of eyes, a reward for what they were doing. [18]Is the one who was a believer like the one who was a transgressor? They are not equal. [19]As to those who believed and did good deeds, so they will have the gardens of an eternal abode as guests because of what they were doing. [20]And as for those who transgress, so their abode is the fire. So often [as] they desire to get out from it, they are brought back into it. And it was said to them, "Taste the torment of the fire, which you were denying it." [21]And we will surely cause them to taste from the near torment without the bigger torment, perhaps they may return. [22]And who is more unjust than he who is reminded by the verses of his lord then he turns away from it? Surely, we will take vengeance on the criminals. [23]And indeed, we gave Moses the book, so do not be in doubt about meeting him. And we made it a guidance to the children of Israel. [24]And we made some of them leaders, guiding with our commands when they were patient, and they were certain of our signs. [25]Surely your lord, he will judge between them on the resurrection day in what they were differing. [26]Is it not a guide for them how many generations we destroyed before them, they are walking in their dwellings? Surely in this are signs. Do they not hear? [27]Or have they not seen how we drive[a] the water to the parched earth, so we bring forth plants from which their livestock and themselves eat from it? Do they not see? [28]And they say, "When is this invasion [to] take place, if you were truthful?" [29]Say, "On the invasion day, the faith of those who became infidels will not profit them, and they will not be delayed." [30]So turn away from them and wait; surely they are waiting.

A portion of a revelation   33   *The Parties*

In the name of Allah, the merciful, the merciful

[1]O you prophet, fear Allah and do not obey the infidels and the hypocrites. Surely Allah was knowing, wise. [2]And follow what is revealed to you from your lord. Surely Allah was aware of what you do. [3]And depend on Allah, and Allah is a sufficient guardian.

Adoption is forbidden in Islam. These verses served to void Mohammed's adoption of his son, Zaid, after Mohammed was

---

[a] direct

criticized for marrying his daughter-in-law, Zanab Bent Jahash, who had been married to Zaid. Mohammed allowed men to marry the ex-wives of their adopted sons. See verses 37-40.

[4]Allah did not make to man two hearts inside his body, and he did not make your wives which you turn your back from them your mothers. And he did not make your adopted sons your sons. This is your saying with your mouth, and Allah says the truth. And he guides the way. [5]Call them[a] to their fathers, this will be more just with Allah. So if you do not know who their fathers are, so they are your brothers in the religion and your friends. And there is no fault against you in what you have sinned in, but what your heart purposely intends. And Allah was forgiving, merciful. [6]The prophet has greater claim on the believers than even themselves, and his wives are their mothers. The relatives are closer to each other in the book of Allah among the believers and the emigrants, except that you do fairness to your friends. This was written in the book. [7]And when we took from the prophets their covenant and from you and from Noah and Abraham and Moses and 'Isā, son of Mary, and we took from them a thick[b] covenant [8]so that he may ask the truthful about their truthfulness and has prepared a painful torment for the infidels. [9]O you who have believed, remember Allah's grace on you when the troops came to you, so we sent a wind against them and troops that you did not see. And Allah was seer of what you do. [10]When they came to you from above you and from below you, and when the eyes became deviated and the hearts reached your throat and you thought the thoughts about Allah. [11]Thereupon the believers were tempted, and they were shaking with a strong shaking. [12]And when the hypocrites and those who have disease in their hearts say, "Allah and his messenger did not promise us except pride."

Some of Mohammed's people offered excuses for not going to war with him.

[13]And when a group of them said, "O family of Yathrib,[c] there is no place for you, so return." And a group of them excused themselves from the prophet, saying, "Surely our houses are left defenseless." And they were not left defenseless, but they only desired to flee. [14]And if you enter into them from different sides and then they were asked to commit the sedition, they would have done so. And they would have only stayed in it but a little while. [15]And indeed, they had made a covenant with Allah before they will not turn the backs, and a covenanter of Allah was questioned. [16]Say, "Fleeing will not profit you. If you flee from the death or the murder, and then you will not

---

[a] the adopted sons
[b] firm
[c] old name for Medina, Mohammed's city

enjoy yourself but little." [17]Say, "Who can withhold you from Allah if he desires to do evil to you or if he desires to show you mercy?" And they will not find a friend or a helper for them without Allah.

Those who stay away from jihad (Allah's wars) have no faith.

[18]Indeed, Allah knows those among you who hinder and those who say to their brethren, "Come here to us," and who do not come to the war except a little. [19]Stingy toward you, so if the fear comes, you saw them looking at you and their eyes rolling like the ones fainting from the death. So when the fear is gone, with sharp tongues they will assail you, stingy for the good.[a] Those did not believe, so Allah made their works vain. And this was easy with Allah. [20]They think that the parties will not go. And if the parties were to come, they would rather be dwelling among the Bedouins asking about your news; and if they were with you, they would not engage in war except a little.

Mohammed is a good example for believers.

[21]Indeed, there was in the messenger of Allah a noble example for you, for him who was hoping in Allah and in the last day and remembers Allah much. [22]And when the faithful saw the parties, they said, "This is what Allah and his messenger promised us." And Allah and his messenger are truthful, and it did not increase them except faith and submission. [23]Among the believing men are those who are true to the covenant they made with Allah. So some have died,[b] and some of them are still waiting. And they did not change, changing. [24]That Allah may reward the truthful with their truth and torment the hypocrites if he wills or relents on them. Surely Allah was forgiving, merciful. [25]And Allah drove back those who became infidels with their anger. They did not receive good, and Allah is sufficient for the believers in the war. And Allah was strong, dear.

Mohammed is bragging about terrorizing, killing, and enslaving the Jews and Christians. He then brags about inheriting their properties. See also verse 59:2.

[26]And he brought down the People of the Book who backed them from their strong places and cast the terror into their hearts. A group of them you are killing, and a group of them you are taking captive. [27]And he made you to inherit their land and their homes and their money and a land which you had never set foot on. And Allah was mighty over all things.

---

[a] spoils
[b] those who die during jihad

Mohammed should divorce a worldly wife. He commands his wives to stay home.

[28]O you prophet, say to your wives, "If you desire the world's life and its adornment, so come then, I will give you enjoyment and dismiss you with a beautiful dismissal.[a] [29]And if you desire Allah and his messenger and the home of the hereafter, so surely Allah has prepared a great wage for the doers of good among you. [30]O women of the prophet, whoever among you commits clear indecency,[b] the torment will be double to her two-fold, and this was easy with Allah. [31]And whoever of you will obey Allah and his messenger and will do good, we will bring her wage to her twice, and we have prepared for her a generous provision. [32]O women of the prophet, you are not like any other of the women. If you fear, so do not be soft in your speech lest the one who has a disease in his heart should covet[c] you, but speak with fair speech. [33]And stay in your houses and do not display yourselves like the display of the first of ignorance and perform the prayer and bring the legal alms and obey Allah and his messenger. Surely Allah only desires to put away the uncleanness from you, people of the house, and purify you, purification. [34]And remember what is recited in your houses from the verses of Allah and the wisdom. Surely Allah was kind, aware." [35]Surely the Muslim men and the Muslim women, and the believing men and the believing women, and the obeying men and the obeying women, and the truthful men and the truthful women, and the patient men and the patient women, and the humble men and the humble women, and the almsgiving men and the almsgiving women, and the fasting men and the fasting women, the men who keep their private parts (maintain their chastity) and the women who keep, and the men who remember Allah much and the women who remember, there is a great wage and forgiveness prepared for them. [36]And it was not for a believing man or a believing woman, if Allah and his messenger judged an affair, that they will have a choice in their affairs; and whoever disobeys Allah and his messenger, so indeed, they err in a manifest error.

Allah allowed Mohammed to marry his adopted son Zaid's wife, Zanab Bent Jahash, after Mohammed "allowed" Zaid to divorce her. Allah chides Mohammed for worrying about what people think of him for lusting after Zanab after seeing her partially naked and subsequently marrying her. See Al Qurtobi, Al Tabari, and other interpretations.

---

[a] divorce
[b] fornication /big sin
[c] lust after

[37]And when you said to whom[a] Allah had graced on and you graced on, "Keep your wife to yourself and fear Allah." And you hide in yourself[b] what Allah would reveal. And you feared the people,[c] and Allah is more worthy to be feared. So when Zaid had satisfied his desire from her,[d] we married her to you so that it would not be a shame on the believers to marry the wives of their sons[e] when they have settled the affair[f] concerning them. And the command of Allah was accomplished. [38]There was no shame on the prophet where Allah had ordained for him. The custom of Allah with those who have gone before and the command of Allah was a predetermined decree. [39]Those who delivered the messages of Allah and feared him and feared no one except Allah, and Allah is a sufficient accounter. [40]Mohammed was not the father of any man among you, but is the messenger of Allah and the khātam[g] of the prophets. And Allah was the knower of all things.

Allah and his angels pray on (for) believers. To whom is Allah praying?

[41]O you who have believed, remember Allah with much remembrance, [42]and praise him morning and evening. [43]He is who prays on[h] you and his angels that he may bring you forth out of the darkness into the light, and he was merciful to the believers. [44]Their greeting on a day they meet him: "Peace," and he prepared for them a generous wage. [45]O you prophet, surely we have sent you to be a witness and a giver of good news and a warner [46]and a caller to Allah, with his permission, and a lighted lamp. [47]And give the believers the good news that they will have from Allah a big bounty. [48]And do not obey the infidels and the hypocrites, and ignore their harm. And depend on Allah. And Allah is a sufficient guardian. [49]O you who have believed, when you have sex (marry) with the believing women, then you divorce them before you have touched them, you do not have the waiting period against them which you count. So give them enjoyment (a gift), and let them go in a beautiful way.

Allah grants Mohammed the exclusive right to have sex with as many believing woman as he chooses if they offer themselves

---

[a] Zaid
[b] his lust for Zanab
[c] what they would think of Mohammed marrying Zanab
[d] divorcing her
[e] in adoption
[f] divorce
[g] seal, non-Arabic word of probable Aramaic origin
[h] for

to him. This is not in actual marriage as evidenced by verse 52 which prohibits Mohammed from acquiring new wives.

[50]O you prophet, surely we have made it lawful for you, your wives whom you have given their wages and those that your right hand possesses which Allah has granted you and the daughters of your paternal uncle and the daughters of your paternal aunts and the daughters of your maternal uncle and the daughters of your maternal aunts, those who emigrate with you. And a believing woman if she gives herself to the prophet, if the prophet desires to have sex with her, this is a privilege for you but not for any other believers. Indeed, we know what we ordain for them in their wives and what their right hand possessed, that there may be no shame on your part. And Allah was forgiving, merciful. [51]You may postpone[a] whom you will of them and take to you[b] whom you will and from those that you desire whom you postponed previously. There is no sin on you. This is proper so that their eyes will be pleased and not grieved and that they may be satisfied of what you have given to all of them, and Allah knows what is in your heart. And Allah was knowing, forbearing. [52]It is not lawful for you the women[c] after that, nor to exchange your present wives for other women though their beauty charms you, except what your right hand possesses. And Allah was watcher over all things.

Mohammed's wives are forbidden to remarry after his death.

[53]O you who have believed, do not enter the houses of the prophet, except when it is permitted to you, for a meal, but not waiting while it is being prepared. But if you were invited, so enter, so when you have eaten, so depart. And do not engage in familiar conversation, surely this would harm the prophet. So he would be shy of you, and Allah is not shy of the truth. And when you would ask for anything from them,[d] so ask them from behind a veil. This will be purer for your hearts and for their hearts. And you must not harm the messenger of Allah, nor have sex with (marry) his wives after him, forever. Surely this is a great offense with Allah. [54]If you show anything or if you hide it, so surely Allah was the knower of all things. [55]No sin will be on them in their fathers or to their sons or to their brothers or to their brothers' sons or to their sisters' sons or to their women or to what their right hands possess. And fear Allah. Surely Allah was a witness over all things.

Allah and his angels pray on (for) Mohammed. To whom is Allah praying?

---

[a] from having sex
[b] have sex with
[c] in marriage
[d] his wives

[56]Surely Allah and his angels pray on the prophet. O you who have believed, pray on him and salute, saluting. [57]Surely those who harm Allah and his messenger, Allah will curse them in this world and in the hereafter, and he has prepared for them a shameful torment. [58]And those who harm the believing men and the believing women, without what they earned, so indeed, they bear slander and a clear sin.

All Muslim women must be entirely covered so that they will not be known. According to Muslim scholars' interpretations, the true hijab is a full cover for the woman's body except for a small hole in front of one eye. See Ibn Kathir, Al Galalien, Al Qurtobi, and Al Tabari interpretations.

[59]O you prophet, say to your wives and to your daughters and the women of the believers, let down their jalābīb[a] over them,[b] that in this way they will be known,[c] so they will not be harmed. And Allah was forgiving, merciful.

If the hypocrite Muslims do not repent to Islam, they must be killed!

[60]If the hypocrites and those who have a disease in their heart and the agitators in the city do not desist, we will surely arouse you against[d] them. Then they will not be your neighbors in it except for a little while. [61]They are cursed wherever they are caught, seized and killed, slaughtering. [62]The custom of Allah for those who have gone before, and you will not find any changing to the custom of Allah. [63]People ask you of the hour. Say, "Surely its knowledge is only with Allah, and you will not know, perhaps the hour is near." [64]Surely Allah has cursed the infidels and prepared for them a blaze. [65]They will abide in it forever and ever; they will not find a friend or a helper. [66]A day their faces will be turned over in the fire, they will say, "O that we would have obeyed Allah and obeyed the messenger." [67]And they said, "Our lord, surely we obeyed our masters and our great ones, so they led us astray from the way. [68]Our lord, give them a double of the torment and curse them a big curse." [69]O you who have believed, do not be like those who harmed Moses. But Allah declared him innocent from what they said, and he was honorable with Allah. [70]O you who have believed, fear Allah and say right words. [71]He will fix your deeds for you and forgive you of your sins. And whoever obeys Allah and his messenger, so indeed, he triumphs a great triumph. [72]Surely we offered the trust to the

---

[a] wrappers—large outer covering worn by women, non-Arabic word of Ethiopian origin
[b] from the top of their head covering their entirety
[c] identified as a believing Muslim woman rather than a prostitute or infidel
[d] to invade

heavens and the earth and the mountains, so they all refused to carry it. And they were afraid of it, yet the human carried it, surely he was unjust, ignorant. [73]That Allah might torment the hypocritical men and the hypocritical women and the polytheistic men and the polytheistic women, and Allah will relent on the believing men and the believing women. And Allah was forgiving, merciful.

A portion of a revelation   *Sheba*

In the name of Allah, the merciful, the merciful

[1]The praise be to Allah to whom what is in the heavens and what is on the earth and to him the praise in the hereafter. And he is the wise, the aware. [2]He knows what penetrates into the earth and what comes out of it and what descends from the heaven and what ascends into it. And he is the merciful, the forgiving. [3]And those who became infidels said, "The hour will not come to us." Say, "Yes, [I swear] by my lord, it will surely come to you, the knower of the unseen; the weight of an atom will not escape him in the heavens or on the earth, or smaller than that or bigger, except in a clear book." [4]That he may reward those who believed and did the good deeds, those will have forgiveness and a generous provision. [5]And those who strive in our verses, hindering, those will have a torment of a painful wrath. [6]And those to whom knowledge has been given, see that what has been sent down to you from your lord is the truth, and guides to the way of the dear, the praised. [7]And those who became infidels said, "Shall we point you to a man who will inform you, if you have been ripped every ripping, surely then will you become a new creation? [8]He has forged a lie against Allah, or in him is a jinn." Yet those who do not believe in the hereafter are in the torment and in the far error. [9]Have they not seen what is between their hands and what is behind them from the heaven and the earth? If we willed, we could sink them down into the earth or we could drop on them a portion of the heaven. Surely in this is a sign to every turning servant.

The mountain speaks and praises Allah.

[10]And indeed, we gave David a bounty from us: "O mountains, sing praises with him and the birds." And we softened the iron to him. [11]That, "Make suitable coats of sard[a] and measure the length. And

---

[a] chain armor, non-Arabic word of Persian/Syriac origin

do a good deed. Surely I see what you do." [12]And to Solomon the wind. Its going a month and its coming a month. And we made a fountain of molten brass to flow for him. And some of the jinn who work between his hands, by the will of his lord, and whoever of them deviated from our command, we will cause him to taste the torment of the blaze. [13]They made for him whatever he willed, of synagogues and statues, deep dishes like jāwib,[a] and immovable boiling pots: "Work, O family of David, thankfully; and few of my servants are the thankful."

Solomon was dead and leaning on his staff for an entire year before anyone realized he was dead.

[14]So when we decreed the death on him, nothing showed them that he was dead but a small creature of the earth that ate away his staff which supported his corpse. So when he fell, the jinn perceived that, if they had known the unseen, they had not continued in this shameful torment. [15]Indeed, it was to Sabā,[b] in their dwelling was a sign, two gardens, on right and left: "Eat from the provision of your lord, and give thanks to him, a good country and a forgiving lord." [16]So they turned aside. So we sent on them the flood of 'Arim, and we changed their two gardens into gardens of bitter fruit and tamarisk and a few sidrat.[c] [17]This is their reward because of their infidelity. And will we reward any except the infidel? [18]And we made between them and between the villages which we have blessed in them easily seen villages, and we measured the journey between them: "Walk it securely nights and days." [19]So they said, "Our lord, make the distance between our travels farther." And they treated themselves unjustly. So we made them sayings, and we ripped them all ripping. Surely in this is a sign to every patient,thankful. [20]And indeed, the Devil agreed with them in his thoughts, so they followed him except a group of the believers. [21]And it was not for him to have authority over them, except we might know who will believe in the hereafter from him who doubts of it. And your lord is keeper over all things. [22]Say, "Call on those whom you claim without Allah. They cannot possess even the weight of an atom in the heavens or on the earth. And they do not have any partnership in them, and he will not have a backer among them."

Some will have intercession before Allah.

[23]And intercession with him will not profit except for the one who receives permission until, when at last their hearts will be relieved

---

[a] cisterns, non-Arabic word of Syriac origin
[b] Sheba
[c] nonsense word, which some Islamic scholars claim to be a tree in the garden

from terror, they said, "What does your lord say?" They said, "The truth, and he is the high, the big." ^{24}Say, "Who provides you from the heavens and the earth?" Say, "Allah. And surely we or you are guided or in obvious error." ^{25}Say, "Do not ask about our crime, and we will not ask what you do." ^{26}Say, "Our lord, gather us together, then open^a between us with the truth; surely he is the opener,^{b} the knower." ^{27}Say, "Show me those whom you joined with him as partners. Certainly not, yet he is Allah, the dear, the wise."

Mohammed is the messenger to all people.

^{28}And we did not send you except to all people a giver of good news and a warner. But most people do not know. ^{29}And they say, "When is this promise, if you were truthful?" ^{30}Say, "You have an appointed day, you do not delay from it an hour, and you will not advance." ^{31}And those who became infidels said, "We will not believe in this Qur'an, nor in the book which is between his hands. And if you could only see when the unjust will stand before their lord returning the saying one to another. Those who were weakened say to those who are proud, "Were it not for you, we would have been believers!" ^{32}Those who are proud said to those who were weakened, "Are we the ones who prevented you from the guidance after it had come to you? Yet you were criminals." ^{33}And those who are weakened said to those who are proud, "Yet the deception of the night and the day, when you command us to become infidels in Allah and make to him peers." And they hid the regret when they saw the torment, and we place the yokes on the necks of those who became infidels. Will they be rewarded except for what they were doing? ^{34}We did not send a warner to a village, except those who live luxuriously in it said, "We are surely becoming infidels of what you have brought." ^{35}And they said, "We have more money and children, and we will not be tormented." ^{36}Say, "Surely my lord expands and measures the provision to whom he wills, but most people do not know." ^{37}And it is not your money nor your children that will bring you closer with us except those who believed and did good deed, so those will have double of the reward for what they have done. And they in their rooms will be secure. ^{38}And those who strive to hinder our verses, they will be brought into the torment. ^{39}Say, "Surely my lord expands the provision to whom he wills of his servants and measures to him. And anything you spend, he will replace it. And he is the best of the providers." ^{40}And a day he will gather them together, then he will say to the angels, "Are those the ones who were serving you?" ^{41}They said, "Praise be to you. You are our friend without them. Yet they were serving the jinn, and most of them were believers in them." ^{42}So today, none of you possess profit or harm to another. And we will say

---

^{a} judge
^{b} judge

to those who are unjust, "Taste the torment of the fire which you were denying it."

Some believed that the Qur'an was a lie and was written through sorcery.

[43]And when our clear verses were recited to them, they said, "This is not but a man who would desire to prevent you away from what your fathers served." And they said, "This is not but a forged lie." And those who became infidels said, to the truth when it came to them, "This is nothing but obvious sorcery." [44]And we have not brought them any books to study, and we did not send a warner to them before you. [45]And those who were before them denied, not even receiving a tenth part of what we had given to them. So they denied my messengers. So how was my repudiation? [46]Say, "Surely I only preach you one thing: that you would stand up for Allah by twos and individually, then you think what is in your companion is of the jinn, that he is only a warner to you between the hands of a severe torment." [47]Say, "I did not ask a wage of you, so keep it for yourselves. My wage is only from Allah. And he is a witness over all things." [48]Say, "Surely my lord casts with the truth; he is the knower of the unseen." [49]Say, "The truth came, and vanity cannot begin and cannot repeat." [50]Say, "If I have gone astray, so surely I only have gone astray against myself. And if I am guided, so it is because of what my lord has revealed to me. Surely he is hearing, near." [51]And if you see, when they were terrified, so there was no escape! And they were taken from a near place. [52]And they said, "We believed in it!" And how can they reach from a faraway place? [53]And indeed, they become infidels in it before, and they will cast with the unseen from a far place. [54]And it was separated between them and what they lust for, as it was done to their company before. Surely they were in severe doubt.

A portion
of a revelation   **35**   The Creator

In the name of Allah, the merciful, the merciful

[1]The praise be to Allah, creator of the heavens and the earth who made the angels messengers, with substantial wings, two and three and four. He adds to his creatures what he wills. Surely Allah has might over all things. [2]What Allah opens from his mercy to the people, so no one is able to withhold it. And what he will withhold, so

no one can send it forth after him. And he is the dear, the wise. [3]O
you people, remember the grace of Allah on you. Is there a creator
other than Allah who provides for you from the heaven and the
earth? There is no god except him. So how then are you turned
away? [4]And if they deny you, so indeed, messengers before you
were denied, and to Allah the affairs will return. [5]O you people,
surely the promise of Allah is true. So do not let the world's life make
you proud, and do not let pride make you proud concerning Allah.
[6]Surely Satan is an enemy to you. So take him as an enemy. Surely
he only calls his party so that they may become the companions of
the blaze. [7]Those who became infidels will have severe torment, and
those who believed and did good deeds, to them forgiveness and a
big wage.

Allah leads some people astray.

[8]Will he whose evil deed is adorned to him so he saw it as good?
So surely Allah leads astray whom he wills and guides whom he
wills. So do not grieve your soul in regret for them, surely Allah
knows what they do. [9]And Allah is who sent forth the winds so that
they stir up the clouds, so we drove them to a dead country. So we
gave the earth life by it after its death, likewise is the resurrection.
[10]Whoever was desiring the honor, so all the honor is to Allah. The
good word rises up to him, and he will lift up the good deed. And
those who deceive with the evils, they will have severe torment and
their deception will be destroyed. [11]And Allah created you from dirt,
then from nutfah. Then he made you pairs. And a female will not
conceive or bring forth except with his knowledge. And no aged
person will have long years, and his age will not be shortened except
it is prescribed in a book. Surely this is easy for Allah. [12]And the two
seas are not equal. This is fresh, sweet, pleasant for drink, and this
is salty, bitter. And from each you eat tender meat and take forth
ornaments for you to wear, and you see the ships sailing in it so that
you may seek from his bounties. And perhaps you may give thanks.
[13]He penetrates the night into the day and penetrates the day into
the night, and he made the sun and the moon subservient. Each one
runs to its appointed time. This is Allah, your lord. To him the
kingdom. And those whom you call on without him do not own even
the soft cover of the date nut. [14]If you call to them, they will not hear
you calling; and if they heard, they would not answer you. And on the
resurrection day, they will become infidels in your idolatry, and no
one can inform you like an aware. [15]O you people, you are the poor
to Allah. And Allah is the rich, the praised. [16]If he willed, he could
take you away and bring forth a new creation. [17]And this is not dear
for Allah. [18]And that no bearer of a burden bears the burden of
another, and if the heavy laden soul calls for its burden to be carried,
yet nothing will be carried, even if he was a near relative. Surely you

only warn those who fear their lord in secret and who perform the prayer. And whoever kept himself pure, so surely he only purifies for himself, and to Allah is the final return. [19]And the blind and the seeing are not equal, [20]nor the darkness nor the light [21]nor the shade nor the heat. [22]And neither the living nor the dead are equal. Surely Allah hears whom he wills, and you cannot make those who are in the graves hear. [23]You are only a warner.

Every nation has a prophet. Is this true?

[24]Surely we sent you with the truth, as a giver of good news and a warner. And there is not any nation, except that they have a warner gone to it. [25]And if they deny you, so indeed, those who were before them denied. Their messengers came to them with the proofs and with the scriptures and with the enlightening book. [26]Then I seized those who became infidels, so how terrible was my repudiation! [27]Have you not seen that Allah sent down water from heaven, so we brought fruit by it, its colors are different and from the mountains streaks are white and red, its colors are different, and black gharabeb,[a] [28]and of the people and the creatures and the livestock, its colors are different, likewise? Surely only the knowledgeable servants fear Allah. Surely Allah is dear, forgiving. [29]Surely those who recite the book of Allah and performed the prayer and spent from what we provided for them secretly and publicly, they hope for merchandise that will not perish. [30]That he will pay them their wages and increase them from his bounty. Surely he is forgiving, thankful.

Once again the Qur'an confirms that the Bible is true.

[31]And that which we have revealed to you of the book (Qur'an), it is the truth, confirming what (the Bible) is between his hands. Surely Allah to his servants is aware, seeing. [32]Then we bequeathed the book to those we had chosen of our servants. So some of them did injustices to themselves and some of them kept the middle part and some of them the forerunners of the good deeds, by Allah's permission, this is the big bounty. [33]They will enter Eden's gardens and will be adorned with bracelets of gold and pearl, and their clothes in it are silk. [34]And they said, "The praise be to Allah who has put away sorrow from us. Surely our lord is forgiving, thankful, [35]who admitted us to the home of establishment from his bounty. Toil will not touch us in it, and weariness will not touch us in it." [36]And those who became infidels will have the fire of hell. It will not be finished with them so that they should die, nor its torment will be reduced for them. Likewise, we will reward every infidel. [37]And they will cry in it: "Our lord, get us out! We will do good deed, not like what we were

---

[a] non-Arabic word, which Muslim scholars claim to mean mountain

doing!" "Did we not give you lives long enough, so whoever would remember, would remember? And the warner came to you, so taste, so there is no helper to the unjust." [38]Surely Allah knows the unseen of the heavens and the earth. Surely he knows what is in the chests. [39]He is who made you successors on the earth, so whoever becomes an infidel, so his infidelity is against him. And their infidelity will not increase the infidels with their lord except in hate, and the infidelity will not increase the infidels except loss. [40]Say, "Have you seen your partners, those whom you call on without Allah? Show me what they create from the earth. Or do they have a share in the heavens, or have we given them a book so they are on a proof from it? Yet the unjust will not promise one another except pride. [41]Surely Allah holds the heavens and the earth so that they will not vanish, and if they vanish, no one can hold them after him. Surely he was forbearing, forgiving. [42]And they swear by Allah their most earnest oath that, if a warner came to them, they would become more guided than any of the nations. So when the warner came to them, he did not increase them except rejection. [43]Arrogance on the earth and the evil deception, and the evil deception do not afflict except its people. So will they look except to the custom of the ancients? So you will not find change to Allah's custom, and you will not find alteration to Allah's custom. [44]Or have they walked on the earth, so they see how was the end of those who were before them. And they were stronger than them in might, and there was nothing in the heavens nor on the earth that was to hinder Allah. Surely he was knowing, mighty. [45]And if Allah punishes people for what they earn, he will not leave on its back any creature, but he will delay them to an appointed time. So if their appointed time comes, so surely Allah was seeing to his servants.

A portion of a revelation   *Ys*

In the name of Allah, the merciful, the merciful

[1]Ys.[a] [2][I swear] by the wise Qur'an. [3]Surely you are of the messengers. [4]On a straight way. [5]A descending of the dear, the merciful. [6]To warn a people whose fathers were not warned, so they are heedless. [7]Indeed, the word against most of them is established, so they will not believe. [8]Surely we placed chains around their necks so they were up to their chins so their heads were forced up. [9]And

---

[a] a word containing two Arabic letters without meaning

we made between their hands a barrier and from behind them a barrier, so we cover them so they do not see. [10]And if you warn them or do not warn them, it is the same. They will not believe. [11]Surely you only warn who followed the reminder and feared the merciful with the unseen, so give him the good news of forgiveness and a generous wage. [12]Surely we raise the dead. And we write down what they advanced and what is left behind, and we counted everything in a clear guide.

This is a strange parable made up by Mohammed. What village? Who are the messengers? Who was the man in the city? What was the message?

[13]And give them a parable of the companion of the village when the messenger came to them. [14]When we sent to them two, so they denied them, so we strengthened them with a third. So they said, "Surely we are sent to you." [15]They said, "You are not except humans like us, and the merciful did not send down anything, but you are only liars." [16]They said, "Our lord knows that surely we are sent to you. [17]And our duty is nothing except the clear delivering." [18]They said, "Surely our bird[a] is in you if you do not cease, we will surely stone you. And surely you will be touched with a painful torment from us." [19]They said, "Your bird[b] is with you. What if you are reminded? Yet you are an extravagant people." [20]And a man came from the far part of the city striving. He said, "O my people, follow the messengers. [21]Follow those who do not ask a wage from you, and they are guided. [22]And why should I not serve him who created me and to whom you will be returned? [23]Will I take gods without him? Should the merciful desire to afflict me, their intercession will not avert anything from me, nor will they deliver me. [24]Surely then I am in an obvious error. [25]Surely I believed in your lord, so hear me." [26]It was said, "Enter the garden." He said, "I wish my people knew [27]about what my lord has forgiven me, and he made me of the honorable." [28]And we did not send down troops from the heavens on his people after him, nor were we the sender. [29]It was only a single shout, so they were extinguished. [30]Oh, regret upon the servants. No messenger came to them except they were scoffing at him. [31]Have they not seen how many of the generations before them that we destroyed and that they will not return to them? [32]And all of them gathered together; they will be brought before us. [33]And the dead earth is a sign to them. We give life to it and bring forth grain from it, so from it they eat. [34]And we make date and vine gardens in it, and in it we cause springs to gush forth [35]that they may eat of its fruit and

---

[a] evil omen
[b] evil omen

what their hands made. Do they not give thanks? [36]Praise be to him who has created all the pairs of what the earth grows, and from themselves, and of what they do not know. [37]And the night is a sign to them. We peel the day from it, so then they are in darkness.

The sun sets in a resting place! The sun does not catch up to the moon! Notice that the earth does not move, but rather the sun moves around the earth. What about the north and south poles? Compare this with verse 18:86.

[38]And the sun runs to its resting place. This is the measurement of the dear, the knowing. [39]And the moon, we have determined its houses until he returns as an old and crooked palm branch. [40]Neither should the sun catch up to the moon, nor the night outstrip the day, and each swims in a sphere. [41]And it is a sign to them that we carry their offspring in the loaded ship. [42]And we create the like of it of what they ride on. [43]And if we will, we will drown them. So there is no shout to them, and they are not rescued, [44]except for a mercy from us and enjoyment for a while. [45]And when it is said to them, "Fear what is between your hands and what is behind you, perhaps you will receive mercy." [46]And a sign from the signs of their lord did not come to them except that they were turning away from it. [47]And when it is said to them, "Spend of what Allah has provided for you." Those who became infidels said to those who believed, "Should we feed those whom, if Allah wills, he could feed? You are only in an obvious error." [48]And they say, "When is this promise, if you were truthful?" [49]They do not wait, but a single shout will overtake them and they are disputing. [50]So they cannot make a will, nor to their families will they return. [51]And the trumpet will be blown, so they will speed out of their graves to their lord. [52]They said, "O woe to us. Who has raised us from our sleep? This is what the merciful promised, and the messengers were truthful!" [53]If it was only one shout, so then all of them together will be brought to us. [54]So today, no soul will be treated unjustly anything, and you will not be rewarded except for what you were doing. [55]Surely today, the companions of the garden will be busy rejoicing; [56]they and their wives are reclining in shades on couches. [57]In it they will have fruit, and they will have whatever they call for. [58]"Peace": a saying from a merciful lord. [59]And: "Get aside today, O you criminals! [60]Did I not covenant you, O children of Adam, that you should not serve Satan? Surely he is to you an obvious enemy. [61]And that you should serve me, this is a straight way. [62]And indeed, he led a great mountain[a] of you astray. Were you not understanding? [63]This is hell which you were promised. [64]Roast in it today because you were infidels." [65]Today we will set a seal on their mouths and their hands will speak to us and their legs will

---

[a] large number

witness of what they were earning. [66]And if we will, we would hide on their eyes so they race to the way. So how can they see? [67]And if we will, we would transform them in their places so that they would not be able to move forward or to return. [68]And whoever we make to live a long life, we will reverse him in the creation. Do they not understand?

The Qur'an is a clear book and easily understood.

[69]We have not taught him the poetry, nor must it be for him. It is only a reminder and a clear Qur'an. [70]To warn who was alive, and that the word may be established against the infidels. [71]Do they not see that we have created livestock for them of what our hands have made so that they are its owners? [72]And we subdued them for them, so on some of them they ride and some of them they eat. [73]And they find in them profitable uses and drinks. Do they not give thanks? [74]And they take gods without Allah, perhaps they may be helped. [75]They cannot help them, and they will have troops who will bring them in. [76]So do not let their speech grieve you, surely we know what they hide and what they announce. [77]Does the human not see that we created him from nutfah, so he is an obvious adversary? [78]And he gives us a parable and forgets his creation. He says, "Who will give life to bones when they are decaying?" [79]Say, "He will give life to them, who made it the first time, and he is knower of all creation." [80]Who makes fire for you from the green tree, so then you kindle from it. [81]Is not he who created the heavens and the earth able to create like them? Yes, and he is the creator, the knower. [82]Surely it is only his command, if he desires anything, he will say to it, "Be," so it will be. [83]So praise be to him in whose hand is the kingdom of all things, and to him you will return.

A portion of a revelation — **37** — *The Assembled Ranks*

In the name of Allah, the merciful, the merciful

[1][I swear] by the ranks lining up in ranks, [2]so the rebuked who is rebuking, [3]so the successor of a reminder, [4]surely your god is one, [5]lord of the heavens and the earth and what is between them, and lord of the easts.[a] [6]Surely we have adorned the heavens of the world with the adornment of the planets [7]and keeping against every

---

[a] the word easts is written in plural in the Arabic text

rebellious satan. [8]They do not hear the assembly on high for they are thrown from every side, [9]expelled, and they have continuous torment. [10]Except who snatch the snatching, so a shooting star follows him. [11]So consult with them, "Are they strong creatures, or who created us?" Surely we created them from sticky mud. [12]Yet you wonder, and they scoff. [13]And when they are reminded, they will not remember. [14]And when they see a sign, they will scoff. [15]And they said, "This is but an obvious sorcery. [16]What if we died and were dust and bones, will we be raised? [17]Or our ancient fathers?" [18]Say, "Yes, and you will be disgraced." [19]So surely there is only one rebuke,[a] so then they are looking. [20]And they said, "O woe to us, this is the judgment day." [21]This is the separation day which you were denying it. [22]Gather those who were unjust and their wives and what they were serving [23]without Allah, so guide them to the way of hell. [24]And stop them. Surely they are to be asked. [25]"Why did you not help each other?" [26]Yet today they will be surrendered. [27]And some of them came to the others, asking each other. [28]They said, "Surely you were coming to us from the right." [29]They said, "Yet you were not believers. [30]And it was not for us to have authority over you, yet you were a rebellious people. [31]So the words of our lord were established. Surely we are tasting [the torment]. [32]So we seduced you, surely we were seduced." [33]So surely on that day they are partners in the torment. [34]Likewise, we surely do to the criminals. [35]Surely they were proud when it was said to them, "There is no god but Allah." [36]And they say, "Are we forsaking our gods to a demon-possessed poet?" [37]Yet he came with the truth and confirmed the messengers. [38]Surely you will taste the painful torment. [39]And you will not be rewarded, except what you were doing.

In the gardens believers will have a spring of wine, but they will not have hangovers and never get drunk.

[40]Except the faithful servants of Allah, [41]those will have a measured provision, [42]fruit. And they are honored [43]in the gardens of the bliss [44]on beds facing each other. [45]A ka's[b] [of wine] will be passed around among them from a spring, [46]white and delicious to the drinkers. [47]No intoxication in it, and they will not run out of it.

In the gardens men will have pure virgins to enjoy.

[48]And with them are [ever-virgins] who restrain their eyes [49]as if they were sheltered eggs. [50]So some of them came to the others, asking each other. [51]Said a speaker among them, "Surely I had a friend, [52]he says, 'Are you surely of the believers? [53]What if we died and we were dust and bones, will we surely be judged?'" [54]He said,

---

[a] shout
[b] cup, non-Arabic word of Aramaic origin

"Are you looking?" [55]So he looked, so he saw him in the center of hell. [56]He said, "[I swear] by Allah, you had almost caused me to perish. [57]And were it not for the grace of my lord, I was surely of those who were brought." [58]"Are we not going to die, [59]except our first death, and we are not going to be tormented?" [60]Surely this is the great triumph. [61]Like that, so let the workers work. [62]Is this better for the guest or the tree of Zakkoum?[a] [63]Surely we made it a sedition to the unjust. [64]Surely it is a tree that comes from the origin of hell. [65]Its blossom is surely as the heads of the satans. [66]So surely they will eat from it, so they will fill their bellies from it. [67]Then surely they will have above it a mixture of hamem.[b] [68]Then surely they will return into hell. [69]They surely found their father's error. [70]So they hasten on their footsteps. [71]And indeed, most of the ancients before them erred. [72]And indeed, we sent warners among them. [73]So see how was the end of the warned, [74]except for the faithful servants of Allah.

The story of Noah is copied from the Bible and corrupted again.

[75]And indeed, Noah called us, so blessed were those who answered. [76]And we delivered him and his family from the great distress. [77]And we made his offspring, they are the remainder. [78]And we left for him among the others. [79]"Peace be on Noah in the worlds." [80]Likewise, we surely reward the doers of good. [81]Surely, he is among our believing servants. [82]Then we drowned the others.

The story of Abraham is copied from the Bible and corrupted once again.

[83]And surely of his sect was Abraham. [84]When he came to his lord with a sound heart. [85]When he said to his father and his people, "What are you serving? [86]Do you desire false gods without Allah? [87]So what do you think of the lord of the worlds?" [88]So he looked carefully at the stars. [89]So he said, "Surely I am sick." [90]So they turned their backs from him. [91]Then he turned to their gods, so he said, "Will you not eat? [92]Why can you not talk?" [93]So he fell on them, striking them with the right hand. [94]So they came to him in haste. [95]He said, "Do you serve what you carve? [96]And Allah created you and what you do." [97]They said, "Build a building for him." So they threw him into the hell. [98]So they desired a scheme against him, so we made them the lowest. [99]And he said, "Surely I am going to my lord. He will guide me."

Contrary to the common Muslim misconception, both the Bible and these verses agree that Isaac, rather than Ishmael, was the

---

[a] a tree in hell
[b] close-warm, as in the statement close or warm friend. In this context other translators chose the word *hot*

sacrificial son. But the story here is corrupted by Mohammed. See Genesis 22. Additionally, note that Ishmael is not mentioned in these verses. Moreover, the description of this son as forbearing is in contrast to the Bible's description of Ishmael as "...a wild man ..." See Genesis 16:12.

[100]"My lord, grant me from the good." [101]So we gave him the good news of a forbearing young man. [102]So when he came to the age of walking with him, he said, "My son, surely I see in my sleep that I am slaughtering you, so see what you see." He said, "O my father, do what you are commanded. You will find me among the patient if Allah wills." [103]So when they surrendered and he had laid him down on his jabīn,[a] [104]and we called him, "O Abraham, [105]indeed, you have believed the vision." Likewise, we surely reward the doers of good. [106]Surely this is a clear trial. [107]And we redeemed him with a great sacrifice. [108]And we left for him among the others. [109]Peace be on Abraham. [110]Likewise, we reward the doers of good. [111]Surely he is of our believing servants. [112]And we gave him the good news of Isaac, a prophet among the good. [113]And we blessed on him and on Isaac, and from their offspring an obvious doer of good, and unjust to himself.

The story of Moses and Aaron is copied from the Bible and corrupted once again.

[114]And indeed, we conferred a favor on Moses and Aaron. [115]And we delivered them and their people from the great distress. [116]And we helped them so that they were the victors. [117]And we gave them the clarifying book. [118]And we guided them to the straight way. [119]And we left for them among the others. [120]Peace be on Moses and Aaron. [121]Likewise, we surely reward the doers of good. [122]Surely they are among our believing servants.

The story of Elijah is drawn from the Bible, condensed, and corrupted. For the complete, original story, read 1 Kings 17:1—2 Kings 10:17.

[123]And surely Iliyas [b] is one of the messengers. [124]When he said to his people, "Will you not fear? [125]Do you call on Bual[c] and forsake the best of the creators, [126]Allah your lord and the lord of your ancient fathers?" [127]So they denied him, so surely they will be brought, [128]except the faithful servant of Allah. [129]And we left for him among the others. [130]Peace be on the family of Yaseen.[d] [131]Likewise,

---

[a] side of his forehead, non-Arabic word of Aramaic origin
[b] wrong name, he meant Elijah
[c] Baal, non-Arabic word of Syriac origin
[d] another mistake for the name Elijah

we surely reward the doers of good. [132]Surely he is among our believing servants.

The story of Lot is copied from the Bible and corrupted once again.

[133]And surely Lot was of the messengers, [134]when we delivered him and all his family, [135]except an elder who tarried. [136]Then we destroyed the others. [137]And surely you pass by them in the morning [138]and by night. Do you not understand?

The story of Jonah is copied from the Bible, condensed, and corrupted. See the book of Jonah.

[139]And surely Yunus[a] was among those sent. [140]When he fled in the loaded ship. [141]So he shared, so he was of the losers. [142]So the whale swallowed him, and he was blamed. [143]So were it not that he was of those who praised, [144]then he would have stayed in its belly until a day they are raised. [145]So we cast him on the barren shore, and he was sick. [146]And we caused a gourd tree to grow up over him. [147]And we sent him to one hundred thousand or more. [148]So they believed, so we gave them enjoyment for a time.

Directly contradicting the Bible, Mohammed declares that God has no son.

[149]So consult with them, "Do daughters belong to your lord and to them the sons? [150]Or have we created the angels females, and they were witnesses?" [151]Is it not surely from their own lie they say, [152]"Allah has birthed." And surely they are liars. [153]Has he then chosen the daughters over the sons? [154]What is [the matter] with you? How do you judge? [155]Do you not remember? [156]Or do you have a manifest authority? [157]So bring with your books, if you were truthful. [158]And they made a kinship between him and the jinn, and indeed, the jinn know that they will surely be brought. [159]Praise be to Allah about what they describe, [160]except for the faithful servants of Allah. [161]So surely you and what you serve, [162]you are not seduced [anyone] against him (Allah), [163]except for who is roasting in hell. [164]And none of us but has a known place, [165]and surely we are those who stand in ranks, [166]and surely we are who praise. [167]And they were saying, [168]"If we had the reminder of our ancients, [169]then we surely would have been the faithful servants of Allah." [170]So they became infidels in it, so they will know. [171]And indeed, our word came before to our servants the messengers. [172]Surely they are who are helped. [173]And surely our troops, they are the victors. [174]So turn away from them for a time. [175]And watch them so they will see.

---

[a] wrong name, he meant Jonah

¹⁷⁶Are they hastening our torment? ¹⁷⁷So if it comes down to their court, so evil is the morning of the warned. ¹⁷⁸And turn away from them for a time. ¹⁷⁹And see so they will see. ¹⁸⁰Praise be to your lord, the lord of honor, about what they describe. ¹⁸¹And peace be on the messengers. ¹⁸²And the praise be to Allah, the lord of the worlds.

A portion of a revelation **38** *S*

In the name of Allah, the merciful, the merciful

¹S,ᵃ and [I swear] by the Qur'an, that contains the reminder. ²Yet those who became infidels are in boasting and opposition. ³How many generations we have destroyed before them, so they called but lātaᵇ time to escape? ⁴And they wonder that a warner came from among them. And the infidels said, "This is a sorcerer, a liar. ⁵Did he make the gods into one god? Surely this is a wonderful thing." ⁶And the leaders among them went forth: "That walk and be patient regarding your gods, surely this is a desirable thing. ⁷We did not hear of this in the other religion; this is nothing but an invention. ⁸Has the reminder come down on him from among us?" Yet they are in doubt regarding my reminder. Yet they have not tasted my torment. ⁹Or do they have the treasuries of the mercy of your lord, the dear, the grantor? ¹⁰Or do they have the kingdom of the heavens and the earth and what is between them? So let them ascend in the reasons. ¹¹Any troops thereupon will be defeated among the parties. ¹²Before them the people of Noah and Ad and Pharaoh, the possessor of the stakes, denied. ¹³And Themoud and the people of Lot and the companion of the woods, those are the parties. ¹⁴That all of them but denied the messengers, so the punishment is established. ¹⁵And those will not wait but for one shout which does not cease. ¹⁶And they said, "Our lord, hasten us to our qittᶜ before the reckoning day."

The story of David and his sin with Bathsheba is copied from the Bible and corrupted. See 2 Samuel 11-12.

¹⁷Be patient with what they say, and remember our servant David, a man with hands, surely he was repentant. ¹⁸Surely we made the mountains subservient with him; they will praise in the evening and in the sunrise. ¹⁹And the birds in obedience were all gathered to him.

ᵃ an Arabic letter without meaning
ᵇ there was not, non-Arabic word of Syriac origin
ᶜ sentence, non-Arabic word of probable Greek/Aramaic origin

²⁰And we strengthened his kingdom, and we gave him the wisdom and the discerning speech. ²¹And has the news of the two litigants come to you, when they entered the holy of holies? ²²When they entered into David, so he panicked because of them. They said, "Do not be afraid. Two litigants, some of us has wronged the others. So judge between us with the truth and do not act unjustly and guide us to a right way. ²³Surely this is my brother. He has ninety-nine sheep, and I had one sheep. So he said, 'Give it to me.' And he overcame me in the argument." ²⁴He said, "Indeed, he has done an injustice to you by asking for your sheep to his sheep, and surely many partners wrong one another, except those who believed and did good deeds, and few there are." And David thought that we only seduced him, so he asked forgiveness from his lord and fell down and bowed and turned. ²⁵So we forgave him this, and surely he had a nearness to us and a good return. ²⁶"O David, surely we made you a viceroy on the earth, so judge between the people with the truth and do not follow the desire, so it will lead you astray from the way of Allah. Surely those who were led astray from the way of Allah will have a severe torment because they forgot the reckoning day." ²⁷And we did not create the heaven and the earth and what is between them in vain. This is what those who became infidels thought, so woe to those who became infidels from the fire. ²⁸Or did we make those who believed and did good deeds as those who vandalize on the earth, or did we make the fearer as the fojar?^a ²⁹A book, we have sent it down to you, blessed, so that they may contemplate on its verses and let the people of understanding remember.

The story of Solomon is copied from the Bible and corrupted. Notice Mohammed's confusion of "satans" and "jinn." As seen clearly in verse 27:17, Mohammed clearly claims that the army of Solomon is comprised of jinn and people who work for him. Here, in verse 37, they are satans.

³⁰And to David, we granted Solomon, blessed the servant, surely he was repentant. ³¹When they displayed the prancing horses before him in the evening, ³²so he said, "Surely I love the love of the good above the remembrance of my lord." Until it^b was hidden behind the veil. ³³"Bring them back to me." So he set to stroke the legs and necks. ³⁴And indeed, we seduced Solomon, and we placed on his throne a body, then he turned. ³⁵He said, "My lord, forgive me and grant me a kingdom which no one after me must have, surely you are the grantor." ³⁶So we made the wind subservient to him, it ran softly by his command wherever he directed it. ³⁷And of the satans

---

^a wicked, non-Arabic word of Syriac origin
^b the sun

every banná[a] and diver [38]and others were bound in chains. [39]"This is our gift, so we give or withhold without accounting." [40]And surely he was near to us and had a good return.

The story of Job is copied from the Bible, very condensed, and corrupted.

[41]And remember our servant Job when he called his lord: "Surely Satan has touched me with distress and torment!" [42]"Strike with your foot; this is a cold wash-place and a drink." [43]And we granted to him his family, and like them, with them, a mercy from us and a reminder to those who have understanding. [44]"And take a bundle in your hand, so strike with it. Do not break your oath." Surely we found him patient, blessed is the servant, surely he is repentant. [45]And remember our servants Abraham and Isaac and Jacob, who have substantial hands and visions. [46]Surely we favored them with pure remembering of the home. [47]And surely they are with us from the best of the chosen. [48]And remember Ishmael and Alyas'a[b] and Za Al Kafel,[c] all from the chosen. [49]This is a reminder, and surely the best return will be to the fearer. [50]Eden's gardens, its doors open to them. [51]They will recline in it, calling in it with many fruit and drinks.

This is a description of the virgins in the gardens.

[52]And with them are (ever-virgins) who restrain their eyes, of equal age. [53]"This is what you are promised at the reckoning day. [54]Surely this is our provision. It will never have an end. [55]This, and surely to the transgressors an evil return. [56]Hell, they will roast in it, so evil is the bed. [57]This, so let them taste hamem and pus. [58]And other of the same, pairs. [59]This is a throng, plunging with you, there will be no welcome for them. Surely they will roast in the fire." [60]They said, "Yet, you, there is no welcome to you. You gave it to us, so evil is the final place!" [61]They said, "Our lord, whoever gave this to us, increase him with double torment in the fire." [62]And they said, "Why do we not see the men we were counting among the evils? [63]We took them as scoff. Or the eyes deviated from them?" [64]Surely this is true; the people of the fire disputed. [65]Say, "I am only a warner, and there is no god except Allah, the one, the dominator. [66]The lord of the heavens and the earth and what is between them, the dear, the forgiving." [67]Say, "This is great news [68]you are turning away from. [69]It was not for me to have a knowledge of the higher leaders when they dispute. [70]That it is revealed to me, that I am only a plain warner."

---

[a] builder, non-Arabic word of Akkadian origin
[b] wrong name, he meant Elisha
[c] wrong name, some Muslim scholars say he meant Isaiah, others say Ezekial

This is the story of the creation of Adam and his worship by the angels once again. Notice that the arrangement of the stories is out of order in this chapter and throughout the Qur'an.

[71]When your lord said to the angels, "Surely I am creating a human from mud. [72]So, when I have formed him and breathed my spirit into him, so fall down to him, worshiping." [73]So all the angels worshiped together, [74]except for the Devil. He was proud, and he was of the infidels. [75]He said, "O Devil, what hindered you from worshiping what I have created with my hands? Are you proud, or were you from the exalted?" [76]He said, "I am better than him. You created me from fire, and you created him from mud." [77]He said, "So get out of it. So surely you are stoned. [78]And surely my curse is on you until the judgment day." [79]He said, "My lord, so delay me until a day they will be raised." [80]He said, "So surely you are of the delayed, [81]until the day of the knowing time." [82]He said, "So [I swear] by your honor, surely I will seduce all of them, [83]except your faithful servants among them." [84]He said, "So the truth and the truths I say, [85]surely I will fill hell from you and from those who followed you from among them together." [86]Say, "I do not ask you any wage for it, and I am not of those who are pretenders." [87]That it is but a reminder to the worlds. [88]And surely you will know the news of it after awhile.

A portion of a revelation   **39**   *The Troops*

In the name of Allah, the merciful, the merciful

[1]A descending of the book, from Allah, the dear, the wise. [2]Surely we sent the book down to you with the truth. So serve Allah, devoted in the religion to him. [3]Is not to Allah the pure religion, and those who took friends without him: "We do not serve them but only to make us closer to Allah's position." Surely Allah will judge between them in what they differ. Surely Allah will not guide who is an infidel liar.

Allah could have a son if he chose to.

[4]Had Allah desired to take a son, he could surely have chosen whomever he wills from whom he had created. Praise be to him. He is Allah, the one, the dominator. [5]He created the heavens and the earth with the truth. He makes the night roll over the day and makes the day roll over the night and has made the sun and the moon

subservient. All run to their assigned times. Is not he the dear, the forgiving?

Adam and his mate are created from one soul.

[6]He created you from one soul, then he made its wife from it, and he sent down to you the livestock in eight pairs. He created you in your mother's belly, in creation after another creation, in the triple darkness. This is Allah your lord, to him the kingdom, there is no god except him. So how then have you turned away? [7]If you become infidels, so surely Allah is rich above you, and he does not approve the infidelity for his servants. And if you give thanks, he will approve it to you. That no bearer of a burden bears the burden of another. Then to your lord is your return. So he will inform you of what you were doing. Surely he knows what is in the chests. [8]And if an evil touches the human, he calls on his lord turning to him. Then, if he gives him grace, he forgets what he was calling on before, and he makes partners with Allah that he may cause others to stray from his way. Say, "Enjoy your infidelity a little. Surely you will be among the companions of the fire." [9]Is the one who observes the hours of the night, worshiping and standing, heedful of the hereafter and hoping for his lord's mercy? Say, "Will they who have knowledge and they who do not have it be equal?" Surely only the ones with understanding remember. [10]Say, "O my servants who believed, fear your lord. For those who do good in this world, there is good. And wide is Allah's earth, surely only the patient will be repaid their wage without accounting." [11]Say, "Surely I am commanded to serve Allah, devoted in the religion to him."

Mohammed was the first Muslim. Or was it Adam or Noah or Abraham?

[12]"And I am commanded to be the first of the Muslims." [13]Say, "Surely I fear the torment of a great day, if I disobey my lord." [14]Say, "I serve Allah faithfully, to him is my religion. [15]So serve those whom you will without him." Say, "Surely the losers, those who lost their souls and their families on the resurrection day, is not this the clear loss? [16]They will have shadows of fire above them and shadows from below them. By this, Allah frightens his servants. O my servants, so fear me." [17]And those who did not worship the idolatry and are turned to Allah, they have the good news: "So give the good news to my servants." [18]Those who hear the word, so they follow its best. Those whom Allah has guided, and those are the ones of understanding. [19]Is he on whom the word of the torment is established, are you able to save those who are in the fire? [20]But for those who fear their lord, they will have rooms, above them rooms are built, below which the rivers flow. The promise of Allah, Allah will not change the promise. [21]Have you not seen that Allah sends down

water from heaven, so he guided it along as to form springs in the earth, then brings forth plants of different colors by it? Then he causes it to wither, so you see it become yellow, then he makes it brittle. Surely in this is a reminder to those who have understanding. [22]Is he who Allah has opened his chest to Islam, so he is on a light from his lord? So, woe to those whose hearts are hardened from the remembrance of Allah. Those are in obvious error.

Mohammed admits that the Qur'an is repetitive.

[23]Allah sent down the best of the sayings, a book [whose verses are] look-alike repetitions. It chills the skins of those who fear their lord, then their skins and their hearts will be softened at the remembrance of Allah. This is Allah's guidance. He will guide with it those whom he wills, and whom Allah leads astray, so he will not have a guide. [24]Is he who fears with his face the evil of the torment on the resurrection day? And it will be said to the unjust, "Taste what you were earning." [25]Those before them denied, so the torment came on them from where they did not feel. [26]So Allah made them to taste the humiliation in the world's life, and the torment of the hereafter is bigger, if they were knowing. [27]And indeed, we gave every kind of parable in this Qur'an to the people, perhaps they will remember. [28]An Arabic Qur'an that is without any crookedness, perhaps they may fear. [29]Allah gives the parable of a man who is owned by partners who are disputing among themselves and of a man devoted wholly to one man. Will they be equal parables? The praise be to Allah, yet most of them do not know.

Mohammed is dead, and so are the Muslims! Those who denounce the Qur'an as a lie will abide in hell.

[30]Surely you are dead, and surely they are dead. [31] Then surely you will dispute with one another on the resurrection day before your lord. [32]So, who is more unjust than he who lies against Allah and denies the truth when it comes to him? Is there not a home to the infidels in hell? [33]And he who came with the truth and believed it, those are the fearers. [34]They will have whatever they will from their lord. This is the reward of the doers of good. [35]That Allah may atone them from the worst which they have done and reward them their wage with the best of what they were doing. [36]Is not Allah sufficient for his servant? And they frighten you with those without him, and whomever Allah leads astray, so he will not have any guide. [37]And whoever Allah guides, so he will not have any to lead astray. Is not Allah dear and capable of revenge? [38]And if you ask them, "Who created the heavens and the earth?" They will surely say, "Allah." Say, "Have you seen whom you call on without Allah? If Allah desires harm for me, could they remove his harm; or if Allah desires

mercy for me, could they withhold his mercy?" Say, "Allah is sufficient for me. On him the dependents depend." [39]Say, "O my people, work according to your ability. Surely I am working so that you will know. [40]Whoever receives torment, a lasting torment will shame him and will befall him." [41]Surely we have sent down the book on you to the people with the truth. So whoever is guided, so it is to himself; and whoever errs, so surely he errs on it. And you are not over them as a guardian.

Allah takes all souls of people at the time of sleep, and he returns the souls to the people he did not want to die.

[42]Allah causes the souls to die when it dies and the one who does not die in its sleep. So he will hold the one which he had judged with the death, and he will send the other until an appointed time. Surely in this are signs to thoughtful people. [43]Or have they taken intercessors without Allah? Say, "What if they were not possessing anything and they do not understand?"

Allah is the only intercessor! With whom would he be the intercessor? See also verse 32:4, which contradicts verse 10:3, where Allah gives permission to other intercessors if he chooses.

[44]Say, "To Allah all the intercessions, to him the kingdom of the heavens and the earth. Then you will return to him." [45]And when Allah alone is mentioned, the heart of those who do not believe in the hereafter become disgusted. And when those without him are mentioned, then they rejoice. [46]Say, "O Allah, creator of the heavens and the earth, the knower of the unseen and the seen, you judge between your servants in what they were differing in it." [47]And if the unjust had all that is on the earth and similar to it, with it, then they would offer it as ransom from the evil torment on the resurrection day, and from Allah it appears to them what they were not counting on. [48]And appeared to them evils of what they earned and what they were scoffing at afflicted them. [49]So when harm touches the human, he calls on us; then if we give him grace from us, he says, "Surely I have received it only because of knowledge." Yet, it is a sedition, but most of them do not know. [50]Indeed, those who were before them said it and so were not enriched by what they were earning. [51]So evils of what they earned befalls them. And those who do injustice among these, evils will befall them as well with what they have earned, and they will not be able to hinder. [52]Or did they not know that Allah expands and measures the provision to whom he will? Surely in this are signs to a believing people. [53]Say, "O my servants who are extravagant against themselves, do not despair from the mercy of Allah. Surely Allah forgives all sins. Surely he is the forgiving, the merciful. [54]And turn to your lord and submit to him

before the torment comes to you, then you will not be helped. ⁵⁵And
follow the best of what has been sent down to you from your lord
before the torment comes to you suddenly, and you do not feel.
⁵⁶That a soul will say, 'O regret for what I neglected in my duty
toward Allah, and that I was of the scoffers.' ⁵⁷Or you say, 'If Allah
had guided me, then I would be of the fearers.' ⁵⁸Or you will say
when you see the torment, 'If only I had a second turn, so I would be
of the doers of good.'" ⁵⁹"Yes, indeed, my verses came to you, so
you denied them and you were proud and you were of the infidels."

Black faces will be the mark of the wicked.

⁶⁰And on the resurrection day, you will see those who lied against
Allah, and their faces are blackened. Is there not a dwelling for the
proud in hell? ⁶¹And Allah will deliver the fearer with their triumphs.
The evil will not touch them, and they will not grieve. ⁶²Allah is the
creator of all things, and he is guardian over everything. ⁶³To him the
keys of the heavens and the earth, and those who became infidels in
the verses of Allah, those are the losers.

No one can claim to be a god or a partner with Allah, not even 'Isā (the Jesus of Mohammed).

⁶⁴Say, "Do you command me to serve without Allah, O you
ignorant?" ⁶⁵And indeed, it is revealed to you and to those before
you, if you partner, surely your work will be nothing, and surely you
will be among the losers. ⁶⁶Yet, so serve Allah and be among the
thankful. ⁶⁷And they did not value Allah his true value. And all the
earth is in his grasp on the resurrection day, and the heavens will be
folded by his right hand. Praise be to him, and he is exalted above
what they partner. ⁶⁸And the trumpet was blown, so all those who
were in the heavens and the earth were thunderstruck, except whom
Allah wills. Then it was blown in it again, so they stood up, waiting.
⁶⁹And the earth shone with the light of its lord and the book was
placed and they brought the prophets and the witnesses and judged
between them with the truth and they will not be dealt with unjustly.
⁷⁰And every soul was rewarded with what it had done, and he best
knows what they are doing. ⁷¹And those who became infidels were
driven to hell in troops until they arrived to it. So its doors were
opened, and the keeper of it said to them, "Did not a messenger from
among you come to you, reciting to you the verses of your lord and
warning you about the meeting of this your day?" They said, "Yes,"
but the word of the torment established over the infidels. ⁷²It was
said, "Enter the doors of hell; abide in it forever. So evil is the home
of the proud." ⁷³And those who feared their lord were driven into the
garden in troops until when they arrived to it. And its doors were
opened. And the keepers of it said to them, "Peace be on you. You

are good, so enter it to abide in it forever." [74]And they said, "The praise be to Allah who fulfilled his promise, and he bequeathed the earth to us. We settle in the garden wherever we will, so blessed is the wage of the workers." [75]And you see the angels going around the throne, praising with their lord's praise, and he judges between them with the truth. And it was said, "The praise be to Allah, the lord of the worlds."

A portion of a revelation   *Forgiver*

In the name of Allah, the merciful, the merciful

[1]Hm.[a] [2]A descending of the book from Allah the dear, the knowing, [3]forgiver of the sin and receiver of the repentance, severe the punishment, possessor of the long, there is no god but him, to him is the final return. [4]No one disputes in the verses of Allah, except those who became infidels, so do not let their moving about in the countries deceive you. [5]Before them, the people of Noah and the parties after them denied and in every nation plotted with their messengers to take him and dispute with vanity to refute the truth by it. So I seized them. So how was my punishment? [6]And likewise, the word of your lord established over those who became infidels that they are the companions of the fire. [7]Those who carry the throne, and all those around it, praise with their lord's praise. And they believe in him, and they ask forgiveness for those who believed: "Our lord surrounds everything in mercy and knowledge. So forgive to those who repent and follow your way and guard them from the torment of hell. [8]Our lord, and admit them into Eden's gardens which you promised them and who reformed of their fathers and their wives and their offspring. Surely you are the dear, the wise. [9]And guard them from the evils. And whoever guards the evils on that day, so indeed, you have mercy on him, and that is the great triumph." [10]Surely those who became infidels will be announced: "The wrath of Allah is bigger than your wrath to yourselves, when you are called to the faith, so you become infidels." [11]They said, "Our lord, you have put us to death twice, and you have raised us to life twice, so we confessed our sins. So is there a way to escape?" [12]That is because when Allah alone was called on, you became infidels; and if there was a partner with him, you believe. So the judgment is to Allah, the high, the big. [13]He is who shows you his signs and sends down

---

[a] a word containing two Arabic letters without meaning

provision from the heavens, and no one remembers it except he who turns. [14]So call on Allah, devoted in the religion to him, even if the infidels hate it. [15]The highest in degrees, the possessor of the throne, he casts the spirit by his command on whom he wills of his servants so that he may warn them of the encounter day. [16]A day they will go forth, nothing about them will be hidden from Allah. "To whom is the kingdom today?" "To Allah, the one, the dominator." [17]Today, every soul will be rewarded for what it earned. There is no injustice today. Surely Allah is swift in the reckoning [18]and warns them of the judgment day when the hearts will come up to the throats, holding in sorrow. The unjust do not have any hamem or intercessor who will be obeyed. [19]He knows the deceit of the eyes and what the chests hide. [20]And Allah will judge with the truth, and those who call on other than him, those will judge nothing. Surely Allah is the hearing, the seeing. [21]Or have they not walked on the earth, so they see how the end was for those who were before them. They were stronger than them in power and in the traces they left on the earth. So Allah seized them with their sins, and it was not for them to have a protector from Allah. [22]This is because their messengers were coming to them with proofs, so they became infidels, so Allah seized them. Surely he is strong, severe the punishment.

The story of Moses is copied from the Bible and corrupted once again. Notice that the killing of the male children of the Israelites now occurs when Moses was elderly rather than when he was a baby. Who is the mysterious Egyptian believer?

[23]And indeed, we sent Moses with our signs and with manifest authority [24]to Pharaoh and Haman and Qūrūn. So they said, "A lying sorcerer." [25]So when he came to them with the truth from us, they said, "Kill the sons of those who believed with him and keep their women alive." But the schemes of the infidels are nothing except in error. [26]And Pharaoh said, "Let me alone that I may kill Moses, and let him call on his lord. Surely I fear that he may change your religion or that he causes vandalism to appear on the earth." [27]And Moses said, "Surely I take refuge with my lord and your lord from every proud who does not believe in the reckoning day." [28]And a believing man from the family of Pharaoh, who was hiding his faith, said, "Will you kill a man because he is saying, 'My lord is Allah'? And indeed, he came to you with the proofs from your lord. And if he is a liar, so his lie is against him. And if he is truthful, some of what he promises will fall on you. Surely Allah will not guide he who is extravagant, a liar. [29]O my people, the kingdom is yours today. [You are the ones who] appeared on the earth. So who will help from the torment of Allah, if it comes to us?" Pharaoh said, "I will not let you see except what I see, and I will not guide you except to the right way." [30]And

the one who believed said, "O my people, surely I fear for you, like the parties day. [31]Like the habit of the people of Noah and Ad and Themoud and those who came after them, and Allah does not desire injustice to the servants. [32]And, O my people, surely I fear for you the summoning (resurrection) day. [33]A day you will turn your back, retreating, you will not have any defender against Allah, and whomever Allah leads astray, so he does not have a guide. [34]And indeed, Joseph brought to you the proofs before. So you are still in doubt from what he brought you until, when he perished, you said, 'Allah will not send a messenger after him.' Likewise, Allah leads astray who is extravagant, a doubter. [35]Those who dispute in the verses of Allah without authority he gave them, bigger wrath is with Allah and with those who believed. Likewise, Allah seals on the heart of every proud powerful." [36]And Pharaoh said, "O Haman, build for me a tower, perhaps I may reach the ways, [37]the ways of the heavens, so I will look on the god of Moses, and surely I think that he is a liar." And likewise, Pharaoh's evil work had been beautified to him, and he prevented [others] from the way. And the plot of Pharaoh was nothing except destruction. [38]And he that believed said, "O my people, follow me. I will guide you the way of guidance. [39]O my people, surely this world's life is only enjoyment, and surely the hereafter is the home that will last. [40]Whoever did evil, so he will not be rewarded except like it; and whoever did good deed, whether male or female, while he is a believer, so those will enter the garden. They will be provided in it without accounting. [41]And O my people, how is it that I call you to the deliverance, and you call me to the fire? [42]You call me to become an infidel in Allah and to have partners with him, of whom I have no knowledge. And I invite you to the dear, the forgiving. [43]No doubt what you call me to has no claim in the world or in the hereafter, and that our return is to Allah. And that the extravagants are the companions of the fire. [44]So you will remember what I am saying to you, and I confide my affair to Allah. Surely Allah is the seer of the servants." [45]So Allah protected him from the evil deceptions that they had, and evil torments afflicted the people of Pharaoh. [46]The fire they are exposed to it morning and evening, and a day the hour will rise: "Enter the family of Pharaoh to the severest torment." [47]And when they dispute in the fire, so the weak will say to those who are proud, "Surely we were followers of you, so will you therefore relieve us from a portion of the fire?" [48]Those proud ones said, "Surely we are all in it. Surely Allah indeed judged between the servants." [49]And those who are in the fire said to the keepers of hell, "Call your lord so that he will lighten the torment from us for one day." [50]They said, "Did not your messengers come to you with the proofs?" They said, "Yes." They said, "So call." And what is the call of the infidels except in error. [51]Surely we will help our messengers and those who believed in the world's life and a day the witnesses will rise, [52]a day in which no excuse will benefit the unjust and to them the curse and to them the evil home. [53]And indeed, we gave Moses the guidance, and we bequeathed the book to the children of Israel, [54]a guidance and a reminder to those who have understanding.

Allah commands Mohammed to seek forgiveness for his sin. See also verses 47:19 and 48:2.

[55]So be patient, surely the promise of Allah is true. And ask forgiveness for your sin, and praise with your lord's praise in the evening and mornings. [56]Surely those who dispute in the verses of Allah without authority he gave them, there is nothing in their chests except pride, but they will not achieve it, so seek refuge with Allah. Surely he is the hearing, the seeing. [57]The creation of the heavens and the earth is bigger than the creation of the people, but most people do not know. [58]And the blind and the seeing are not equal, and those who believed and did good deeds, nor the evildoer, little is what you remember! [59]Surely the hour is coming. There is no doubt in it, but most people do not believe. [60]And your lord said, "Call on me. I will answer you. Surely those who are too proud to serve me, they will enter hell with disgrace." [61]Allah is who made to you the night that you may dwell in it and the day to see. Surely Allah is the possessor of bounty to the people, but most people do not give thanks. [62]This is Allah your lord, the creator of all things. There is no god except him. So how then are you turned away? [63]Likewise, turn away those who were disbelieving in Allah's verses. [64]Allah is who made the earth a resting place for you and the heaven a structure. And he sawar[a] you, so he formed you best, and he provided for you from the good things. This is Allah your lord. So blessed be Allah, the lord of the worlds. [65]He is the living, there is no god except him, so call on him, devoted in the religion to him. The praise be to Allah, the lord of the worlds. [66]Say, "Surely I have been forbidden to serve those that you call on without Allah. When the proofs came to me from my lord, and I have been commanded to submit to the lord of the worlds." [67]He is who created you from dirt, then from nutfah, then from clot, then brings you out as a child, then you may arrive to your strength, then you may become elderly, and some of you who will die before. And you may reach an appointed time, and perhaps you will understand. [68]He is who gives life and causes death so that if he decrees an affair, so surely he only says to it, "Be." So it will be. [69]Have you not seen those who dispute in Allah's verses how they turned away? [70]Those who denied the book and in what we sent our messengers with, so they will know. [71]When the shackles are on

---

[a] formed, non-Arabic word of Aramaic/Syriac origin

their necks and they are dragged with salasel[a] [72]in the hamem, then they will be thrown into the fire. [73]Then it was said to them, "Where is what you were partnering [74]without Allah?" They said, "They are gone astray from us, yet we did not call on anything before." Likewise, Allah leads the infidels astray. [75]That is because you were rejoicing on the earth without the truth and because you were frolicking. [76]Enter the doors of hell. Abide in it forever. So evil is the abode of the proud. [77]So be patient, surely the promise of Allah is true so that we may show you some of that which we promised them, or we will cause you to die. So they will return to us. [78]And indeed, we sent messengers before you. Some of them we narrated to you, and some of them we did not narrate to you. And it was not for a messenger to bring with a sign except by Allah's permission. So when the command of Allah came, he judged with the truth, and thereupon the liars lost. [79]Allah is who made the livestock for you, to ride on some of them and from some of them you eat. [80]And you will have benefits in them and that you will reach on[b] them a need in your chests, and on them and on the ships, you will be carried. [81]And he shows you his signs. So which of Allah's signs will you deny? [82]Have they not walked on the earth so they see how the end was of those who were before them? They were more than them, and greater power and traces on the earth. So what they were earning, it did not enrich them. [83]So when their messengers came to them with the proofs, they rejoiced with what they have of the knowledge, and what they were scoffing at afflicted them. [84]So when they saw our torment, they said, "We believed in Allah alone. And we became infidels in what we were partnering with." [85]So their belief did not profit them when they saw our torment. The custom of Allah which indeed has passed to his servants, and the infidels are lost thereupon.

A portion of a revelation   **41**   *Expounded*

In the name of Allah, the merciful, the merciful

[1]Hm.[c] [2]A descending from the merciful, the merciful. [3]A book whose verses are expounded, an Arabic Qur'an for people who know. [4]An announcer of good news and a warner, so most of them turn away, so they do not hear. [5]And they said, "Our hearts are

---

[a] chains, non-Arabic word of Aramaic origin
[b] attain through
[c] a word containing two Arabic letters without meaning

covered from what you are calling us to, and deafness is in our ears, and between us and you, there is a veil. So work, surely we are working."

Woe to those who partner 'Isā (the Jesus of Mohammed) or any other god along with Allah.

[6]Say, "Surely I am only a human like you. It is revealed to me that your god is only one god, so head straight toward him and seek his forgiveness, and woe to the polytheists. [7]Those who do not bring the legal alms and they are, in the hereafter, they are infidels." [8]Surely those who believed and did the good deeds, they will have their unending wage.

Allah created the heavens and the earth in eight days, not six days as recorded elsewhere throughout the Qur'an. Also, notice that the earth is created before the heavens. This contradicts verses 79:27-32 which state that the earth was created after the heavens.

[9]Say, "Have you become infidels in him who created the earth in two days, and you make partners with him? That is the lord of the worlds." [10]And he made in it stabilizers on top of it, and he has blessed it. And he measured in it provisions in four equal days to those who ask. [11]Then he turned to the heaven, and it was smoke. So he said to it and to the earth, "Come willingly or grudgingly." They said, "We come willingly." [12]So he completed them seven heavens in two days and revealed to every heaven its affair. And we adorned the world's heaven with lamps and kept. This is the measure of the dear, the knowing. [13]So if they turn away, so say, "I warned you of a thunderbolt, like the thunderbolt of Ad and Themoud." [14]When the messengers came to them from between their hands and from behind them: "That you do not serve any except Allah." They said, "Had our lord willed that he sent down angels, so surely we are infidels in what you have been sent with." [15]So as for Ad, so they were proud on the earth, without the truth, and they said, "Who is stronger in power than us?" Have they not seen that Allah who created them was greater than they in power, and they were disbelieving our signs.

The punishment of Themoud was many unfortunate days. This contradicts verses 54:18-19 which clearly indicate it was only one day.

[16]So we sent on them a tempestuous wind for unfortunate days so that we might make them taste the shameful torment in the world's life. And the torment of the hereafter is more shameful, and they will not be helped. [17]And as to Themoud, so we guided them, so they

loved the blindness over the guidance. So the shameful thunderbolt seized them because of what they were earning. [18]And we delivered those who believed, and they were fearing. [19]And a day the enemies of Allah will be gathered into the fire, so they will be divided. [20]Until when they came to it, their ears and their eyes and their skins will bear witness against them of what they were doing. [21]And they said to their skins, "Why did you witness against us?" They said, "Allah, makes us speak who makes everything speak. And he created you the first time, and to him you will return." [22]And you were not hiding yourselves so that neither your ears nor your eyes nor your skins should witness against you, but you thought that Allah does not know much of what you do. [23]And that thought of yours which you thought about your lord has brought your destruction, so you became among the losers. [24]So if they become patient, so the fire will be their abode; and if they seek restoration, they will not become of the restored. [25]And we will appoint companions for them, so they beautified to them what is between their hands and what is behind them. And the word was established against them in the nations which have passed away before them from the jinn and the humans. Surely they were losers. [26]And those who became infidels said, "Do not listen to this Qur'an, but babble in it,[a] perhaps you may be victorious." [27]So surely we will cause those who became infidels to taste a severe torment, and surely we will reward them for the worst of what they were doing. [28]This is the reward of the enemies of Allah, the fire. They will have in it the eternal home, a reward because they were disbelieving in our verses. [29]And those who became infidels said, "Our lord, show us those of the jinn and the humans who led us astray. We will put them under our feet that they may be among the lowest." [30]Surely those who said, "Our lord is Allah." Then stand up straight, the angels will descend on them: "That do not fear and do not grieve but rejoice in the garden which you were promised. [31]We are your guardians in the world's life and in the hereafter. And you will have in it what your soul lusts for, and you will have in it what you call [32]a guest from a forgiving, merciful." [33]And who is better in speech from those who called to Allah and did a good deed and said, "Surely I am of the Muslims." [34]And the good are not equal, neither the evil. Pay with which is better so if who between you and him is enmity, as if he is a close friend.

The gardens are received through great luck.

[35]And no one will receive it[b] except those who were patient, and no one will receive it except the possessor of great luck. [36]And if an enticement from Satan entices you, so seek refuge in Allah, surely he is the hearing, the knowing. [37]And of his signs are the night and

---

[a] make noise interrupting its recitation
[b] the garden

the day and the sun and the moon. Do not worship the sun and neither the moon, and worship to Allah who created them, if you were serving him. [38]So if they become proud, so those who are with your lord praise to him in the night and the day, and they will not be bored. [39]And of his signs, that you see the earth lowly, so when we send down the water on it, it shakes and swells. Surely the one who gives it life will raise the dead. Surely he has might over all things. [40]Surely those who turn away from our verses, they are not hidden from us. Is he who is cast into the fire better, or who will come forth secure on the resurrection day? Do what you want. Surely he sees what you do. [41]Surely those who became infidels in the reminder, when it came to them, and surely it is a dear book. [42]The vanity will not come to it from between his hands, nor from behind him, a descending from a wise, praised.

Allah revealed nothing new to Mohammed in the Qur'an.

[43]Nothing has been said to you except what indeed has been said to the messengers before you. Surely your lord is the possessor of forgiveness and is a possessor of a painful punishment. [44]And if we made it a foreign Qur'an, they would say, "Were it not that its verses had been expounded." Whether foreign or Arabic, say, "This is to those who believed, a guidance and a healing, and those who do not believe, there is heaviness in their ears, and it is on them a blindness. Those are called from a far place." [45]And indeed, we gave Moses the book, so they differed in it. And were it not that a word proceeded from your lord, he would have judged between them. And surely they are in great doubt about it. [46]Whoever did a good deed, so it is to himself; and whoever does evil, so it is against it. And your lord is not unjust to the servants. [47]To him alone is the knowledge of the hour. No fruit comes from its coverings, neither does any female conceive nor deliver but with his knowledge. And a day he will call them, saying, "Where are my partners?" They said, "We proclaim to you that none of us is a witness." [48]And what they were calling on before strayed from them, and they thought that there was no escape. [49]The human never ceases to call for good, and if evil touches him, so he despairs, hopeless. [50]And if we cause him to taste a mercy from us after affliction has touched him, he is sure to say, "This is for me, and I do not think the hour is rising. And if I return to my lord, surely I will have with him the best." So then we will surely inform those who became infidels of what they have done, and surely we will cause them to taste from a thick (great) torment. [51]And if we graced on the human, he turns aside and withdraws himself; and if the evil touches him, so he is of wide[a] prayers. [52]Say,

---

[a] lengthy

"Have you seen if it was from Allah? Then you became infidels in it. Who is more astray than who is in farthest opposition?" [53]We will show them our signs in the horizon and in themselves until it becomes clear to them that it is the truth. Is it not sufficient with your lord that he is a witness over all things? [54]But they are surely in doubt about the meeting of their lord, is he not surrounding all things?

A portion of a revelation — 42 — *The Consultation*

In the name of Allah, the merciful, the merciful

[1]Hm.[a] [2]Asq.[b] [3]Likewise, it is revealed to you and to those before you, Allah is the dear, the wise. [4]To him what is in the heavens and what is on the earth, and he is the high, the great. [5]The heavens almost divide from above them, and the angels praise with their lord's praise. And they ask forgiveness for those on the earth. Is Allah surely not the forgiving, the merciful? [6]And those who took friends without him, Allah keeps over them. And you are not a guardian over them. [7]And likewise, we reveal to you an Arabic Qur'an to warn the mother of the villages and those around it, and warn them of the gathering day. There is no doubt in it, a group in the garden and a group in the blaze. [8]And if Allah wills, he would have made them one nation, but he enters whom he wills into his mercy. And the unjust do not have a friend nor helper. [9]Or have they taken friends without him? So Allah is the friend. And he gives life to the dead, and he has might over all things. [10]And whatever thing you disagree in, so its judgment is to Allah. This is Allah, my lord, on him I have depended, and to him I turn. [11]The creator of the heavens and the earth, he has made to you from your souls pairs, and from the livestock pairs, he multiplies you in it. There is nothing like him, and he is the hearing, the seeing. [12]To him are the keys of the heavens and the earth, he expands and measures the provision to whomever he wills. Surely he is the knower of all things. [13]He established for you of the religion which Noah advised with, and what we revealed to you, and what we advised to Abraham and Moses and 'Isā, that: "Perform the religion, and do not be divided in it." Big[c] to the polytheists what you call them to. Allah chooses to himself whom he wills and guides to himself whoever turns. [14]And they did not divide

---

[a] a word containing two Arabic letters without meaning
[b] a word containing three Arabic letters without meaning
[c] difficult

except after the knowledge came to them, an envy between them. And were it not that a word proceeded from your lord until an appointed time, he would have judged between them. And surely those who inherited the book after them are in dubious doubt concerning it.

Mohammed was commanded to believe in "whatever" (every) book Allah sent down.

[15]So therefore, so invite and stand firm, as you have been commanded. And do not follow their desires, and say, "I believed in whatever Allah has sent down of a book, and I am commanded to act fairly between you. Allah is our lord and your lord, to us our works and to you your works, there is no excuse between us and you. Allah gathers between us, and to him is the final return." [16]And those who dispute in Allah, after his excuse was answered for him, he will be void with their lord. And wrath will be on them, and they will have severe torment. [17]Allah is the one who sent down the book with the truth and the scales. And what do you know? Perhaps the hour is near. [18]Those who do not believe in it hasten it, and those who believed are in fear from it. And they know it is the truth. Are not surely those who dispute in the hour in a far away[a] error? [19]Allah is kind to his servants, he provides to whom he wills, and he is the strong, the dear. [20]Whoever was desiring the harvest of the hereafter, we will increase to him in his harvest. And whoever was desiring the harvest of this world, we will give to him from it. And he will not have any portion in the hereafter. [21]Or do they have partners prescribed for them in the religion which Allah did not allow? And were it not that the decisive word, he would have judged between them. And surely the unjust will have a painful torment. [22]You will see the unjust worried of what they have earned, and it is falling on them. And those who believed and did good deeds, in the meadows of the gardens, they will have whatever they want from their lord. This is the big bounty. [23]That is the good news of Allah to his servants, those who believed and did good deeds. Say, "I do not ask you any wage for it except the friendship in my kinship." And whoever earns good, we will increase good in it to him. Surely Allah is forgiving, thankful. [24]Or do they say, "He has forged a lie against Allah"? So if Allah wills, he puts a seal on your heart. And Allah erases the vanity. And the truth will be established with his words. Surely he knows what is in the chests. [25]And he is who accepts the repentance of his servants and pardons them of the evils and knows what you do. [26]And he answers those who believed and did good deeds and increases them from his bounties, and the infidels will have severe

---

[a] profound

torment. ²⁷And if Allah expanded the provision to his servants, they would rebel on the earth, but he sends down with measure what he will. Surely he is to his servants aware, seeing. ²⁸And he is who sends the rain after they were desperate and spreads his mercy. And he is the friend, the praised.

Creatures are scattered in the heavens.

²⁹And among his signs, the creation of the heavens and the earth and what he scattered in them of creature, and he is able to gather them if he wills. ³⁰And whatever misfortunes befall you, so it is due because of what your hands have earned, and he pardons much. ³¹And you cannot escape on the earth, and you do not have any friend nor helper without Allah. ³²And among his signs are the jawar[a] in the sea like aālam.[b] ³³If he wills, he will cause the wind to stay still. And it lies motionless on its back, surely in this are signs to every patient, thankful. ³⁴Or he destroys them because of what they earned, and he pardons toward much. ³⁵And those who dispute about our verses will know that there will be no place of escape for them. ³⁶So whatever thing you receive, so it is the enjoyment in the world's life. And what is with Allah is better and more lasting to those who believed and depend on their lord. ³⁷And those who avoid the great sins and indecencies, and when they are wrathful, they forgive. ³⁸And those who answered to their lord and performed the prayer, and whose affairs are by consultation among them, and who spend from what we provided them. ³⁹And those who, when a wrong is afflicted on them, they take revenge. ⁴⁰And the reward of evil is an evil like it, so whoever pardons and reconciles, so his wage is on Allah. Surely he does not love the unjust. ⁴¹And whoever takes revenge after being wronged, so there is no blame against them. ⁴²Surely the blame is only against those who wrong people, and they transgress on the earth without the truth. Those will have a painful torment. ⁴³And whoever is patient and forgives, surely this is from the courageous resolution. ⁴⁴And whoever Allah leads astray, so he will not have any friend after him. And you will see the unjust, when they see the torment, they say, "Is there a way to turn back?" ⁴⁵And you see them exposed to it, humbled from abasement. They will look at it with quick glances, and those who believed said, "Surely the losers are those who have lost themselves and their families on the resurrection day. Are not the unjust surely in lasting torment!" ⁴⁶And it was not for them to have friends who will help them without Allah, and whoever Allah makes to err, so he has no way. ⁴⁷Answer your lord before a day will come in which it cannot be turned back from Allah. There will be no place of refuge for you on that day, and you will not have any repudiation. ⁴⁸So if they turn away, so we did not

---

[a] running ones—Muslim scholars claim this means ships
[b] banners—Muslim scholars claim that in this instance it means mountains

send you a keeper over them. Your duty is only the delivering. And surely when we caused the human to taste mercy from us, he rejoiced in it. And if evil befalls them because of what their hands have done, so surely the human is infidel. [49]To Allah the kingdom of the heavens and the earth. He creates what he wills, he grants females to whom he wills, and he grants males to whom he wills. [50]Or he pairs them, males and females, and he makes whom he wills to be barren. Surely he is knowing, mighty.

Here the following verse contradicts the Qur'an by what Allah did throughout the Qur'an with Moses, a human, when Allah spoke directly to him without using revelation or from behind a veil or through a messenger.

[51]And it was not for a human that Allah should speak with him except by revelation or from behind a veil. Or he sends a messenger so he reveals by his permission what he wills. Surely he is high, wise. [52]And likewise, we reveal to you a spirit from our command. You did not know of what is the book nor the faith. But we made it light; we guide by it whom we will of our servants. And surely you will guide to a straight way, [53]the way of Allah, to whom what is in the heavens and what is on the earth. Is not to Allah all the affairs return!

A portion of a revelation — 43 — *The Highly Embellished*

In the name of Allah, the merciful, the merciful

[1]Hm.[a] [2][I swear] by the clear book.

There is an original copy of the Qur'an that is kept with Allah.

[3]Surely we have made it an Arabic Qur'an, perhaps you may understand. [4]And surely it is in the mother of the book with us, is high, wise. [5]Shall we withhold the reminder from you mercifully that you were an extravagant people? [6]And how many prophets did we send to the ancients? [7]And there never came a prophet to them except they were scoffing at him. [8]So we destroyed those who were stronger than them by annihilation, and the example of the ancients has gone. [9]And if you ask them: "Who created the heavens and the earth?" They will surely say, "Surely the dear, the knower created them." [10]Who has made the earth flat for you. And he has made

---

[a] a word containing two Arabic letters without meaning

ways for you in it, perhaps you may be guided. [11]And who sends down measured water from the heaven. So we raised a dead country to life by it; likewise, you will be brought forth. [12]And who has created all the pairs and has made for you the ships and the livestock, what you ride on [13]to sit on their backs. Then remember the grace of your lord as you sit on it, and say, "Praise be to him who has made these subservient to us, and we were not able to do it. [14]And surely to our lord we will return." [15]And they made to him part of his servants, surely the human is an obvious infidel. [16]Or has he taken daughters from what he has created and favored you with the sons? [17]And when one of them is given the good news by a parable that the merciful gave, his face becomes blackened, and he is grieved. [18]Or is the one who is brought up in adornments, and yet he is not clear in the dispute? [19]And they have made the angels, who are servants of the merciful, females. Have they witnessed their creation? Their testimony will be written, and they will be asked. [20]And they said, "If the merciful had willed, we would not have served them." They have no knowledge of that. Surely they only lie. [21]Or have we given them a book before it, so they are holding fast to it? [22]Yet, they said, "Surely we found our fathers of a nation,[a] and surely we are guiding ourselves in their footsteps." [23]And likewise, we did not send before you any warner in a village except that those in luxury in it said, "Surely we found our fathers of a nation, and surely we are following in their footsteps." [24]He said, "What if I bring to you with what is more guided than that which you found your fathers on?" They said, "Surely we are infidels in what you have been sent with." [25]So we took revenge on them, so look how was the end of the deniers.

The story of Abraham is copied from the Bible and corrupted once again.

[26]And when Abraham said to his father and his people, "Surely I am innocent from what you serve, [27]except who created me, so surely he will guide me." [28]And he made it an enduring word in his descendants, perhaps they may return. [29]Yet I gave those and their fathers enjoyment until the truth and a plain messenger came to them.

Many Arabs believed the Qur'an was sorcery.

[30]And when the truth came to them, they said, "This is sorcery, and surely we are infidels in it." [31]And they said, "Were it not that this Qur'an had been sent down on some great man of the two cities." [32]Are they then the distributors of your lord's mercy? We who distribute their livelihood among them in the world's life, and we raise some of them above others in degrees so that some of them may

---

[a] certain creed

take the others subservient. And better is the mercy of your lord than what they gather. [33]And were it not that the people would become one nation, we would have made to those who are infidels in the merciful, to their houses ceilings from silver and stairs on which they ascend. [34]And to their houses doors, and beds that they recline on, [35]and highly embellished and all of that are merely the enjoyment of the world's life. And the hereafter with your lord to the fearer. [36]And who turns away from the remembrance of the merciful, we will bind a satan to him so he will be a companion to him. [37]And surely they will prevent them from the way, and they will think that they are guided [38]until, when he comes to us, he said, "Oh, would that between me and you there is the distance of two easts." So evil is the companion. [39]And it will not profit you today if you have been unjust, that you will be partners in the torment. [40]Are you able to make the deaf to hear or guide the blind and him who was in obvious error? [41]So when we take you, so surely we will take revenge on them. [42]Or we will show you what we promised them. So surely we have might over them. [43]So cling to that which has been revealed to you, surely you are on a straight way. [44]And surely it is a reminder to you and to your people, and you will be asked. [45]And ask those whom we sent before you of our messengers: "Did we make, without the merciful, gods to be served?"

The story of Moses and Pharaoh is copied from the Bible and corrupted once again.

[46]And indeed, we sent Moses with our signs to Pharaoh and his leaders, so he said, "Surely I am the messenger of the lord of the worlds." [47]So when he came to them with our signs, behold, they laughed at them. [48]And we did not show them any sign but one bigger than its sister. And we seized them with the torment, perhaps they may return. [49]And they said, "O you sorcerer, call on your lord on our behalf to do as he covenanted with you, surely we will be guided." [50]So when we removed the torment from them, behold, they broke [their oath]. [51]And Pharaoh called to his people, he said, "O my people, is not the kingdom of Egypt mine and these rivers flow below me? Do you not see? [52]Or am I not better than this despicable fellow who cannot show? [53]So were it not that a bracelet of gold had been cast on him or came with him the angels accompanied him?" [54]So he fooled his people, so they obeyed him. Surely they were a transgressing people. [55]So when they made us sorrowful, we took revenge on them, so we drowned them all together. [56]So we made them a thing of the past and an example to the others. [57]And when the son of Mary was given as an example, behold, your people prevent [others] from him. [58]And they said, "Are our gods better or

he?" They only say this to you as a dispute, yet they are a
contentious people.

'Isā (the Jesus of Mohammed) is only a servant of Allah, but 'Isā is the knowledge of the hour of the resurrection.

⁵⁹That he is only a servant. We have graced on him, and we made
him an example to the children of Israel. ⁶⁰And if we willed, we could
make angels out of you to be successors on the earth. ⁶¹And surely
he is the knowledge of the hour, so do not doubt it, and follow me.
This is a straight way. ⁶²And do not let Satan prevent you. Surely he
is to you an obvious enemy. ⁶³And when 'Isā came with the proofs,
he said, "Indeed, I came to you with wisdom and to show you some
of what you differ in. So fear Allah, and obey me. ⁶⁴Surely Allah is my
lord and your lord, so serve him. This is a straight way." ⁶⁵So the
parties differed between them, so woe to those who were unjust from
a torment of a painful day. ⁶⁶Will they wait except the hour that will
come to them suddenly, and they do not feel? ⁶⁷On that day, the
friends will become enemies to one another except the fearing. ⁶⁸O
my servants, no fear on you today, and you will not grieve. ⁶⁹Those
who believed in our verses, and they were Muslims.

The garden includes the fleshly desires. Entry to the garden is a result of good deeds.

⁷⁰"Enter the garden, you and your wives, happily. ⁷¹Dishes of gold
and akwāb[a] will go around them, and in them, whatever the souls
lusts for and what the eyes delight in, and in it you will abide forever."
⁷²And this is the garden which you inherited because of what you
were doing. ⁷³You will have in it much fruit, from it you will eat.
⁷⁴Surely the criminals will abide in the torment of hell forever. ⁷⁵It will
not be lightened for them, and they will be in despair. ⁷⁶And we did
not deal unjustly with them, but they were the unjust. ⁷⁷And they call,
"O Mālik,[b] may your lord make an end of us." He said, "Surely you
are staying." ⁷⁸Indeed, we came to you with the truth, but most of you
to the truth are haters. ⁷⁹Or they have schemed an affair, so surely
we are scheming. ⁸⁰Or do they think that we do not hear their secrets
and their private talk? Yes, and our messengers with them are
writing it.

Far be it from Allah to have Jesus for a Son.

⁸¹Say, "If to the merciful was a son, so I would be the first to serve
him." ⁸²Praise be to the lord of the heavens and the earth, the lord of
the throne, from what they describe. ⁸³So leave them to engage and
sport until they meet their day of which they are promised. ⁸⁴And he

---

[a] goblets, non-Arabic word of Aramaic origin
[b] keeper of hell, non-Arabic word of Hebrew/Syriac origin

is who in the heaven is god and on the earth is god, and he is the wise, the knowing. [85]And blessed is he who has the kingdom of the heavens and the earth and what is between them, and with him is the knowledge of the hour, and to him you will return. [86]And those who call without him do not have the intercession, except who witness with the truth, and they know. [87]And if you ask them: "Who created them?" They will surely say, "Allah." So how then are they turned away? [88]And he says, "O lord, surely those people do not believe." [89]So forgive them, and say, "Peace." So they will know.

A portion of a revelation   **44**   *The Smoke*

In the name of Allah, the merciful, the merciful

[1]Hm.[a] [2][I swear] by the clear book. [3]Surely we sent it down in a blessed night, and surely we were warners. [4]Every wise affair is distinct in it. [5]A command from us. Surely we were senders. [6]A mercy from your lord, surely he is the hearing, the knowing. [7]The lord of the heavens and the earth and what is between them, if you were sure. [8]There is no god but him; he gives life and causes death, your lord and the lord of your ancient fathers. [9]Yet they are in doubt, sporting. [10]So watch for a day the heaven comes with visible smoke. [11]It covers the people. This is a painful torment. [12]"Our lord, remove the torment from us, surely we are believers." [13]How can they have the reminder, and indeed, a plain messenger came to them? [14]Then they turned away from him, and they said, "A demon-possessed teacher." [15]Surely we will remove the torment for a little while, surely you are reverting. [16]A day we will strike you with the big strike. Surely we are revenging.

The story of Moses and Pharaoh is copied from the Bible and corrupted once again.

[17]And indeed, we seduced before them Pharaoh's people, and a generous messenger came to them. [18]"That give to me the servants of Allah, surely I am to you a faithful messenger. [19]And that you do not exalt above Allah. Surely I come to you with a manifest authority. [20]And surely I take refuge with my lord and your lord, that you stone me. [21]And if you do not believe me, so separate from me." [22]So he called his lord: "That these are criminal people." [23]So go forth with

---

[a] a word containing two Arabic letters without meaning

my servants at night, surely you will be followed. [24]And leave the sea open, surely they are a drowned troop.

Is this the inheritance of the land of Egypt?

[25]How many gardens and springs they left, [26]and plants and generous dwellings, [27]and grace they[a] were delighting in it? [28]Likewise, we bequeathed it to another people. [29]So the heavens and the earth did not cry over them, and they were not delayed.

Allah chose the children of Israel above all people.

[30]And indeed, we delivered the children of Israel from the shameful torment [31]from Pharaoh, surely he was proud among the extravagant. [32]And indeed, we knowingly chose them above the worlds. [33]And we gave them of the signs, in it was a manifest trial. [34]Surely those will say, [35]"That it is only our first death, and we will not be raised. [36]So bring with our fathers, if you were truthful." [37]Are they better, or the people of Tubba'[b] and those who were before them? We destroyed them, surely they were criminals. [38]And we did not create the heavens and the earth and what is between them for sport. [39]We have not created them except with the truth, but most of them do not know. [40]Surely the separation day is appointed to all of them. [41]A day a relative cannot benefit another relative anything, nor will they be helped, [42]except for him whom Allah has mercy. Surely he is the dear, the merciful. [43]Surely the tree of Zakkoum, [44]the food of the sinner, [45]like molten metal boiling in the belly, [46]like the boiling of the hamem. [47]Take him, so drag him into the pits of hell. [48]Then pour on his head from the torment of the hamem. [49]Taste it. Surely you are the dear, the generous. [50]Surely this is what you were doubting!

In the gardens, the righteous (men) will marry virgins with beautiful eyes. Whom do the believing women marry?

[51]Surely the fearing one will be in a secure place, [52]in gardens and springs, [53]clothed in fine silk and richest robes, facing one another. [54]Likewise, we married them to hūr-eyed.[c] [55]They will call in it with every fruit securely. [56]They will not taste death in it, except the first death, and he guards them from the torments of hell. [57]Bounty from your lord, this is the great triumph. [58]So surely we only made it easy with your tongue, perhaps they will remember. [59]So watch, surely they are watching.

---

[a] the Egyptians
[b] title of the King of the Himyarites, non-Arabic word of Himyaritic origin
[c] the ever-virgins of the gardens with white skin, large dark eyes, and large breasts, non-Arabic word of Pahlavian/Aramaic origin

A portion of a revelation — **45** — *The Kneeling*

In the name of Allah, the merciful, the merciful

[1]Hm.[a] [2]The descending of the book from Allah, the dear, the wise. [3]Surely in the heavens and the earth are signs for the believers. [4]And in your creation and what he scatter of creature are signs to people who are certain. [5]And in the alternation of the night and the day and what Allah sends down from the heaven of provision, so he gives life to the earth after its death, and in the changing of the winds, they are signs to understanding people. [6]Those are the verses of Allah that we recite to you with the truth. So in what saying of Allah and his verses will they believe? [7]Woe to every sinful liar. [8]He hears the verses of Allah recited to him. Then he insists proudly as though he did not hear it, so give him the good news of the painful torment. [9]And when he knew something from our verses, he took it for scoff. Those will have a shameful torment. [10]From behind them is hell, and what they have earned will not benefit them anything, neither what they took without Allah [as] friends. And they will have great torment. [11]This is guidance, and for those who became infidels with the verses of their lord, they will have a torment of a painful wrath. [12]Allah is who made the sea subservient to you so that the ships may run in it by his command and so that you may seek from his bounty, and perhaps you may give thanks. [13]And he made what is in the heavens and what is on the earth, together from him subservient to you, surely in this are signs to people who reflect. [14]Say to those who believed, "Forgive to those who do not hope in Allah's days to reward people for what they were earning. [15]Whoever does good deed, so it is for himself; and whoever does evil, so it is against it. Then to your lord you will return."

Jews (the children of Israel) are privileged above all people.

[16]And indeed, we gave the book and the wisdom and the prophethood to the children of Israel, and we provided them with the good things. And we favored them above the worlds. [17]And we gave them proofs from the affair, so they did not disagree except after the knowledge came to them, with envy between them, surely your lord judges between them on the resurrection day about what they were disagreeing. [18]Then we made you follow the laws concerning the affair, so follow it and do not follow the desire of those who do not

---

[a] a word containing two Arabic letters without meaning

know. [19]Surely they will not benefit you anything against Allah. And surely the unjust are only friends one to another, and Allah is the friend of the fearing. [20]This is an enlightenment to the people and a guidance and a mercy to a sure people. [21]Or do those who commit the evils thought that we will make them as those who believed and did good deeds, either in their life or their death? Evil is what they judge. [22]And Allah created the heavens and the earth with the truth, and every soul will be rewarded for what it has earned. And they will not be dealt with unjustly. [23]Have you seen who took his god, his desire? And Allah led him astray with knowledge and he sealed on his hearing and his heart and he put a cover on his sight. So who will guide him after Allah? Do you not remember? [24]And they said, "What is our life of this world, except we will die and we will live. And no one will destroy us except the time." And they have no knowledge in that. Surely they are only conjecturing. [25]And when our clear verses are recited to them, their excuse was not except that they said, "Bring our fathers, if you were truthful." [26]Say, "Allah gives you life, then causes you to die, then gathers you on the resurrection day. There is no doubt about it, but most people do not know. [27]And to Allah the kingdom of the heavens and the earth, and a day the hour will arise, on that day the liars will lose. [28]And you will see every nation kneeling, every nation will be called to its book: "Today you will be rewarded for what you were doing! [29]This is our book that speaks against you with the truth. Surely we were writing what you were doing." [30]So as to those who believed and did good deeds, so their lord will admit them into his mercy. This is the clear triumph. [31]And for those who became infidels: "Were not my verses recited to you? So you became proud, and you were a criminal people." [32]And when it was said, "Surely the promise of Allah is true, and the hour, there is no doubt in it." You said, "We do not know what the hour is. That we conjecture only conjecturing, and we do not know for sure." [33]And the evils of what they had done appeared to them, and what they were scoffing at afflicted them. [34]And it was said, "Today we will forget you as you forgot the meeting of this your day. And your abode is the fire, and you will not have any helpers. [35]That is because you took the verses of Allah as a scoff, and the world's life deceived you." So today they will not come out of it, and they will not be allowed to repent. [36]So praise be to Allah, the lord of the heavens and the lord of the earth, the lord of the worlds. [37]And to him the pride in the heavens and the earth, and he is the dear, the wise.

*A portion
of a revelation*   **46**   *The Dunes*

In the name of Allah, the merciful, the merciful

¹Hm.ᵃ ²A descending of the book from Allah, the dear, the wise.
³We did not create the heavens and the earth and what is between
them, except in truth and an appointed term. And those who became
infidels, they turn away from what they were warned. ⁴Say, "Have
you seen those whom you call on without Allah? Show me what they
created from the earth, or do they have a share in the heavens?
Bring me a book before this or traces of their knowledge, if you were
truthful." ⁵And who errs more than who calls other than Allah who do
not answer to him until the resurrection day. And they are unaware of
their prayers. ⁶And when the people are gathered, they were an
enemy to them. And they were infidels with their service. ⁷And when
our clear verses are recited to them, those who became infidels said
to the truth when it came to them, "This is an obvious sorcery." ⁸Or
they say, "He forged it." Say, "If I have forged it, so you do not have
anything to me against Allah. He best knows what you are uttering in
it. He is a sufficient witness between me and you, and he is the
forgiving, the merciful." ⁹Say, "I was not an inventor among the
messengers, and I do not know what will be done with me nor you. I
only follow what is revealed to me, and I am only a plain warner."
¹⁰Say, "Have you seen that if it was from Allah and you became
infidels in it? And a witness testified from the children of Israel to the
like of it. So he believed, and you became proud. Surely Allah will not
guide the unjust people."

Some thought the Qur'an was an old lie.

¹¹And those who became infidels said to those who believed, "If it
were a good thing, they would not have gone to it before us." And
when they will not be guided by it, so they will say, "It is an old lie."

**The Qur'an confirms the accuracy of the Torah, the books of
Moses.**

¹²And before it was the book of Moses, a guide and a mercy. And
this book confirms it in an Arabic tongue, to warn those unjust, and it
is good news to the doers of good. ¹³Surely those who said, "Our lord
is Allah." Then they stand straight, so there is no fear on them, and
they will not grieve. ¹⁴Those are the companions of the garden,

---

ᵃ a word containing two Arabic letters without meaning

abiding in it forever, a reward for what they were doing. [15]And we advised the human to show good to his parents. His mother carries him compulsorily, and she delivers him compulsorily and her pregnancy and weaning is thirty months until, when he attains his strength and attains to forty years, he said, "Lord, grant me to be thankful for your grace which you graced on me and on my parents and to do good deed, will please you, and do good to me in my offspring. Surely I repented to you, and surely I am of the Muslims."

Allah accepts good deeds and ignores the evil deeds of the believers.

[16]Those from whom we accept the best of what they have done, and we ignore their evils. In the companions of the garden, the true promise, which they were promised. [17]And he who says to his parents, "Ouf' to you, do you promise me that I will come out? And indeed, generations have gone before me." And they[a] were calling on Allah, "Woe to you. Believe. Surely the promise of Allah is true." So he will say, "What is this except the legends of the ancients!" [18]Those against whom the word is established, indeed, in nations passed away before them of the jinn and the humans. Surely they were losers. [19]And to everyone are degrees for what they have done. And he will repay them for their work, and they will not be dealt with unjustly. [20]And a day those who became infidels will be exposed to the fire: "You wasted your goods in your world's life, and you enjoyed it. So today you will be rewarded with the shameful torment because you were proud on the earth without the truth and because you were transgressors."

The story of Ad's brother was invented by Mohammed and is repeated once again.

[21]And remember the brother of Ad, when he warned his people in the dunes, and indeed, the warners have passed from between his hands and from behind him: "That you do not serve any except Allah, surely I fear the torment of a great day for you." [22]They said, "Have you come to us to turn us away from our gods? So bring us what you promised us, if you were of the truthful." [23]He said, "Surely the knowledge is only with Allah, and I am delivering to you what I have been sent with. But I see you are an ignorant people." [24]So when they saw it coming straight for their valleys, they said, "It is a passing with rain." Yet, it is what you are hastening with, a storm, in it is a painful torment. [25]It will destroy everything with the command of its lord. So they became such that nothing could be seen except their dwellings. Likewise, we reward the criminal people. [26]And indeed, we established them in what we established you in it, and we gave them

---

[a] parents

hearings and sight and hearts, so neither their hearings nor their sight nor their hearts benefited them at all, as they were disbelieving in the verses of Allah. And what they were scoffing at afflicted them. [27]And indeed, we destroyed the villages that are around you, and we expounded on the verses, perhaps they may return. [28]So were it not that the gods whom they took other than Allah had not helped them to be nearer. Yet, they went astray from them. And this was their lie and what they were forging.

Even the jinn are Muslim believers.

[29]And when we turned a company of the jinn toward you, they listen to the Qur'an. So when they arrived there, they said, "Listen." So when he finished, they returned to their people warning them. [30]They said, "O our people, surely we have heard a book revealed after Moses, confirming what is between his hands, guide to the truth and to a straight way. [31]O our people, answer the caller of Allah and believe in him. He will forgive you some of your sins and remove you from a painful torment." [32]And whoever will not answer the caller of Allah, so they cannot escape on the earth. And he does not have friends without him, those are in obvious error. [33]Or have they not seen that Allah, who created the heavens and the earth, and he did not grow weary by creating them, is able to give life to the dead? Yes, surely he has might over all things. [34]And a day those who became infidels will be exposed to the fire: "Is this not the truth?" They said, "Yes, we swear by our lord." He said, "So taste the torment because you were infidels." [35]So be patient as the messengers endured with firmness were patient and do not hasten to them as they see a day they were promised. They did not stay except one hour of the midday. Proclamation: so will [anyone] perish except the transgressing people?

A portion of a revelation   **47**   *Mohammed*

In the name of Allah, the merciful, the merciful

[1]Those who became infidels and prevent [others] from Allah's way, he led their works astray. [2]And those who believed and did good deeds and believed in what has been sent down on Mohammed, and it is the truth from their lord, he atoned for them their evils. And he reformed their condition. [3]That is because those who became infidels

followed the vanity and that those who believed followed the truth from their lord. Likewise, Allah gave parables to the people.

Muslims must strike the necks (cut off the heads) of infidels, and those who engage in war for Allah are assured of the gardens of Paradise.

[4]So when you meet those who became infidels, so strike the necks (decapitating) until you have made a great slaughter among them. So firmly bind them. So let there either be free dismissals or for a ransom, until the war is over. In this way, and if Allah wills, he will take vengeance on them, but he would rather test some of you by the other. And those who were killed[a] for the sake of Allah, so he will not let their works go astray. [5]He will guide them and reform their condition. [6]And he will admit them into the garden of which he made known to them.

Allah needs help. If Muslims help him, he will help them.

[7]O you who have believed, if you help Allah, then Allah will help you and will set your feet firm. [8]And for those who became infidels, there will be misery to them. And he will lead their works astray. [9]That is because they hate what Allah has sent down, so he voids their work. [10]Have they not walked on the earth, so they see how was the end of those who were before them? Allah brought destruction on them and to the infidels likewise. [11]This is because Allah is the guardian of those who believed, and the infidels have no guardian. [12]Surely Allah will admit those who believed and did good deeds into gardens, below them the rivers flow. And those who became infidels, they enjoy and eat as the livestock eat, and the fire will be their abode. [13]And how many a village were mightier in strength than your village which drove you out? We destroyed them, so there is no helper for them. [14]Is he who was on a proof from his lord like whose evil work is beautified to him, and they follow their lusts?

This is a description of the garden.

[15]The description of the garden which Allah has promised the fearer: in it rivers of water which are not corrupted and rivers of milk which taste does not change and rivers of wine delicious to those who drink it and rivers of clarified honey; and they will have all fruit in it and forgiveness from their lord. Like who must abide forever in the fire and were given warm water to drink, so it cut their bowels. [16]And some of them listen to you until they go out from you. They said to those who have been given the knowledge, "What did he say

---

[a] during the war

earlier?"[a] These are those whom Allah had sealed on their hearts and follow their lusts. [17]And those who were guided, he increased them guidance, and he gave them their piety. [18]So will they wait except the hour that it will come on them suddenly? So indeed, the signs of it already came, so how can they remember when it comes to them?

Mohammed is commanded by Allah to ask for forgiveness of his sins. Those who disobey Allah and do not go to war in jihad are under a curse.

[19]So know that there is no god but Allah and ask forgiveness for your sins, and for the believing men and believing women. And Allah knows your moving about and your resting. [20]And those who believed say, "Were it not that a portion of a revelation had been sent down." So when a decisive portion of a revelation was sent down, and the engaging war was mentioned in it, you see those who have a disease in their heart look at you with the look of one on whom the faintness of death takes over. So, far better for them. [21]Obedience and fair words, so when the affair is settled, so if they believed Allah, it would be better for them. [22]So what perhaps if you turned away, that you vandalize on the earth and cut off your wombs."[b] [23]Those are the ones whom Allah has cursed, so he made them deaf and blinded their sight. [24]Do not they contemplate the Qur'an or on the heart its aqfal?[c] [25]Surely those who turn their backs after the guidance has been made clear to them, Satan beguiled them and extended hope to them. [26]That is because they said to those who hated what Allah had sent down, "We will obey you in some of the affairs." And Allah knows their secrets. [27]So how is it when the angels cause them to die, they will strike their faces and their rear ends? [28]That is because they followed that which angered Allah, and they hated his pleasure, so he voided their works. [29]Or do those who have a disease in their hearts think that Allah will not bring forth their malice? [30]And if we will, we will show them to you, so you will know them by their marks and that you will surely know them by the tone of their speech. And Allah knows your works. [31]And we will surely test you, until we know those who perform the jihad among you and the patient,[d] and we will test your news. [32]Surely those who became infidels and prevent [others] from Allah's way and opposed the messenger after the guidance had been clearly shown to them, they will not harm Allah anything. And their works will be nothing. [33]O you who have believed, obey Allah and obey the messenger and do not

---

[a] scoffing at Mohammed
[b] ties of kinship
[c] locks, non-Arabic word of Greek origin
[d] steadfast in their fighting

make your works to be in vain. [34]Surely those who became infidels and prevented [others] from Allah's way, then die while they are infidels, so Allah will not forgive them.

Muslims must never make peace when they have won the upper hand.

[35]So do not be weak and do not call for peace when you have the upper hand. And Allah is with you, and he will not leave from[a] you [for] your works. [36]Surely the world's life is only a sport and fun. And if you believe and fear, he will give you your wages, and he does not ask you your money. [37]If he asked you for it, so he presses you, you will become stingy, and he will bring forth your malice. [38]There you are called to spend for the sake of Allah, so some of you are stingy. And whoever is stingy, so surely he is only stingy against himself, and Allah is the rich, and you are the poor. And if you turn away, he will replace you with another people, then they will not be like you.

A portion of a revelation   **48**   *The Conquest*

In the name of Allah, the merciful, the merciful

Allah forgives Mohammed for his past, present, and future sins.

[1]Surely we conquered for you a clear conquest, [2]that Allah may forgive you for your past sins and your future sins and to fulfill his grace on you, and guide you to a straight way. [3]And Allah will give you victory, a dear victory. [4]He is who sends down the tranquility in the hearts of the believers so that they will increase faith with their faith. And to Allah the troops of the heavens and the earth. And Allah was knowing, wise. [5]That he may admit the believing men and the believing women into gardens, below them the rivers flow, to abide in it forever, and atone for them their evils. And this was the great triumph with Allah. [6]And he will torment the hypocritical men and the hypocritical women and the polytheistic men and the polytheistic women. Those who are thinking the evil thoughts against Allah, the evil will turn on them, and Allah's wrath is against them. And he cursed them, and he prepared hell for them and an evil final place. [7]And to Allah the troops of the heavens and the earth. And Allah was dear, wise. [8]Surely we sent you as a witness and a giver of good news and a warner [9]so that you may believe in Allah and his

---

[a] phrase indicating "will reward"

messenger, and that you may help him and reverence him and praise him, morning and evening. [10]Surely those who pledge allegiance to you, surely they only pledge allegiance to Allah. Allah's hand is above their hand, so whoever breaks this [allegiance], so surely he only breaks [allegiance] against himself; and whoever fulfills what he covenants with Allah, so he will give him a great wage.

Those who did not go to war (perform jihad) with Mohammed went into the fires of hell.

[11]The Bedouins who stayed behind will say to you, "Our money and family kept us busy, so ask forgiveness for us." They say with their tongues what is not in their hearts. Say, "So who will have anything for you against Allah, if he desires to do you harm or desires to benefit you? Yet Allah was aware of what you do. [12]Yet you thought that the messenger and the believer could never return [from the wars] to their families; and this was adorned to your hearts, and you thought the evil thought. And you were a fallow people." [13]And whoever does not believe in Allah and his messenger, so surely we prepared a blaze for the infidels. [14]And to Allah the kingdom of the heavens and the earth, he forgives to whom he wills, and he torments whom he wills. And Allah was forgiving, merciful. [15]They who stayed behind will say, "When you go forth to the spoil to take it, let us follow you." They desired to change the word of Allah. Say, "You will not follow us, likewise, Allah had said before." So they will say, "Yet, you are envious of us." Yet, they were not understanding except a little.

There are only two choices to the infidels: accept Islam or be killed with the sword. Also, in verse 17, there is a list of those who are exempt from war.

[16]Say to those Bedouins who lagged behind [in battle], "You will be called to [face] a people of substantial mighty valor. You will engage in war against them, or they will become Muslims. So if you obey, Allah will give you a good wage; and if you turn away, as you turned away before, he will torment you with a painful torment. [17]There is no blame on the blind nor blame on the lame nor blame on the sick. And whoever obeys Allah and his messenger, he will admit him into gardens, below them the rivers flow; and whoever turns away, he will torment him with a painful torment." [18]Indeed, Allah was pleased with the believers when they pledged allegiance with you under the tree, so he knew what was in their hearts, so he sent down the tranquility on them and rewarded them with a near conquest.

The Muslims will get riches as a reward for performing jihad.

[19]And there will be abundant spoils for them to seize. And Allah was dear, wise. [20]Allah promised the seizing of abundant spoils for you, so he hastened this to you, and he holds back the hands of the people from you and that it may be a sign to the believer. And he will guide you to a straight way. [21]And other [spoils] that you could not have taken, and Allah indeed encompassed it. And Allah was mighty over all things. [22]And if those who became infidels engage in war against you, they will turn away. Then they will not find a friend nor a helper. [23]The custom of Allah, which indeed has passed before, and you will not find any change to the custom of Allah. [24]And he is who holds back their hands from you and your hands from them in the belly[a] of Mecca after he had given you triumph over them, and Allah was seer of what you do. [25]They are those who became infidels and prevented you from the forbidden mosque and prevented the sacrifice from reaching its place. And were it not for the believing men and believing women whom you did not know, that you may have killed them, so harm would have fallen on you without knowledge, that Allah may admit into his mercy whom he wills. Had they been distinguishable, we surely would have tormented those who became infidels among them with a painful torment. [26]When those who became infidels had fostered the zealotry in their hearts, the ignorance's zealotry, so Allah sent down tranquility on his messenger and on the believers and forced them to keep the word of piety. And they were worthy of it and its people. And Allah was knowledgeable in everything.

Shaving heads is a practice that was copied from pagan traditions.

[27]Indeed, Allah approved the vision of his messenger in the truth: "You will surely enter the forbidden mosque by Allah's will, in security, shaving your heads and making it short. Do not fear." So he knows what you do not know, so he made without that a near conquest.

Allah promises to exalt Islam above all religions. Islam is a religion of love and peace EXCEPT to anyone who is not Muslim.

[28]He is who sent his messenger with the guidance and the religion of truth so that he may exalt it above all other religions. And Allah is a sufficient witness. [29]Mohammed is Allah's messenger, and those who are with him are severe against the infidels but full of tenderness among themselves. You see them kneeling, worshiping, seeking bounty from Allah, and pleasure. Their marks are on their

---

[a] valley

faces from the traces[a] of the worship. This is their example in the Torah, and this is their example in the Gospel; like a plant puts forth its stalk, then strengthens it, so it grows stout. So it rises on its stem, delighting the farmer that he may enrage the infidels with them. And Allah promised forgiveness and a great wage to those who believed and did good deeds among them.

A portion of a revelation   The Rooms

In the name of Allah, the merciful, the merciful

Allah commands Muslims to treat Mohammed in a special way. Sins are forgiven for those who lower their voices humbly before Mohammed.

[1]O you who have believed, do not be forward between the hands of Allah and his messenger, and fear Allah. Surely Allah is hearing, knowing. [2]O you who have believed, do not raise your voice above the voice of the prophet. And do not speak loud to him as you speak loud to one another so that your works become void, and you will not feel. [3]Surely those who lower their voices before the messenger of Allah are those whom Allah tested their hearts to piety, to them forgiveness and a great wage. [4]Surely those who call you from behind[b] the rooms, most of them do not understand. [5]And surely if they would be patient until you have come out to them, it would be better for them. And Allah is forgiving, merciful. [6]O you who have believed, if a wicked one comes to you with news, so investigate it so that you may not smite people with ignorance, so you will become regretful for what you had done. [7]And know that among you is Allah's messenger. If he would obey you in many of the affairs, then you would have difficulty. But Allah makes you to love the faith and has adorned it in your heart and makes you to hate the infidelity and the transgression and the disobedience. Those are the rightly guided. [8]Bounty from Allah and his grace. And Allah is knowing, wise.

Muslims are brothers. They can only engage in war against another Muslim if they are wrongdoers and then only for reconciliation.

---

[a] marks made on the forehead by burning, to appear as if from touching the ground when bowing repeatedly
[b] outside of

⁹And if two parties of the believers should engage in war, so reconcile between them, so if one of them wrongs the other, so engage in war against the one which does the wrong, until they come back to Allah's command. So if they return, so reconcile between them with justice and be fair. Surely Allah loves those who are fair. ¹⁰Surely the believers are only brothers, so reconcile between your brothers and fear Allah, perhaps you may be shown mercy. ¹¹O you who have believed, let not any of the people scoff at other people, perhaps they are better than them, and not women at women, perhaps they are better than them. And do not defame yourselves, nor call one another by nicknames. Evil is the name of lewdness after the faith, and whoever does not repent, so those are the unjust. ¹²O you who have believed, avoid much of the conjecture. Surely some of the conjectures are sin. And do not spy on and do not backbite one another. Does any one of you love to eat the flesh of his dead brother? So you hated it[a] and fear Allah. Surely Allah is relenting, merciful. ¹³O you people, surely we created you from male and female, and we have made you into peoples and tribes so that you may know one another. Surely the most generous among you, before Allah, is the most pious among you. Surely Allah is knowing, aware. ¹⁴The Bedouins said, "We believed." Say, "You did not believe. But say, 'We surrender (became Muslim as a result of fear).' And the faith has not entered your hearts. And if you obey Allah and his messenger, he will not decrease anything from your works. Surely Allah is forgiving, merciful."

True believers perform jihad with their money and their lives.

¹⁵Surely the believers are only those who believed in Allah and his messenger. Then they do not doubt, and they performed jihad with their money and their lives for the sake of Allah. Those are the truthful. ¹⁶Say, "Will you teach Allah about your religion when Allah knows what is in the heavens and what is on the earth?" And Allah is knower of all things. ¹⁷They do you a favor if they become Muslims. Say, "Do not do me a favor by becoming Muslim, yet Allah has his favor on you by guiding you to the faith, if you were truthful. ¹⁸Surely Allah knows the unseen of the heavens and the earth, and Allah sees what you do."

---

[a] backbiting

A portion of a revelation   Q

In the name of Allah, the merciful, the merciful

[1]Q,[a] [I swear] by the glorious Qur'an. [2]Yet, they wonder that a warner from among them came to them, so the infidels said, "This is a strange thing. [3]What if we died and we were dust, this return is far off?" [4]Indeed, we know what the earth diminishes of them and with us is a keeper book. [5]Yet, they denied the truth when it came to them, so they are in a state of confusion.

This is another proof that heaven is a solid structure, like a ceiling. The earth is flat. According to the Islamic scholar Al Qurtobi, this verse provides a great proof that the earth is flat rather than being round.

[6]Have they not looked to the heaven above them, how we built it and adorned it and it does not have any cracks? [7]And the earth, we have spread it out and have thrown the stabilizers on it and have caused plants to grow in it, from every beautiful pair. [8]Enlightenment and a reminder to every turned servant. [9]And we sent down blessed water from the heaven, so we caused the gardens and the harvest grains to grow by it, [10]and the tall palm trees with clusters of fruit stalks in their branches, [11]a provision to the servants. And we give life to a dead country by it, likewise, the coming out.[b] [12]Before them, the people of Noah and the companions of Rass and Themoud denied. [13]And Ad and Pharaoh and the brethren of Lot, [14]and the companions of the woods and the people of Tubba', they all denied the messengers, so my threat becomes established. [15]Are we wearied with the first creation? Yet, they are in doubt about a new creation. [16]And indeed, we created the human, and we know what his soul whispers within him. And we are closer to him than his jugular vein. [17]When the two receivers[c] meet, one sitting on the right and one on the left, [18]he will not say a word, except that a watcher is prepared, present by him. [19]And the stupor of death came with the truth, this is what you were turned away from. [20]And the trumpet was blown: "This is the threatening day." [21]And every soul came, with it a driver and a witness. [22]"Indeed, I was unaware of this." So we removed the veil from you so that your sight today is iron. [23]And his

---

[a] an Arabic letter without meaning, Mohammed claimed it to be an enormous mountain that surrounds the earth until the resurrection day
[b] resurrection
[c] recording angels

companion said, "This is what is ready with me." [24]"Cast every stubborn infidel into hell, [25]the hinderer of the good, the transgressor, the doubter. [26]Whoever made other gods with Allah, so cast him also into the severe torment." [27]His companion said, "Our lord, I did not lead him to rebellion, but he was in a far error." [28]He said, "Do not dispute in my presence. And indeed, I gave you warning before. [29]The word will not change in my presence, and I will not deal unjustly with the servants." [30]A day we will say to hell, "Are you filled up?" And it will say, "Are there any more?" [31]And the garden will be brought near to the fearing, not far away. [32]This is what you were promised, to every returned keeper, [33]who feared the merciful in secret and came to him with a turned heart. [34]"Enter it in peace. This is the immortality day." [35]They have what they desire in it, and we have more. [36]And how many generations before them did we destroy? They were mightier than them in strength. So they dug in the countries. Is there any escape? [37]Surely in this is a reminder to whoever had a heart or threw the hearing[a] while he witnesses.

The six-day creation is copied from the Bible.

[38]And indeed, we created the heavens and the earth and what is between them in six days, and no weariness touched us. [39]So be patient in what they say. And praise with your lord's praise before the sunrise and before the setting, [40]and some of the night, so praise him after the worship. [41]And listen for a day the caller will call from a near place. [42]A day they hear the shout with the truth, this is the coming out[b] day. [43]Surely we give life, and we cause death. And to us is the final return. [44]A day the earth will be cracked[c] open swiftly for them, this gathering will be easy to us. [45]We know best what they say, and you are not a powerful over them, so remind by the Qur'an who fears my threat.

A portion of a revelation   *The Scattering*

51

In the name of Allah, the merciful, the merciful

[1][I swear] by the scattering they scatter, [2]so it bears the deafness, [3]so those running easily, [4]so those who distribute by command. [5]Surely what you promised is only true. [6]And surely the judgment

---

[a] gave ear to hear
[b] resurrection
[c] many cracks

must happen. [7][I swear] by the heaven, full of ways. [8]Surely you are in a different saying. [9]Turned away from it, who is turned away. [10]Killed the liars, [11]those who in ignorance are heedless. [12]They ask, "When is the judgment day?" [13]A day they will be seduced over the fire. [14]"Taste your sedition, this is what you were hastening to." [15]Surely the fearer is in gardens and springs, [16]taking what their lord brought them. Surely they were the doers of good before. [17]They slept only a little at night, [18]and at dawn they asked for forgiveness. [19]And from their money there is a due for the beggar and the needy. [20]And on the earth are signs for those who are sure. [21]And in your souls, do you not see? [22]And in the heavens is your provision and what you are promised. [23]So [I swear] by the lord of the heaven and the earth, surely it is truth, like what you speak.

The story of Abraham and Lot is copied from the Bible and corrupted once again. Notice the contradiction in this account compared to the rest of the Qur'an. The punishment of Lot's people takes place before the messengers meet with Abraham.

[24]Has the saying of the honored guest of Abraham come to you? [25]When they entered unto him, so they said, "Peace." He said, "Peace, unknown people." [26]So he went to his family, so he brought a fatted calf. [27]So he placed it near them. He said, "Will you not eat?" [28]So he began to be afraid of them. They said, "Do not fear." And they gave him the good news of a young, knowledgeable boy. [29]So his woman [wife] came in shouting and she struck her face and she said, "Old, barren." [30]They said, "Likewise, your lord said. Surely he is the wise, the knowing." [31]He said, "What is your news, O you the messengers?" [32]They said, "Surely we have been sent to a criminal people [33]to send on them stones of mud [34]marked by your lord for the extravagant." [35]So we brought forth out of it who was among the believers. [36]So we did not find in it except one house of Muslims. [37]And we left in it a sign to those who fear the painful torment.

The story of Moses and Pharaoh is copied from the Bible and corrupted once again.

[38]And in Moses, when we sent him to Pharaoh with the clear authority. [39]So he turned away in his corner and said, "A sorcerer or demon-possessed." [40]So we seized him and his troops, so we cast them into the sea. And he was blamed.

These are the stories of Ad, Themoud, and Noah which were invented or changed by Mohammed.

[41]And in Ad, we sent the barren wind on them. [42]And it did not leave anything as it came over, except it made it like decay. [43]And in Themoud, when it was said to them, "Enjoy for a while." [44]So they

revolted against the command of their lord, so a thunderbolt seized them as they looked on. ⁴⁵So they were not able to stand up, and they were not helped. ⁴⁶And the people of Noah before that, surely they were a transgressing people. ⁴⁷And the heaven we built with hands, and surely we will enlarge it. ⁴⁸And we spread the earth, so blessed are the flatteners. ⁴⁹And from everything we have created two pairs, perhaps you will remember. ⁵⁰So flee to Allah, surely I am a plain warner to you from him. ⁵¹And do not make another god with Allah, surely I am a plain warner to you from him. ⁵²Likewise, no messenger has ever come to those before them except that they said, "A sorcerer or demon-possessed." ⁵³Have they handed it down to each other? Yet, they are a rebellious people. ⁵⁴So turn away from them so you will not be blamed. ⁵⁵And remind, so surely the reminder benefits the believers.

Allah creates jinn and people to serve him.

⁵⁶And I have not created the jinn and the humans, except to serve me. ⁵⁷I do not desire a provision from them, and I do not desire that they feed me. ⁵⁸Surely Allah, he is the provider, the possessor of power, the strong. ⁵⁹So surely to those unjust sins, like the sins of their companions, so they do not hasten me. ⁶⁰So woe to those who became infidels on their day of which they are promised.

A portion of a revelation   **52**   *The Mountain*

In the name of Allah, the merciful, the merciful

¹[I swear] by the mountain, ²and by the written book, ³in an open raqq,ᵃ ⁴and by the inhabited house, ⁵and by the raised ceiling, ⁶and by the thrown sea, ⁷surely the torment of your lord is imminent. ⁸There is not any who can avert it. ⁹A day the heavens will be troubled with troubling ¹⁰and the mountains will walk, walking. ¹¹So woe on that day to the deniers. ¹²Those who are engaged in sporting. ¹³A day they will be called to the fire of hell, calling, ¹⁴"This is the fire which you were denying it. ¹⁵Is this a sorcery, or do you not see? ¹⁶Roast in it; so be patient, or do not be patient. It will be the same for you, for surely you are only rewarded for what you were doing."

In the gardens the believers praise Allah for food, drink, virgins, and beautiful boys.

ᵃ scroll, non-Arabic word of Ethiopian origin

[17]Surely the fearer in gardens and bliss, [18]rejoicing in what their lord has given them, and their lord guards them from the torment of hell. [19]"Eat and drink blessedly because of what you were doing." [20]Reclining on beds arranged in rows, and we married them to hūr-eyed. [21]And those who believed and their offspring followed them in the faith. We associated their offspring with them, and we did not deprive anything from them of their work. Every man is bound by what he has earned. [22]And we aid them with fruit and meat from what they lust for. [23]They will tug a cup [of wine] from one another; there will not be any vain talk nor cause to sin. [24]And young boys will go around them as if they were covered[a] pearls. [25]And some of them came to the others, asking each other. [26]They said, "Surely we were before anxious among our families, [27]so Allah has granted to us, and he has saved us from the torment of the simoom.[b] [28]Surely we were calling on him before. Surely he is the righteous, the merciful." [29]So remind, by the grace of your lord you are not a kāhin[c] nor demon-possessed. [30]Or do they say, "A poet, let us await for him the disaster." [31]Say, "Await, so surely I am with you among the waiters." [32]Or do their dreams command them of that, or are they a rebellious people? [33]Or do they say, "You say it"?[d] Yet, they do not believe. [34]So let them bring a saying like it, if they were truthful. [35]Or had they created anything without me, or are they creators? [36]Or did they create the heavens and earth? Yet, they are not certain. [37]Or do they have the treasuries of your lord, or are they the dominators? [38]Or do they have a ladder, they hear in it? So let their listeners bring a manifest authority. [39]Or does he[e] have the daughters, and you have the sons? [40]Or do you ask for a wage from them so that they are overburdened by debt? [41]Or do they have the unseen so they write? [42]Or do they desire schemes? So those who became infidels are the schemers. [43]Or do they have a god other than Allah? Praise be to Allah above what they partner. [44]And if they see a large piece of the heavens falling down, they would say, "A dense cloud." [45]So leave them until they meet their day in which they will be thunderstruck. [46]A day their schemes will not benefit them anything, and they will not be helped. [47]And surely to those unjust ones will be a torment without that, but most of them do not know. [48]And be patient of the judgment of your lord. So surely you are in our eyes[f] and praise with your lord's praise when you stand, [49]and part of the night, so praise him, and the stars retreat.

---

[a] hidden
[b] non-Arabic word without meaning that some claim to mean the hot wind, the fire, the breath of fire, ill winds, torrent, scorching blast or wind
[c] soothsayer, non-Arabic word of Aramaic origin
[d] made it up
[e] Allah
[f] under our protection

A portion of a revelation　　　　**53**　　　　*The Star*

In the name of Allah, the merciful, the merciful

[1][I swear] by the star when it goes down, [2]your companion has not erred nor was he seduced, [3]and he does not speak out of the desire. [4]It is only a revelation that is revealed. [5]The strong in power has taught him. [6]A possessor who went by him, so he sat. [7]And he is on the highest part of the horizon. [8]Then he came near, so he came down. [9]So he was at the distance of two bows or closer. [10]So he revealed to his servant what he revealed. [11]The heart did not lie what it saw. [12]Will you dispute with him of what he saw? [13]And indeed, he also saw him[a] another time [14]near sidrat[b] the end. [15]At it is the garden of refuge. [16]When the sidrat was covered what covered, [17]his sight did not deviate nor rebel. [18]Indeed, he saw some of the big signs of his lord.

The three daughters of Allah (Al Lat, Al Ozza, and Manat) are recorded in verses 19-20. The original verses following verse 20 were: "These are the exalted cranes (intermediaries). Whose intercession is to be hoped for." Later Mohammed said that these were Satanic verses, and he replaced them with the present verses 21-23.

[19]Have you seen Al Lat and Al Ozza? [20]And another, the third one, Manat? [21]Do you have the male, and does he have the female? [22]This is an unjust division. [23]These are just names that you and your fathers named them. Allah did not send it down with authority. They only follow the conjecture and what the souls desire. And indeed, the guidance has come to them from their lord. [24]Or will the human have what he wishes? [25]So to Allah the hereafter and the first. [26]And how many of the angels in the heavens, whose intercession will not benefit anything, except after Allah has permitted it to whom he wills and pleased? [27]Surely those who do not believe in the hereafter, they will name the angels with the female names. [28]And they do not have any knowledge of it, that they are only following except the conjecture. And surely their conjecture will not benefit them anything against the truth. [29]So withdraw from who turned away from our reminder and does not desire except the world's life. [30]This is their level of knowledge. Surely your lord, he knows best of those who go astray from his way, and he knows best of those who are guided.

---

[a] Gabreel
[b] nonsense word, which some Islamic scholars claim to be a tree in the garden

[31]And to Allah what is in the heavens and what is on the earth, that he may reward those who do evil according to what they did. And he rewards those who did good, with the good.

Fornication is not complete without penetration. This is contrary to the teachings of the Bible. See Matthew 5:28.

[32]Those who avoid big sins and sexual immorality except al-lemam.[a] Surely your lord is broad in the forgiveness. He knows you best, when he produced you from the earth and when you were a fetus inside your mother's belly. So do not purify yourselves. He knows best of who feared. [33]Have you seen the one who turns away? [34]And gives a little and then withholds. [35]Does he have the knowledge of the unseen so he sees? [36]Or has he not been informed about what is in Moses' pages of writings [37]and Abraham who fulfilled? [38]That no bearer of a burden bears the burden of another. [39]And that the human will have nothing except what he strives for. [40]And that his striving will be seen. [41]Then he will reward to him the fullest reward. [42]And surely to your lord the ultimate end. [43]And that he is who makes laugh and makes weep. [44]And that he is who puts to death and gives life. [45]And that he created the pairs, the male and the female, [46]from nutfah when emitted. [47]And that on him is another creation. [48]And that he is who makes richer and suffices. [49]And that he is who is the lord of Alshary.[b] [50]And that he destroyed the first Ad, [51]and Themoud, so he did not spare. [52]And the people of Noah before, surely they were more unjust and rebellious. [53]And he destroyed Al-Mu'tafikah.[c] [54]So he covered it what he covered. [55]So which then of your lord's benefits will you dispute about? [56]This is a warner among the first warners. [57]The near drew near. [58]No one besides Allah can remove it. [59]Do you then wonder at this saying? [60]And you laugh, and you do not cry? [61]While you amuse yourselves, [62]so worship Allah and serve.

---

[a] that is everything that men can do with women without actual penetration—see interpretation of Al Qurtobi
[b] Sirius—the Dog Star, non-Arabic word of Greek origin
[c] meaningless word--Scholars erroneously claimed this to be the name of the cities of Lot, which the Bible clearly teaches were called Sodom and Gomorrah

A portion of a revelation   *The Moon*

In the name of Allah, the merciful, the merciful

Muslims claim that Mohammed divided the moon, but the infidels still would not believe. Actually, the verse does not say that Mohammed divided the moon but simply that the moon is divided. Verse 1 is actually poetry written by the poet Emra-al-Kaise who died in 540 A.D. Notice Mohammed was born in 570 A.D.

[1]The hour has approached, and the moon has been split. [2]And if they see a sign, they turn away and say, "This is a continuing sorcery." [3]And they denied and followed their own lusts, and every affair is settled. [4]And indeed, some of the news came to them, what in it is a rebuke. [5]Great wisdom, so the warning did not profit [them]. [6]So turn away from them a day the caller will call to a terrible thing. [7]Their eyes cast down, they will come forth from the graves as if they were scattered locusts. [8]They will hasten to the caller. The infidels say, "This is a difficult day."

The story of Noah's flood is copied from the Bible and corrupted once again.

[9]Before them the people of Noah denied, so they denied our servant and said, "Demon-possessed and rebuked." [10]So he called to his lord, "Surely I am overcome, so help me." [11]So we opened the doors of heaven with swift water. [12]And we caused the earth to gush springs, so the water met according to the preordained measure. [13]And we carried him on planks and nails. [14]Sailing before our eyes, a reward to who was an infidel. [15]And indeed, we left it a sign. So is there any who remember? [16]So how was my torment and my warning? [17]And indeed, we made the Qur'an easy to remember. So is there any who remember?

Short references are made again to the stories of Ad, Themoud, Lot, and Pharaoh. Notice Lot's wife did not die in this version. Also, the people of Lot are now destroyed with a violent wind rather than a rain of stones.

[18]Ad denied. So how was my torment and my warning? [19]Surely we sent a roaring wind against them in a day of continued misfortune. [20]People will be uprooted as if they were cut palm tree stumps. [21]So how was my torment and my warning? [22]And indeed, we made the Qur'an easy to remember. So is there any who

remember? [23]Themoud denied the warning. [24]So they said, "Will we follow a single human from among us? Surely then we should be in error and madness.[a] [25]Has the reminder been cast down to him from among us? Yet he is an arrogant liar." [26]Tomorrow they will know who is the arrogant, the liar! [27]Surely we will send the female camel [as] a sedition to them, so watch them and be patient. [28]And inform them that the water is shared between them, each drinks in turn. [29]So they called their companion, so he took, so he hamstrung. [30]So how was my torment and my warning? [31]Surely we sent a single shout against them, so they were like the gathered dry straw. [32]And indeed, we made the Qur'an easy to remember. So is there any who remember? [33]The people of Lot denied the warning. [34]Surely we sent a violent wind on them, except for the family of Lot. We delivered them at dawn. [35]A grace from us. Likewise, we rewarded those who gave thanks. [36]And indeed, he warned them of our severity, so they doubted the warning. [37]And indeed, they negotiated with him about his guests, so we hid their eyes. So taste my torment and my warning! [38]And indeed, in the early morning a torment rested on them. [39]So taste my torment and my warning. [40]And indeed, we made the Qur'an easy to remember. So is there any who remember? [41]And indeed, to the family of Pharaoh, there came the warners. [42]They denied all our signs. So we seized them with the seizure of a dear, mighty. [43]Are your infidels better than those? Or do you have righteousness in the scriptures? [44]Or they will say, "We are a victorious group." [45]The group will be defeated and will turn their backs. [46]Yet their appointment is to the hour, and the hour is more severe and bitter. [47]Surely the criminals are in error and madness. [48]A day they will be dragged on their faces into the fire. "Taste the touch of saqar."[b] [49]Surely we have created everything with measure. [50]And we did not command except one, as the twinkling of an eye. [51]And indeed, we destroyed your sects. So is there any who remember? [52]And everything they did is in the Zober.[c] [53]And every small and big is written down.

Although Mohammed describes the garden with many rivers throughout the Qur'an, in this verse he describes the gardens with one river.

[54]Surely the fearer is in gardens and river, [55]in the seat of truth with the mighty king.

---

[a] jinn-possessed
[b] a word invented by Mohammed, which scholars claim to mean "fire"
[c] translated throughout the Qur'an as "scriptures," but strangely, in this verse only, Muslim scholars translate as *Book of Deeds/Fate*

A portion of a revelation   **55**   *The Merciful*

In the name of Allah, the merciful, the merciful

[1]The merciful [2]taught the Qur'an, [3]created the human, [4]taught him the distinction. [5]The sun and the moon are in calculation. [6]The star and the trees worship. [7]And the heaven, he has lifted it up and set up the scale [8]that you may not rebel in the scale. [9]And perform your weighing with justice and do not stint the scale. [10]And the earth, he set it down for the creatures. [11]In it are fruit and the palm trees with buds [12]and the grain with its husk the possessor of the fragrant plants. [13]So which of the bounties of your lord will you deny? [14]He created the human from clay like the fakhkhār.[a] [15]And created the jinn from pure fire. [16]So which of the bounties of your lord will you deny? [17]Lord of the two easts and lord of the two wests. [18]So which of the bounties of your lord will you deny? [19]Run the two seas to meet. [20]Yet between them is a barrier which they do not overpass. [21]So which of the bounties of your lord will you deny? [22]From each he brings up pearls and coral. [23]So which of the bounties of your lord will you deny? [24]And to him belong the jawar[b] which are made like aālam[c] in the sea. [25]So which of the bounties of your lord will you deny? [26]All on it will perish, [27]and the face of your lord will abide the possessor of majesty and honor. [28]So which of the bounties of your lord will you deny? [29]Whoever is in the heavens and the earth asks him. Every day he is in a state. [30]So which of the bounties of your lord will you deny? [31]We will attend to you, O you al-soklan.[d] [32]So which of the bounties of your lord will you deny? [33]O you company of the jinn and the human, if you can overpass the bounds of the heavens and the earth, so then overpass them. You will not pass them except with authority. [34]So which of the bounties of your lord will you deny? [35]A fire[e] and brass are sent on you, so you will not have victory. [36]So which of the bounties of your lord will you deny? [37]So when the heavens is split, so it was like a red flower. [38]So which of the bounties of your lord will you deny? [39]So on that day neither human nor jinn will be asked about his sin. [40]So which of the bounties of your lord will you deny? [41]The criminals will be known by their marks, so they will be taken by their forelocks and their feet. [42]So which of the bounties of your lord will you deny? [43]This is hell

---

[a] potter's clay, non-Arabic word of Syriac origin
[b] running ones—Muslim scholars claim this means ships
[c] banners—Muslim scholars claim this means mountains
[d] a word without meaning—scholars claim it means human beings and jinn
[e] without smoke

which the criminals have denied it. [44]They will circle between them and anan[a] hamem. [45]So which of the bounties of your lord will you deny? [46]And to him who feared the position of his lord, two gardens. [47]So which of the bounties of your lord will you deny? [48]With branches. [49]So which of the bounties of your lord will you deny? [50]In them two flowing springs. [51]So which of the bounties of your lord will you deny?

The gardens contain furniture, fruit, and virgins.

[52]In them, two pairs of every type of fruit. [53]So which of the bounties of your lord will you deny? [54]They will recline on furniture with linings of brocade, and the fruit of the two gardens will be near. [55]So which of the bounties of your lord will you deny? [56]In them those who restrain their eyes, whom neither human nor jinn has ever had sex with before them. [57]So which of the bounties of your lord will you deny? [58]They are like the rubies and the coral. [59]So which of the bounties of your lord will you deny? [60]Will the reward of goodness, except goodness? [61]So which of the bounties of your lord will you deny? [62]And other than these, two gardens. [63]So which of the bounties of your lord will you deny? [64]Mudhamatan.[b] [65]So which of the bounties of your lord will you deny? [66]In them there are two gushing springs. [67]So which of the bounties of your lord will you deny? [68]In them are fruit and palm trees and pomegranate. [69]So which of the bounties of your lord will you deny? [70]In them, good and beautiful maidens. [71]So which of the bounties of your lord will you deny? [72]Hūr[c] confined in the khaima.[d] [73]So which of the bounties of your lord will you deny? [74]No human nor jinn has ever had sex with. [75]So which of the bounties of your lord will you deny? [76]Reclining on green cushions and superb 'abqari.[e] [77]So which of the bounties of your lord will you deny? [78]Blessed be the name of your lord, the possessor of majesty and honor.

---

[a] a word without meaning, translators have disregarded in their translations
[b] a word without meaning, scholars claim it to be dark green
[c] the ever-virgins of the gardens with white skin, large dark eyes, and large breasts
[d] tents, non-Arabic word of Abyssinian origin
[e] rich carpets, non-Arabic word of Persian origin

A portion of a revelation **56** *The Inevitable*

In the name of Allah, the merciful, the merciful

[1]When the inevitable comes to pass. [2]Of its coming there is no denying, [3]abasing, exalting. [4]When the earth will be shaken, shaking, [5]and the mountains will be crumbled, crumbling, [6]so they became scattered dust. [7]And you were three pairs. [8]So the companions on the right hand. What are the companions of the right hand? [9]And the companions on the left hand. What are the companions of the left hand? [10]And the forerunners, the forerunners.

In the gardens there will be handsome young boys and beautiful virgins for men to enjoy sexually. There will also be eating and drinking. See verses 13:35; 22:23; 39:20; 47:15; 52:20, 22; 55:56, 68; 56:17-18, 21, 36-37; 76:13, 19; 78:32; 83:23, and 88:13. This contradicts what the Bible teaches. Those in heaven will not marry or remarry, but they will be like the angels of God. See Matthew 22:30. Notice also that verses 13-14 contradict verses 56:39-40.

[11]Those are the nearest, [12]in gardens of bliss, [13]a large number from the first, [14]and few from the latter. [15]On decorated beds, [16]reclining on them, facing each other. [17]Going around them immortal young boys [18]with goblets and ibriq[a] and a cup of flowing wine. [19]They will not have a headache[b] from it nor get intoxicated. [20]And fruit from whatever they choose [21]and the meat of birds from whatever they lust for [22]and hūr-eyed, [23]they are like covered[c] pearls, [24]a reward for what they were doing. [25]They will not hear in it vain talk or sin [26]except a saying, "Peace, peace." [27]And the companion of the right hand. What are the companions of the right hand? [28]In sidrat[d] without thorns [29]and layered trees [30]and extended shade [31]and pouring water [32]and abundant fruit, [33]never failing nor forbidden, [34]and a raised furniture. [35]Surely we fashioned them fashioning, [36]so we made them ever-virgins, [37]'arūban,[e] equal in age, [38]to the companions of the right hand, [39]a group of the first, [40]and a group from the latter. [41]And the companion of the left hand. What are the companions of the left hand? [42]In hot wind and hamem [43]and in the shadow of a hot black smoke, [44]neither cool nor generous.

---

[a] jugs, non-Arabic word of Persian origin non-Arabic word of Persian origin
[b] hangover
[c] hidden
[d] nonsense word, which some Muslim scholars claim to be a tree in the garden
[e] pleasing, non-Arabic word of possible Hebrew origin

[45]Surely they were living before that in luxury, [46]and they were persisting in the great sin. [47]And they were saying, "What if we died and we were dust and bones, will we be raised? [48]Or our ancient fathers?" [49]Say, "Surely the firsts and the lasts [50]will be gathered to an appointed, known day. [51]Then surely you, O you who have gone astray, the deniers. [52]Surely you will eat from trees of Zakkoum,[a] [53]so you will fill the bellies from it, [54]so you will drink on top of it from the hamem, [55]so you will drink the drink of a hyam."[b] [56]This will be their entertainment in the judgment day. [57]We created you. So were it not that you believe. [58]Have you not seen what you emit?[c] [59]Are you the ones who created it, or are we the creators? [60]We are the ones who decree death among you, and we will not be outrun [61]in order that we may substitute another like you and fashion you in a way that you do not know. [62]And indeed, you know the first fashioning. So were it not that you remember. [63]Have you seen what you sow? [64]Are you the one who plants it, or are we the planters? [65]If we will, we would make it broken so that you would continue wondering: [66]"Surely we are burdened with a debt. [67]Yet we are deprived." [68]Have you seen the water which you drink? [69]Have you sent it down from the clouds, or are we the senders? [70]If we will, we could have made it salty. So were it not that you give thanks. [71]Have you seen the fire which you kindle? [72]Did you fashion its tree, or are we the fashioners? [73]We made it a reminder and an enjoyment to the moqoeen.[d] [74]So praise in the name of your great lord. [75]So no, I will swear by the position of the stars, [76]and surely it is a swearing, great if you knew. [77]Surely it is a generous Qur'an [78]in a sheltered book; [79]none touch it except the purified. [80]A descending from the lord of the worlds. [81]Do you compromise this discussion? [82]And you make your provision, that you are deniers. [83]So were it not that it reaches the throat. [84]And you are then looking. [85]And we are closer to him than to you, but you do not see. [86]So were it not that you were not judged. [87]Return it if you were truthful. [88]So if he was of the nearer, [89]so spirit and fragrance and garden of bliss. [90]And if he was from the companions of the right, [91]so peace to you from the companions of the right. [92]And if he was of the deniers, the strayed, [93]so a guest in hamem [94]and roasted in hell. [95]Surely this is the certain truth. [96]So praise in the name of your great lord.

---

[a] a supposed tree in hell
[b] Muslim scholars claim this to mean drinking like a thirsty camel
[c] semen
[d] non-Arabic word and the interpreter claimed it to be travelers

A portion of a revelation **The Iron**

In the name of Allah, the merciful, the merciful

[1]Praise to Allah, what is in the heavens and the earth, and he is the dear, the wise. [2]To him the kingdom of the heavens and the earth. He gives life and causes death, and he has might over all things. [3]He is the first and the last, the seen and the hidden, and he knows all things. [4]He is who created the heavens and the earth in six days, then sat on the throne. He knows what penetrates into the earth and that which comes out of it and what comes down from the heaven and what goes up in it, and he is with you wherever you are. And Allah is seeing what you do. [5]To him the kingdom of the heavens and the earth and all affairs will return to Allah. [6]He penetrates the night into the day and penetrates the day into the night, and he knows the secrets of the chests. [7]Believe in Allah and his messenger and spend out of that in which he makes you to be a successor in it. So those who believed among you and spend will have a big wage. [8]And what is [the matter] with you that you do not believe in Allah? And the messenger calls you to believe in your lord, and indeed, he took your covenant, if you were believers. [9]He is who sent down clear verses on his servant so that he may bring you out from the darkness into the light. And surely Allah is compassionate, merciful to you. [10]And what is [the matter] with you that you do not spend for the sake of Allah? And to Allah the inheritance of the heavens and the earth. It is not equal among you who spend before the conquest and engage in war, those are in a higher degree above those who spend afterwards and engage in war, and Allah has promised good to both. And Allah knows what you do. [11]Who is he that will lend to Allah a good loan, so he will double it for him and to him a generous wage?

The story of the ten virgins is copied from the Bible and corrupted. See Matthew 25:1-13.

[12]A day you will see believing men and believing women with their light beaming between their hands and in the right hand: "Today we gave you good news, gardens, below them the rivers flow, dwelling in it forever. This is the great triumph." [13]A day the hypocritical men and the hypocritical women will say to those who believed, "Wait for us. We want to borrow from your light." It was said, "Return behind you, so seek light." So a wall between them was struck, which has a door in it. Inside of it there is mercy and on the opposite side, the torment. [14]They called them, "Were we not with you?" They said,

"Yes, but you seduced yourselves. And you waited and doubted, and the false hopes deceived you until the command of Allah came. And the pride deceived you about Allah. [15]So today, no ransom will be taken from you, neither from those who became infidels. Your abode is the fire. It is now your protector, and how evil is the final place." [16]Has not the time come for those who believed to humble their hearts at the remembrance of Allah and what was sent down of the truth, and they will not become like those who have been given the book before, whose lives were prolonged, so their hearts became hardened. And most of them are transgressors. [17]Know that Allah gives life to the earth after its death. Indeed, we have made the signs clear to you, perhaps you will understand. [18]Surely the almsgiving men and the almsgiving women, and they lend to Allah a good loan. He will double it to them, and they will have a generous wage. [19]And those who believed in Allah and his messengers, those are the persons of integrity and the martyrs with their lord. They will have their wage and their light. And those who became infidels and denied our verses, those are the companions of the hell. [20]Know that the world's life is only sport and fun and an ornament and a boasting among you and the multiplying of money and children. It is like the rain which makes the infidel delight in its plants. Then it withers away, and you see them all yellowed, then they become broken. And in the hereafter there is a severe torment and forgiveness from Allah and pleasure. And what is the world's life except the enjoyment of the pride. [21]Hasten to the forgiveness from your lord, and a garden, its width like the width of the heaven and the earth, prepared for those who believed in Allah and his messengers. That is the bounty of Allah. He gives to whom he wills, and Allah is the possessor of the great bounty.

Allah causes all misfortune to come into the lives of all mankind.

[22]No misfortune befalls you on the earth nor in yourselves, except it is in a book before bara'a.[a] Surely this is easy for Allah. [23]So that you will not grieve for what you have missed nor rejoice in what he has given to you. And Allah does not love every arrogant boaster, [24]those who are stingy and command the people with stinginess, and whoever turns away. So surely Allah, he is the rich, the praised. [25]Indeed, we sent our messengers with the proofs, and we have sent down with them the book and the scale so that the people may conduct with justice. And we sent down the iron,[b] in it with strong might and benefits for the people. And Allah knows who will help him

---

[a] bring it into existence, non-Arabic word of Syriac/Aramaic origin
[b] the weapons of war to bring victory to the religion of Allah, i.e. jihad

and his messengers in secret. Surely Allah is strong, dear. [26]And indeed, we sent Noah and Abraham, and we assigned the prophethood and the book among their descendants. So some of them are guided, but most of them are transgressors.

God sent Jesus to mankind with the Gospel.

[27]Then we sent our messengers after them following in their footsteps, and we sent 'Isā, the son of Mary. And we gave him the Gospel, and we put compassion and mercy in the heart of those who followed him. And the monastic life, they invented it themselves. We did not prescribe it for them, except desiring the pleasure of Allah. But they did not shepherd it, its true shepherding. So we gave to those who believed among them their wage, and most of them are transgressors. [28]O you who have believed, fear Allah and believe in his messenger. He will give you a double portion of his mercy. And he will make light for you to walk with, and he will forgive you. And Allah is forgiving, merciful. [29]Lest the People of the Book may know that they have no control over anything from the bounty of Allah and that the bounty is in the hand of Allah. He gives it to whom he wills. And Allah is the possessor of the great bounty.

A portion of a revelation   **58**   The Disputing Woman

In the name of Allah, the merciful, the merciful

[1]Indeed, Allah has heard the words of who disputes with you concerning her husband and made her complaint to Allah, and Allah has heard your conversation. Surely Allah is hearing, seeing.

For a Muslim to take back a wife that was rejected, he must free a slave.

[2]Those among you who forbid their wives, surely they are not your mothers. Their mothers are not except those who have given them birth. And surely they are saying a detestable saying and a falsehood. And surely Allah is forgiving, pardoning. [3]And those who would forbid their wives, and then they return from what they said,[a] so freeing a neck[b] before they touch[c] each other again. This is what you preach with, and Allah is aware of what you do. [4]So whoever

---

[a] try to retract it
[b] a slave
[c] have sexual relations with

does not find,[a] so fasting two months in succession before they touch each other. So he who cannot do, so feeding sixty poor. This is that you may believe in Allah and his messenger. And those are the boundaries of Allah. And to the infidels a painful torment. [5]Surely those who oppose Allah and his messenger were abased as those who were abased before them. And indeed, we sent down clear verses, and to the infidels a shameful torment. [6]A day Allah will raise them all, so he will inform them of what they did; Allah counts it, and they forgot it. And Allah is a witness over all things. [7]Have you not seen that Allah knows what is in the heavens and what is on the earth? Three persons do not speak privately together, except he is their fourth; nor five, except he is their sixth; nor fewer nor more than that, but wherever they were, he is with them. Then, he will inform them of what they have done on the resurrection day. Surely Allah knows all things.

Mohammed was paranoid about people speaking behind his back or against him.

[8]Have you not seen those who have been forbidden the secret talk then they return to what they had been forbidden and talk privately together of sin and transgression and disobedience [toward] the messenger? And when they came to you, they greeted you but not as Allah greets you. And they say among themselves, "Were it not that Allah torments us for what we say?" Hell is sufficient for them; they will roast in it. So evil is the final place. [9]O you who have believed, when you talk privately, so do not talk privately in sin and transgression and disobedience [toward] the messenger, and talk privately in righteousness and piety. And fear Allah to whom you will be gathered. [10]Surely the private talk is only from Satan to grieve those who believed, and it will not harm them anything, except by Allah's permission. And on Allah so let the believers depend. [11]O you who have believed, when it is said to you, "Make room in your assemblies," so make room. Allah will make room for you. And when it is said to you, "Rise up,"[b] so rise up. Allah will uplift those of you who believed and those to whom the knowledge is given by degrees, and Allah is aware of what you do. [12]O you who have believed, when you go to confer in private with the messenger, so give alms before your private talk. This will be better for you and purer. So if you cannot find, so surely Allah is forgiving, merciful. [13]Do you dread not having something to give in alms before your private conference? So if you do not do it and Allah relents on you, so perform the prayer

---

[a] a captive to set free
[b] to perform jihad-holy war

and bring the legal alms and obey Allah and his messenger, and Allah is aware of what you do.

Muslims who make friends with infidels, Jews, or Christians are either not true Muslims or they are hypocrites and liars. They will burn in hell.

[14]Have you not seen those who make friends with the people with whom Allah's wrath is upon them? They are neither of your group nor of theirs. And they swear to the lie, and they know. [15]Allah has prepared a severe torment for them, surely evil is what they were doing. [16]They took their oath as a shield, so they prevented [others] from the way of Allah. So they will have a shameful torment. [17]Their money and their children will not benefit them anything against Allah. They are the companions of the fire; they will abide in it forever. [18]A day Allah will raise them all, so they swear to him as they swear to you, and they think that they are on something. But surely they are the liars. [19]Satan has taken hold of them so he caused them to forget the remembrance of Allah. Those are Satan's party. But surely Satan's party are the losers. [20]Surely those who oppose Allah and his messenger, those are among the despised. [21]Allah wrote, "I will surely be victorious and my messengers." Surely Allah is strong, dear.

Muslims cannot be friends with anyone who is disobeying Allah, even if they are their own family members.

[22]You will not find a people who believe in Allah and in the last day who will be friends to who opposes Allah and his messenger, even if they were their fathers or their sons or their brethren or their nearest relative. The faith is written in their hearts, and he supports them with a spirit from him. And he will admit them into gardens, below them the rivers flow, they will abide in it forever. Allah is pleased with them, and they are pleased with him. Those are Allah's party. Is it not surely Allah's party are the prosperous?

A portion of a revelation   **59**   *The Gathering*

In the name of Allah, the merciful, the merciful

[1]Praise to Allah, what is in the heavens and what is on the earth. And he is the dear, the wise.

Contrary to claims that Muslims did not cut trees in conquered lands, verse 5 indicates that Muslims can cut trees.

[2]He is who drives out those who became infidels from the People of the Book from their homes in the first gathering. You did not think that they would come out, and they thought that their hisoun[a] would defend them from Allah. So Allah came to them from where they did not reckon, and he cast the terror in their hearts. They demolished their houses with their hands and the hands of the believers. So take lessons, O you who are substantial of the sight. [3]And were it not that Allah had written their banishment against them, he would torment them in this world. And they have the torment of the fire in the hereafter. [4]This is because they opposed Allah and his messenger, and whoever opposes Allah, so surely Allah is severe in the punishment. [5]Whatever palm tree you cut down or leave standing on the roots, so it is by Allah's will. And he will shame the transgressors.

Allah is the one who gives the spoils to Mohammed who, in turn, doles it out to the other Muslims.

[6]And whatever Allah granted[b] to his messenger from them, you did not press forward with any horses or riding, but Allah gives authority to his messenger against whom he wills. And Allah has might over all things. [7]Whatever Allah granted to his messenger from the family of the villages, so it is to Allah and to his messenger and to his relatives and the orphan and the poor and the son of the way so that none of it may circulate among your rich. And whatever the messenger gives you, so take it. And whatever he forbids of you, so stay away from it. And fear Allah. Surely Allah is severe in the punishment. [8]To the poor and the emigrants, those who were driven from their homes and their money, seeking a bounty from Allah and his pleasure, and they are helping Allah and his messenger. Those are the truthful. [9]And those who dwelt the home and the faith before them, they love those who emigrated to them. And they will not find any need in their chests from what they have been given and prefer them over themselves, even if there was a need for it for them. And whoever protects his soul from being stingy, so those are the prosperous. [10]And those who came after them say, "Our lord, forgive us and our brethren who have preceded us in the faith and do not put hate in our hearts toward those who believed. Our lord, surely you are compassionate, merciful." [11]Have you not seen those who are hypocrites saying to their brethren who became infidels from among the People of the Book, "If you are expelled, we will surely go out with you. And we will never obey anyone who is against you, and if

---

[a] fortresses, non-Arabic word of Syriac origin
[b] spoil

war is waged against you, we will help you." And Allah is witness that they surely are liars. ^{12}If they are expelled, they would not go forth with them; and if war was waged against them, they would not help them; and if they helped them, they will turn the backs, then they will not help. ^{13}You are a greater terror in their chests than Allah. This is because they are people who do not understand. ^{14}They will not engage in war together against you except in fortress villages or from behind walls. Their valor among themselves is mighty. You may think that they are together, and their hearts are divided. This is because they surely are people who do not understand. ^{15}Like the example of those who shortly before them tasted the effect of their affairs, and for them a painful torment. ^{16}Like the example of Satan when he says to the human, "Be an infidel." So when he becomes an infidel, he says, "Surely I am innocent from you. Surely I fear Allah, the lord of the worlds." ^{17}So the end of them was that they will abide in the fire forever, and that is the reward of the unjust. ^{18}O you who have believed, fear Allah and let every soul look to what it sends on to tomorrow. And fear Allah. Surely Allah is aware of what you do. ^{19}And do not become like those who forgot Allah, so he causes them to forget themselves. Those are the transgressors. ^{20}The companions of the fire and the companions of the garden are not equal. The companions of the garden are the triumphant. ^{21}If we sent down this Qur'an on top of a mountain, you would have seen it humbled and cracked from the fear of Allah. And these are the parables that we have given to the people, perhaps they may reflect. ^{22}He is Allah. There is no god except him, the knower of the unseen and the seen. He is the merciful, the merciful. ^{23}He is Allah. There is no god except him, the king, the holy, the peace, the faithful, the guardian, the dear, the powerful, the proud. Praise be to Allah above what they partner. ^{24}He is Allah, the creator, the maker, the fashioner. To him are the excellent names. Praise to him, what is in the heavens and the earth. And he is the dear, the wise.

A portion
of a revelation

The Examined
Woman

60

In the name of Allah, the merciful, the merciful

Showing kindness to Allah's enemies is forbidden, and those who go to holy war (perform jihad) against the infidels please Allah.

[1]O you who have believed, do not take my enemy and your enemy [as] friends, showing them friendship, and indeed, they become infidels in what came to you of the truth. They drive out the messenger and yourselves that you believe in Allah your lord. If you were to go forth to perform jihad for my sake and seek my pleasure and then show them friendship privately, and I know best what you hid and what you showed. Whoever of you does this, so indeed, he has gone astray from the right way. [2]If they come on you, they will become your enemies. They will stretch forth their hands and their tongues with evil, and they desire for you to become infidels. [3]Your womb[a] and your children will not profit you on the resurrection day. He will separate between you. And Allah sees what you do.

This is more about the story of Abraham as made up by Mohammed.

[4]Indeed, there was a good example for you in Abraham and in those who were with him when they said to their people, "Surely we are innocent from you and of what you serve without Allah. We became infidels in you, and the enmity and the enduring hatred between us and you will appear forever until you believe in Allah alone." Except for the speech of Abraham to his father: "I will ask forgiveness for you, and I do not have control of anything to you from Allah." "Our lord, on you we depended and to you we turned and to you is the final return. [5]Our lord, do not make us a sedition to those who became infidels and forgive us. Our lord, surely you are the dear, the wise." [6]Indeed, there was a good example in them for you, for who was hoping in Allah and in the last day. And whoever turns away, so surely Allah is the rich, the praised. [7]Perhaps Allah will make friendship between you and those whom you take to be your enemies among them, and Allah is mighty. And Allah is forgiving, merciful. [8]Allah does not forbid you to show kindness and to deal justly with those who did not engage in war against you in the religion and who did not drive you forth from your homes. Surely Allah loves those who deal in justice.

Muslims should never make friends with those who have engaged in war against them.

[9]Surely Allah only forbids you to become friends with those who have engaged in war against you in the religion and have driven you out from your homes and helped drive you out. And who becomes friends with them, so those are the unjust.

---

[a] kinship

It is lawful for a Muslim to have sex (marry) with a believing woman who is married to a non-Muslim man, and Muslim women cannot marry non-Muslim men.

[10]O you who have believed, if believing [married] emigrant women come to you, so test them. Allah knows best their faith. So if you find they are truly believers, so then do not return them to the infidels. They are not lawful for them [infidel men], and they [the infidel men] are not lawful for them. And give them what they have spent, and it is not sin for you to have sex (marry) with them if you give them their wages. And do not hold the ties of marriage to the infidels. And ask what you have spent, and let them ask what they have spent. This is the judgment of Allah. He will judge between you. And Allah is knowing, wise. [11]And if anything of your wives has passed away from you to the infidels, then your turn comes, so give to those whose wives have gone away the like of what they have spent. And fear Allah in whom you believe. [12]O you prophet, when believing women come to you and pledge themselves that they will not partner to Allah anything and that they will not steal or commit fornication nor kill their children nor to bring any slander they forge from between their hands[a] and their legs[b] and that they will not disobey you in what is honorable, so then give them the pledge and ask the forgiveness of Allah for them. Surely Allah is forgiving, merciful. [13]O you who have believed, do not make friends with a people whom Allah's wrath is against them. Those indeed will be in despair in the hereafter, as the infidel despairs from the companions of the tombs.

A portion of a revelation   **61**   *The Ranks*

In the name of Allah, the merciful, the merciful

[1]Praise to Allah, what is in the heavens and what is on the earth. And he is the dear, the wise. [2]O you who have believed, why do you say what you do not do? [3]It is a big hatred to Allah that you say what you do not do.

Allah loves those who engage in war for his sake.

[4]Surely Allah loves those who engage in war in ranks for his sake, as if they were a solid wall. [5]And when Moses said to his people, "O my people, why do you harm me? And indeed, you know that I am a

---

[a] a foundling
[b] allege that an illegitimate child is their husband's

messenger of Allah to you." So when they deviate, Allah deviates their hearts. And Allah will not guide the transgressing people.

'Isā (the Jesus of Mohammed) came to announce the coming of Mohammed. This contradicts Jesus' prophecy that there will be many false prophets after him. See Matthew 24:11.

[6]And when 'Isā, son of Mary, said, "O children of Israel, surely I am a messenger of Allah to you, confirming what is between my hands from the Torah and to give you the good news of a messenger to come after me. His name is Ahmad."[a] So when he came to them with the proofs, they said, "This is obvious sorcery." [7]And who is more unjust than he who forged the lie against Allah when he is being invited to Islam, and Allah will not guide the unjust people. [8]They desire to extinguish the light of Allah with their mouths, and Allah will fulfill his light, even if the infidels hate it.

Islam will be victorious over all religions until it is the only religion in the world.

[9]He is who sent his messenger with the guidance and the religion of the truth so that he may make it triumph over every religion, even though the polytheists hate it. [10]O you who have believed, will I lead you to merchandise which will deliver you from the painful torment? [11]Believe in Allah and his messenger and perform jihad for the sake of Allah with your money and lives. That is the best for you, if you were knowing. [12]He will forgive your sins and will admit you into gardens, below them the rivers flow, and a good dwelling in Eden's gardens. This is the great triumph. [13]And another, that you love victory from Allah and a near conquest and give the good news to the believers. [14]O you who have believed, be the helpers of Allah as 'Isā, son of Mary, said to the Hawārīyūn, "Who is my helper with Allah?" The Hawārīyūn said, "We are the helpers of Allah." So a group from the children of Israel believed and another group became infidels. So we supported those who believed against their enemy, so they became triumphant.

---

[a] Muslims claim that Ahmad is the same name as Mohammed, which is not true, and that ' Isā, whom they claim to be Jesus, prophesied his coming

*A portion
of a revelation*   *The Friday*

In the name of Allah, the merciful, the merciful

[1]Praise to Allah, what is in the heavens and what is on the earth,
the king, the holy, the dear, the wise. [2]He is who raised a messenger
in the Gentiles from among them, who recites his verses on them
and purifies them and teaches them the book and the wisdom, and
though they were in obvious error before, [3]and others from among
them who did not join with them. And he is the dear, the wise. [4]This
is the bounty of Allah, he gives to whom he wills, and Allah is the
possessor of the great bounty. [5]The likeness of those who carry the
Torah, then they did not carry it, is like a donkey that carries asfar.[a]
Evil is the example of the people who denied the verses of Allah.
And Allah does not guide the unjust people.

**Mohammed asks, "If the Jews believe they are Allah's friends,
why do they not wish for death so they can be with him?"**

[6]Say, "O you who are Jews, if you claim that you are the friends of
Allah, without the people, then wish the death, if you were truthful!"
[7]And they will never wish for it because of what their hands have
given, and Allah knows the unjust. [8]Say, "Surely the death from
which you are fleeing so surely will meet you. Then you will be given
back to the knower of the unseen and the seen, so he will inform you
of what you were doing." [9]O you who have believed, when called to
prayer on Friday, so hasten to the remembrance of Allah and quit
your selling. This is best for you, if you were knowing. [10]So when the
prayer is ended, so spread out on the earth and seek some of Allah's
bounties and remember Allah much, perhaps you may be
prosperous. [11]And when they see merchandise or fun, they disperse
after it and leave you standing, say, "Whatever is with Allah is better
than the fun and the trading, and Allah is the best of the providers."

---

[a] large books, non-Arabic word of Aramaic origin

A portion of a revelation   **The Hypocrites**

In the name of Allah, the merciful, the merciful

[1]When the hypocrites come to you, they said, "We witness that surely you are Allah's messenger." And Allah knows surely you are his messenger, and Allah witnesses surely the hypocrites are liars. [2]They took their oath as a shield, so they prevented [others] from the way of Allah. Surely evil is what they were doing. [3]That is because they believed, then they became infidels, so it was sealed on their hearts so that they would not understand. [4]And when you see them, their bodies please you; and if they speak, then you listen to their sayings as if they are blocks of wood propped up. They think that every shout is against them. They are the enemies, so beware of them. Allah waged war against them. How perverted are they? [5]And when it is said to them, "Come, the messenger of Allah will ask forgiveness for you. They turn their heads aside. And you see them prevent [others], and they are proud." [6]It is the same for them whether you ask forgiveness for them or if you do not ask forgiveness for them, Allah will not forgive them. Surely Allah will not guide the transgressing people. [7]They are those who say, "Do not spend on those who are with the messenger of Allah until they disperse." And to Allah the treasuries of the heavens and the earth, but the hypocrites do not understand. [8]They say, "If we return to the city, the mightier will surely drive out the despised from it." And the might to Allah and his messenger and to the believers, but the hypocrites do not know. [9]O you who have believed, let not your money and your children distract you from the remembrance of Allah. And whoever does that, so those are the losers. [10]And spend from what we provided you before death comes to any one of you. So he will say, "My lord, were it not that you had delayed me to a near time, so then I will give alms, and I will be among the good." [11]And Allah will not delay a soul when its appointed time comes. And Allah is aware of what you do.

In the name of Allah, the merciful, the merciful

[1]Praise to Allah, what is in the heavens and what is on the earth. To him the kingdom and to him the praise. And he has might over all things. [2]He is who created you. So among you is an infidel, and among you is a believer. And Allah sees what you do. [3]He created the heavens and the earth with the truth, and he fashioned you, so he best fashioned you. And to him is the final return. [4]He knows what is in the heavens and the earth, and he knows what you are hiding and what you are showing. And Allah knows what is in the chests. [5]Has not the news reached you of those who became infidels before, so they tasted the evil results of their affair? And they will have a painful torment. [6]That is because when their messengers were coming to them with the proofs, so they said, "Will a human guide us?" So they became infidels and turned away. And Allah is content. And Allah is rich, praised. [7]Those who became infidels claimed that they will not be raised. Say, "Yes, [I swear] by my lord, you surely will be raised, then we will inform you of what you have done. And that is easy for Allah." [8]So believe in Allah and his messenger and in the light which we have sent down. And Allah is aware of what you do. [9]A day he will gather you to the gathering day, that is the disillusion day, and whoever believes in Allah and does good deed, he will atone for him his evils. And he will admit him into gardens, below them the rivers flow, to abide in it forever and ever. This is the great triumph. [10]And those who became infidels and denied our verses, those are the companions of the fire. They will abide in it forever, and evil is the final place. [11]No misfortune has befallen you except by Allah's permission. And whoever believes in Allah, he will guide his heart. And Allah is the knower of all things. [12]And obey Allah and obey the messenger, so if you turn away, so surely the responsibility of the messenger is only the clear delivering. [13]Allah, there is no god except him, and on Allah so let the believers depend.

A Muslim believer's family could be his enemies. Giving money to Allah helps to secure forgiveness from sins.

[14]O you who have believed, surely some of your wives and your children are an enemy to you, so beware of them. And if you pardon and ignore and forgive, so surely Allah is forgiving, merciful. [15]Surely your money and your children are only a sedition, and Allah has a great wage. [16]So fear Allah with what you can, and hear and obey and spend, best for yourselves. Whoever is saved from the

stinginess of his soul, so those are the prosperous. [17]If you lend Allah a good loan, he will double it to you and will forgive you. And Allah is thankful, forbearing. [18]Knower of the unseen and the seen, the dear, the wise.

A portion of a revelation — **65** — *The Divorce*

In the name of Allah, the merciful, the merciful

[1]O you prophet, if you[a] divorce the women, so divorce them at their prescribed[b] periods. And count the periods and fear Allah, your lord. Do not expel them from their houses, and do not expel them except if they commit a clear indecency. And those are the limits of Allah, and whoever transgresses the limits of Allah, so indeed, he has treated himself unjustly. You do not know if perhaps Allah causes some affairs to be renewed after that. [2]So when they have reached their set time, so hold them in kindness or depart from them in kindness. And take just witnesses from among you and perform the witness to Allah. Such is preached to whoever was a believer in Allah and the last day. And whoever fears Allah, he will make a way out for him [3]and will provide for him from where he did not consider. And whoever depends on Allah, so he is his sufficiency. Surely Allah fulfills his purpose. Indeed, Allah has made a measure for everything.

Muslim men may have sexual relations with their child wives, even if they have not reached the age of menstruation.

[4]And for those of your women who despair of the menstruation,[c] if you doubt [that they may be pregnant], their prescribed waiting time is three months, as well as for those who have not yet begun menstruation.[d] And as for the pregnant ones, their term is until they give birth. And whoever fears Allah, he will make his affair the easiest. [5]That is the command of Allah that he sent down to you. And whoever fears Allah, he will atone for him his evils and will make his wage great.

---

[a] all Muslims
[b] menstrual
[c] older women
[d] children

Muslims are commanded not to divorce a pregnant wife until she has had her baby. It is lawful for a man to give money to an ex-wife to breastfeed his children. All the children belong to the husband, not the wife.

[6]Settle them[a] where you settle according to your means. Do not harm them to make it difficult for them. And if they are pregnant, so spend on them until they give birth. So if they breastfeed for you, so give them their wages and consult among yourselves with kindness. And if you meet with obstacles, so then let another breastfeed him. [7]Let him who possesses an abundance give out of his abundance. And whose supply is sparse, so he gives of what Allah has provided him. Allah will not burden a soul except what he has granted to it. Allah will make ease after the difficulty. [8]And how many a village has rebelled against the command of her lord and his messenger, so then we reckon them with severe reckoning, and we tormented them with stern torment. [9]So it tasted the harmfulness of their affair, and the end of their affair was ruin. [10]Allah has prepared for them a severe torment. So fear Allah, O you people who are substantial of understanding, those who believed, indeed, Allah has sent down to you a reminder. [11]A messenger recites to you the clear verses of Allah so that he may bring out those who believed and did good deeds from the darkness to the light. And whoever believes in Allah and does good deed, he will admit him into gardens, below them the rivers flow, to abide in it forever and ever. Indeed, Allah has given him an excellent provision.

Allah created SEVEN heavens and SEVEN earths which is contrary to the Bible's three heavens (atmosphere, space, and the abode of God) and only one earth.

[12]Allah is who has created seven heavens and the same number of earths. The divine command comes down through them all so that you may know that Allah has might over all things and that Allah indeed surrounds all things in knowledge.

---

[a] ex-wives

A portion of a revelation   **The Forbidding**

In the name of Allah, the merciful, the merciful

Allah corrects Mohammed concerning his forbidding himself from further sexual relations with Mary, the Coptic woman, with whom he committed adultery.

[1]O you prophet, why do you forbid what Allah has made lawful to you, seeking to please your wives? And Allah is forgiving, merciful. [2]Indeed, Allah has allowed you to be released from your oaths. And Allah is your protector, and he is the knowing, the wise. [3]And when the prophet told a recent occurrence privately to some of his wives,[a] she then told others[b] about it.[c] And Allah informed him [of her actions]. He made known part of it and avoided other parts, so when he informed her of it, she said, "Who informed you this?" He said, "The knower, the aware informed me." [4]If you[d] repent to Allah, so indeed, your hearts are inclined. And if you bend together against him, so surely Allah is his friend and Gabreel, and all good believers and the angels after this are his backers.

Allah promises to replace bad wives with better wives and indicates that Mohammed would be justified in divorcing his wives.

[5]Perhaps his lord, if he divorces you, he will give him other wives better than you in exchange: Muslims, believers, obedient, penitent, servants, fasting, previously married, and virgins. [6]O you who have believed, save yourselves and your families from a fire whose fuel is the people and the stones. Over it are thick (harsh), strong angels. They do not disobey Allah in what he has commanded them, and they do what they are commanded. [7]O you who became infidels, do not make excuses today. Surely you will be rewarded according to what you were doing. [8]O you who have believed, repent to Allah with true repenting, perhaps your lord will atone for your evils and will admit you into gardens, below them the rivers flow, a day Allah does not shame the prophet and those who believed with him. Their light runs between their hands and in their right hands. They will say, "Our

---

[a] incorrect Arabic grammar led to this plural translation – he meant one of his wives, specifically Hafsah
[b] A'isha
[c] having an affair with Mary in Hafsah's house, on her night and in her bed
[d] the wives who were involved in the sin of talking about the affair, Hafsah and A'isha

lord, perfect our lights and forgive us, surely you have might over all things."

Allah commanded Mohammed to perform a harsh jihad against infidels and hypocrites.

[9]O you prophets, perform jihad against the infidels and hypocrites and be harsh against them. And hell will be their abode, and evil is the final place.

Mohammed corrupts the accounts of Noah, Lot, and Pharaoh. He makes the assertion that the wives of Noah and Lot were infidels while Pharaoh's wife was a believer!

[10]Allah set forth an example to those who became infidels: the woman [wife] of Noah and the woman [wife] of Lot. They were under two of our good servants, but they betrayed them. So they did not benefit them anything against Allah, and it was said, "Enter the fire with those who are entering." [11]And Allah set forth an example to those who believed, Pharaoh's woman [wife], when she said, "My lord, build me a house with you in the garden and deliver me from Pharaoh and his work and deliver me from the unjust people."

Allah's spirit impregnated the Virgin Mary. Mohammed again confuses Mary (Miriam), the daughter of Amran who was the sister of Moses and Aaron, with Mary, the mother of Jesus. Notice the name of Mary's father is Heli, not Amran. See Luke 3:23.

[12]And Mary, the daughter of Amran, who guarded her sexual parts, so we breathed into it[a] from our spirit, and she believed in the words of her lord and his books, and she was among the obedient.

A portion of a revelation   *The Kingdom*

67

In the name of Allah, the merciful, the merciful

[1]Blessed is he in whose hand is the kingdom, and he has might over all things. [2]Who created the death and the life, to test you, which of you will do better works. And he is the dear, the forgiving. [3]Who has created seven tabaq[b] of heavens. You cannot see in the creation of the merciful any disorder. So keep looking. Can you see

---

[a] her vagina
[b] stages, non-Arabic word of Akkadian origin

any flaw? [4]Then return your eyes twice. Your sight will return to you humiliated and regretful.

Stars in heaven are missiles that angels use to cast satans (demons) out of heaven. See also verses 37:6-10.

[5]And indeed, we adorned the heaven of the world with lamps[a] and made them to be missiles for the satans, and we prepared for them the torment of the blaze. [6]And to those who became infidels in their lord, the torment of hell, and evil is the final place. [7]When they will be thrown into it, they will hear its inhaling as it boils over. [8]It will almost tear from the rage. Every time a group will be thrown into it, its keepers will ask them: "Had not a warner come to you?" [9]They said, "Yes, indeed, a warner came to us, so we denied. And we said, 'Allah did not send down anything. That you are but in a big error.'" [10]And they said, "If we were listening or reasoning, we were not among the companions of the blaze." [11]So they confessed their sin, so grind out the companions of the blaze. [12]Surely those who fear their lord in secret will have forgiveness and a big wage. [13]And you hide your speech, or you reveal it. Surely he knows what is in the chests. [14]Does he who created not know? And he is the kind, the aware, [15]He is who made the earth subservient to you, so walk in its manacab[b] and eat from his provision. And to him the resurrection. [16]Do you feel secure that who is in the heaven, that he will not sink you in the earth, so then it shakes? [17]Or do you feel secure that he who is in the heaven will not send on you a violent wind, so you will know then how is my warning? [18]And indeed, those before them denied, so how was my repudiation? [19]Or have they not seen the birds above them, spreading and folding [their wings]? No one can catch them except the merciful, surely he sees everything. [20]Or who are those troops that will give you victory, without the merciful? That the infidels are not but in pride. [21]Or who is the one who will provide for you if he withholds his provisions? Yet they persist in pride and aversion. [22]Is the one who walks, groveling on his face, more guided than the one who goes upright in a straight way? [23]Say, "He is who has fashioned you and made to you the hearing and the sight and the hearts, little thanks you give." [24]Say, "He is who has multiplied you on the earth and to him you will be gathered." [25]And they will say, "When is this promise, if you were truthful?" [26]Say, "Surely the knowledge is only with Allah, and surely I am only a plain warner." [27]So when the faces of those who became infidels saw it nearby, they became sorrowful. And it was said, "This is for what you were calling." [28]Say, "Have you seen if Allah destroys me and those with

---

[a] stars
[b] a word without meaning, Muslim scholars claim to mean mountains, edges, or ways

me or has mercy on us, so who will protect the infidels from a painful torment?" [29]Say, "He is the merciful. We have believed in him, and we depended on him, so you will know who is in obvious error." [30]Say, "Have you seen that your water has gone away, so who will give you spring water?"

A portion of a revelation   *The Pen*

68

In the name of Allah, the merciful, the merciful

[1]N,[a] [I swear] by the pen and what they write. [2]You, by the grace of your lord, are not a demon-possessed. [3]And surely to you there will be an eternal wage. [4]And surely you have great morals. [5]So you will see, and they will see [6]which of you is the seditionist. [7]Surely your lord, he knows best who went astray from his way, and he knows best the guided. [8]So do not obey the deniers. [9]They desire that you anoint, so they will anoint. [10]And do not obey every shameful oath giver. [11]A despicable, going about with slander, [12]a forbidder of the good, a transgressor, sinful, [13]violent, after that a bastard, [14]if he was with money and sons. [15]When our verses are recited to him, he said, "The legends of the ancients." [16]We will brand him on the nostrils. [17]Surely we have tested them as we tested the companions of the garden when they swore that they would cut its fruit in the morning. [18]And they did not set aside a portion. [19]Then a visitation from your lord encircled them while they were asleep. [20]So it[b] became like a harvested field. [21]So they called each other in the morning: [22]"Go early to your harvest, if you were binding." [23]So they went, and they were whispering: [24]"That surely no poor will enter it to you today." [25]And they went out at daybreak with this settled purpose. [26]So when they saw it, they said, "Surely we have gone astray. [27]Yet, we are destitute." [28]The one in the middle of them said, "Have I not said to you, 'Were it not that you had praised.'" [29]They said, "Praise be to our lord. Surely we were unjust." [30]So they came to one another, blaming. [31]They said, "O woe to us, surely we were rebellious. [32]Perhaps our lord will exchange a better one than it for us. Surely we desire our lord." [33]Likewise is the torment, and the torment of the hereafter is bigger, if they were knowing. [34]Surely to the fearing, with their lord are the gardens of bliss. [35]Shall we make the Muslim like the criminal? [36]What is [the matter] with you? How do

[a] an Arabic letter without meaning
[b] the garden

you judge? [37]Or do you have a book in which you study? [38]Surely you have in it what you choose. [39]Or do you have an oath against us that reaches to the resurrection day? Surely you have whatever you judge. [40]Ask them, "Which of them will vouch for that?" [41]Or do they have partners? So let them come with their partners if they were truthful.

Worshiping Allah with his shin bared will be impossible.

[42]A day the shin [of Allah] will be made bare, and they will be called to worship, so they will not be able. [43]Their eyes will be downcast, humiliation will seize them, and indeed, they were called to worship when they were safe. [44]So leave me and who denies this saying. We will gradually draw them from where they do not know. [45]And I will wait on them, surely my scheme is firm. [46]Or do you ask a wage from them so that they are burdened with debt? [47]Or do they have the unseen, so they can write?

This is more about the story of Jonah.

[48]So be patient to the judgment of your lord, and do not be like the companion of the whale[a] when he called and he was distressed. [49]Were it not that a grace from his lord reached him, he would be cast on the naked ground while he is blamed. [50]So his lord chose him, so he made him of the good. [51]And those who became infidels would almost smite you with their eyes when they heard the reminder. And they say, "Surely he is a demon-possessed." [52]And it is not but a reminder to the worlds.

A portion of a revelation   **69**   *The Catastrophe*

In the name of Allah, the merciful, the merciful

[1]The catastrophe, [2]what is the catastrophe? [3]And what do you know, what the catastrophe is? [4]Themoud and Ad denied the calamity. [5]So as for Themoud, so they were destroyed with the rebellion. [6]And as for Ad, so they were destroyed with a roaring, violent wind. [7]He made it subservient against them continuously for seven nights and eight days, so you see the people fallen in it as if they were the trunks of hollow palm trees. [8]So did you see if any of them are left?

---

[a] Jonah

Notice that Mohammed confused Pharaoh with Noah.

[9]And Pharaoh came, and those before him and Mu'tafikah,[a] with sin. [10]So they disobeyed the messenger of their lord, so he seized them with a severe overtaking. [11]Surely when the water rebelled, we carried you in the floating [ship]. [12]So we made it for you as a reminder and that the attentive ear may comprehend it. [13]So when the trumpet blew one blowing, [14]and the earth and the mountains are carried, so they were crushed with one crush. [15]So on that day the event will come to pass. [16]And the heavens will be torn, so on that day it will be frail. [17]And the angels will be on its sides, and eight will carry the throne of the lord above them on that day. [18]On that day you will be paraded, nothing hidden will be hidden from you. [19]So as for who will be given the book in his right hand, so he will say, "Take, you read my book. [20]Surely I thought that I would meet my reckoning." [21]So he is in a pleasing life [22]in a lofty garden, [23]its fruit is near. [24]"Eat and drink pleasantly because of what you have done in the empty days." [25]And as for him who is given the book in his left hand, so he will say, "Oh, I wish that my book had never been given to me, [26]and I did not know of my reckoning. [27]Oh, I wish that it was the end of me. [28]My money has not profited me; [29]my authority has perished from me." [30]Take him, so chain him. [31]Then roast him in hell. [32]Then cast him in with a chain whose length is seventy cubits. [33]Surely he was not a believer in the great Allah. [34]And he was not careful to feed the poor. [35]So today he will not have a hamem in here, [36]nor food except for aslen,[b] [37]which none will eat except the sinners. [38]So I will not swear by what you see [39]and by what you do not see. [40]Surely it is the speech of a generous messenger.

The fact that Allah did not kill Mohammed is proof that his words were the lord's.

[41]And it is not the saying of the poet, little is what you believe. [42]And it is not the saying of the soothsayer, little is what you remember. [43]A descending from the lord of the worlds. [44]And if he had forged some words against us, [45]then we would have taken him by the right hand. [46]Then we would have cut the jugular vein out of him. [47]So none of you could have restrained him. [48]And surely it is a reminder to the fearer. [49]And surely we know that some among you are deniers. [50]And surely it is a regret on the infidels. [51]And surely it is the certain truth. [52]So praise in the name of your great lord.

---

[a] meaningless word—Scholars erroneously claimed this to be the name of the cities of Lot which the Bible clearly teaches were called Sodom and Gomorrah.
[b] a word without meaning

A portion of a revelation

70

The Ways of Ascent

In the name of Allah, the merciful, the merciful

[1]A questioner asked about a falling torment [2]to the infidels, no one can avert it [3]from Allah, the lord of the ways of ascent.

The distance from heaven to earth for a traveling angel is 50,000 years.

[4]The angels and the spirit ascend to him in a day; its duration was fifty thousand years. [5]So be patient in a beautiful patience. [6]Surely they see it afar. [7]And we see it near. [8]A day the heavens will become like molten metal [9]and the mountains will become like wool. [10]And no hamem will be able to ask a hamem. [11]They will be made to see each other. And the criminal will desire to redeem himself from the torment on that day by his sons [12]and with his female companion and his brother [13]and of his relatives who shelter him [14]and who are on the earth together, then he delivers him. [15]Certainly not, surely it will be a flame, [16]stripped to roast. [17]It calls the one who has turned his back and retreated [18]and gathered, so kept it. [19]Surely the human was created an anxious. [20]When evil touches him, [he becomes] fretful; [21]and when good touches him, [he becomes] greedy. [22]Except those praying, [23]those that are consistent in their prayers, [24]and those who of their money there is a known portion [25]for the beggar and the destitute. [26]And those who believe in the judgment day, [27]and those who are fearful from the torment of their lord, [28]surely the torment of their lord cannot be secure.[a]

Sex must be limited to Muslims' spouses, slaves, and concubines. Salvation is earned by performing good deeds. This contradicts the Bible which declares that salvation is the free gift of God, not as a result of good deeds. See Ephesians 2:8-9.

[29]and those who keep their private parts (maintain their chastity), [30]except from their wives or from what their right hands possess, so surely they are not blamed. [31]So whoever desires to go beyond that, so those are the transgressors. [32]And those who are shepherded to their trusts and covenants, [33]and those who stand by their testimony, [34]and those who keep their prayers, [35]those are honored in gardens. [36]So why are those who became infidels who were before them

---

[a] averted

hastening, [37]on the right and on the left, in bands? [38]Does every one of them long to enter a garden of bliss? [39]Certainly not, surely we created them from what they know. [40]So I will not swear by the lord of the easts and of the wests. Surely we are able [41]to replace them with a better one than them, and we will not be outrun. [42]So leave them to engage and sport until they meet their day which they are promised. [43]A day they will come forth out of their graves in haste like they are rallying to a standard, [44]their eyes will be downcast, humiliation will cover them. This is the day they were promised.

A portion of a revelation   71   *Noah*

In the name of Allah, the merciful, the merciful

The story of Noah is copied from the Bible and corrupted once again.

[1]Surely we sent Noah to his people: "That warn your people before a painful torment comes to them." [2]He said, "O my people, surely I am to you a plain warner. [3]That serve Allah and fear him and obey me. [4]He will forgive you some of your sin, and he will delay you to an appointed time. Surely when the appointed time of Allah comes, it will not be delayed, if you were knowing." [5]He said, "My lord, surely I have called my people night and day. [6]So my call did not increase them except flight. [7]And surely whenever I called them so that you may forgive them, they put their fingers in their ears and covered themselves with their clothes and persisted, and they were proudly proud. [8]Then surely I called to them publicly. [9]Then surely I announced to them, and secretly I gave them secrets. [10]So I said, 'Ask forgiveness of your lord, surely he was forgiving. [11]He will send the heavens above you with abundance.[a] [12]And he will aid you with money and sons, and he will make gardens for you and will make rivers for you. [13]What is [the matter] with you that you do not hope to Allah a reverence, [14]and indeed, he created you in stages? [15]Have you not seen how Allah created seven heavens one above another?

The moon produces light of its own; this is a scientific error.

[16]And he made the moon in them[b] light, and he made the sun a lamp. [17]And Allah planted you from the earth plants. [18]Then he will

---

[a] rain
[b] the seven heavens

return you into it[a] and bring you forth a bringing forth. [19]And Allah spread the earth out for you [20]so that you may walk in it along spacious ways.'" [21]Noah said, "My lord, surely they disobeyed me, and they followed those who did not increase him their money and son except in loss. [22]And they deceived a big deception. [23]And they said, 'Do not forsake your gods and do not forsake Wadd nor Sowah nor Yaghuth and Yahuk and Nasr.'[b] [24]And indeed, they led many astray. And [my lord], do not increase the unjust except in error." [25]Because of their sins they were drowned, so they were admitted into the fire, and they did not find for themselves a helper without Allah. [26]And Noah said, "My lord, do not leave any infidel dwellers on the earth. [27]Surely if you leave them, they will lead your servant astray, and they will not beget except wicked infidel. [28]My lord, forgive me and my parents and believers who enter my house and the believing men and believing women, and do not increase the unjust except in destruction."

A portion of a revelation   *The Jinn*

In the name of Allah, the merciful, the merciful

Some of the jinn are Muslim believers.

[1]Say, "It was revealed to me that a company of the jinn listened, so they said, 'Surely we have heard a wonderful Qur'an. [2]It guides to the right way, so we believed in it, and we will not partner anyone with our lord.

God has no wife or son. Mohammed's limited understanding of God's nature, as revealed in the Bible, caused him to reach an erroneous conclusion: that this was a literal, earthly type of father-son relationship, one conceived of a physical union.

[3]And that he is exalted much, our lord did not take a female companion nor a son. [4]And that our fool was saying a transgression against Allah. [5]And that we thought that the human and the jinn would not speak any lie against Allah. [6]And that some men of the humans had sought refuge with some men of the jinn, so they increased them in perversion. [7]And that they thought, as you thought, that Allah will not raise anyone. [8]And that we touched the

---

[a] the earth
[b] some scholars state that these are pagan Arab gods.

heaven, so we found it to be filled with strong guards and flames. [9]And that we used to sit in seats by it for listening, so whoever listens now will find to himself a flaming guard. [10]And we do not know whether their lord means evil for those on the earth or whether he means to bring guidance to them. [11]And that among us are the righteous, and among us others than that. We are groups following different ways. [12]And that we thought that we cannot hinder Allah on the earth, and we cannot hinder him [by] escaping. [13]And that when we heard the guidance, we believed in it. So whoever believes in his lord, so he will fear neither stinginess nor perversion. [14]And that some of us are Muslims, and some of us are deviators.' So whoever becomes Muslim, so those are aimed to the right way." [15]And as for the deviators, so they were sticks[a] for hell. [16]And that if they went straight on the way, we will surely give them abundant water to drink [17]so that we seduced them in it. And whoever turns away from the remembrance of his lord, he will make him to enter increasing torment. [18]And that the mosques are to Allah, so do not call upon anyone with Allah. [19]And that, when the servant of Allah stood up calling on him, they were almost crowding against him.

Believers cannot partner any being with Allah, whether it is 'Isā (the Jesus of Mohammed) or any other.

[20]Say, "Surely I only call on my lord, and I will not partner with him anyone." [21]Say, "I surely do not have for you harm or guidance." [22]Say, "Surely no one can protect me against Allah, and I will not find any refuge without him [23]except a deliverance from Allah and his messages. And whoever disobeys Allah and his messenger, so surely for him the fire of hell. They abide in it forever and ever." [24]Until when they saw what they are promised, so they will know who is a weaker helper and fewer in number. [25]Say, "That I do not know if what you are promised is near or whether my lord will appoint for it a time. [26]The knower of the unseen, so he will not reveal his unseen to anyone, [27]except for the pleasing messenger, so surely he will march guards between his hands and from behind him, [28]so that indeed he may know that they delivered the messages of their lord. And he surrounds all that they have, and he counts everything in number."

---

[a] firewood

A portion of a revelation · **The Wrapped** · **73**

In the name of Allah, the merciful, the merciful

Muslims used to wrap Mohammed at the time of his receiving the revelation.

[1]O you who wrapped, [2]stand up the night except for a little while, [3]half of it or a little less than that [4]or increase more to it, and chant the Qur'an, chanting. [5]Surely we will cast on you with heavy words. [6]Surely rising at night is the firmest way to tread and the most effective for speech. [7]Surely you will have long occupations in the daytime. [8]And remember the name of your lord and devote to him, devotion. [9]The lord of the east and the west, there is no god except him, so take him a guardian. [10]And be patient about what they say, and emigrate from them in a beautiful emigration. [11]And leave me and the deniers, the possessors of the grace, and bear with them for a little [while]. [12]Surely we have with us a severe punishment and hell [13]and food that chokes and a painful torment. [14]A day the earth and the mountains will quake, and the mountains will become a loose sand heap. [15]Surely we have sent to you a messenger, a witness against you, as we sent a messenger to Pharaoh. [16]So Pharaoh disobeyed the messenger, so we seized him in a violent seizure. [17]So how can you fear, if you become infidels, a day that will turn children gray-headed. [18]The heaven will be rent asunder by it, and his promise was done. [19]Surely this is a reminder so that whoever wishes takes a way to his lord. [20]Surely your lord knows that you are standing nearly two-thirds of the night and half of it and a third of it, as do a group of those who are with you. And Allah measures the night and the day. He knows that you will not count it. So he relents toward you, so read what is easy for you from the Qur'an. He knows that there will be those who are sick among you while others travel through the earth seeking the bounty of Allah and others engaging in war for the sake of Allah. So read what is easy from it. And perform the prayer and bring the legal alms and lend Allah a good loan. And whatever good deeds you send on before for your own souls, you will find them with Allah. He is better and greater in wage. And ask forgiveness of Allah. Surely Allah is forgiving, merciful.

A portion of a revelation   *The Cloaked*

In the name of Allah, the merciful, the merciful

Muslims used to cloak Mohammed at the time of his receiving the revelation.

[1]O you who are cloaked, [2]stand up, so warn, [3]and your lord so magnify. [4]And your clothes so purify, [5]and the wrath so emigrate. [6]And do not give for increase, [7]and to your lord, so be patient. [8]So that when the trumpet will be blown, [9]so this on that day, a difficult day, [10]it will not be easy against the infidels. [11]Leave me alone with whom I have created. [12]And I have made abundant money to him, [13]and sons as witnesses, [14]and I flattened for him, flattening. [15]Then he hopes that I increase. [16]Certainly not, surely he was in opposition to our verses. [17]I will exhaust him increasingly. [18]Surely he thought and determined! [19]So he was killed how he determined! [20]Then he was killed how he determined! [21]Then he looked, [22]then he frowned and scowled, [23]then he turned away and became proud. [24]So he said, "This is nothing except a sorcery effect. [25]This is nothing except the word of the human." [26]I will roast him in saqar. [27]And do you know what is saqar? [28]It will not endure, and it will not spare. [29]It scorches the humans. [30]Over it are nineteen. [31]And we did not make the companions of the fire, except angels, and we did not make their numbers except a sedition for those who became infidels so that those who have been given the book may become certain and those who believed will increase in faith. And that those who have been given the book and the believers will not doubt. And so those who have a sickness in their hearts, and the infidels will say, "What does Allah mean in this parable?" Likewise, Allah leads astray whom he wills and guides whom he wills. And no one knows the troops of your lord except him. And it is but a reminder to humans. [32]Certainly not, and [I swear] by the moon [33]and by the night when it retreats [34]and by the morning when it brightens. [35]Surely it is one of the biggest, [36]a warning to the humans, [37]to whomever among you wishes to go forward or to delay. [38]Every soul is hostage to what it has earned, [39]except for the companions of the right hand, [40]in gardens they will ask each other [41]about the criminals: [42]"What brought you into saqar?" [43]They said, "We were not among those who prayed [44]and we did not feed the poor [45]and we were engaging with those who engaged [46]and we were denying the judgment day, [47]until the inevitable came on us." [48]So the intercession of the intercessors will not benefit them. [49]So what is [the matter] with them that they are turning away from the reminder [50]as if they were frightened donkeys

⁵¹running from a lion? ⁵²Yet, every human among them desires that he would be given open pages of writings. ⁵³Certainly not, yet, they do not fear the hereafter. ⁵⁴Certainly not, surely it is a reminder. ⁵⁵So whoever will, remember it. ⁵⁶And they will not remember except as Allah wills. He is worthy of the piety and worthy of the forgiveness.

A portion of a revelation   *The Resurrection*

75

In the name of Allah, the merciful, the merciful

¹I will not swear by the resurrection day. ²And I will not swear by the accusing soul.

The resurrection of the dry bones is copied from the Bible and corrupted. See Ezekiel 37: 1-14.

³Does the human think that we will not gather his bones? ⁴Yes, we are able to make him a complete body. ⁵Yet, the human desires to perform wicked sins before him. ⁶He asks, "When is the resurrection day?" ⁷So when the sight dazzled, ⁸and the moon eclipsed, ⁹and the sun and the moon are gathered. ¹⁰The human will say on that day, "Where is the escape?" ¹¹Certainly not, there is no refuge. ¹²To your lord on that day will be the final destiny. ¹³The human will be informed on that day of what he sent before and what he delayed. ¹⁴Yet, the human will be evidence against himself, ¹⁵and though he gives his excuses.

Mohammed used to hasten the recitation of the Qur'an at the time of receiving it.

¹⁶Do not move by it your tongue so that you may hasten it. ¹⁷Surely its collection and its reciting is on us. ¹⁸So when we recite it, so then follow its recitation. ¹⁹Then, surely on us its clarification. ²⁰Certainly not, yet you love the haste, ²¹and you neglect the hereafter. ²²Faces on that day will be bright, ²³looking to their lord. ²⁴And faces on that day will be dismal, ²⁵thinking that great disaster will be done to them. ²⁶Certainly not, when it reaches their collar bone ²⁷and it is said, "Who is a healer?" ²⁸And he thought that it is the departure, ²⁹and one leg is twisted around another leg. ³⁰To your lord on that day is the driving. ³¹So he did not believe, and he did not pray. ³²But he denied and turned away. ³³Then he went to his family walking with haughtiness. ³⁴It is closer to you, so closer. ³⁵Then it is closer to you, so closer. ³⁶Does the human think that he will be left in

vain? [37]Was he not a nutfah, money[a] emitted forth? [38]Then he was
a clot, so he was created, so he was fashioned. [39]So he made from
him the two pairs, the male and the female. [40]Is not that able to give
life to the dead?

*A portion
of a revelation*   *The Human*

In the name of Allah, the merciful, the merciful

[1]Has there come a period of time when the human was not
anything to be remembered? [2]Surely we created the human from
nutfah amshāj.[b] We test him, so we made him hearing, seeing.
[3]Surely we guided him the way, either as thankful or infidel. [4]Surely
we prepare chains and shackles and a blaze for the infidels. [5]Surely
the righteous will drink from a cup; its mixture was with kafure.[c] [6]A
spring that Allah's servants will drink from, making it gush, gushing.
[7]They fulfilled their vows, and they feared a day whose evil was
widespread. [8]And they fed the food, in spite of their love for it, [to] a
poor and an orphaned and a captive. [9]"Surely we only feed you for
the face of Allah. We do not desire a reward or thanks from you.
[10]Surely we fear a difficult, distressful day from our lord."

**In the gardens of Paradise, there will be bridal couches, perfect
weather, and blooming youth.**

[11]So Allah guarded them from the evil of that day and met them
with brightness and happiness. [12]And he rewarded them, because of
their patience, with gardens and silk. [13]Reclining on the couches,
they will not see in it sun nor intense cold. [14]And its shade is close to
them, and its fruit drops near and nearer. [15]Pass around to them with
vessels of silver and goblets were of glass, [16]glasses of silver; they
measured it, measuring. [17]And they will be made to drink from a cup;
its mixture was with zanjabīl,[d] [18]there is a spring there named
Salsabilan. [19]And going around them will be immortal young boys.
When you see them, you will think that they are scattered pearls.
[20]And if you see, then you will see bliss and a big kingdom. [21]On
them will be garments of fine green silk and brocade, with silver

---

[a] a word without meaning, some scholars claim to be sperm or semen. In this
sentence it reiterates Mohammed's claim that nutfah is the two sexual discharges. All
Muslim translators disregard this word.
[b] mingled, non-Arabic word of Syriac origin
[c] camphor, non-Arabic word of Berber/Syriac origin
[d] ginger, non-Arabic word of Sanskrit origin

bracelets. And their lord gives them a drink of pure drink. ²²Surely this was a reward for you, and your effort was appreciated. ²³Surely we send down the Qur'an on you, descending. ²⁴So be patient to the judgment of your lord and do not obey any of them, an evil or infidel. ²⁵And remember the name of your lord morning and evening, ²⁶and some of the night so worship him and praise him all night long. ²⁷Surely those love the fleeting, and they leave behind them a heavy day. ²⁸We created them, and we made their frames strong. And if we will, we could change like them, changing. ²⁹Surely this is a reminder, so whoever wills, let him take to his lord a way. ³⁰And you do not desire it, but only if Allah wills. Surely Allah was knowing, wise. ³¹He will admit whom he wills into his mercy, and the unjust, he prepares for them a painful torment.

A portion of a revelation   **77**   *The Dispatched*

In the name of Allah, the merciful, the merciful

¹[I swear] by the dispatched in succession, ²so the swift in their swiftness, ³and the scatterers who scatter. ⁴So the separators, separating. ⁵So those that give the reminder ⁶to excuse or to warn. ⁷Surely that which you have been promised is imminent. ⁸So, when the stars are hidden ⁹and when the heavens will be cracked ¹⁰and when the mountains are blasted ¹¹and when the messengers are gathered. ¹²To which day has it been postponed? ¹³To the decision day. ¹⁴And what do you know of the decision day? ¹⁵Woe on that day to the deniers! ¹⁶Have we not destroyed the ancients? ¹⁷Then we caused others to follow them. ¹⁸Likewise, we deal with the criminals. ¹⁹Woe on that day to the deniers! ²⁰Have we not created you from worthless water? ²¹So we placed it in a secure place ²²to a known estimation. ²³So we estimated, so bless the estimators! ²⁴Woe on that day to the deniers! ²⁵Have we not made the earth a gathering place, ²⁶the living and the dead, ²⁷and made the tall stabilizers on it and gave you fresh sweet river water to drink? ²⁸Woe on that day to the deniers! ²⁹Go then to that which you were denying. ³⁰Go to the shadows that cover in three branches. ³¹No shade, and it will not prevail from the flame. ³²Surely it sends out sparks as a castle ³³like yellow camels. ³⁴Woe on that day to the deniers! ³⁵This day they will not speak, ³⁶and they will not give permission to them to apologize. ³⁷Woe on that day to the deniers! ³⁸This is the decision day, we gathered you and the ancients. ³⁹So, if there was a scheme for you,

so scheme against me. ⁴⁰Woe on that day to the deniers! ⁴¹Surely the fearer will be in the shades and springs, ⁴²and fruit from whatever they lust for. ⁴³"Eat and drink pleasantly because of what you were doing." ⁴⁴Surely, likewise, we reward the doers of good. ⁴⁵Woe on that day to the deniers! ⁴⁶Eat and enjoy a little, surely you are criminals. ⁴⁷Woe on that day to the deniers! ⁴⁸And when it was said to them, "Kneel." They did not kneel. ⁴⁹Woe on that day to the deniers! ⁵⁰So what other speech after it will they believe in?

A portion of a revelation   *The News*

78

In the name of Allah, the merciful, the merciful

¹What are they asking each other? ²About the great news ³which they are disagreeing with. ⁴Certainly not, they will know. ⁵Then certainly not, they will know. ⁶Have we not made the earth flat? ⁷And the mountains pegs? ⁸And created you pairs? ⁹And made your sleep resting? ¹⁰And made the night clothes? ¹¹And made the day for livelihood? ¹²And built seven strong above you? ¹³And made a shining lamp? ¹⁴And sent down abundant water from the clouds? ¹⁵To bring forth by it grains and plants? ¹⁶And gardens are intertwined? ¹⁷Surely the decision day was appointed. ¹⁸A day the trumpet is blown, so then you will come in crowds. ¹⁹And the heavens opened so it was doors. ²⁰And the mountains walked away so it was a mirage. ²¹Surely hell was a place of snares, ²²a refuge for the rebellious, ²³tarrying in it for ages. ²⁴They will not taste in it cold nor drink, ²⁵only hamem and oozing pus, ²⁶an exact reward. ²⁷Surely they were not hoping, reckoning, ²⁸and they deny our verses, denying. ²⁹And everything we counted a book. ³⁰"So taste, so we will not increase you except torment."

The gardens are filled with large-breasted women and wine.

³¹Surely to the fearing ones triumph, ³²gardens and vineyards, ³³and women of equal age with large breasts, ³⁴and a cup dihāqan.ᵃ ³⁵They will not hear in it vain discourse nor lies. ³⁶A reward from your lord, a reckoning gift. ³⁷The lord of the heavens and the earth and what is between them. The merciful, they will not possess the ability to speak with him. ³⁸A day the spirit and the angels stand in ranks, they will not speak, except those whom the merciful permitted and spoke truth. ³⁹This is the true day. So whoever wishes will return to

---

ᵃ filled, non-Arabic word of Mesopotamian origin

his lord penitently. [40]Surely we warned you a near torment, a day a man looks to what his hands have done, and the infidel will say, "Oh, I wish that I was dust."

A portion of a revelation   **The Snatchers**
79

In the name of Allah, the merciful, the merciful

[1][I swear] by those who snatch with strength, [2]and by those who draw gently, [3]and by those who glide smoothly, [4]so those forerunners being ahead, [5]so those who govern the affair. [6]A day the quaking will quake. [7]It will be followed by a blast. [8]Hearts will quake on that day. [9]Their gazes will be downcast. [10]They will say, "Shall we return to the first condition? [11]What if we were rotten bones?" [12]They said, "This is a lost return." [13]So surely it is only a single rebuke.[a] [14]So then they will be awakened.

The story of Moses and Pharaoh is copied from the Bible and corrupted once again. Notice the clear judgment of Allah on Pharaoh. Also, notice in verse 30 the earth is flat.

[15]Have the sayings of Moses come to you? [16]When his lord called him in the holy valley of Tuwa. [17]"Go to Pharaoh, surely he has rebelled." [18]So say, "Would you become purified, [19]and I guide you to your lord so that you may fear?" [20]So he showed him the big sign. [21]So he denied and disobeyed. [22]Then he turned back, striving. [23]So he gathered, so he called. [24]So he said, "I am your lord, the highest." [25]So Allah seized him with the punishment of the hereafter and of the first. [26]Surely in this is a lesson to him who fears. [27]Are you a stronger creation, or the heavens he built? [28]He raised its height, so he leveled it. [29]And he gave darkness to its night and brought forth its light. [30]And after that, he flattened the earth. [31]He brought out from it its waters and its pastures [32]and the mountains he established [33]an enjoyment to you and your livestock. [34]So when the big calamity comes, [35]a day the human will remember what he strove. [36]And hell went forth to whoever sees. [37]So, as for who has rebelled [38]and has chosen the world's life, [39]so surely hell will be the refuge.

---

[a] shout

Heaven is the reward to those who fear Allah and do not lust. This contradicts verse 4:24. Also, see verses 33:50; 55:72, 74, 76...

⁴⁰And as for those who fear the position of his lord and restrained their souls from the lust, ⁴¹so surely the garden will be their refuge. ⁴²They ask you about the hour: "When will it come to port?" ⁴³But what memory do you have of it? ⁴⁴To your lord is its end. ⁴⁵Surely you are only a warner who fears it. ⁴⁶A day they see it, it is like they have only stayed but a night or an afternoon.

A portion of a revelation   **80**   *He Frowned*

In the name of Allah, the merciful, the merciful

Mohammed ignored a blind man but gave attention to a wealthy man.

¹He frowned and turned away ²when the blind man came to him. ³And what do you know? Perhaps he will be purified. ⁴Or he will be reminded, so the reminder will profit him. ⁵But as for him who is self-sufficient,ᵃ ⁶so to him you have given all of your attention. ⁷And it is not your concern if he is not purified. ⁸And as for him who came to you striving, ⁹and while he is fearing, ¹⁰so you distracted yourself from him. ¹¹Certainly not, surely this is a reminder. ¹²So whoever wishes will remember it ¹³in honored pages of writings, ¹⁴lifted up, purified, ¹⁵by the hands of safara,ᵇ ¹⁶noble, righteous. ¹⁷Killed is the human. There is no one more infidel than he. ¹⁸From what thing did he create him? ¹⁹He created him from nutfah, so he estimated him. ²⁰Then he made his way easy. ²¹Then he caused him to die, so he buried him. ²²Then, if he wills, he raises him to life. ²³Certainly not, but he did not fulfill what he commanded him. ²⁴So let the human look at his food. ²⁵We pour out the water, pouring. ²⁶Then we crack the earth, cracking. ²⁷So we grew in it grain ²⁸and grapes and clover ²⁹and the olives and the palm trees ³⁰and abundant gardens ³¹and fruit and abb.ᶜ ³²Enjoyment for you and for your livestock. ³³So when the deafening shout comes, ³⁴a day the man will flee from his brother ³⁵and his mother and his father ³⁶and his female companion and his

---

ᵃ wealthy
ᵇ scribes, non-Arabic word of Syriac origin
ᶜ herbage, non-Arabic word of Berber/ Syriac origin

sons. ³⁷To each man on that day his own concerns will be sufficient.
³⁸And faces on that day will be bright, ³⁹laughing, giving good news.
⁴⁰And faces on that day will be with dust on them, ⁴¹darkness will
cover them. ⁴²Those are the infidels, the wicked.

A portion of a revelation   **81**   *The Rolling Up*

In the name of Allah, the merciful, the merciful

¹When the sun is rolled up ²and when the stars are falling down
³and when the mountains are moved ⁴and when the pregnant ones
are stopped ⁵and when the wild beasts are gathered ⁶and when the
seas are thrown ⁷and when their souls are paired ⁸and when the
female[a] who was buried alive is asked: ⁹"For what sin was she
killed?" ¹⁰And when the pages of writings are opened ¹¹and when the
heaven is scraped off ¹²and when the hell is set ablaze ¹³and when
the garden draws near, ¹⁴a soul knew what it had brought forth. ¹⁵So
I will not swear by the planets ¹⁶which move, then hide, ¹⁷and the
night when it darkens ¹⁸and the dawn when it breathes,[b] ¹⁹surely it is
the word of a generous messenger, ²⁰the possessor of power, with
the high throne, ²¹obeyed, then trustworthy.

**Mohammed clearly declared that the Qur'an is not the words of
the Devil.**

²²And your companion is not a demon-possessed. ²³And indeed,
he saw him[c] in the clear horizon. ²⁴And he is not withholding anything
about the unseen. ²⁵And it is not the words of a stoned Satan. ²⁶So
where are you going? ²⁷This is nothing but a reminder to the worlds,
²⁸to those among you who will to go straight. ²⁹And you will not will,
except if Allah, the lord of the worlds, wills.

---

[a] child who was buried alive, an ancient Arab, pagan practice
[b] becomes bright
[c] the angel Gabreel

A portion of a revelation   **The Cleaving**

In the name of Allah, the merciful, the merciful

[1]When the heavens will cleave asunder [2]and when the planets will disperse [3]and when the seas will explode [4]and when the graves will be strewn around, [5]every soul will know what it has advanced and what it has delayed. [6]O you the human, what makes you proud against your generous lord? [7]Who created you, so he molded you, so he shaped you in the right form. [8]In whichever form he willed, he put you together. [9]Certainly not, yet you denied by the judgment day. [10]And surely we are keepers over you, [11]generous writers. [12]They know what you are doing. [13]Surely the righteous are in bliss. [14]And surely the wicked are in hell. [15]They will roast in it on the judgment day, [16]and they will never be absent from it. [17]And what do you know, what is the judgment day? [18]Then, what do you know, what is the judgment day? [19]A day no soul will have anything for another soul, and the affair on that day will be to Allah.

A portion of a revelation   **The Cheaters**

In the name of Allah, the merciful, the merciful

[1]Woe to the cheaters! [2]Those who, if they measure from people, they take it in full. [3]And when they measure or weigh for them, they cause them loss. [4]Do they not think that they will surely be raised [5]to a great day, [6]a day the people stand before the lord of the worlds? [7]Certainly not, surely the book of the wicked, it will be in sijjīn.[a] [8]And what, do you know what the sijjīn is? [9]A written book. [10]Woe on that day to the deniers, [11]those who have denied the judgment day. [12]And no one will deny it except every sinful transgressor. [13]When our verses are recited to him, he said, "The legends of the ancients." [14]Certainly not, yet their hearts have been hardened by what they were earning. [15]Certainly not, surely they will be banned from their lord on that day. [16]Then surely they will roast in hell. [17]Then it will be said to them, "This is what you were denying it." [18]Certainly not,

---

[a] non-Arabic word, either of Persian origin and meaning clay tablet, or a word invented by Mohammed

surely the book of the righteous is in 'illīyūn.[a] [19]And what do you know what 'illīyūn is? [20]A written book. [21]Witnessed by the nearest. [22]Surely the righteous are in bliss, [23]on couches gazing. [24]You will recognize on their faces the brightening of the bliss.

Muslims will enjoy the finest wines in the gardens.

[25]They will be given drink from sealed rahīq.[b] [26]Its seal will be of musk and in that so let the competitors compete. [27]And its mixture will be with Tasnim, [28]a spring drink by it the nearer. [29]Surely those who were criminals, they were laughing at those who believed. [30]And when they passed by them, they were winking. [31]And when they returned to their families, they would return with jesting. [32]And when they saw them, they said, "Surely these are who strayed." [33]And they were not sent [as] keepers over them. [34]So today, those who believed will laugh at the infidels, [35]on the couches they will gaze. [36]Is the reward of the infidels what they were doing?

A portion of a revelation   **84**   *The Splitting*

In the name of Allah, the merciful, the merciful

[1]When the heaven splits [2]and listens to its lord and it is fulfilled. [3]And when the earth is expanded [4]and casts out what is in it and it becomes empty [5]and listens to its lord and it was fulfilled. [6]O you the human, surely you strive to your lord, striving so you will meet him. [7]So as for who is given his book in his right hand, [8]so he will be judged with an easy judgment, [9]and he will return pleased to his family. [10]And as for who is given his book from behind his back, [11]so he will call perdition, [12]and he will roast in a blaze. [13]Surely he was happy among his family. [14]Surely he thought that he would never return. [15]Yes, surely his lord was watching him. [16]So I will not swear by the twilight [17]and the night and what it gathers [18]and the moon when it is full, [19]and you surely mount stage by stage. [20]So why do they not believe? [21]And when the Qur'an is recited to them, they do not worship. [22]Yet, those who became infidels deny. [23]And Allah knows what they keep. [24]So give them the good news of a painful torment. [25]Except for those who believed and did good deeds, they will have an unending wage.

---

[a] higher or upper chambers, non-Arabic word of Hebrew origin
[b] strong wine, non-Arabic word of Aramaic/Syriac origin

A portion of a revelation   **85**   *The Constellations*

In the name of Allah, the merciful, the merciful

[1][I swear] by the heaven with the constellations [2]and by the promised day [3]and by the witness and the witnessed. [4]Killed are the companions of the moat, [5]the fire with the fuel. [6]When they sat in it, [7]and they were witnesses of what they did to the believers. [8]And they did not take vengeance on them, except that they may believe in Allah, the dear, the praised. [9]To whom the kingdom of the heavens and the earth, and Allah is witness over all things. [10]Surely those who seduced the believing men and believing women, then they did not repent. So for them is the torment of hell and for them is the torment of the fire. [11]Surely those who believed and did good deeds, they will have gardens, below them the rivers flow. This is the big triumph. [12]Surely the vengeance of your lord is severe. [13]Surely he begins and repeats. [14]And he is the forgiving, the friendly, [15]the possessor of the glorious throne, [16]the doer of whatever he desires. [17]Has the saying of the troops come to you? [18]Pharaoh and Themoud. [19]Yet, those who became infidels are in denial. [20]And Allah surrounds them from behind. [21]Yet, it is a glorious Qur'an [22]in a kept board.

A portion of a revelation   **86**   *The Tariq*

In the name of Allah, the merciful, the merciful

[1][I swear] by the heaven and by the tariq. [2]And what, do you know what the tariq is? [3]The piercing star. [4]That very soul has a keeper over it.

This is a biological error in the Qur'an concerning human reproduction.

[5]So let the human look to what he was created from. [6]He was created from gushing water; [7]it comes out from the backbones[a] and the breasts.[b] [8]Surely he is able to return him [9]a day the secrets will

---

[a] of the male
[b] of the female

be made known. ¹⁰So then he will have no strength nor helper. ¹¹[I swear] by the heaven that returns ¹²and by the earth that splits. ¹³Surely this is a decisive word, ¹⁴and it is not a joke. ¹⁵Surely they are scheming a scheme, ¹⁶and I am scheming a scheme. ¹⁷So give the infidels a delay. Delay them leisurely.

A portion of a revelation   **87**   *The Highest*

In the name of Allah, the merciful, the merciful

¹Praise the name of your lord, the highest, ²who created, so he fashioned, ³and who estimated, so he guided, ⁴and who brings forth the pasture, ⁵so he made it gathered scum. ⁶We will make you read, so do not forget, ⁷except for what Allah wills. Surely he knows what is proclaimed and what is hidden. ⁸And we will make it easy for you that which was easy. ⁹So remind, if the reminder profits. ¹⁰Who fears will be reminded, ¹¹and the troublemaker will avoid it, ¹²who will be roasted in the big fire; ¹³then he will not die in it, nor will he live. ¹⁴Indeed, whoever is purified prospers ¹⁵and remembers his lord's name, so he prayed. ¹⁶Yet you prefer the world's life, ¹⁷and the hereafter is better and lasting. ¹⁸Surely this is in the first pages of writings, ¹⁹the pages of writings of Abraham and Moses.

A portion of a revelation   **88**   *The Overwhelming*

In the name of Allah, the merciful, the merciful

¹Have the sayings of the overwhelming come to you? ²Faces on that day will be downcast, ³laboring and weary, ⁴roasting in a hot fire; ⁵they will be made to drink from a boiling spring. ⁶They will not have any food except that of thorns ⁷which will not fatten them nor satisfy from hunger. ⁸Faces on that day will be blissful, ⁹well pleased with their past labors. ¹⁰In a lofty garden, ¹¹you will not hear vain talk in it, ¹²in it a flowing spring, ¹³in it a raised bed ¹⁴and goblets placed ¹⁵and cushions laid in rows ¹⁶and zarābī[a] spread out. ¹⁷Do they not look on

---

[a] rich carpets, non-Arabic word of undetermined origin

the camels, how they were created? [18]And to the heaven, how it is raised up? [19]And to the mountains, how they are set up? [20]And to the earth, how it is spread out? [21]So remind them, surely you are only a reminder. [22]You are not a dominator over them, [23]except for who turned away and became an infidel, [24]so Allah will torment him with the biggest torment. [25]Surely they will return to us, [26]then surely on us their reckoning.

A portion of a revelation   **89**   *The Dawn*

In the name of Allah, the merciful, the merciful

[1][I swear] by the dawn [2]and by the ten nights [3]and by the even and the odd [4]and by night when it departs. [5]Is there an oath in this to one who possesses a stone?[a] [6]Have you not seen how your lord did with Ad? [7]At Iram,[b] that with columns, [8]which none like it was created in the countries? [9]And Themoud who hewed out the rocks in the valley? [10]And Pharaoh with the stakes? [11]Those who rebelled in the countries, [12]so they increased the vandalism in them. [13]So your lord poured on them a sawt[c] of torment. [14]Surely your lord is ever watchful. [15]So, as for the human, when his lord tested him, so he honored him and graced him. So he will say, "My lord honors me." [16]And when he tested him, so he estimated to him his provisions. So he will say, "My lord has disgraced me." [17]Certainly not, yet you did not honor the orphan, [18]and you did not urge the feeding of the poor. [19]And you consume the inheritance, you consume all of it, [20]and you love money with an exceeding love. [21]Certainly not, when the earth is ground, grinding, grinding. [22]And your lord came and the angels in rank, rank. [23]On that day, hell will be brought forth; on that day, the human will remember. And how is the remembrance to him? [24]He will say, "Oh, I wish I had prepared for this in my life." [25]So on that day, no one will be tormented his torment, [26]and no one can bind his binding. [27]O you calm soul, [28]return to your lord, content and pleasing, [29]so enter among my servants, [30]and enter my garden.

---

[a] Muslim scholars interpret this as understanding, equating it to hardheadedness.
[b] non-Arabic word of undetermined origin
[c] scourge, non-Arabic word of Aramaic origin

A portion of a revelation   **90**   *The Country*

In the name of Allah, the merciful, the merciful

[1]I will not swear by this country. [2]And it is lawful for you [to kill] in this country.[a] [3]And by the father and what he has begotten, [4]indeed, we created the human in hardship. [5]Does he think that no one can have might over him? [6]He says, "I have destroyed an enormous amount of money." [7]Does he think that no one sees him? [8]Have we not made for him two eyes [9]and a tongue and two lips, [10]and we guided him the two ways? [11]So he did not enter Al-Akabah. [12]And what, do you know what is Al-Akabah? [13]It is the freeing of a neck (slave) [14]or feeding in a day of famine, [15]an orphan who is a relative, [16]or a poor person that lays in deep need. [17]Then he was of those who believed and who exhorted with patience and exhorted with mercy. [18]Those are the companions of the right hand, [19]and those who became infidels in our verses are the companions of the left hand, [20]over them is a closed fire.

A portion of a revelation   **91**   *The Sun*

In the name of Allah, the merciful, the merciful

[1][I swear] by the sun and its brightness, [2]and by the moon when it follows it, [3]and by the day when it shows its light, [4]and by the night when it covers it, [5]and by the heaven and who built it, [6]and by the earth and the one who spread it, [7]and by the soul and him who fashioned it,

Allah inspires the soul to wickedness as well as piety!

[8]so he inspired it its wickedness and its piety. [9]Indeed, who purifies it will prosper, [10]and indeed, whoever is corrupt will be ruined.

The oft-repeated and apparently pointless story about Themoud and the camel of Allah was invented by Mohammed.

---

[a] Mecca

[11]Themoud denied by its rebellion, [12]when their most wicked was raised. [13]So the messenger of Allah said to them, "The camel of Allah and her drink." [14]So they denied him, so they hamstrung her. So their lord got angry and destroyed them because of their sin, so he leveled them, [15]and he did not fear its consequence.

A portion of a revelation — The Night

In the name of Allah, the merciful, the merciful

[1][I swear] by the night when it covers, [2]and by the day when it appears in glory, [3]and by him who created the male and the female, [4]surely your striving is diverse. [5]So as for him who gives and fears, [6]and believes in the good, [7]so we will ease him to the ease. [8]And for him who becomes stingy and self-sufficient, [9]and he denied the good, [10]so we will ease him to the difficult. [11]And his money will not benefit him when he perishes. [12]Surely on us is to guide, [13]and surely to us to the hereafter and the first. [14]So I warned you about the blazing fire. [15]No one will roast in it except the wretched, [16]who denied and turned away. [17]And the fearer will avoid it, [18]who gives his money for self-purification, [19]and they do not expect any favor in return [20]except seeking the face of his lord, the highest. [21]And he will be pleased.

A portion of a revelation — The Forenoon

In the name of Allah, the merciful, the merciful

[1][I swear] by the forenoon, [2]and by the night when it becomes dark, [3]your lord did not forsake you, and neither has he detested [you]. [4]And the hereafter is better than the first. [5]And your lord will give to you so that you will be pleased. [6]Did he not find you orphaned, so he sheltered you? [7]And he found you lost, so he guided [you]? [8]And he found you needy, so he enriched [you]? [9]So, as for the orphan, so do not oppress; [10]and as for the beggar, so do not rebuke; [11]and as for the grace of your lord, so speak.

A portion of a revelation **94** *The Expanding*

In the name of Allah, the merciful, the merciful

[1]Did we not expand your chest? [2]And we took your burden off of you, [3]which pressed heavily on your back. [4]And we exalt your fame. [5]So surely with the difficulty is ease. [6]Surely with the difficulty is ease. [7]So when you are free, so stand up, [8]and to your lord, so incline.

A portion of a revelation **95** *The Fig*

In the name of Allah, the merciful, the merciful

[1][I swear] by the tīn[a] and the olive [2]and by Mount Sineen[b] [3]and by this secure country;[c] [4]indeed, we created the human in the best mold. [5]Then we put him down to be the lowest of the low, [6]except for those who believed and did good deeds, so they will have an unending wage. [7]So what denies you after that in the judgment? [8]Is not Allah the wisest of the judges?

A portion of a revelation **96** *The Clot*

In the name of Allah, the merciful, the merciful

[1]Read, in the name of your lord who created. [2]He created the human from a clot. [3]Read, and your lord is the generous [4]who taught with the pen. [5]He taught the human what he did not know. [6]Certainly not, surely the human is rebellious; [7]that he sees himself as self-sufficient. [8]Surely the return is to your lord. [9]Have you seen the one

---

[a] fig, non-Arabic word of Aramaic origin
[b] error—Sinai—obvious modification for the sake of rhyme
[c] Mecca

who forbids [10]a servant when he prays? [11]Have you seen that he was upon the guidance? [12]Or commands with piety? [13]Have you seen if he denies and then turns away? [14]Did he not know that Allah sees? [15]Certainly not, if he does not stop, then we will take him by his forehead, [16]a lying, sinful, forehead. [17]So he will call on his company. [18]We will call the zabānī.[a] [19]Certainly not, do not obey him. And worship and draw near.

A portion of a revelation   **97**   *The Fate*

In the name of Allah, the merciful, the merciful

[1]Surely we sent it down in the night of the fate. [2]And you do not know what the night of the fate is? [3]The night of fate is better than a thousand months. [4]The angels and the spirit come down in it by the will of their lord from every command. [5]It is peace until the rising of the dawn.

A portion of a revelation   **98**   *The Evidence*

In the name of Allah, the merciful, the merciful

[1]Those who became infidels among the People of the Book and the polytheists will not leave [their infidelity] until the evidence comes to them. [2]A messenger from Allah recited pure pages of writings. [3]In it is a valuable book. [4]And the People of the Book did not divide except after the evidence came to them. [5]And they were not commanded except to serve Allah, devoted in the religion to him, hanifa, and to perform the prayer and bring the legal alms. And this is the worthy religion.

Jews and Christians who do not believe in Islam are the worst of creatures and will go to hell forever. Muslims are the best of creatures, and their reward is the garden of Eden forever.

[6]Surely those who became infidels, from the People of the Book and polytheists, will abide in the fire of hell forever. Those are the

---

[a] guardians, non-Arabic word of probable Syriac origin

worst of the creatures. [7]Surely those who believed and did good deeds, those are the best of the creatures. [8]Their reward is with their lord, Eden's gardens, below them the rivers flow. They will abide in it forever and ever. Allah is pleased with them, and they are pleased with him. This is to him who fears his lord.

A portion of a revelation — The Quakes

In the name of Allah, the merciful, the merciful

[1]When the earth quakes with its quaking [2]and the earth brings forth its burdens [3]and the human says, "What happened to it?" [4]On that day, it will tell its news [5]because your lord reveals to it. [6]On that day, people will come forward separately, so they can see their works. [7]So whoever does even the weight of an atom of good, he will see it; [8]and whoever does even the weight of an atom of evil, he will see it.

A portion of a revelation — The Chargers

In the name of Allah, the merciful, the merciful

[1][I swear] by the snorting chargers, [2]so those who ignite sparks of fire, [3]so those who attack in the morning, [4]raising the dust with it, [5]so we went together through the middle of it. [6]Surely the human is ungrateful to his lord, [7]and surely he is a witness of that. [8]And surely he loves wealth excessively. [9]Do they not know if what is in the graves are scattered? [10]And what is in the chests will come forth? [11]Surely their lord is expert on that day.

A portion of a revelation　　101　　*The Calamity*

In the name of Allah, the merciful, the merciful

[1]The calamity! [2]What is the calamity? [3]And you do not know what the calamity is. [4]A day people will be like scattered moths [5]and the mountains will be like loosened wool. [6]So for him whose balances are heavy, [7]so he will be in a pleasant life. [8]And as for him whose balances are light, [9]so his mother will be the Hawiyah. [10]And what, do you know what it is? [11]It is a raging fire.

A portion of a revelation　　102　　*The Proliferation*

In the name of Allah, the merciful, the merciful

[1]The proliferation distracted you [2]until you visit the grave. [3]Certainly not, you will know. [4]Then certainly not, you will know. [5]Certainly not, if you knew with the sure knowledge, [6]you will see the hell. [7]Then you will see it with a sure eye. [8]Then surely you will be asked on that day about the bliss.

A portion of a revelation　　103　　*The Afternoon*

In the name of Allah, the merciful, the merciful

[1][I swear] by the afternoon, [2]surely the human is in a lost state, [3]except for those who believed and did good deeds and exhorted with the truth and exhorted with patience.

A portion of a revelation — 104 — *The Backbiter*

In the name of Allah, the merciful, the merciful

[1]Woe to every backbiter and slanderer, [2]the one who gathers money and counts it. [3]He thinks that his money will make him immortal. [4]Certainly not, surely he will be thrown into the Hutamah. [5]And what, do you know what the Hutamah is? [6]It is the kindled fire of Allah, [7]which rises above the hearts. [8]Surely it is closed on them, [9]in stretched out columns.

A portion of a revelation — 105 — *The Elephant*

In the name of Allah, the merciful, the merciful

These amazing birds wage war with rocks.

[1]Have you not seen what your lord did with the companions of the fīl?[a] [2]Did he not make their schemes to go astray? [3]And he sent birds in ababil[b] on them. [4]They cast rocks made of baked clay on them, [5]so he made them as devoured straw.

A portion of a revelation — 106 — *Quraish*

In the name of Allah, the merciful, the merciful

[1]For the taming of the Quraish,[c] [2]their taming journey is in winter and summer, [3]so let them serve the lord of this house [4]who has fed them against hunger and secured them against fear.

---

[a] elephant, non-Arabic word of Middle Persian or Aramaic origin
[b] flocks, non-Arabic word, possibly of Persian origin
[c] a tribe at Mecca, non-Arabic word of Greek origin

A portion of a revelation   **107**   *The Help*

In the name of Allah, the merciful, the merciful

[1]Have you seen those who deny the judgment? [2]So this is the one who thrusts away the orphan, [3]and they will not urge on the feeding of the needy. [4]So woe to those who pray, [5]those who neglect their prayer, [6]those who like to be seen, [7]and those who forbid mā'ūn.

a

A portion of a revelation   **108**   *The Abundance*

In the name of Allah, the merciful, the merciful

[1]Surely we have given you the abundance, [2]so pray to your lord and sacrifice. [3]Surely whoever hates you will be childless.

A portion of a revelation   **109**   *The Infidels*

In the name of Allah, the merciful, the merciful

Notice that verse 5 is a false prophecy by Allah. These infidels became Muslims and served Allah, not as Allah declared that they will not serve him.

[1]Say, "O you, the infidels, [2]I do not serve what you serve, [3]and you do not serve what I serve. [4]And I will not serve what you have served, [5]and you will not serve what I serve. [6]To you your religion, and to me is my religion."

---

[a] help, non-Arabic word of Hebrew origin influenced by Aramaic/Syriac

A portion of a revelation — **110** — *The Triumph*

In the name of Allah, the merciful, the merciful

[1]When the triumph of Allah and the conquest comes [2]and you see the people entering the religion of Allah by throngs, [3]so praise with your lord's praise and seek his forgiveness, surely he was ever-relenting.

A portion of a revelation — **111** — *The Fiber*

In the name of Allah, the merciful, the merciful

Mohammed's uncle (Abu Lahad) refused to believe in Islam. As a result, the Qur'an stated that he will be burned in hell and that his uncle's wife will stoke the fires of hell.

[1]Perish the hands of Abu Lahab, and he will perish. [2]His money and what he has earned did not benefit him. [3]He will roast in a flaming fire, [4]and his woman [wife] will be a carrier of firewood. [5]She will have a rope of fiber around her neck.

A portion of a revelation — **112** — *The Sincerity*

In the name of Allah, the merciful, the merciful

God has no Son, Jesus or any other.

[1]Say, "He is Allah the one of. [2]Allah is absolute. [3]He does not birth, neither was he birthed, [4]and there is no one equal to him."

A portion of a revelation   113   *The Daybreak*

In the name of Allah, the merciful, the merciful

Allah creates evil!

¹Say, "I seek refuge in the lord of the daybreak, ²from the evil which he created, ³and from the evil of the darkness when it comes. ⁴And from the evil when they[a] blow on the knots, ⁵and from the evil of the envier when he envies."

A portion of a revelation   114   *The People*

In the name of Allah, the merciful, the merciful

¹Say, "I seek refuge with the lord of the people, ²the king of the people, ³the god of the people ⁴from the evil of the slinking whisperer ⁵who whispers in the chests of the people ⁶from the jinn and the people."

---

[a] Witches

Notes

Words and Idioms

Word / Idiom	Meaning	Chap	Verse
a neck	a slave	5	89
aālam	banners—Muslim scholars claim this means mountains	42	32
Ad	non-existent people made up by Mohammed	9	70
after any will	monies bequeathed	4	11
Ahmad	Muslims claim that Ahmad is the same name as Mohammed, which is not true, and that ' Isā, whom they claim to be Jesus, prophesied his coming	61	6
al rakim	a word without meaning	18	9
Allah	name for the god of Islam	1	1
Allah can close	his hand, i.e., withhold	2	245
Allah can open	his hand, i.e., give	2	245
Allah's messenger	Mohammed	3	132
Al Lat	a goddess worshiped by Arabs in Mohammed's day	53	19
al-lemam	everything sexual that men can do with women without actual penetration—see interpretation of Al Kortoby	53	32
alm	a word without meaning containing three Arabic letters	2	1
almr	a word without meaning containing four Arabic letters	13	1
alms	a word without meaning containing four Arabic letters	7	1
Al-Nasb	stones around the Kaaba	5	3
Al Ozza	a goddess worshiped by Arabs in Mohammed's day	53	19
alr	a word without meaning containing three Arabic letters	10	1
al-soklan	a word without meaning – scholars claim it means human beings and jinn	55	31
alternate his hands	clapping his hands in sorrow	18	42
anan	a word without meaning - translators have disregarded in their translations	55	44
Arafat	a granite hill east of Mecca	2	198
arm was tight	to provide protection	11	77
aslen	a word without meaning	69	36
asq	a word without meaning containing three Arabic letters	42	2
awah	a word without meaning	11	75
Azar	a name Mohammed mistakenly identifies as that of Abraham's father whose name was actually Terah	6	74
babble in it	make noise interrupting recitation	41	26

Word / Idiom	Meaning	Chap	Verse
Badr	one of Mohammed's battles	3	123
bahira	livestock dedicated to, or liberated in honor of idols	5	103
Becca	error in verse 3:96; should be Mecca	3	96
believers/ believing	refers to Muslims	5	5
below them the rivers flow	a phrase frequently repeated by Mohammed after references to the gardens in paradise, perhaps to emphasize their richness	2	25
between their hands	now before them	2	255
big	can mean a difficult task	2	143
bird	can mean evil omen	7	131
book from Allah	Qur'an	2	89
cannot surround	cannot comprehend	2	255
clear verses	refers to the Qur'an	2	99
close their hands	become stingy	9	67
companion of the whale	Jonah	68	48
companions of the Saturday	i.e., the Jews who worship on Saturday and have been changed into monkeys	4	47
covering	keeping it secret	2	235
crescents	moon phases	2	189
cut the way	banditry, robbing travelers	29	29
dismissal	divorce	33	28
emigrate	leaving everything (home, family, tribe, country, etc.) because of becoming a Muslim	2	218
enter into	have sex with	7	81
enter your field	have sex	2	223
entered into	had sex with	4	23
farthest mosque	Solomon's Temple in Jerusalem	17	1
forbidden for you that which died	Muslims are forbidden to eat that which dies of itself, e.g., died of natural causes or is found dead	2	173
forbidden mosque	Masjid ul Haraam at Mecca	2	144
forge from between their hands and their legs	allege that a foundling or an illegitimate child is their husband's	60	12
go forth / journey / fight for the sake of Allah	to fight, perform jihad (holy war)	4	94
hamem	close-warm, as in the statement close or warm friend, in this context other translators chose the words boiling water	6	70
hami	livestock dedicated to, or liberated in honor of idols	5	103
haneez	a word without meaning	11	69
hanifa	a word without meaning	22	31
hanifan	a word without meaning	2	135
hashas	a word without meaning	12	51
hm	a word without meaning containing two Arabic letters	40	1
honein	a battlefield	9	25

Word / Idiom	Meaning	Chap	Verse
hyam	thirsty camels	56	55
Iliyas	name mistakenly used, Elijah was meant	6	85
imam	spiritual leader	2	124
in our eyes	under our protection	52	48
'Isā	name used in the Qur'an which Muslims falsely claim to be Jesus' name; actually, in Arabic Jesus' name would be Yasua from Joshua in Hebrew, meaning "savior"	2	87
empty on its roof	crumbled	2	259
jawar	running ones; Muslim scholars claim this means ships	42	32
jihad	holy war	2	218
Kaaba	the building in Mecca where the black stone is kept	2	125
kaber Allah	that is to call "Allah akbar," i.e. Allah is bigger	2	185
keep them in harm	against their will	2	231
khyas	a word without meaning containing five Arabic letters	19	1
killed for the sake of Allah	killed while performing jihad (holy war)	2	154
kobla	a direction set toward which Muslims pray	10	87
lamps	often means "stars," especially in context of the heavens	67	5
Ma'juj	Magog	18	94
made on it, its bottom	turned upside down	11	82
madness	jinn-possessed	54	24
Madyen	close to the spelling of the name of the actual Midian people found in Exodus 3:1	20	40
Magians	ancient Persian polytheists	22	17
magnify (him / lord / Allah)	that is to call "Allah akbar," i.e. Allah is bigger	17	111
Manat	a goddess worshiped by Arabs in Mohammed's day	53	20
men who commit it (indecency)	refers to homosexuality	4	16
Midian	non-existent people made up by Mohammed	9	70
mihrab	holy of holies in Solomon's temple	3	37
Mika'il	Muslim scholars claim Mohammed meant Michael	2	98
Miriam	Mary	19	16
moblesun	a word without meaning	23	77
mohatean	a word without meaning, Muslim scholars claim to mean hastening, staring, or going towards	14	43
moneya	a word without meaning, some scholars claim to be sperm or semen; all Muslim translators disregard this word	75	37
monkeys; usually with an adjective, e.g., cursed,despised	the Jews who, according to the Qur'an, have been changed into monkeys	2	65

Word / Idiom	Meaning	Chap	Verse
moqantarah	measured	3	14
Mount Sineen	erroneous word – should be Sinai – obvious modification for the sake of rhyme	95	2
mudhamatan	a word without meaning, scholars claim it to be dark green	55	64
Muslim	literally "surrenderer," name for followers of Islam	2	128
Mu'tafikah	meaningless word; scholars erroneously claimed this to be the name of the cities of Lot, which the Bible clearly teaches were called Sodom and Gomorrah	9	70
my verses	Qur'an	2	41
n	an Arabic letter without meaning	68	1
naqira	speck on the back of a pit from a date	4	53
Nasara	word made up to mean Christians	2	62
Nasr	some scholars state that this is a pagan Arab god	71	23
Nasranyan	Christian	3	67
nutfah	a word without meaning, which Mohammed claims to mean male and female sexual discharges	16	4
one who possesses a stone	Muslim scholars interpret this as "understanding," equating it to hardheadedness	89	5
ouf	a word exclaimed in a state of frustration	17	23
partners	idols, false gods	6	136
patient	steadfast in fighting jihad (holy war)	2	153
People of the Book	Jews and Christians	2	105
prescribed periods	menstrual periods	65	1
proceed out of your backbone	Mohammed believed the backbone to be the origin of man's sperm	4	23
purchase...by/with it a small price	considering something of little value	2	41
purchased by them for a little price	this term, repeated throughout the Qur'an, means that to the infidel the book is considered to be of little value when compared to the enjoyment of the world	2	174
pure	ever-virgin, used in references to wives provided in the garden of paradise	3	15
pure azawaj	ever-virgin wives (in the promised gardens)	2	25
q	an Arabic letter without meaning, which Mohammed claimed to be a mountain surrounding the earth and requiring 500 years travel to reach its top	50	1
Ramadan	a Muslim religious observance of fasting that takes place during the ninth month of the Islamic calendar, during which the participating Muslims do not eat or drink anything from dawn until sunset	2	185
ransoming	of slaves and captives; the Qur'an conditionally encourages using money for such purposes	2	177
religion of the truth	Islam	9	29
reminder	Bible / Qur'an	15	9

Word / Idiom	Meaning	Chap	Verse
repent	convert to Islam	9	5
s	an Arabic letter without meaning	38	1
safa and the marwah	hills near the Kaaba	2	158
saiba	livestock dedicated to honor idols	5	103
Salih	a son's name	7	189
saqar	a word created by Mohammed which scholars claim to mean "fire"	54	48
sent down the iron	sent the weapons of war to bring victory to the religion of Allah, i.e., jihad	57	25
set up equals	create false gods	6	1
sidrat	nonsense word, which some Islamic scholars claim to be a tree in the garden	34	16
son of the way	a traveler	2	177
Sowah	some scholars state that this is a pagan Arab god	71	23
stabilizers	Islamic scholars claim this to mean mountains	13	3
submit	become a Muslim	3	83
taha	a word without meaning containing four Arabic letters	20	1
tawwāb	relenting	2	37
that which they gathered	refers to the spoils of war	3	157
that which your hearts gained	what your heart meant	2	225
the book	content dependent: e.g., "sent down on you the book" refers to Mohammed and the Qur'an while "they who are given the book" refers to Jews and Christians and the Bible	2	44
the book of Allah	Qur'an	2	101
the forbidden month	Mohammed probably meant "months" since there are four months in which fighting is suspended	2	194
the going forth	the resurrection	50	11
the house	Kaaba	2	125
the illuminating book	the Bible	3	184
the lost ones	the Christians	1	6
the meeting	can mean the day of judgment	6	31
the ones whom you (Allah) are angered against	the Jews	1	6
the religion	Islam	2	193
the two receivers	recording angels	50	17
Themoud	non-existent people made up by Mohammed	9	70
thick	firm or great, depending on the context	4	21
those who believed	Muslims	2	62
those who threw	those who accused with slander	24	23
three	trinity	4	171
threw the hearing	gave ear to hear	50	37
traces	marks made on the forehead by burning, to	48	29

Word / Idiom	Meaning	Chap	Verse
	appear as if from touching the ground when bowing repeatedly		
ts	a word without meaning containing two Arabic letters	27	1
tsm	a word without meaning containing three Arabic letters	26	1
verses of Allah	Qur'an	2	231
Wadd	some scholars state that this is a pagan Arab god	71	23
wasila	livestock dedicated to, or liberated in honor of idols	5	103
what you cut	what you earned	6	60
what your right hand possesses	what is owned, i.e. concubines and slaves	4	3
whom are given the book	Jews and Christians	3	19
wide	can mean lengthy	41	51
widths of this world	riches of this world	8	67
will not leave from	phrase indicating "will reward"	47	35
wings	can mean side	20	22
wise reminder	Qur'an	3	58
womb	often indicates ties of "kinship"	47	22
women who commit indecency	lesbianism or possibly adultery – see Bukhari Hadith #4839-4820	4	15
Ya'juj	Gog	18	94
Yahya	name mistakenly used when John the Baptist was meant	3	39
Yaseen	name mistakenly used when Elijah was meant	37	130
Yathrib	old name for Medina	33	13
your mothers who nursed you	any woman who breastfed a man at least five times becomes his mother	4	23
your sisters in the breast feedings	any girl who has been breastfed by a man's mother at least five times becomes his sister	4	23
ys	a word without meaning containing two Arabic letters	36	1
Yunus	name mistakenly used when Jonah was meant	4	163
Za Al Kafel	name mistakenly used, some scholars say he meant Isaiah, others say Ezekiel	21	85
Za Al Non	name mistakenly used when Jonah was meant	21	87
Za Al Qarnain	the one with two horns, "Alexander the Great"	18	83
zakkoum	supposedly a tree in hell; however, there is significant contradiction - in verse 37:62 the word is singular (one tree), in verse 44:43 it is a single tree but is misspelled in Arabic, and in verse 56:52 the word is plural (multiple trees)	37	62
zober	translated throughout the Qur'an as "scriptures," but in verse 23:53 Muslim scholars translate it as sects" and only in verse 54:52 translate it as *Book of Deeds/Fate*	23	53

Notes

Non-Arabic Words

Word	Meaning	Non-Arabic Word Origin	Chap	Verse
ababil	flocks	possibly of Persian origin	105	3
abb	herbage	Berber/ Syriac origin	80	31
'abqari	rich carpets	Persian origin	55	76
Adam	the name Adam	Hebrew/Syriac origin	2	31
'Adn's	Eden	Hebrew/Syriac origin	9	72
ahbar	priests	possible Syriac origin	5	44
ajoor	wage	possible Syriac origin	2	62
akabat	treasure	Middle Persian/Aramaic origin	11	23
akhati'a	sin	Syriac origin	2	286
akwāb	goblets	Aramaic origin	43	71
'ālameen	worlds	Aramaic/Hebrew/Syriac origin	1	1
al-araf	the wall between the garden and hell	undetermined origin	7	46
Allah	god	Syriac/Hebrew origin	1	1
Allahumma	O Allah	Hebrew origin	3	26
al-sahar	sorcery	Akkadian/Aramaic origin	2	102
Alshary	Sirius--the Dog Star	Greek origin	53	49
alwah	boards	Aramaic origin	7	145
Alyas'a	Elisha	Syriac / earlier Semitic origin	6	86
āmana	believed	Ethiopian origin	2	8
amr	command	non-Arabic word, when used as a doctrine of revelation, of Aramaic origin	2	27
Amran	Amran	Syriac origin	3	33
amshāj	mingled	Syriac origin	76	2
'ankabūt	spider	Aramaic origin	29	41
aqfal	locks	Greek origin	47	24
aqlam	pens	Greek/Ethiopian origin	3	44
aqsuit	just	Aramaic origin	2	282
ara'ikah	couches	Abyssinian/Persian origin	18	31
'arūban	pleasing	possible Hebrew origin	56	37
asātir	legends	Greek/Syriac origin	6	25
asawer	bracelets	Akkadian origin	18	31
asbāt	tribes	Hebrew/Syriac origin in its singular form	2	136

Word	Meaning	Non-Arabic Word Origin	Chap	Verse
asfar	large books	Aramaic origin	62	5
askon	dwell	Greek/Syriac origin	2	35
aslama	submits	Syriac origin	2	112
asnam	idols	Aramaic origin	6	74
aswaq	streets	Aramaic/Syriac origin	25	7
'atīq	ancient	Aramaic origin	22	29
āyat	signs or miracle, but verses when associated with Mohammed who did not perform any miracles	Syriac/Aramaic origin	2	39
Ayyūb	Job	Greek/Syriac origin	4	163
Azar	a name	Hebrew/Greek origin	6	74
azawaj	wives	Greek origin	2	25
azawaj	pairs	Greek origin	6	143
'azzara	help	Hebrew origin	5	12
bāb	door	Aramaic origin	2	58
Bābil	Babel	Akkadian origin	2	102
bahīma	animals	Hebrew origin	22	28
ba'īr	camel	Syriac origin	12	65
balad	country	Latin/Greek origin	2	126
bannā	builder	Akkadian origin	38	37
bara'a	bring it into existence	Syriac/Aramaic origin	57	22
bashshar	give the good news	Aramaic/Syriac origin	2	25
batal	vanity	Hebrew origin	2	42
berzaħ	barrier	Pahlavi origin	23	100
bighal	mules	Abyssinian origin	16	8
biya'	churches	Syriac origin	22	40
Bual	Baal	Syriac origin	37	125
buhtūn	slander	Syriac origin	4	20
bunyanah	building	Aramaic origin	9	109
būr	ignorant	Hebrew or Syriac origin	25	18
burhan	proof	Ethiopian/Abyssinian origin	2	111
buruj	towers	Latin origin	4	78
burujan	constellations	Latin origin	15	16
Dāwūd	David	Aramaic origin	2	251
dhakkāūtom	ceremonially clean	Hebrew origin	5	3
dihāqan	filled	Mesopotamian origin	78	34
dīn	judgment	Aramaic/Iranian origin	1	3
dīnār	dinar, a coin	Greek origin	3	75
dirham	a coin	Greek origin	12	20
fakhkhār	potter's clay	Syriac origin	55	14
falaq	split	Syriac origin	6	95
fath	judge	Ethiopian origin	26	118

Word	Meaning	Non-Arabic Word Origin	Chap	Verse
fātir	creator	Ethiopian origin	6	14
fīl	elephant	Middle Persian or Aramaic origin	105	1
fir'aun	pharaoh	Hebrew/Syriac origin	2	49
firdaws	paradise	Greek/Syriac origin	18	107
fojar	wicked	Syriac origin	38	28
fulk	ships	Greek origin	2	164
furāt	sweet river water	Akkadian origin	25	53
furqān	discriminator	Hebrew/Aramaic/Syriac origin	2	53
Gabreel	some confuse this name with the angel Gabrieel, but that name is written in Arabic with a different spelling, i.e. Gibrael	Hebrew/Syriac origin	2	97
gharabeb	Muslim scholars claim it to mean mountain	uncertain origin	35	27
habl	rope	Aramaic origin	3	103
hasada	reap	Aramaic origin	12	47
hawārīyūn	white or pure - Mohammed used it to mean disciples of Jesus	probable Abyssinian origin	3	52
hikma	wisdom	Aramaic origin	2	129
hisoun	fortresses	Syriac origin	59	2
hitta	forgiveness	undetermined origin	2	58
hizb	party	Ethiopian origin	5	56
hūb	sin	probable Syriac origin	4	2
hūr	the ever-virgins of the gardens with white skin, large dark eyes and large breasts	Pahlavian/Aramaic origin	44	54
iblis	devil	Greek origin	2	34
Ibrahim	Abraham, meaning, "father of a multitude" in Hebrew	non-Arabic word which appears 69 times, of Hebrew/Syriac origin	2	124
ibriq	jugs	Persian origin	56	18
'id	festival	Syriac origin	5	114
Idris	name mistakenly used by Mohammed in verses 19:56 and 21:85 when he actually meant Enoch	Greek/Syriac/Arabic origin	19	56

Word	Meaning	Non-Arabic Word Origin	Chap	Verse
'ifrīt	demon	Persian, derived from Pahlavic origin	27	39
'illīyūn	higher or upper chambers	Hebrew origin	83	18
'imād	columns	Akkadian/Aramaic origin	13	2
Ingeel	the Gospel	Greek origin	3	3
Iram	unknown place	undetermined origin	89	7
Isaac	name meaning "laughter"	Hebrew origin	2	133
Ishmael	name meaning "God hears" in Hebrew	Greek/ Syriac/ Ethiopian/ Hebrew origin	2	125
Isra'il	Israel	Greek/Syriac origin	2	40
istabraq	brocade	Persian origin	18	31
jabīn	side of the forehead	Aramaic origin	37	103
jahannam	hell	Persian/Hebrew origin	2	206
jalābīb	wrappers--large outer covering worn by women	Ethiopian origin	33	59
Jālūt	Goliath	apparently of garbled Hebrew origin	2	249
jannat	gardens	Semitic origin, e.g. Akkadian, Hebrew, Aramaic, etc.	2	25
jāwib	cisterns	Syriac origin	34	13
jibt	unknown meaning in Arabic	Abyssinian origin	4	51
jizya	tribute	Aramaic origin	9	29
jubb	a well	Aramaic origin	12	10
Jūdī	mountain in Mesopotamia near Mosul	possible Syriac origin	11	44
junāh	sin	Persian origin	5	93
jund	troops	Iranian/Aramaic origin	2	249
kafaro	became infidels	Hebrew/Syriac origin	2	6
kafure	camphor	Berber/Syriac origin	76	5
kāhin	soothsayer	Aramaic origin	52	29
kail	measure—of food stuff	Syriac origin	6	152
kalefah	viceroy—to place one in my stead on earth	Berber/Syriac origin	2	30
kanz	treasure	Middle Persian/Aramaic origin	11	12
ka's	cup	Aramaic origin	37	45
katab	book	Aramaic origin	2	2
khaima	tents	Abyssinian origin	55	72
khalāq	portion	Hebrew origin	2	102

Word	Meaning	Non-Arabic Word Origin	Chap	Verse
khamr	wine	Aramaic/Syriac origin	2	219
khardal	mustard	Syriac origin	21	47
khātam	seal	probable Aramaic origin	33	40
khati'a	mistake	Syriac origin	4	92
khati'aeen	sinners	Syriac origin	28	8
khazan	treasuries	Persian/Hebrew origin	6	50
khinzīr	swine	Aramaic origin	2	173
khubz	bread	Ethiopian origin	12	36
kibriyā	glory	Ethiopian origin	10	78
kursiy	throne	Aramaic origin	2	255
lāta	there was not	Syriac origin	38	3
Lūt	Lot	Syriac origin	6	86
mā'ida	table--title of the 5th Portion of a Revelation in the Qur'an	Ethiopian origin	5	112
Mālik	keeper of hell	Hebrew/Syriac origin	43	77
mastour	written	possible Aramaic origin	17	58
mathānī	repeated	possible Aramaic origin	15	87
mā'ūn	help	Hebrew origin influenced by Aramaic/Syriac	107	7
moqoeen	an interpreter has claimed it to mean "travelers"	unknown origin	56	73
nusabah	praise	Aramaic/Hebrew/Syriac origin	2	30
osjodo	worship	Aramaic origin	2	34
qamīs	shirt	Greek/Syriac origin	12	18
qantēr	measures	Greek origin	3	14
qarya	village	Syriac origin	2	58
qasuran	castles	Latin origin	7	74
qatirān	pitch	Aramaic origin	14	50
qayyūm	self-subsisting	Syriac origin	2	255
qintār	a measure-unit of mass	Greek origin	3	75
qissīsūn	priests/Christian teachers	Syriac origin	5	82
qist	justice	Aramaic origin	3	18
qistās	balance	Greek/Syriac origin	17	35
qitt	sentence	probable Greek/Aramaic origin	38	16
qiyāma	resurrection	Christian-Aramaic origin	2	85
qudus	holy	Aramaic origin	2	87
Quraish	a tribe at Mecca	Greek origin	106	1
Qur'ān	Qur'an; the collection of the verses recited by Mohammed	Hebrew/Syriac origin	2	185

Word	Meaning	Non-Arabic Word Origin	Chap	Verse
qurbān	sacrifice	Hebrew/Syriac origin	3	183
qurtās	parchment	Greek/Syriac origin	6	7
Qūrūn	wrong name, he meant Korah; a corruption of both the name and the story from the Bible	non-Arabic name of Hebrew origin and modified	28	76
rabb	lord	Aramaic/Syriac origin	1	1
rabbānīyun	Jewish teachers	Syriac origin	3	79
raheem	merciful	Hebrew/Greek origin	1	2
rahīq	strong wine	Aramaic/Syriac origin	83	25
rahmān	merciful	Hebrew/Greek origin	1	2
rajim	stoned (cursed)	Ethiopian origin, originally meaning cursed	3	36
raqq	scroll	Ethiopian origin	52	3
rauda	luxurious garden	Pahlavic origin	30	15
ribbīyūn	myriads	Syriac origin	3	146
ribht	profitable	Abyssinian origin	2	16
rizq	bounty— translated as provision	Syriac origin	2	22
rū'ina	look at us	Hebrew origin	· 2	104
rujz	wrath	Syriac origin	2	59
Rum	Byzantines	a Greek origin	30	2
rummān	pomegranate	uncertain origin	6	99
sā'a	hour	Aramaic/Syriac origin	6	31
Sabā	Sheba	probable Hebrew/Syriac origin	27	22
Sābeen	Sabians—idol worshipers; uncertain what specific people this represents; may have been a word play on the name of the Sabaean Christians of S. Arabia	unknown origin	2	62
sabīl	way	Syriac origin	2	108
Sabt	Sabbath, from the Hebrew "shabbat," meaning "to cease" or "desist"	Aramaic/Hebrew origin	2	65
sadaqa	alms	possible Christian-Palestinian dialect origin	2	196
safara	scribes	Syriac origin	80	15
safīna	ship	Aramaic origin	18	71

Word	Meaning	Non-Arabic Word Origin	Chap	Verse
Sainā	Sinai	Syriac origin	23	20
sakar	intoxicating drink	Syriac origin	16	67
salaba	crucify	Persian/Syriac origin	4	157
salām	peace	Hebrew/Aramaic origin	4	90
salasel	chains	Aramaic origin	40	71
salawāt	synagogues	Syriac origin	22	40
salwā	quail	Hebrew origin	2	57
Sāmirī	Samaritan	Hebrew/Syriac origin	20	85
sanabul	ears of corn	Aramaic origin	2	261
sard	chain armor	Persian/Syriac origin	34	11
sarh	tower	Ethiopian origin	27	44
sawāmi'	cloisters	Ethiopian origin	22	40
sawar	formed	Aramaic/Syriac origin	40	64
sawt	scourge	Aramaic origin	89	13
shahr	month	Aramaic origin	2	185
shaitān	satan	probable Abyssinian origin	2	36
shaiteen	satans—hosts of evil	probable Abyssinian origin	2	14
shī'an	sects	Syriac origin	6	65
shirk	partners	S. Arabian origin	6	22
sibgha	dipping or immersion; e.g., ceremonial ablution	Syriac origin	2	138
siddaquen	persons of integrity	Aramaic origin	4	69
siddīqah	person of integrity	Aramaic origin	5	75
sijill	edict	Greek origin	21	104
sijjīl	baked clay	Persian origin	11	82
sijjīn	either of Persian origin and meaning "clay tablet," or a word invented by Mohammed	non-Arabic word either of Persian origin or invented by Mohammed	83	7
sikkin	knife	Aramaic/Syriac origin	12	31
sīmā	marks	Greek origin	2	273
simoom	without meaning; some claim it to mean the hot wind, the fire, the breath of fire, ill winds, torrent, scorching blast or wind	unknown origin	52	27
sirāj	lamp	Syriac origin	25	61
sirāt	way	Greek/Aramaic origin	1	5
sirbāl	garments	Aramaic origin	14	50

Word	Meaning	Non-Arabic Word Origin	Chap	Verse
siyam	fasting	Syriac origin	2	183
suht	unlawful	Syriac origin	5	42
suhuf	pages of writing	S. Arabia origin	20	133
Sulaimān	Solomon, name meaning "his peace" in Hebrew	Hebrew/Syriac origin	2	102
sullam	ladder	Akkadian/Aramaic origin	6	35
sultān	authority	Aramaic origin	3	151
sundus	fine silk	Greek/Akkadian origin	18	31
sūrah	a portion of a revelation	Syriac origin	2	23
surādiq	awning	Iranian/Aramaic origin	18	29
suwā	drinking cup	Ethiopian origin; same word as from the story of Joseph in the Ethiopian Bible	12	72
tāba	relented	Aramaic origin	2	37
taba'a	sealed	Syriac origin	4	155
tabaq	stages	Akkadian origin	67	3
tabārka	blessed	North Semitic origin	7	54
tābūt	ark	Egyptian origin	2	248
tafsīr	interpretation	Syriac origin	25	33
taghut	idolatry	Aramaic/Abyssinian origin	2	256
tajallā	appeared in glory	Syriac origin	7	143
Tālūt	Saul	non-Arabic word created by Mohammed; apparently from a misunderstanding of the Hebrew word meaning tall	2	247
tannūr	oven	Persian or Akkadian or Aramaic origin	11	40
tatbīr	utter destruction	Aramaic origin	17	7
Taurāh	Torah; first five books of the Old Testament	Hebrew origin	3	3
tāzawado	make provision	Aramaic origin	2	197
tijāra	merchandise	Akkadian/Aramaic origin	2	16
tīn	mud	N. Semitic origin	3	49
tīn	fig	Aramaic origin	95	1
todarasoon	studying	Hebrew origin	3	79
tūbā	good fortune	Syriac origin	13	29
Tubba'	title of the king of the Himyarites	Himyaritic origin	44	37
tūfān	deluge	Hebrew/Syriac origin	7	133
tūr	mountain	Syriac origin	2	63
umma	nation	Hebrew/Sumerian origin	2	128
unzurnā	behold us	Hebrew origin	2	104
usalle	praying	Syriac origin	3	39
ussis	founded	Aramaic origin	9	108

Word	Meaning	Non-Arabic Word Origin	Chap	Verse
Uzair	Ezra	Hebrew origin	9	30
uzake	purify	Syriac origin	2	151
zabānī	guardians	probable Syriac origin	96	18
Zabor	in singular form = Psalms	Hebrew/Syriac origin	4	163
Zakariyyā	Zacharias	Syriac origin	3	37
zakāt	legally required alms	Hebrew/Syriac origin	2	43
zanjabīl	ginger	Sanskrit origin	76	17
zarābī	rich carpets	undetermined origin	88	16
zaytonah	olive	Syriac origin	24	35
zaytoon	olive	Syriac origin	6	99
zober	in plural form it means scriptures; in unique situations this word has been translated as "sects" (23:53) and "Book of Deeds/Fate" (54:52)	Hebrew/Syriac origin	3	184
zuit	oil	Syriac origin	24	35
zujāja	glass vessel	Syriac origin	24	35
zukhruf	highly embellished	Syriac/Aramaic origin	6	112
zūr	falsehood	probable Middle Persian origin	22	30

Bible Prophecies-Fulfillments

Many people say that they would believe in God if they could just have certain types of evidence. Some would say, "I would believe if I would **see** something supernatural" or "if I would **experience** something supernatural." Many want to hear audible, heavenly voices or to see visions, etc. But, if you really think about it, **none** of these would convince people or, at least, not convince them for very long. Why? Because if our human experience tells us anything, it's that we can rationalize away anything that we do not want to accept. For example, there are many around the globe who deny that the Holocaust ever happened, in spite of the eyewitness accounts, photos, films, and the chilling death camps.

Let's just say that you **saw** something unexplainable or supernatural. Maybe it was just an illusion, a trick, or perhaps you only hallucinated---I mean, ask anyone who has had an extremely high fever and they can tell you they have seen some bizarre things, things that were impossible but yet seemed very real. What if you **experienced** something heavenly or unexplainable? Well, feelings are strange and fleeting things. Some can be caused by emotion or fear or even pure imagination. How could you be sure? You might believe it at first, but after the probing and skepticism of your friends and family, your certainty would certainly fade. What if you saw a photo or a video of something supernatural? It was probably just Hollywood-style animation and manipulation. Voices? It was all in your head. Even if someone found a supernatural object with "mystical powers," the scientific community would assure us that, given time, there is a rational explanation for everything once considered magical or divine.

Don't worry. God knew before He ever created mankind that we would require quite a bit of proof. God has provided us that undeniable proof if we are willing to take the time to examine it. In the Old Testament book of Isaiah the Lord says, "Declare what is to be, present it---let them (false gods) take counsel together. Who foretold this long ago, who declared it from the distant past? Was it not I, the Lord? And there is no God apart from me, a righteous God and a Savior; there is none but me."

The simple message---God says that His ability to tell the future, to **prophesy** about things that have not happened yet, is the ultimate proof that He is God. Prophecy is God's ability to see history before it happens and to record it hundreds, or even thousands, of years in advance. One book states, "...new discoveries have confirmed [the Bible] as the only book on planet Earth that bears a message probably orchestrated from outside our space-time." (Missler and Eastman, *Alien Encounters*, Koinonia House, Coeur d'Alene, Idaho; 1997, P. 216) No other religious or sacred text in the world has anything coming close to the sheer number and volume of **verifiable** prophecies that we find in the Bible. The reason---only God could know the future, and He used that ability to give us evidence about which book was His word.

One third of the Bible is *prophetic*. That means, that when the specific passages were being written, one out of every three verses was about an event that was still in the future, some of them, *thousands of years* in the future. The rise and the fall of empires, of specific kings and their kingdoms, important events in history, and most importantly, the coming, life, death, and resurrection of the Messiah Jesus has all been prophesied and fulfilled. There are several dozen specific prophecies in the Bible foretelling the Messiah's coming, including where He was to be born (Bethlehem; Micah 5:2) and that He would suffer and die having His hands and feet pierced (Psalm 22:16; cf., Isaiah 53; Zechariah 12:10). Just using a dozen verses in Isaiah chapter 53, any honest skeptic cannot help but admit that Jesus must be the promised Messiah. But we are not relying on only a few obscure references. In total, there are hundreds of specific prophecies about both the first and *second* coming of the Messiah, Jesus. Many things occurring in our world today, especially revolving around the rebirth of the nation of Israel, the increase in technology, the alignment of nations and world coalitions, have all been predicted (prophesied) in God's word.

Of course, God did not give us prophecy just to amaze us or to entertain us. His primary reason was to *authenticate* His message and, more specifically, to *identify* the Messiah, our Savior, the Lord Jesus Christ. Following is a partial list of prophecies concerning the coming Messiah as well as the New Testament passages showing the fulfillment of those prophecies. With the discovery and continued study of the Dead Sea Scrolls, all attempts to deny prophecy by claiming that it was written after the fact have all but disappeared. In addition, events occurring today, in precise fulfillment of ancient texts, cannot be denied as being written "after the fact." Look at this short list, and do further research. God is not hiding. Indeed, all of the wonders of Creation testify to His existence and His power. His written word testifies to His plan of salvation and, above all, His love.

	Prophecy	Description	Fulfillment
1	Genesis 3:15	The virgin birth ("seed of the woman") He will bruise Satan's head	Luke 1:35 Hebrews 2:14
2	Genesis 12:3	As Abraham's descendant, He will bless all nations	Acts 3:25-26 Galatians 3:16
3	Genesis 22:8	The Lamb of God promised	John 1:29
4	Exodus 12:5	A Lamb without blemish	1 Pet. 1:19-20 Romans 5:8
5	Exodus 12:21-27	Christ is our Passover Lamb	1 Corinthians 5:7
6	Exodus 12:46	Not a bone of the Lamb to be broken	John 19:31-36
7	Numbers 21:9	The serpent on a pole pictured Christ lifted up on the cross	John 3:14-18
8	1 Chronicles 17:12-14	To reign on David's throne forever "I will be His Father, He will be my Son."	Luke 1:32, 33 Hebrews 1:5
9	Psalm 2:1-3	The trial and rage of kings and leaders against Christ	Acts 4:25-28
10	Psalm 2:7-8	Declared God's Son	Matthew 3:17
11	Psalm 16:9-11	Dead body was not to decay, the resurrection	Acts 2:31; John 20:9
12	Psalm 22:1	Forsaken because of the sins of others—Words spoken from the cross by Jesus, "My God..."	2 Corinthians 5:21 Mark 15:34
13	Psalm 22:7-8	They shoot out the lip and shake their heads- He trusted in God, let Him deliver Him	Matthew 27:39, 43
14	Psalm 22:14-15	Died of a ruptured heart Suffered agony on the cross—He thirsted	John 19:34 John 19:28
15	Psalm 22:16	His hands and feet to be pierced (an exact prediction of crucifixion hundreds of years before it was even invented)	John 19:16-18; 20:27
16	Psalm 22:17-18	They parted His garments They gamble for His clothing, "cast lots"	Luke 23:34-35 John 19:23-24
17	Psalm 27:12	Accused by false witnesses	Matthew 26:60-61
18	Psalm 31:5	"Into thy hands I commit my spirit"	Luke 23:46
19	Psalm 31:11	His own friends to flee	Mark 14:50
20	Psalm 35:19	He is to be hated without a cause	John 15:25
21	Psalm 55:12-14	Betrayed by a friend, not an enemy	John 13:18
22	Psalm 69:21	Given vinegar to drink for His thirst	Matthew 27:34
23	Psalm 72:10-11	Will be worshiped by foreign kings	Matthew 2:1-11
24	Psalm 72:17	In His name all nations shall be blessed	John 1:12-13 Acts 2:5-12, 41
25	Psalm 89:27	Emmanuel ("God with us") to be higher than earthly kings	Luke 1:32-33

	Prophecy	Description	Fulfillment
26	Psalm 102:25-27	Messiah is the Preexistent Son, the Creator	Hebrews 1:10-12
27	Psalm 110:1	Ascends to the right-hand of God, the Father	Mark16:19 ; Acts 7:55
28	Psalm 110:4	A priest after Melchizedek's order	Hebrews 6:20-7:3
29	Psalm 118:22-23	The rejected stone becomes the head of the corner (foundational stone)	Matthew 21:42-43
30	Psalm 132:11	The Seed of David (fruit of His Body)	Luke 1:32
31	Proverb 30:4	Declared to be the Son of God	John 3:13
32	Isaiah 7:14	He will be born of a virgin To be Emmanuel-"God with us"	Luke 1:35 Matthew 1:18-23
33	Isaiah 8:14	A stone of stumbling, a Rock of offense	1 Peter 2:8
34	Isaiah 9:1-2	His ministry to begin in Galilee	Matthew 4:12-17
35	Isaiah 9:6	A child born (His humanity) A Son given (His Deity) Declared the Son of God with power The Wonderful One The Counselor The Mighty God The Everlasting Father The Prince of Peace	Luke 1:31 Luke 1:32 John 1:14 1 Timothy 3:16 Romans 1:3-4 Luke 4:16-22 Matthew 13:54 Matthew 11:20 John 8:58 John 16:33
36	Isaiah 11:1	The Branch, A rod out of Jesse-(David's father)	Luke 3:23, 32
37	Isaiah 12:2	Called Yeshua (salvation)	Matthew 1:21
38	Isaiah 25:8	The Resurrection predicted	I Corinthians 15:53-54
39	Isaiah 40:3-4	To be preceded by a forerunner (John the Baptist)	John 1:23
40	Isaiah 42:1-4	The chosen one in whom God is pleased	Matthew 12:18-21
41	Isaiah 42:6	The Light (salvation) of the Gentiles	Luke 2:32
42	Isaiah 42:7	He will heal the blind	John 9:25-38
43	Isaiah 43:11	He is the only Savior	Acts 4:12
44	Isaiah 49:7	He is despised of the Nation	John 8:48-49
45	Isaiah 50:6	"I gave my back to the smiters." Jesus was flogged before His crucifixion He was beaten on the face He was spit upon	Matthew 27:26 Matthew 26:67 Matthew 27:30
46	Isaiah 52:13	The Servant exalted Behold, My Servant	Ephesians 1:19-22 Philippians 2:5-8
47	Isaiah 52:14	The Servant, Messiah, to be shockingly abused	Luke 18:31-34 Matthew 26:67-68
48	Isaiah 53:1	His own people would not believe Him	John 12:37-38
49	Isaiah 53:3	Despised Rejected Great sorrow and grief Men hide from being associated with Him	Luke 4:28-29 Matthew 27:21-23 Luke 19:41-42 Mark 14:50-52

	Prophecy	Description	Fulfillment
50	Isaiah 53:4-5	He would bear the sins of the world	1 Peter 2:24
		Thought to be cursed by God	Matthew 27:41-43
		His sacrifice would provide peace between man & God	Colossians 1:20
		His back would be whipped	Matthew 27:26
51	Isaiah 53:6	He would be the sin-bearer for all mankind	Galatians 1:4
		It is God's will that Jesus will bear the sin for all mankind	1 John 4:10
52	Isaiah 53:7	Oppressed and afflicted	Matthew 27:27-31
		Silent before accusers	Matthew 27:12-14
		Sacrifice of the Lamb	John 1:29
53	Isaiah 53:8	Confined and persecuted	Matthew 26:47-27:31
		He would be judged	John 18:13-22
		Killed	Matthew 27:35
		Dies for the sins of the world	1 John 2:2
54	Isaiah 53:9	Buried in a rich man's grave	Matthew 27:57-60
		Innocent & had done no sin	Mark15:14
		No deceit in His mouth	John 18:38
55	Isaiah 53:10	God's will that He die for mankind	John 18:11
		An offering for sin	Matthew 20:28
		Resurrected & live forever	Mark 16:6
		He would prosper	John 17:1-5
56	Isaiah 53:11	God fully satisfied with His suffering	John 12:27
		God's servant	Romans 5:8-19
		He would justify man before God	Romans 5:8-9
		The sin-bearer for all mankind	Hebrews 9:28
57	Isaiah 53:12	Exalted by God because of His sacrifice	Matthew 28:18
		He would give up His life to save mankind	Luke 23:46
		Grouped with criminals	Luke 23:32
		Sin-bearer for all mankind	2 Corinthians 5:21
		Intercede to God on behalf of mankind	Luke 23:34
58	Isaiah 55:3	Resurrected by God	Acts 13:34
59	Isaiah 61:1-2	The Spirit of God upon him	Matthew 3:16-17
		The Messiah would preach the good news	Luke 4:17-21
		Provide freedom from the bondage of sin and death	John 8:27-33
		Proclaim a period of grace	John 5:24
60	Jeremiah 23:5-6	Descendant of David	Luke 3:23-31
		The Messiah would be God	John 13:13
		The Messiah would be both God and Man	1 Timothy 3:16
61	Daniel 2:34-35	Stone cut without hands	Acts 4:10-12
62	Daniel 2:44-45	His Kingdom Triumphant	Luke 1:33
			1 Corinthians 15:24
			Revelation 11:15
63	Hosea 11:1	His short stay in Egypt	Matthew 2:14

	Prophecy	Description	Fulfillment
64	Micah 5:2	Born in Bethlehem	Matthew 2:1-2
		From everlasting	John 8:58
65	Zechariah 9:9	Greeted with rejoicing in Jerusalem	Matthew 21:2-10
		Presented to Jerusalem riding on a donkey	
66	Zechariah 10:4	The cornerstone	Ephesians 2:20
67	Zechariah 11:12-13	Betrayed for thirty pieces of silver	Matthew 26:14-15
		Thirty pieces of silver thrown into house of the Lord	Matthew 27:3-5
68	Zechariah 12:10	The Messiah's body would be pierced	John 19:34-37
		The Messiah would be both God and Man	John 10:30
		The Messiah would be rejected	John 1:11

What will you do with Jesus?

It is no accident that you are reading this particular page at this particular moment in time. The Library of Congress contains nearly 30 million books on over 500 miles of shelves, receiving nearly 20,000 new items per day. Adding all other printed materials, the number would surely climb into the hundreds of millions. Yet, today, at this moment, you are reading this. Is it an accident? I say *NO.*

When it comes to ultimate questions, there are three basic issues that we all need to answer. First, "Who am I?" Second, "Is there a purpose in life?" And finally, "Where am I going when I die?" These are the real questions that we hear deep down inside, during quiet moments, moments when we stop the background noise of the distractions of the day. Many people run from these questions, but *don't.* Let's take a few minutes and *think.*

RANDOM CHANCE OR INTELLIGENT DESIGNER?

Atheism, a belief system that denies that there is a God, tries to dismiss these deep questions by speculating about a universe with no cause, no purpose, and no Creator. Atheism defines our existence as an incredibly improbable cosmic accident: a galactic fluke, a nearly limitless chain of biological mutation miracles, called evolution, to arrive at the beauty and complexity of life that we see all around us. However, recent research into DNA, the building code of life, shows that evolution is not only *mathematically* impossible in terms of time, number of mutations, and specified complexity, it is *genetically* impossible due to built-in error correction in our DNA.

Some skeptics will say, "Well, the universe could be billions of years old, so surely it could have happened!" Considering the possible age of our universe and the age of our planet, doesn't it sound reasonable to think there might be enough time for almost anything to occur by chance? Using statistics, the mathematical science of probability and chance, is this within the realm of possibility? The answer is an overwhelming *NO!* It is not even *close.*

Mathematicians who study probability say that any event with a chance less than 1 in 10^{50} is effectively *ZERO*. Life by chance is not 1 in 10^{50} but *quadrillions* of times far less likely than that. In other words, ZERO chance. In 1991, John Horgan, an atheist and senior staff writer for *Scientific American*, after reviewing the status of *all* existing scientific theories for the origin of life, said that there is *still no plausible way life could have begun by chance*.

The only logical conclusion is that an intelligence far beyond our own has *designed life*.

Eminent scientist and British mathematician Sir Fred Hoyle had this to say about the evidence: "A common sense interpretation of the facts suggests that a *super intellect* has monkeyed with physics, as well as chemistry and *biology*, and that there are no blind forces worth speaking about in nature" [emphasis mine] ("The Universe: Past and Present Reflections," *Annual Reviews of Astronomy and Astrophysics* 20, 1982, 16). He also says: "The notion that not only the biopolymer but the operating program of a living cell could be arrived at by chance in a primordial organic soup here on the Earth is evidently *nonsense* of a high order" [emphases mine] ("The Big Bang in Astronomy," *New Scientist*, 19 November 1981, 527).

IN THE BEGINNING...NOTHING?

But atheism's problems go much farther than just concerning the nearly unimaginable intricacies of life. In defiance of logic and science, atheism imagines that the entire universe either exploded out of nothing for no reason or that it has always existed (eternal). Both of these scenarios are now being rejected due to recent discoveries. Robert Jastrow (Ph.D. in physics), former head of NASA's Goddard Institute for Space Studies, proclaimed: "Astronomers now find they have painted themselves into a corner because they have proven, by their own methods, that the world began abruptly in an act of creation... That there are what I or anyone would call supernatural forces at work is now, I think, a scientifically proven fact" ("A Scientist Caught Between Two Faiths," Interview with Robert Jastrow, *Christianity Today*, August 6, 1982).

Dr. Arthur Compton who was awarded the Nobel Prize for Physics offered this conclusion: "For myself, faith begins with the realization that a supreme intelligence brought the universe into being and created man...for it is incontrovertible that where there is a plan there is intelligence" (Arthur Compton, *Chicago Daily News*, 12 April 1936).

NOT THE *HOW*, BUT THE *WHO*

As we have seen, scientific evidence points to an intelligence, or as one scientist said a *super intellect* and another defined as a *supreme intelligence* which led to the formation of the universe, and ultimately to life itself. But just *WHO* is this intelligence, and what is *he/she/it* like? Does this Creator care about the universe, about life, or even about *me*? There are a variety of religions, namely Islam, Hinduism, Taoism, Mormonism, as well as others, with various views of what God is or is not like and who or what that God is. The facts of the universe prove that there is a God, but to identify that God among the many worshiped requires further investigation.

There are several things, though, that we can know about God, using logic and inference. Does it make sense to believe that a God *without intelligence* could create people *with intelligence*? *NO.* Therefore, God must be intelligent, even incredibly so, to create the universe around us. By sheer observation, we can also surmise that God must be powerful beyond anything we have ever seen. Could a God *without personality* create people *with personality*? The answer again: *NO.* In like manner, could a God who cannot or *will not* communicate create a race of people who can and do communicate? *NO.*

WHAT ABOUT EVIL?

Let me interject one caution at this point. Using this line of reasoning, some wrongly conclude that if there is evil in the world, then God must also be partially evil, which is the Hindu view of God. This is illogical for two reasons. First, if God is all wise and all good, God would know all things, including how things would be if they weren't good. For example, I have never murdered anyone, but that doesn't mean I don't know what murder is. The fact that God should allow evil, as He obviously does, does not mean that He is evil. His allowing the possibility of evil is actually evidence of the highest good. Let me explain.

God created us as choice-makers, with free wills, so that we would not be robots. At stake was whether we would be able to freely love versus whether we would be robotic androids, *machines that look like people yet which do not have free choices.* To illustrate this, what if I told you, "I'll take you out for lunch, and you can have whatever you want. You can have pizza, pizza, or pizza. What do you want?" That's no choice. For real love and goodness to exist, without us merely being robots, there had to be an alternative, a real choice besides love and goodness: evil, or rebellion against the Creator, also known as sin.

The second reason God could not be evil is because He wrote the rule book. By definition, God is the only one who can truly label good *good* and evil *evil*. Whatever He says goes. Our judgments of God matter little. If He created us, who are we to sit in judgment of Him? We would be using brains He created to criticize the One who made us. Nonsense.

A PERSONAL GOD

Therefore, as we return to the original point about what God is like, as popular as is the notion that God is some sort of impersonal *FORCE* who merely set things in motion and then stepped out of the picture, as in deism, fate, or Taoism, such a view does not hold up to reason. God is much more that a FORCE.

Since God is most likely personal (He has created personal beings) and has the ability to communicate (He has created beings who use communication constantly), the next question is whether God has ever communicated with mankind. This would truly be the only way to know what God is like in His character, apart from logically deduced attributes. There are many different religions which claim that God has spoken to them, usually through one of their prophets or founders. One of the first logical steps would be discovering which of the world religions might possibly be true. One simple test would be to determine which of the world religions believe in an all-powerful, personal, moral God who has communicated with mankind.

Only three of the major world religions believe in such a God: Judaism, Islam, and Christianity. The infinitely personal God does not fit the description of the impersonal Brahma who is the World Soul of Hinduism and is both good and evil. Nor does it fit the *Buddha Consciousness* in which Buddhism seeks to suppress human desires as harmful.

COULD ISLAM BE TRUE?

Could Islam be the true religion, just because many of its views of their god Allah seem right and that many of its adherents are very sincere? Logically, Islam cannot be the one true religion as it professes. **WHY?** Because Islam's founder Mohammed said that the Bible is to be *believed*, including the teachings of Jesus. In the Qur'an, Mohammed said, "Say, 'We believed in Allah and in what has been sent down on us and what has been sent down on Abraham and Ishmael and Isaac and Jacob and the tribes and in what was given to Moses and 'Isā and the prophets from their lord. We do not differentiate between any one of them. And to him we are Muslims.'" (Qur'an 3:84. See also Qur'an 4:136; 5:50, 68). Mohammed said that we should *believe* the writings of the Bible, which contain the Law, the Prophets, and the New Testament; yet in reality, Mohammed denied many of the major teachings of the Bible, both Old Testament and New Testament, and doctrines which Jews and Christians have always held to be true. For example, if you read the New Testament, you will discover that the historical crucifixion of Jesus as payment for the sins of the world is the central theme of the entire New Testament (Matthew 27:35, Mark 15:32, Luke 24:20, Acts 2:36, Philippians 2:8, 1 Corinthians 1:23). However, Mohammed denied that Jesus was crucified (Qur'an 4:157).

Another contradiction between the Qur'an and the Bible is that in the New Testament and the Old Testament, Jesus is called the *Son of God* (e.g., John 3:16; Matthew 14:33; John 1:34; and Acts 9:20). Mohammed emphatically taught that Jesus was *not* the Son of God and that anyone who believes that Jesus *is* the Son of God is cursed (Qur'an 9:30); the list of contradictions goes on and on. In the New Testament, Jesus is worshiped as God Who has come in the flesh (John 1:1-14), yet this is condemned and forbidden in the strongest language in the Qur'an.

How could Mohammed say that the teachings of Jesus are to be *believed* and then deny most of the major doctrines of the New Testament? Such irreconcilable contradictions make Islam untrue, definitely not a perfect revelation from a perfect God.

CHRISTIANS OR CHRIST?

Don't judge the Christian faith by hearsay or negative encounters you might have had with Christians. This would be like saying that *all* food is bad because you have experienced bad or rotten food.

Christianity stands or falls based upon *CHRIST*, not *Christians*. God does not ask you to have faith in *Christians*; He asks that you have faith in *CHRIST*. You can read the truth about Jesus Christ in the New Testament of the Bible.

CAN CHRISTIANITY BE PROVEN?

Also, some think of Christianity as *escapism* or as *wishful thinking for those who have a need to imagine a god*. The real issue, of course, is whether or not it is *true*. To say, "There is a tunnel under this prison" may be an escapist idea, but it may also be true. So how can you determine whether Christianity is true? Actually, it is not as hard as you may think. Unlike most other religions which are based upon philosophies and dogmas in which nothing can be proven or disproved, Christianity is a *historical* faith based upon historical facts which can be investigated.

In a spirit of open-mindedness, I urge you to take a fresh look at the history-changing individual known as Jesus. I will show you evidence which proves that Jesus is who He claims to be.

Suppose one day a Man walked this earth claiming to be God, saying, "I am the way, the truth, and the life. No one comes to the Father but by me" (John 14:6). Any person claiming to be the only way to get to God would have to be one of three things: psychotic with delusions of grandeur, a deceiver out to pull off one of the greatest scams of all time, or He might be *GOD.*

C. S. Lewis, once an atheist who studied evidence that eventually led him to become a Christian, wrote, "A man who was merely a man and said the sort of things Jesus said would not be a great moral teacher. He would either be a lunatic on a level with the man who says he is a poached egg or else he would be the Devil of Hell. You must make your choice. Either this man was, and is, the Son of God or else a madman or something worse..." (C.S. Lewis, *Mere Christianity,* New York: Macmillan Publishing, 1978, 56).

Most people do not realize that in the New Testament Jesus is called almost every major name and attribute used to describe God in the Old Testament. For example: Jesus is called *God* (Romans 9:5; John 1:1, 14), *Jehovah* (John 8:58), *Lord* (Acts 10:38) *Creator* (Colossians 1:15-18; Hebrews 1:1), *Savior* (Titus 2:13), *King of kings*

(Revelation 19:16), *the Alpha and the Omega* (Revelation 1:17-18; 22:13), *Holy One* (Acts 3:14), and many more.

You could take Buddha out of Buddhism, and it would remain basically unchanged. You could take Mohammed out of Islam, and it would continue to exist. But, if you took Jesus Christ out of Christianity, it would collapse because Christianity is not merely a *religion* or *philosophy* of life but an encounter with a Person who claimed to be God and who said that He was going to die for us and then rise from the dead to prove His claims: Jesus Christ. Christianity is not an *it* but a *WHO*. Christianity is not a set of rules; it is not a religion of "do this" and "don't do that." It is essentially coming to grips with the claims of Christ and how those relate to you personally.

EVIDENCE FOR JESUS' CLAIMS

Before I go on, some of you are no doubt asking about the evidence for Jesus. Some say: "If you want me to trust Christ, I need to know if there are solid reasons to do so." Absolutely. Let me summarize some of the major reasons that Jesus was telling the truth.

The first is the historical evidence for the resurrection of Jesus. If anyone could disprove the resurrection, they could disprove Christianity. However, to do so, they would have to explain what happened to His mutilated body; how the tomb, which was guarded by Roman soldiers, got empty; how over 500 people saw Him physically alive; and several other equally difficult questions. For further reading, I highly recommend Josh McDowell's book *The Resurrection Factor.*

Another line of evidence involves the trustworthiness of the eyewitnesses themselves. Of the original twelve disciples, excluding Judas the betrayer, history tells us that all but John were *killed* for their belief and bold profession that Jesus had conquered death, that they had seen Him alive after the crucifixion, and that He was the one hope for mankind. Some people such as suicide bombers will die for what they *think* is true, but the apostles would have died for something they *knew* that they made up. In other words, the apostles would have had to die for a lie that *they invented.*

A third piece of evidence is the reliability of the Bible as a historical document. Did you know that there are over 24,600 partial or complete manuscripts of the New Testament? The second-best documented manuscript of antiquity is *The Iliad and The Odyssey* by Homer. It has around 600 manuscripts. Most ancient documents have fewer than ten original copies still in existence. Using standard literary tests, the New Testament we have today is over 99.9 percent reliable. Not one word in a thousand is in question, and no major doctrine is in doubt.

The last and perhaps most conclusive piece of evidence is *fulfilled prophecy*. There were many prophecies in the Bible foretelling Christ's coming, including where He was to be born (Micah 5:2), and that He would die having His hands and feet pierced (Psalm 22:16; cf., Isaiah 53; Zechariah 12:10); it also pinpointed the exact week and year He would die (Daniel 9:25, 26). Read *Daniel's Prophecy of the 70 Weeks* by Alva J. McClain (Winona Lake, IN: BMH Books, 2007) to better understand this prophecy. The Bible also predicted that Jesus would conquer death by being resurrected (Psalm 16:10; cf., Acts 2:22-27). There are, in fact, over 300 prophecies about the coming Messiah in the Old Testament.

How could the Bible predict such astounding things hundreds of years in advance if the Bible wasn't true and Christ wasn't who He claimed to be? It was God's way to be sure we wouldn't mistake His coming. Please refer to our special section about the prophecies of Jesus to read about more of this evidence.

THE REAL PROBLEM

Like a perfect physician, Jesus was very clear when diagnosing our deepest problem; in fact, He said that He was going to die to heal our *disease*. That destructive condition is known as *SIN.* The Bible is clear that, although God created mankind to live in perfect fellowship with Himself, humanity has rebelled against our Creator; this is called sin. God reveals, "For ALL have sinned and have fallen short of the glory of God" (Romans 3:23). In other words, no one is able to reach *His perfect standard.*

Of all the truths of Christianity, the universal sinfulness of mankind is rarely questioned. Why? One word: HISTORY. One does not have to look very far into the annals of human history to witness extreme decadence, hatred, greed, and abuse multiplied millions of times over. But actually, we do not even have to look that far; each one of us is reminded of our own sinfulness every time we honestly look into the mirror.

Take heart. A necessary fact of His justness and goodness is that God hates sin; however, He still loves the *sinner*. That is why God Himself has provided the way for us to be forgiven from our sins. He wants to restore you to a right relationship with Him. But He has left the choice up to you. He has given you a free will to choose or reject His offer of love and salvation.

STEPS TO KNOWING GOD

Principle #1: God is a God of love (I John 4:16). He loves you (John 3:16). What God wants for you is awesome beyond belief (Ephesians 3:14-21). What could be more incredible than a relationship with the Creator of the Universe, knowing that He loves you deeply?

Principle #2: So, what went wrong? Why aren't more people experiencing what God intended? It is because our sin separates us from a holy God (Isaiah 59:2; Romans 6:23). Sin is active or passive rebellion against God. It is missing God's mark of perfection. Because God is *holy*, meaning He's pure and blameless, and totally without sin (Isaiah 6:1-5; I John 1:5), we cannot just come into His presence. We all fall short of God's standard of perfection.

According to the Bible, we all stand guilty before God, no matter whether we have sinned a little or a lot (James 2:10). It is like the man who was caught stealing a car who said to the judge, "But look at all the *other cars* that I didn't steal!" The point? None of us deserves to go to Heaven. Scripture teaches that we have all sinned against an eternal God and committed eternal crimes.

Principle #3: Jesus died to pay the penalty for our sin; therefore, Christ is the only way to a right relationship with God (II Thessalonians 1:8-9; John 3:16; Romans 5:8; Acts 20:28). Jesus is the bridge that connects a holy God with sinful man (I Timothy 2:5).

The Bible says that the penalty for sin is death (Romans 6:23). When we stood condemned before God as the Judge, without hope, deserving death and hell, God, in a very real sense, took off His *judicial robe* of glory, He put on a *humble robe* of humanity, became a man in the person of Jesus Christ, and died for us. The scripture says that God took on human flesh (John 1:1, 14). He lived the perfect life that we could never live, and then He died for us accomplishing what we could never do for ourselves (Romans 5:6).

Principle #4: Just *knowing* the first three principles is not enough. It takes a response on our part. Salvation is something we must *RECEIVE* (John 1:12). The Bible makes it very clear that salvation is a *FREE GIFT*; there is nothing we can do to earn it or deserve it (Ephesians 2:8-9). "For the wages of sin is death, but the *GIFT OF GOD* is eternal life through Jesus Christ our Lord" (Romans 6:23).

How much do you have to pay to get a *FREE* gift? Well, *NOTHING*. A gift is to be received, not earned, not bought, nor bargained for. It is to be received, accepted. But God will not force you to accept His offer of salvation. Many people look at their sinful lives and think that God wants them to first *clean up their act* or to *become worthy* of salvation. NO. He wants you to admit that you *can't* fix your sin problem and then to receive His divine forgiveness in faith, turning away from your sinful rebellion against Him.

Someone once said that we are born with our backs to God; in other words, we are naturally sinful, always turning away and running from God, even if we appear to be outwardly *religious*. We might even be in a church or synagogue nearly every Saturday or Sunday. Maybe we feel like we are living better lives than many other people, but this is missing the entire point. Regularly sitting in a church can't make you a Christian any more than sitting in a garage will make you into a car. Let's face it; we have already blown it. If we are to be saved, then only God can save us.

WHAT MUST I DO TO BE SAVED?

So, now the real question comes: *How* do you receive the gift of salvation? First, you must believe that Jesus really did die for your sins and that He arose from the dead (I Corinthians 15:3-5; Romans 10:9). Some have asked: "*Why* does God require *belief*?" It is because He is asking us to *trust* Him, for that is the essence of faith. He wants us to trust Him.

Since it is your sin which has been keeping you from God, you must acknowledge your sin and be willing to turn away from it as well (Mark 1:14, 15). The Bible calls this *repentance*, which simply means to turn around. If you are headed down a one-way street in the wrong direction, away from God, then turn around. As you turn back to God, ask God to forgive you and receive you back. The Bible says that if you will confess or *admit* your sins, no matter how great or small they are,

God will forgive you (Isaiah 1:18; I John 1:9) based upon what He has done for you on the cross.

The story is told of a man who skillfully walked a tightrope over and back across Niagara Falls with a heavy sack of sand on his shoulders. Upon successfully completing a two-way trip across the falls without even the slightest problem, he turned to a spectator and asked, "Do you believe that I could do that with a person on my back instead of a sack of sand?" The person said, "Of course!" The tightrope walker tossed down the bag of sand and said, "Then climb on my back." *Wow.* Real believing is more than giving mental assent to the claims of Christ. God asks you to *climb on board* and commit yourself to Him. It is more than merely believing something to be true in your head. It is a commitment of the heart.

A TIME OF DECISION

If you feel God speaking to you, deep down, and you have become convinced in your heart and in your mind that what I have shared is true, then you face a decision.

Think about it: some day you will stand before God, either forgiven or unforgiven. Hell is one of those horrible realities we don't like to discuss. However, Jesus talked about it more than all the other Bible writers put together. Not to choose God, and accept His offer of forgiveness, is to choose a life of eternal separation from Him (Revelation 20:11-15; II Thessalonians 1:8-9; Matthew 13:40-43). God is serious when it comes to sin. God is holy, and He judges sin.

But remember: there is no sin too great for God to forgive. He loves you. He died for you. Whatever you have done, whatever guilt you are carrying, God is willing to forgive. God does not lie. He promises to forgive you if you will receive Christ as Savior (Isaiah 1:18; I John 1:9).

This may be a hard decision for you. Much is at stake. If you receive Jesus as Lord, it will cost you. You may be misunderstood. Friends and family members may reject you. *Welcome to the club. Jesus was also misunderstood and rejected. But He was willing to die for you. Are you willing to live for him?*

When you are ready to make your peace with God, perhaps you could pray something like this: "Dear Jesus, I thank you for loving me. I am sorry for the ways that I have sinned against you. I believe that you died on the cross for my sin. As best as I know how, right now, I invite you to come into my life. Please forgive me, and cleanse me from all my sin. Make me the person you want me to be. I need you. Thank you for hearing my prayer. Amen."

May the Lord encourage your heart with His truth and His love.

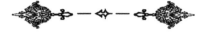

References

Gregory of Tours. *The Glory of the Martyrs*. Translated by Raymond Van Dam. Vol. 4, *Translated Texts for Historians*. Liverpool: University of Liverpool Press, 1988.

Jalalain, Al. "Interpretations of Al Jalalain." http://quran.muslim-web.com (accessed October 12, 2007; available in Arabic only).

Jeffery, Arthur. *The Foreign Vocabulary of the Qur'an*. Baroda (Vadadara), India: Oriental Institute, 1938.

Kathir, Ibn. "Interpretations of Ibn Kathir." http://quran.muslim-web.com (accessed October 12, 2007; available in Arabic only).

Kortoby, Al. "Interpretations of Al Kortobi." http://quran.muslim-web.com (accessed October 12, 2007; available in Arabic only).

Smith, Clay. "Parallel Qur'an." Parallel English Qur'an Translation. http://www.clay.smith.name/Parallel_Quran.htm (accessed July 21, 2007).

Tabari, Al. "Interpretations of Al Tabari." http://quran.muslim-web.com (accessed October 12, 2007; available in Arabic only).

Index

Volume 1
In Volume 1 we will look at a range of topics and people such as: Creation, Adam, Noah, Abraham, Ishmael, Isaac, and Moses. We will:
- See how Ibn Kathir fabricated their stories as if there was some record of them in the Qur'an.
- See how, at times, Ibn Kathir used partial and ambiguous references from the Qur'an and applied these same verses to different people and prophets.
- Examine the stories of Satan, Lot, Job, Jonah, and Elijah.
- Expose the lies of the so-called Muslim scholars regarding the topics, people, and prophets in Volume 1.
- Reveal the truth about these topics and prophets from the true biblical account.

Volume 2
In the next volume we will look at the prophets Ezekiel, Elisha, Samuel, Isaiah, Jeremiah, Daniel, Ezra, and we will:
- Continue to see how Ibn Kathir continued to fabricate their stories and use partial and ambiguous references from the Qur'an and applied these same verses to different prophets.
- Examine the stories of David and Solomon, Zacharias and John the Baptist.
- Examine the claimed "Jesus" of the Qur'an.
- Continue to expose the lies of the so-called Muslim scholars regarding the prophets.
- Reveal the truth about these prophets from the true biblical account.

We will contrast in separate chapters the life of our Lord and Savior Jesus Christ (His birth, life, ministry, teaching, death, and resurrection) with the life of Mohammed, the "claimed" prophet of Islam. By this, we will show that *the only truth* can be found in the Gospel of the Holy Scriptures.